GIFTED & TALENTED®
WORKBOOKS

A SUPER EDITION

WORKBOOK

For Grades 1–2

Gifted & Talented®
WORKBOOKS

A SUPER EDITION WORKBOOK

For Grades 1–2

Written by Martha Cheney, Susan Amerikaner, Nancy Casolaro, Kaye Furlong, and Diane Bockwoldt

Illustrated by Kerry Manwaring, Leesa Whitten, and Larry Nolte

LOWELL HOUSE JUVENILE

LOS ANGELES

CONTEMPORARY BOOKS

CHICAGO

Requests for such permissions should be addressed to:
Lowell House Juvenile
2020 Avenue of the Stars, Suite 300
Los Angeles, CA 90067

Lowell House books can be purchased at special discounts when ordered in bulk for premiums and special sales. Contact Department TC at the above address.

Manufactured in the United States of America

ISBN: 1-56565-832-9

10 9 8 7 6 5 4 3 2

Contents

Note to Parents and Teachers

THE GIFTED & TALENTED® SUPER EDITION WORKBOOK will help develop your child's natural talents and gifts by providing activities to enhance critical and creative thinking skills. These skills of logic and reasoning teach children **how** to think. They are precisely the skills emphasized by teachers of gifted and talented children.

Thinking skills are the skills needed to be able to learn anything at any time. Unlike events, words, and teaching methods, thinking skills never change. If a child has a grasp of how to think, school success and even success in life will become more assured. In addition, the child will become self-confident as he or she approaches new tasks with the ability to think them through and discover solutions.

THE GIFTED & TALENTED® SUPER EDITION WORKBOOK presents these skills in a unique way, combining the basic subject areas of phonics, reading, language arts, and math with thinking skills. The top of each page is labeled to indicate the specific thinking skill being developed. Here are some of the skills you will find:

- Analogy—the ability to find similarities between two things that may otherwise be unalike
- Classification—the ability to group or arrange similar items into categories
- Creative Thinking—the ability to generate unique ideas; to compare and contrast the same elements in different situations; to present imaginative solutions to problems
- Deduction—the ability to reach a logical conclusion by interpreting clues
- Inference—the ability to reach a logical conclusion from given or assumed evidence
- Memory—the ability to recall information previously learned
- Sequencing—the ability to organize events, numbers; to recognize patterns

- Understanding Relationships—the ability to recognize and identify how objects, shapes, and words are similar or dissimilar
- Visual Discrimination—the ability to recognize similarities and differences by how objects look

Each section of this workbook contains activities that challenge children. The activities range from easier to more difficult. You may need to work with your child on many of the pages, especially with the child who is a non-reader. However, even a non-reader can master thinking skills, and the sooner your child learns how to think, the better. Read the directions to your child and, if necessary, explain them. Let your child choose to do the activities that interest him or her. When interest wanes, stop. A page or two at a time may be enough, as the child should have fun while learning.

It is important to remember that these activities are designed to teach your child **how to think,** not how to find the right answer. Teachers of gifted children are never surprised when a child discovers a new "right" answer. For example, a child may be asked to choose the object that doesn't belong in this group: a table, a chair, a book, a desk. The best answer is **book,** since all the others are furniture. But a child could respond that all of them belong because they all could be found in an office or a library. The best way to react to this type of response is to praise the child and gently point out that there is another answer, too. While creativity should be encouraged, your child should choose the best and most **suitable** answer.

Where your child is asked to write, remember that the expression of his or her ideas is more important than spelling. At this age, the child should be encouraged to record the letter sounds that he or she hears without fear of mistakes. This process is known as **invented spelling**. If children only write words they know they can spell correctly, they will limit their written expression. Using invented spelling permits your child's spoken vocabulary to be available to him or her for writing. This vocabulary is vastly greater than the list of words that a six- or seven-year-old can spell correctly.

For example, if your child writes *dnosr* for *dinosaur*, that's okay! Praise your child for the sounds he or she heard. You can encourage the child to listen for the missing vowels as you say the word and write it out so that the child can see the correct form. Just keep the emphasis on his or her success—the letters your child did hear—and not on his or her "error." The youngster needs to grow in confidence and exhibit curiosity about the sounds of the letters and how they go together to make words. The experience of attempting new words requires careful thought about the sounds of the letters and makes them more and more the child's own.

THE GIFTED & TALENTED® SUPER EDITION WORKBOOK has been written and endorsed by educators. It will benefit any child who demonstrates curiosity, imagination, a sense of fun and wonder about the world, and a desire to learn. The book will open your child's mind to new experiences and help fulfill his or her true potential.

PHONICS

This section is designed to give children an opportunity to explore and play with the sounds of the alphabet. This study of letter sounds is known as phonics, and it is fundamental in helping children learn how to read. Reference charts depicting the sounds of letters appear on the next few pages. Help your child use the charts whenever he or she needs a reminder.

Consonant Chart

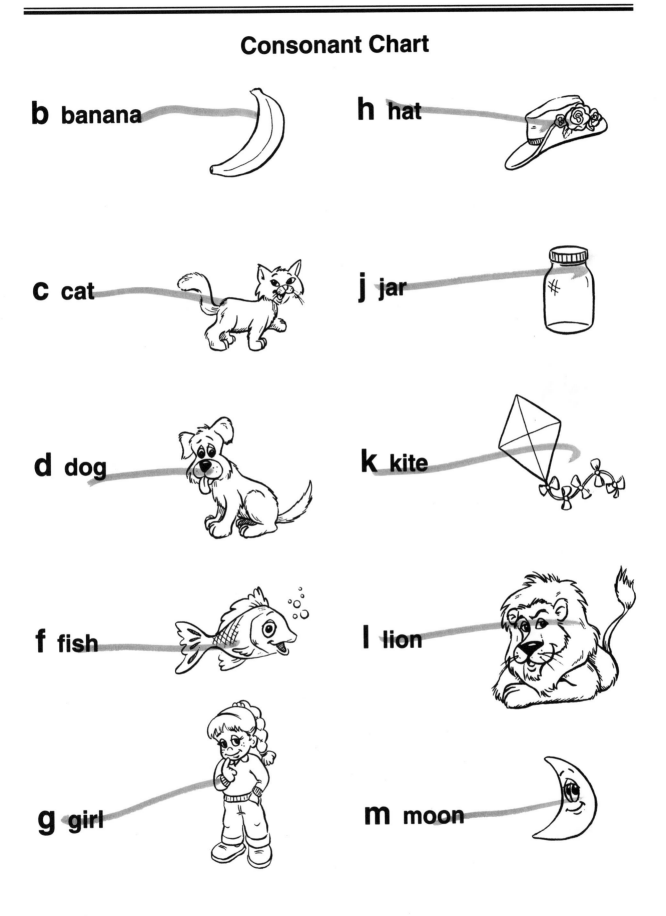

b banana

c cat

d dog

f fish

g girl

h hat

j jar

k kite

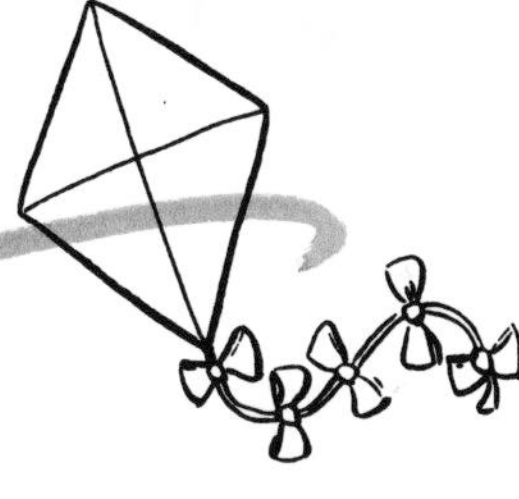

l lion

m moon

n nest
p penguin
q queen
r raccoon
s sun
t telephone
v violin
w wagon
x X ray
y yarn
z zebra

Vowel Chart

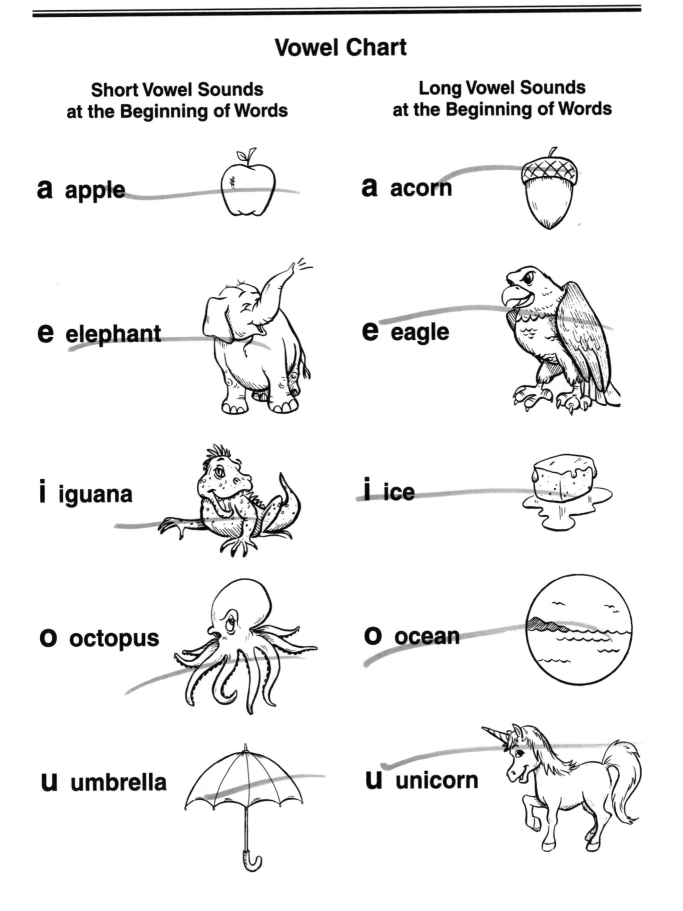

Short Vowel Sounds at the Beginning of Words		Long Vowel Sounds at the Beginning of Words	
a apple		**a** acorn	
e elephant		**e** eagle	
i iguana		**i** ice	
o octopus		**o** ocean	
u umbrella		**u** unicorn	

Vowel Chart

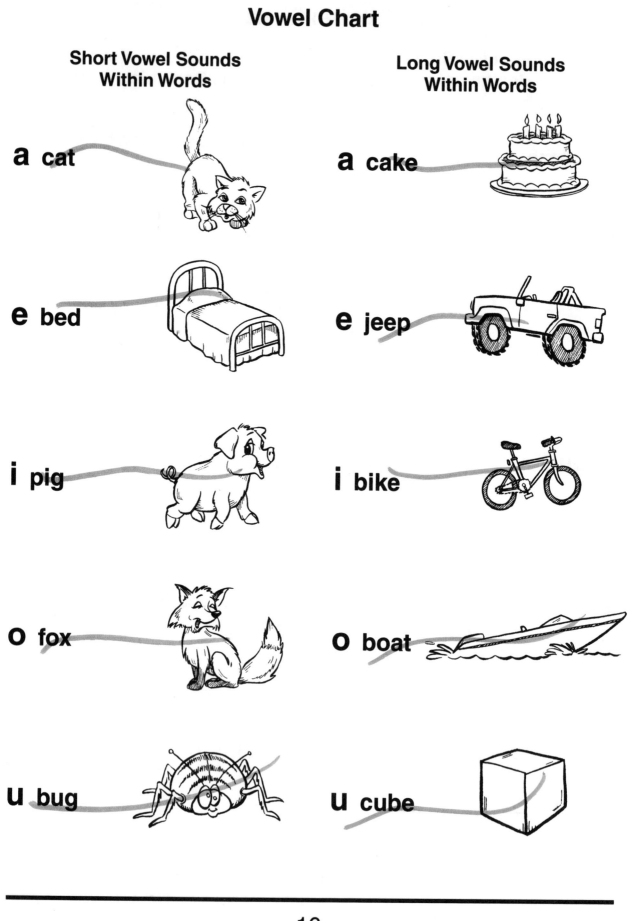

Short Vowel Sounds Within Words	Long Vowel Sounds Within Words
a cat	**a** cake
e bed	**e** jeep
i pig	**i** bike

Letter Combinations Chart

Some of the Most Frequently Used Letter Combinations

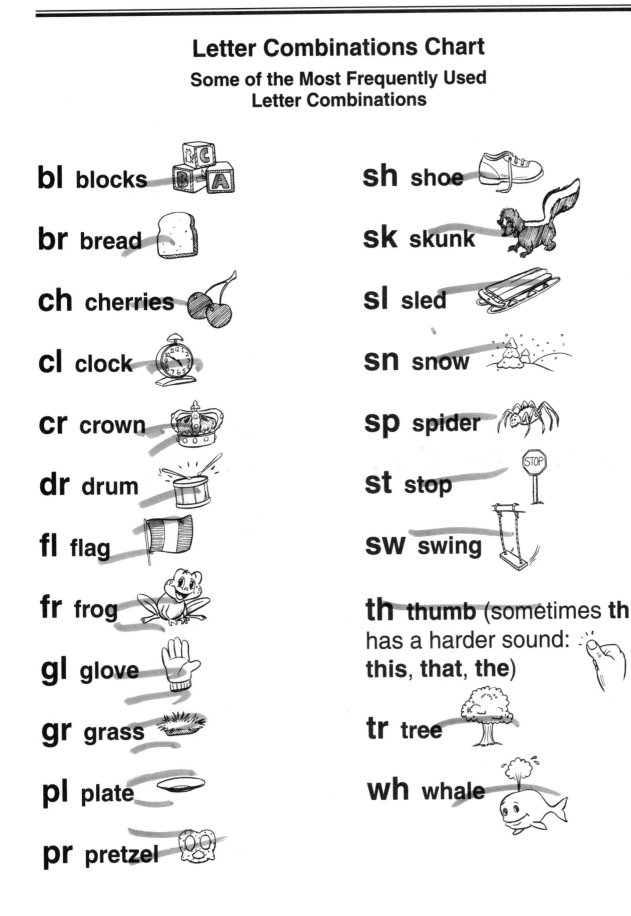

bl **blocks** 

br **bread** 

ch **cherries** 

cl **clock** 

cr **crown** 

dr **drum** 

fl **flag** 

fr **frog** 

gl **glove** 

gr **grass**

pl **plate**

pr **pretzel** 

sh **shoe**

sk **skunk** 

sl **sled** 

sn **snow** 

sp **spider** 

st **stop** 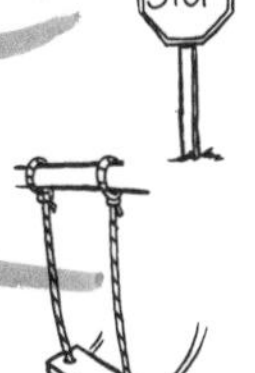

sw **swing**

th **thumb** (sometimes **th** has a harder sound: **this, that, the**)

tr **tree** 

wh **whale** 

They Go Together!

Each box contains a list of words that begin with the same letter. The words name objects that are alike in some way. Add as many more objects as you can think of to each list. Make sure each addition belongs with the others.

moose Moose
man
mouse
monkey

Explain how these objects are alike: thay are bothe animalls

corn
carrot carrot
cucumber

Explain how these objects are alike:

They Go Together!

Each box contains a list of words that begin with the same letter. The words name objects that are alike in some way. Add as many more objects as you can think of to each list. Make sure each addition belongs with the others.

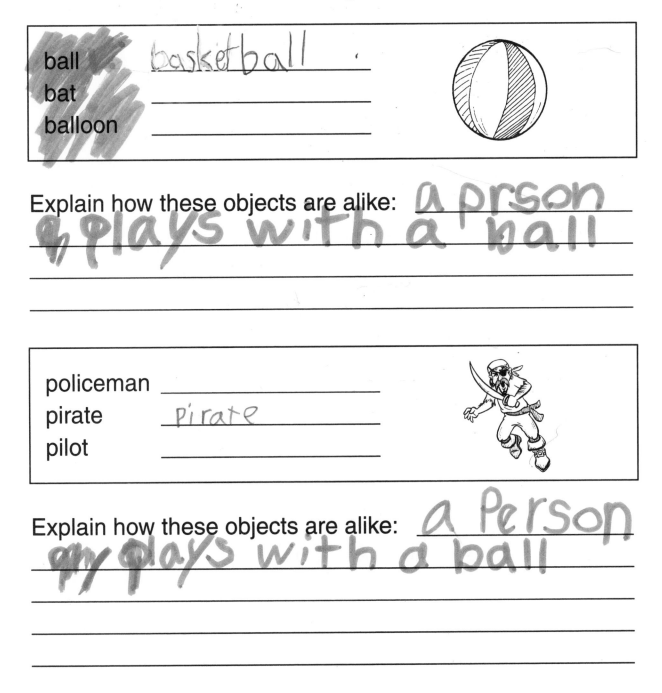

ball basketball
bat
balloon

Explain how these objects are alike: a prson plays with a ball

policeman
pirate pirate
pilot

Explain how these objects are alike: a Person plays with a ball

Mystery Letters

Use the same letter combination to fill in each blank in the sentence below. Do the same for the other sentences.

We can __ __are the fi__ __.

Please __ __ing your __ __other to the party.

__ __y to play the __ __umpet while you ride the __ __icycle.

Mystery Letters

Use the same letter combination to fill in each blank in the sentence below. Do the same for the other sentences.

__ __ich kind of __ __ale is usually __ __ite?

I would like a __ __eese sandwi__ __ and some __ __erries for lun__ __.

Bo__ __ of us __ __ought we heard a __ __ump.

Mystery Letters

Use the same letter combination to fill in each blank in the sentence below. Do the same for the other sentences.

The __ __ond boy __ __owing bubbles wore a __ __ue shirt and __ __ack shoes.

Sarah __ __ayed with the __ __ane while she ate a __ __um.

The __ __ea __ __ung himself across the __ __oor and did a __ __ip.

Mystery Letters

Use the same letter combination to fill in each blank in the sentence below. Do the same for the other sentences.

Daniel and his ___ ___other had ___ ___own ___ ___ead and ___ ___occoli for lunch.

The ___ ___een plant ___ ___ows out of the ___ ___ound.

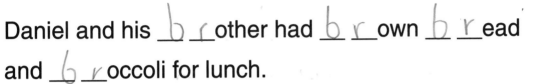

The ___ ___agon ___ ___ank a soda while he played the ___ ___ums.

Calling All Vowels

Fill in the blank spaces with long and short vowels. Make sure the words you form make sense in the story! Add a sentence of your own to finish the story. Draw a picture to illustrate your ending.

J__n and T__m found a b__x. They opened the l__d and peeked __n. The tw__ k__ds could n__t believe wh__t they s__w. __t the bottom of the b__x there w__s a n__st. S__tting __n the n__st was a gigantic __gg. __s they w__tched, the __gg b__gan to sh__ke and sh__ver.

____

____

____

Calling All Vowels

Fill in the blank spaces with long and short vowels. Make sure the words you form make sense in the story! Add a sentence of your own to finish the story. Draw a picture to illustrate your ending.

Laura and Tricia w___nt f___shing wh___n the s___n was j___st c___ming ___p. They d___g some w___rms out of the d___rt in the g___rden. They p___cked a l___nch to eat at n___ ___n. They p___t on their h___ts and w___lked d___wn to the str___ ___m. As soon as Laura put her l___ne in the w___ter, a f___sh began to t___g at it. The p___le began to b___nd.

____

____

____

Calling All Consonants

Fill in the blank spaces with consonants. Make sure the words you form make sense in the story! Add a sentence of your own to finish the story. Draw a picture to illustrate your ending.

Sue and Josh __anted to __ake a __ake. They __ot out __ilk, egg__, __ __our, __ugar, __anilla, and __aking pow__er. They foun__ a __ __eat __ig __owl. They mi__ed e__erything __ogether in the bow__ and __oured the __atter into a __an. They pu__ the __an in the ove__ and __aited.

____

____

____

Calling All Consonants

Fill in the blank spaces with consonants. Make sure the words you form make sense in the story! Add a sentence of your own to finish the story. Draw a picture to illustrate your ending.

One __aturday, Gary __ent for a __ide on his ho__se, Shorty. They went up to the __op of the __ountain to ha__e a __icnic lun__ __. Gary __ __ought a __andwich and so__e coo__ies for __imself. He brough__ a ca__ __ot and an a__ __le for Shorty. Whi__e they we__e ea__ing __unch, they hear__ a __oud boo__.

Zoom!

Label each picture on this page. Each word will contain the **oo** sound that you hear when you say **zoom**. Remember, there are several letter combinations that can make the same sound, such as **oo, ue,** and **ew**.

Add two more pictures that belong on this page and label them.

Sail Away!

Label each picture on this page. Each word will contain the **ay** sound that you hear when you say **sail** or **away**. Remember, there are several letter combinations that can make the same sound, such as **ay, ai,** and **eigh**.

Add two more pictures that belong on this page and label them.

Turtle Talk

Label each picture on this page. Each word will contain the **er** sound that you hear when you say **turtle**. Remember, there are several letter combinations that can make the same sound, such as **er, ur,** and **ir**.

Add two more pictures that belong on this page and label them.

How Now, Brown Cow!

Label each picture on this page. Each word will contain the **ow** sound that you hear when you say **cow**. Remember, there are a few letter combinations that can make the same sound, such as **ow** or **ou**.

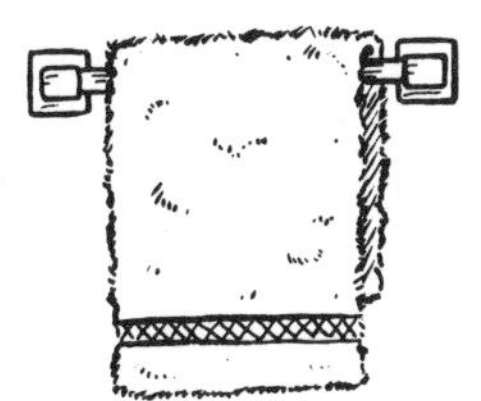

Add two more pictures that belong on this page and label them.

The Sounds of C

The letter **C** has no sound of its own. When **C** is in front of the vowels **i** and **e,** it sounds like the letter **S**. When it is in front of the vowels **a** and **o,** it sounds like the letter **K**.

Look at the pictures on the page. List the name of each picture under the correct heading below.

Sounds Like **S**	Sounds Like **K**
______________________	______________________
______________________	______________________
______________________	______________________
______________________	______________________

The Sounds of G

The letter **G** sometimes borrows the sound of the letter **J**. When **G** is in front of the vowels **i** and **e,** it usually sounds like the letter **J**. When it is in front of the vowels **a, o,** and **u,** it usually sounds like the letter **G**. Can you think of any words that start with **G** that are exceptions to these rules?

Look at the pictures on the page. List the name of each picture under the correct heading below.

Sounds Like **J**

____

____

____

____

Sounds Like **G**

____

____

____

____

Tongue Twister

"Peter Piper picked a peck of pickled peppers . . . " is the beginning of a well-known tongue twister. There are many items in the picture below that begin with the letter **P**. Use the lines below to make up a tongue twister using some or all of the words for the items that you found. Add some other words that begin with **P** if you can!

Write your tongue twister here.

Tongue Twister

"She sells seashells . . . " is the beginning of a well-known tongue twister. There are many items in the picture below that begin with the letters **CL**. Use the lines below to make up a tongue twister using some or all of the words for the items that you found. Add some other words that begin with **CL** if you can!

Write your tongue twister here.

Tongue Twister

"How much wood would a woodchuck chuck . . . " is the beginning of a well-known tongue twister. There are many items in the picture below that begin with the letter **V**. Use the lines to make up a tongue twister using some or all of the words for the items that you found. Add some other words that begin with **V** if you can!

Write your tongue twister here.

____

____

____

____

Poetry Corner

There are many items in the picture below that end with the letters **AT**. Use the lines below to make up a poem using some or all of the words for the items that you found. Add some other words that end with **AT** if you can!

Write your poem here.

Poetry Corner

There are many items in the picture below that end with the letters **OLD**. Use the lines below to make up a poem using some or all of the words for the items that you found. Add some other words that end with **OLD** if you can!

Write your poem here.

Poetry Corner

There are many items in the picture below that end with the letters **AIL**. Use the lines below to make up a poem using some or all of the words for the items that you found. Add some other words that end with **AIL** if you can!

Write your poem here.

Poetry Corner

There are many items in the picture below that end with the letters **IN**. Use the lines below to make up a poem using some or all of the words for the items that you found. Add some other words that end with **IN** if you can!

Write your poem here.

____

____

____

____

Read and Draw

Read the sentences below. Complete the picture using the information in the sentences. Look for a silent letter in each underlined word! Circle all the silent letters.

<u>Two</u> little <u>ghosts</u> went for a <u>walk</u> in the darkest <u>hour</u> of the <u>night</u>. They saw a <u>bright</u> <u>light</u> shining from a <u>house</u>, so they went up to the door and turned the <u>knob</u>.

What happened next? Write your answer below. Try to use some words that have silent letters.

____

____

____

____

Read and Draw

Read the sentences below. Complete the picture using the information in the sentences. Look for a silent letter in each underlined word! Circle all the silent letters.

Sally said, "I can't do anything <u>right</u> today! I hit my <u>thumb</u> with a hammer. I fell and skinned my <u>knee</u>. I put my shoes on the <u>wrong</u> feet. My socks do not <u>match</u>."

What did Sally say next? Write your answer below. Try to use some words that have silent letters.

____

____

____

____

Letter-Sound Riddles

I am yummy to eat. I am red and sweet. I grow on trees. My name begins with the same sound as [cheese] and [chair].

What am I? Draw a circle around me.

Write a sentence about me!

____

____

I am a pest. People do not like to have me around. I am small and black. My name ends with a long **i** sound.

What am I? Draw a circle around me.

  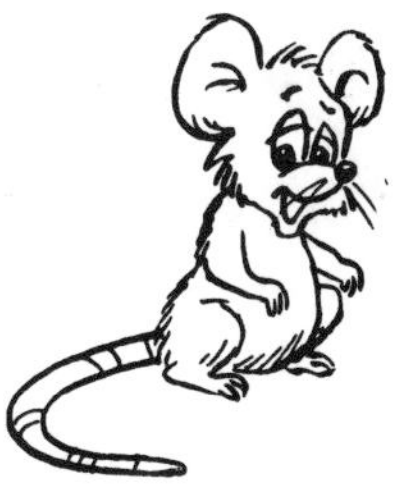

Write a sentence about me!

____

____

Letter-Sound Riddles

I am white. Sometimes I am slippery. Sometimes I am wet. My name has the same vowel sound as .

What am I? Draw a circle around me.

Write a sentence about me!

I can fly. I come in many different sizes and colors. There are no silent letters in my name.

What am I? Draw a circle around me.

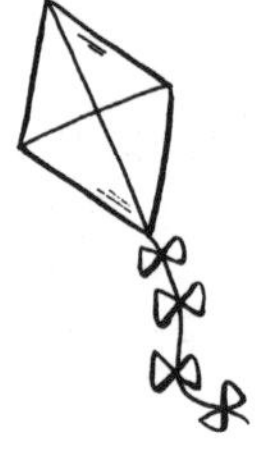

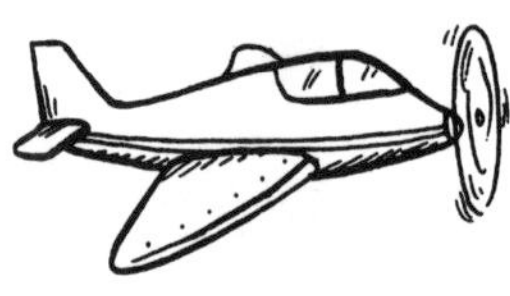

Write a sentence about me!

Letter-Sound Riddles

I am small. I can fit in a pocket. I am usually made of plastic. I am useful! I have a silent letter in my name.

What am I? Draw a circle around me.

Write a sentence about me!

I have wheels. It is fun to ride on me. I can go fast! My name has the same vowel sound as .

What am I? Draw a circle around me.

Write a sentence about me!

Rhyming Riddles

I am very beautiful. I come in many shapes and colors. I am a living thing. I rhyme with .

What am I? ________________

Write a short poem about me. Use some rhyming words!

___

___

___

I am something you eat for breakfast. I am crunchy. I am brown. I rhyme with something that is part of a fence.

What am I? ________________ Draw a picture of a yummy breakfast. Be sure to include me!

Rhyming Riddles

I am an animal. I lay eggs. I can make a lot of noise!

I rhyme with  .

What am I? ________________

Write a short poem about me. Use some rhyming words!

____

____

____

I am something you see in the sky. Sometimes I am very bright. Usually you see me at night. I rhyme with something you use to eat soup.

What am I? ________________ Draw a picture of me in the night sky.

Silent E

Change each word on the list to a new word by adding an **e** to the end of the word. This **e** is silent, but powerful, because it changes the short vowel sound to a long vowel sound. Write a sentence using each pair of words.

Example:

fin fine

The fin on the fish is in fine shape.

1. hid ____________

____

2. bit ____________

____

3. hop ____________

____

4. pan ____________

____

5. cub ____________

____

Silent E

Change each word on the list to a new word by adding an **e** to the end of the word. This **e** is silent, but powerful, because it changes the short vowel sound to a long vowel sound. Write a sentence using each pair of words.

Example:

man mane

The man held on to the horse's mane.

1. Sam ____________

____

2. spin ____________

____

3. scrap ____________

____

4. plan ____________

____

5. hat ____________

____

Fractured-Word Puzzles

Fill in the blanks to complete each word. The picture clues will help you. Put the letters from the blanks together to form a new word.

Example:

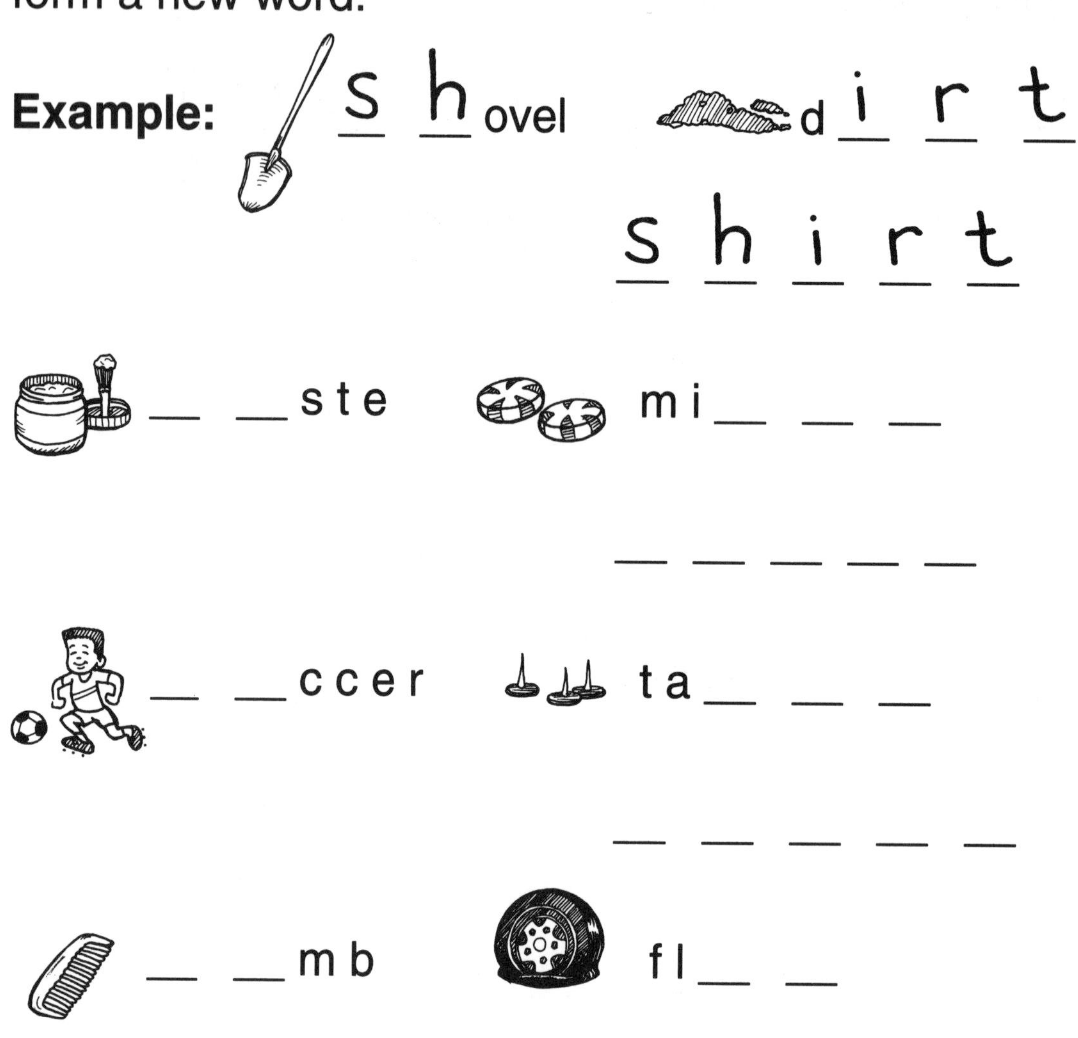

Why do all the new words belong together? On a separate piece of paper, make up your own fractured-word puzzle that goes with the other puzzles on the page! Ask a friend or family member to solve it.

Fractured-Word Puzzles

Fill in the blanks to complete each word. The picture clues will help you. Then put the letters from the blanks together to form a new word.

Why do all the new words belong together? On a separate piece of paper, make up your own fractured-word puzzle that goes with the other puzzles on the page! Ask a friend or family member to solve it.

Follow the Letter

Make up a "follow the letter" sentence. Make sure that each word in your sentence begins with the letter that the word before it ends with. The first word in the sentence can begin with any letter.

Example:

Th**e** **e**lephan**t** **t**oo**k** **K**in**g** **G**erald'**s** **s**ilve**r** **r**ing.

Write your "follow the letter" sentence on the lines below. Then draw a picture to illustrate your sentence.

Follow the Letter

Make up a "follow the letter" sentence. Make sure that each word in your sentence begins with the letter that the word before it ends with. The first word in the sentence can begin with any letter.

Example:

Ever**y** **y**oun**g** **g**ir**l** **l**ike**s** **s**wee**t** **t**reats.

Write your "follow the letter" sentence on the lines below. Then draw a picture to illustrate your sentence.

Follow the Letter

Make up a "follow the letter" sentence. Make sure that each word in your sentence begins with the letter that the word before it ends with. The first word in the sentence can begin with any letter.

Example:

Pu**t** **t**omat**o** **o**n Nick'**s** **s**andwich.

Write your "follow the letter" sentence on the lines below. Then draw a picture to illustrate your sentence.

Follow the Letter

Make up a "follow the letter" sentence. Make sure that each word in your sentence begins with the letter that the word before it ends with. The first word in the sentence can begin with any letter.

Example:

Ho**w** **will** **Lee** **eat** **two** **o**melets?

Write your "follow the letter" sentence on the lines below. Then draw a picture to illustrate your sentence.

Hidden Words

In each sentence below you will find a hidden word. All the hidden words belong together. Do you know why? Circle the hidden words.

Example: The lit**tle g**irl ran to her mother.

The car might run out of gas.

My mom gives me some honey every morning.

The address on the letter is 221 Spring Street.

The elevator always gets stuck on this floor.

This is the fourth umbrella that I have broken!

Now write your own hidden-word sentences. Choose any subject you like for your words.

____

____

____

____

Hidden Words

In each sentence below you will find a hidden word. All the hidden words belong together. Do you know why? Circle the hidden words.

Example: Ta**p each** toe twice to keep the beat.

Put the napkin in your lap please.

The little monkey played in the tree.

He should have been home long before now.

These tomatoes are ripe aren't they?

Those dresses are pretty enough for angels to wear.

Now write your own hidden-word sentences. Choose any subject you like for your words.

____

____

____

____

Word Scrambles

Unscramble each word on the following list. Then write a sentence using only those words. Draw a picture to illustrate the sentence.

shrsoe ____________________

rove ____________________

teh ____________________

lishl ____________________

nevse ____________________

pallog ____________________

Word Scrambles

Unscramble each word on the following list. Then write a sentence using only those words. Draw a picture to illustrate the sentence.

dwnis ____________________

olcd ____________________

twnire ____________________

wobl ____________________

dan ____________________

liwd ____________________

Word Scrambles

Unscramble each word on the following list. Then write a sentence using only those words. Draw a picture to illustrate the sentence.

omse ____________________

spinkump ____________________

drnclhie ____________________

greona ____________________

levtew ____________________

odfun ____________________

____

____

Word Scrambles

Unscramble each word on the following list. Then write a sentence using only those words. Draw a picture to illustrate the sentence.

drastuya ____________________

uro ____________________

rcdas ____________________

ylmfia ____________________

gtinh ____________________

ydalep ____________________

Word Pyramid

Complete the word pyramid by writing a new word on each line. Work from top to bottom. The first word you write must have two letters and must include the letter at the top of the pyramid. The next word must have three letters and include both letters from the previous word. The letters do not have to be in the same order. Try to fill in the whole pyramid.

Example:

Word Pyramid

Complete the word pyramid by writing a new word on each line. Work from top to bottom. The first word you write must have two letters and must include the letter at the top of the pyramid. The next word must have three letters and include both letters from the previous word. The letters do not have to be in the same order. Try to fill in the whole pyramid.

Example:

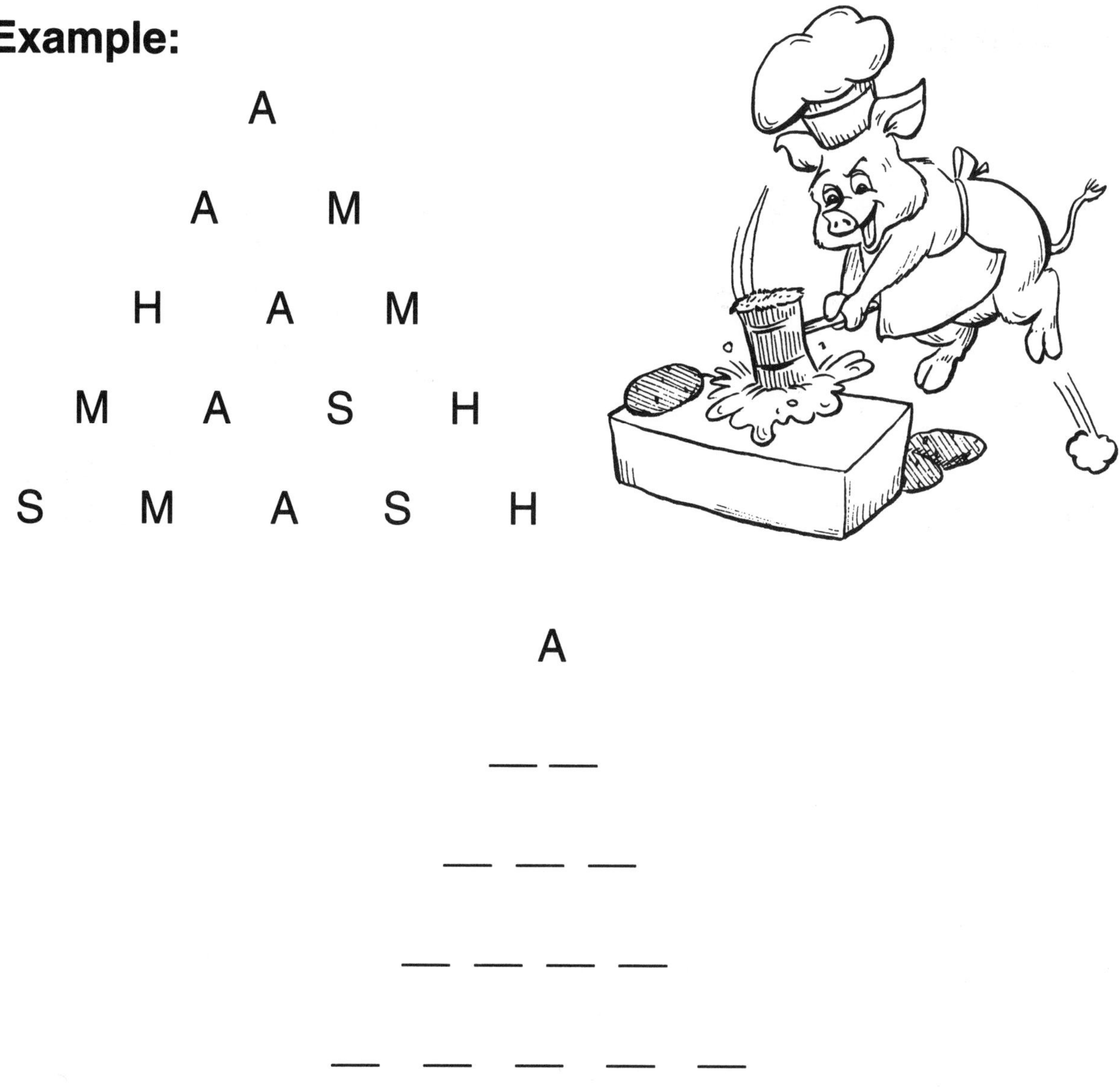

A

A M

H A M

M A S H

S M A S H

A

__ __

__ __ __

__ __ __ __

__ __ __ __ __

Word Pyramids

Complete the word pyramids by writing a new word on each line. Work from top to bottom. The first word you write must have two letters and must include the letter at the top of the pyramid. The next word must have three letters and include both letters from the previous word. The letters do not have to be in the same order. Try to build two different pyramids using the same letter.

O

__ __

__ __ __

__ __ __ __

__ __ __ __ __

O

__ __

__ __ __

__ __ __ __

__ __ __ __ __

Word Pyramids

Complete the word pyramids by writing a new word on each line. Work from top to bottom. The first word you write must have two letters and must include the letter at the top of the pyramid. The next word must have three letters and include both letters from the previous word. The letters do not have to be in the same order. Try to build two different pyramids using the same letter.

E

__ __

__ __ __

__ __ __ __

__ __ __ __ __

E

__ __

__ __ __

__ __ __ __

__ __ __ __ __

Story Time

Write a story about the picture. Use words with long and short vowels. Try to use words with consonants that look the same but sound differently from one another. Also try to use some words with silent letters.

Story Time

Write a story about the picture. Use words with long and short vowels. Try to use words with consonants that look the same but sound differently from one another. Also try to use some words with silent letters.

Story Time

Write a story about the picture. Use words with long and short vowels. Try to use words with consonants that look the same but sound differently from one another. Also try to use some words with silent letters.

READING

This section features exercises to help children practice and develop their reading comprehension skills. Deduction and inference play a large role in this section, as children are asked to draw conclusions and assess information using the clues and facts provided. In addition to working through the exercises, read aloud to your child, or have him or her read aloud to you. Make reading an everyday activity with your child. As your child grows, the love of reading you have fostered in him or her will carry through into adulthood.

Princess Nancy dreams about a knight in shining armor. Read all about him. Which one of the knights is Nancy dreaming about? Write his name.

He has long, straight hair.
His face is smooth and clean.
His shield has the royal seal.
His name is
________________.
Barry
Lester
Alan
Alberto

Who robbed the cookie store? Ms. Riley saw the robber. Read her description. Then write his name below.

He had curly hair and a scar over his right eye. He had a mustache. He was very thin.
Zak
Sam
Harry
Albert
Ralph
Max

The thief is ____.

Read all the clues. Then write the name of each girl below her. Make sure you read **all** the clues first!

1. Carol is wearing a hat. She is between Leesa and Joyce.

2. Alana is not wearing shoes. She is next to Leesa.

3. Helen is holding a ball.

4. Where is Joyce?

Six girls are having a pajama party. Read all the clues. Then write each girl's name in the correct place.

1. Susan is across from Hilary.
2. Mary is next to Susan, who is closest to the food.
3. Maria is not next to Mary or Hilary.
4. Jill is having a pillow fight with Maria.
5. Where is Yolanda?

Seven people live in this apartment house. Read all the clues. Then write each person's name in the correct place.

1. Adam loves flowers. He lives on the bottom floor next to Tony.
2. Carl is on the top floor.
3. Carl lives above two boys. One of them is Willy.
4. Sherry lives between Mike and Tony.
5. Where does Sophia live?

For each number, cross out the one thing that you **don't** need to know.

1. To fix a bike you need to know
   a. what tools to use
   b. what time the bike broke
   c. how a bike works

2. To build a doghouse you need to know
   a. the size of the dog
   b. where your tools are
   c. what the dog eats for dinner

3. To go camping you need to know
   a. where your friends camped last summer
   b. the weather report
   c. how to start a fire

4. To wash the car you need to know
   a. how to hook up the hose
   b. how to drive
   c. where the soap is

For each number, cross out the one thing that you **don't** need to know.

1. To go on vacation you need to know
   a. what time you are going
   b. how big the hotel is
   c. what clothes to pack

2. To make spaghetti you need to know
   a. how to set the table
   b. how many people will be eating
   c. how to boil water

3. To give a book report you need to know
   a. who the author is
   b. what the story is about
   c. who else has read the book

4. To go sailing you need to know
   a. what the sail is made of
   b. how fast the wind is blowing
   c. which way the wind is blowing

Circle the picture that is the same as the one in the box, but turned in a different way. The first one is done for you.

Circle the picture that is the same as the one in the box, but turned in a different way.

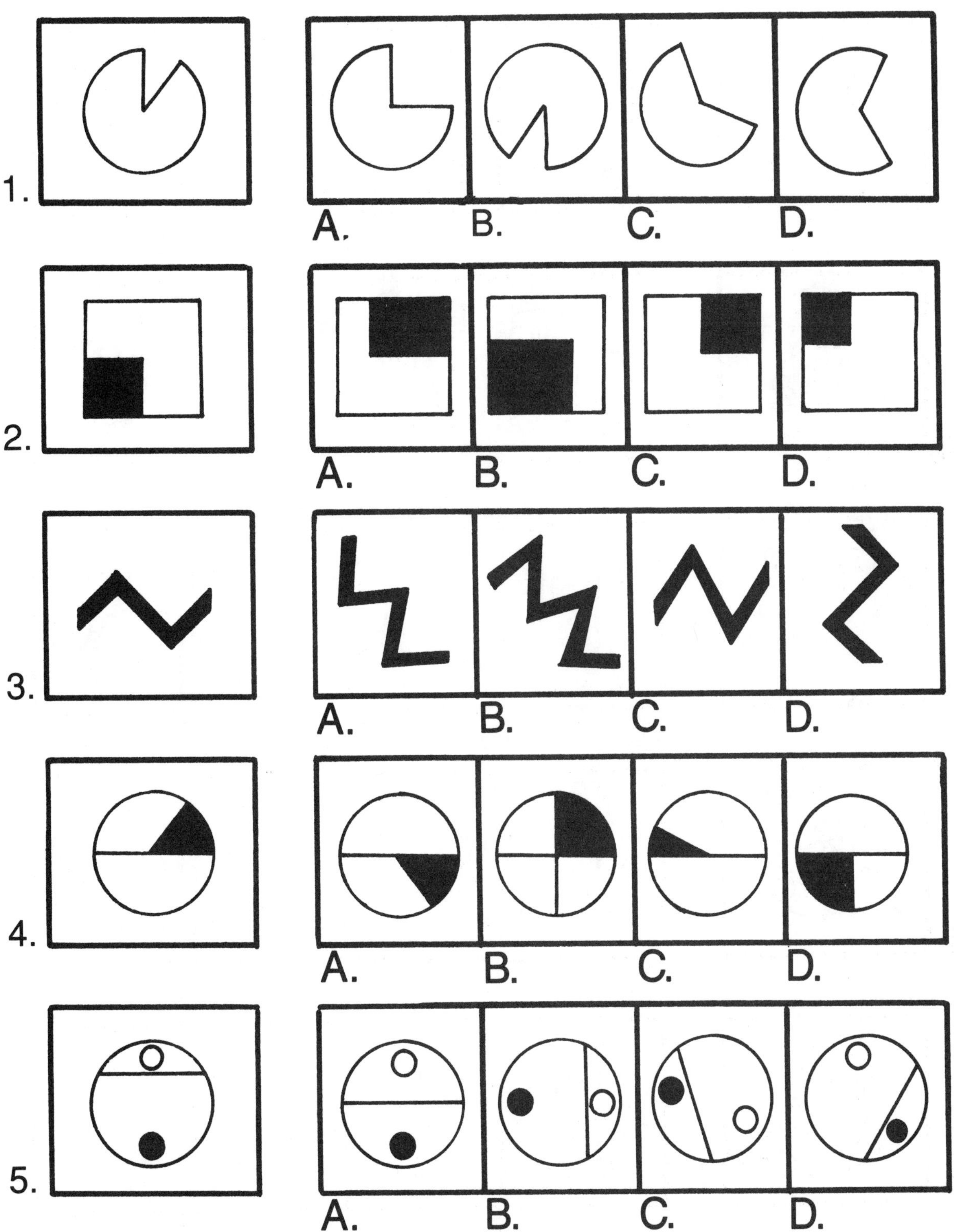

Circle the picture that is the same as the one in the box, but turned upside down.

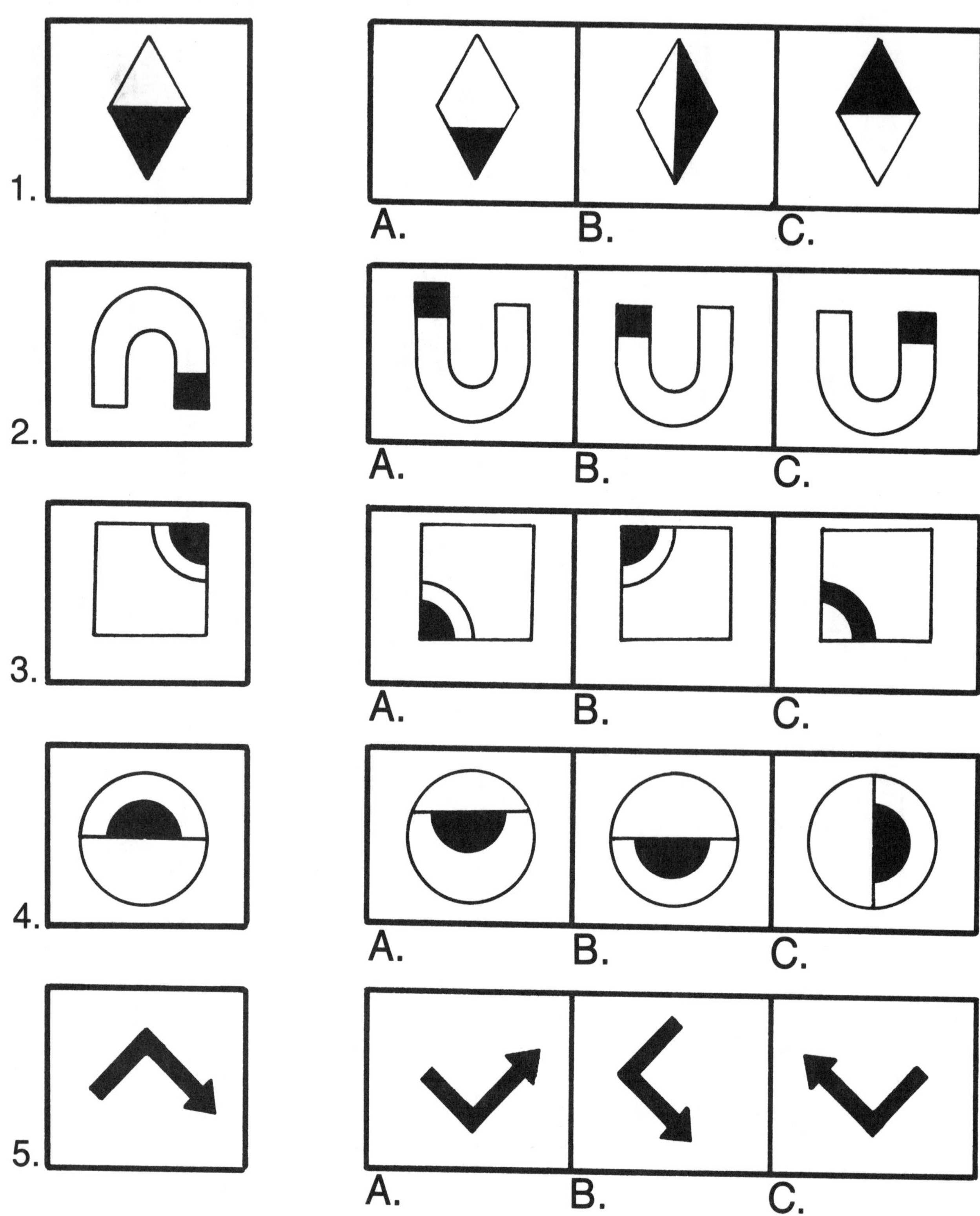

Circle the picture that is the same as the one in the box, but turned upside down.

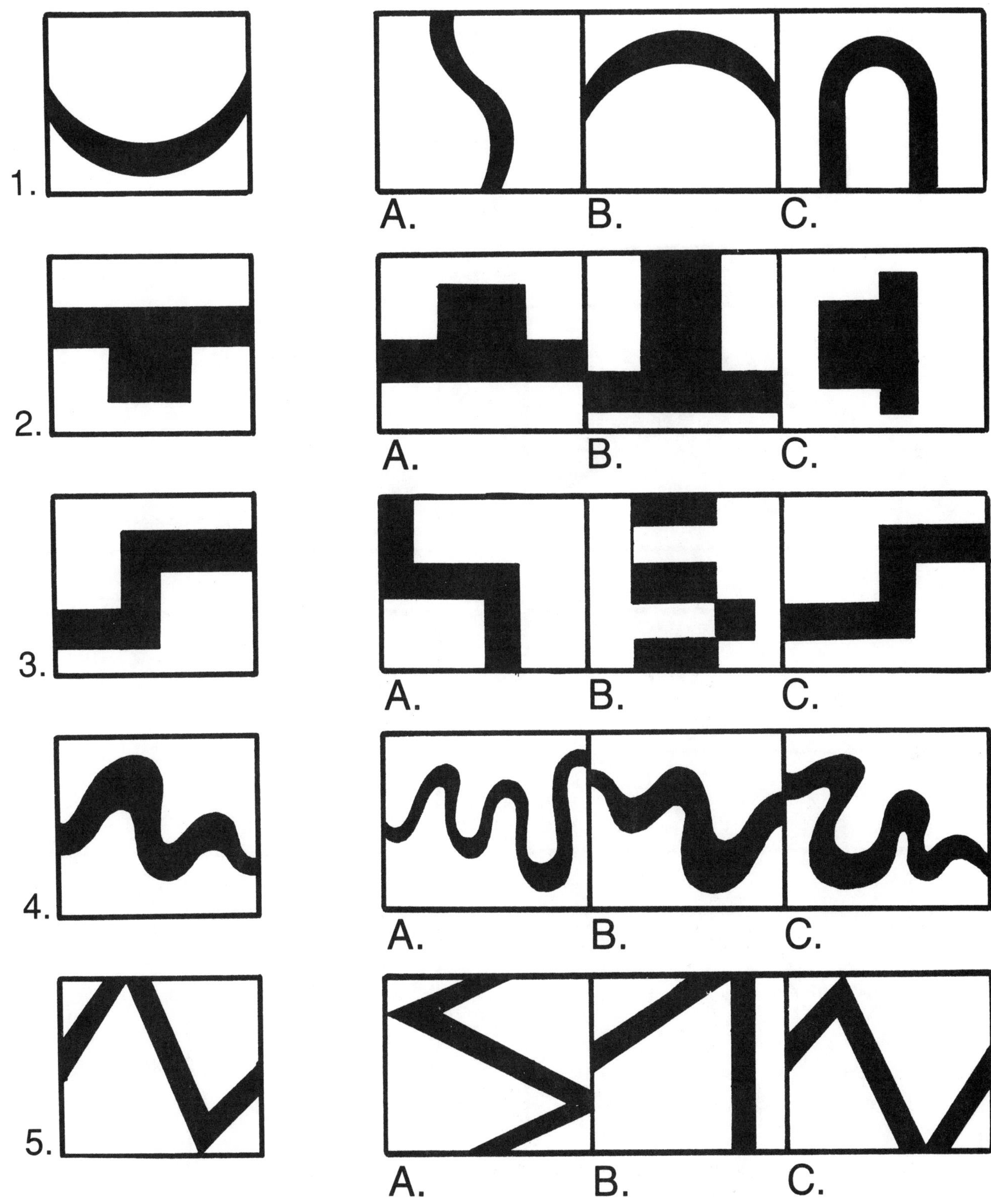

Draw each picture again — but draw it upside down. Think carefully before you draw!

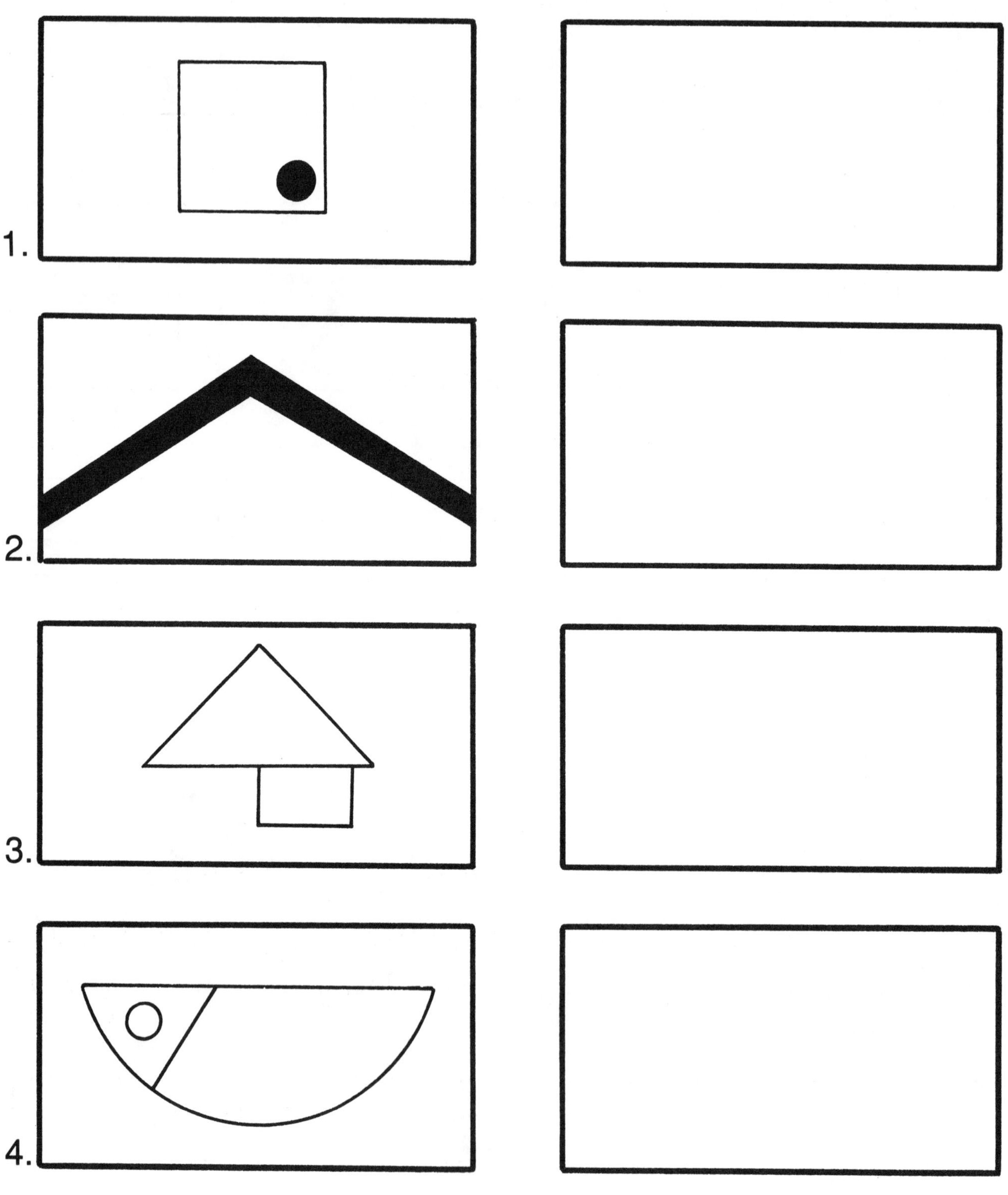

Cross out the incorrect word in each sentence. Find the correct word in the word list and write it at the end of the sentence. **One** sentence is correct just as it is! Put a check at the end of it.

1. Tyrone put boats on his feet to keep them dry. ____________

2. Angela was late. She talked very fast to catch the bus. ____________

3. The lemon was sweet and juicy. ____________

4. We could see fish swimming under our car. ____________

5. We went roller-skating on the frozen pond. ____________

6. The chocolate froze in the hot sun. ____________

7. Did you see that show? ____________

8. The dog parked all night long. ____________

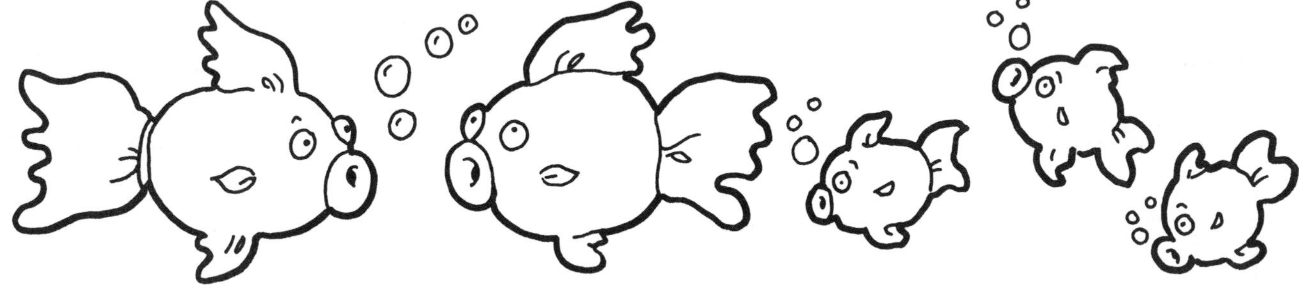

boat	mat	see	laughed
ice-skating	walked	sea	barked
melted	yellow	boots	cold

Cross out the incorrect word in each sentence. Find the correct word in the word list and write it at the end of the sentence. **One** sentence is correct just as it is! Put a check at the end of it.

1. Washington, D.C. is the middle of our country. ________________

2. She didn't **here** a thing I said. ________________

3. Ann was smiling. She was sorry she came to the party. ________________

4. He walked so fast we couldn't understand him. ________________

5. She fell and scraped her knee. ________________

6. The fire burned for hours. There was much left of the house. ________________

____

7. Her parents were proud of her. Her report card was awful. ________________

8. She could hear smoke. She knew something was burning. ________________

glad	more	top	hear
smell	capital	pet	feel
talked	wasn't	great	green

Cross out the incorrect word in each sentence. Find the correct word in the word list and write it at the end of the sentence. **One** sentence is correct just as it is! Put a check at the end of it.

1. Are you crazy? Have you locked your marbles? ____________
2. After swimming, she felt dead in one ear. ____________
3. We hurried so we wouldn't miss the end of the movie. ____________
4. The newspaper was yellow and stiff. It was old. ____________
5. She knocked over the milk. Her pants were sold. ____________
6. Luisa hit a home run just in time to win the football game. ____________
   ____
7. The park opens after dark. ____________
8. Larry put on a wool glove to keep his head warm. ____________

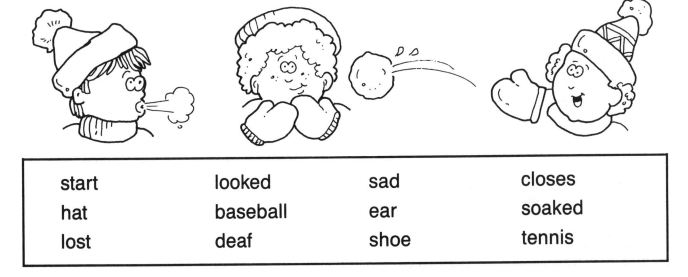

start	looked	sad	closes
hat	baseball	ear	soaked
lost	deaf	shoe	tennis

Princess Roxanne has a lot to do today before she goes to the Wizard for her magic lesson. She made a list of errands, but they are not in the right order. Number her errands in the **best** order so she can get to the Wizard's house on time.

Princess Roxanne's Castle
Wizard's House
Dragon's Cave
Crown Computers
Royal Bakery
Pet Shop
Highness Hardware

A. ____ Pick up her computer.

B. ____ Buy nails to repair castle doors.

C. ____ Kill the dragon.

D. ____ Buy food for the alligators in the moat.

E. ____ Get cake for the royal feast.

Mr. Smith has many errands to do before he goes to work at the bank today. Number the errands in the **best** order so he can get to work on time.

A. ____ Return library books.

B. ____ Pick up his shoes.

C. ____ Buy bread.

D. ____ Get gas.

E. ____ Borrow sugar from Ms. Brown.

F. ____ Get his teeth cleaned.

Red Riding Hood and the Wolf are both going to visit Grandma, but their directions are all mixed up. Put their directions in order by numbering them from 1 to 3.

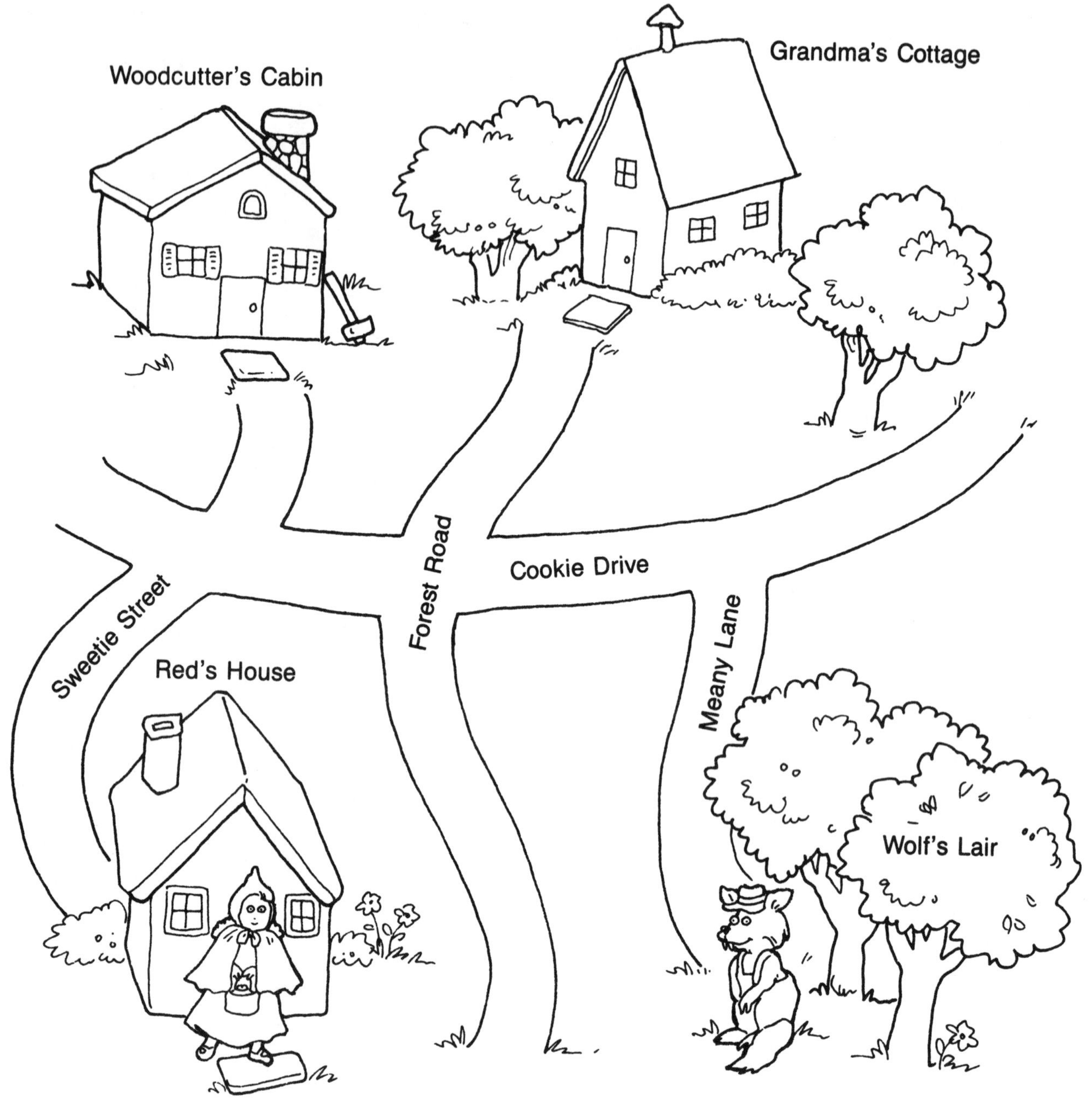

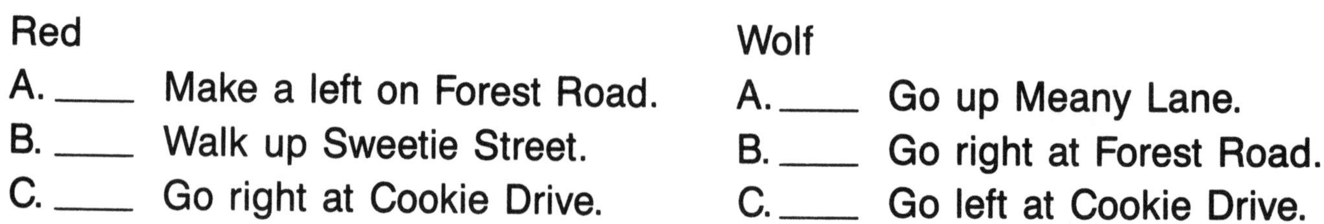

Red

A. ____ Make a left on Forest Road.

B. ____ Walk up Sweetie Street.

C. ____ Go right at Cookie Drive.

Wolf

A. ____ Go up Meany Lane.

B. ____ Go right at Forest Road.

C. ____ Go left at Cookie Drive.

Sam and Dan are going to the market. Their directions are mixed up. Put their directions in order by numbering from 1 to 4.

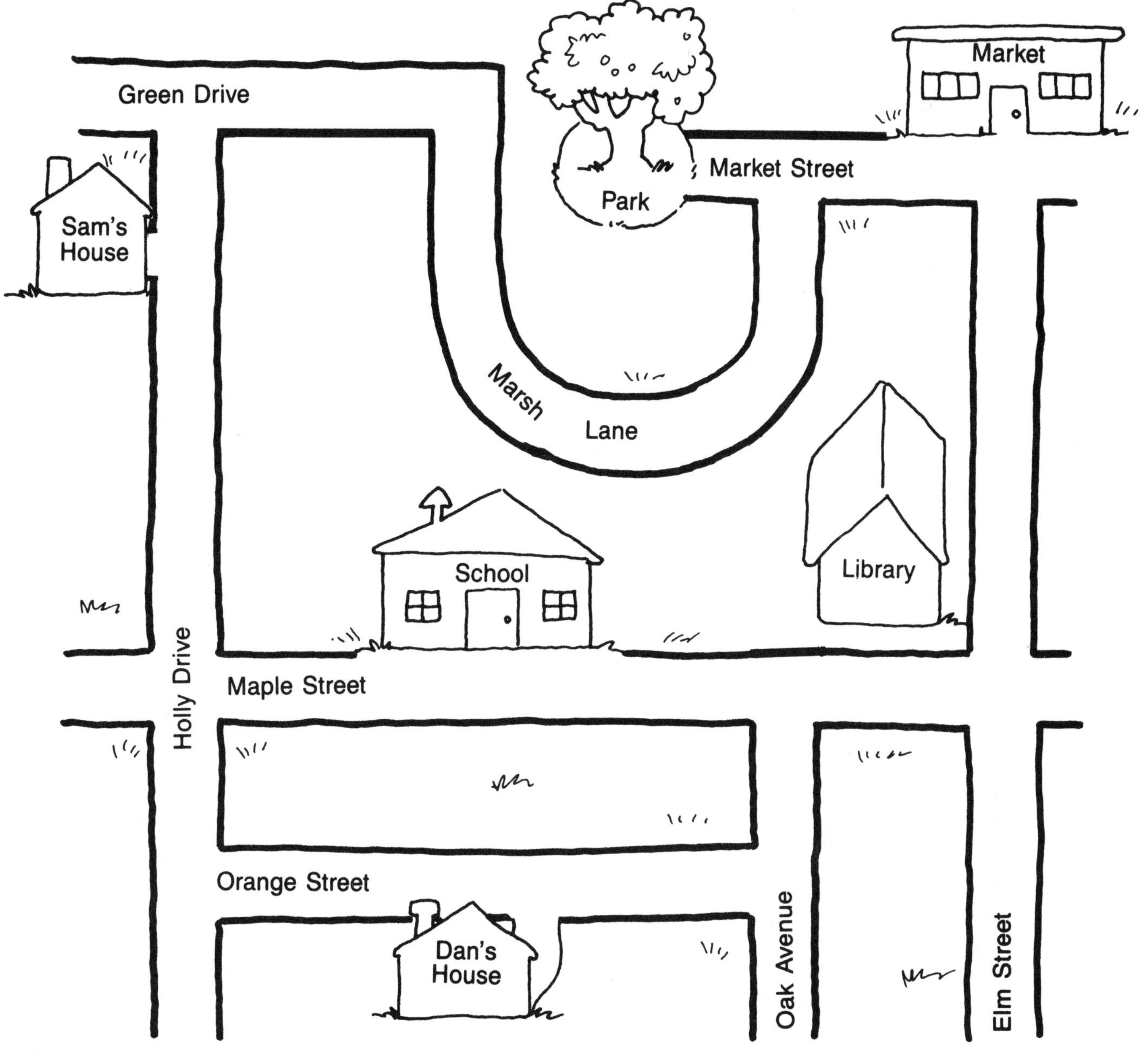

Sam

A.____ Make a right on Marsh Lane.

B.____ Go right on Market Street.

C.____ Go left on Holly Drive.

D.____ Go right on Green Drive.

Dan

A.____ Go right on Maple Street.

B.____ Go left on Elm Street.

C.____ Make a left on Oak Avenue.

D.____ Go right on Orange Street.

How is each pair of words alike? Use the word bank to complete each sentence. The first one has been done for you.

1. Grass and lettuce are green.
2. Red and yellow are ______________________.
3. Bananas and apples are ______________________.
4. Houses and castles are ______________________.
5. Tennis and baseball are ______________________.
6. Computers and cars are ______________________.
7. Hammers and rulers are ______________________.
8. Kittens and puppies are ______________________.
9. Amy and Susan are ______________________.
10. Hurricanes and tornadoes are ______________________.

salty	green	cars	girls
sports	hats	machines	buildings
storms	fruits	tools	slow
babies	clothes	colors	

How is each pair of words alike? Use the word bank to complete each sentence.

1. Snow and cotton are ______________________________.
2. Birds and kites ______________________________.
3. Wheels and records ______________________________.
4. Children and hair ______________________________.
5. Mexico and France are ______________________________.
6. London and Paris are ______________________________.
7. Doors and windows ______________________________.
8. Spring and fall are ______________________________.
9. Mark and Adam are ______________________________.
10. Balloons and feathers are ______________________________.

light	heavy	lakes	go around
seasons	boys	countries	fly
grow	open	cities	shows
run fast	hot	white	

How is each pair alike and different? The first one is done for you.

A unicorn and a cow

Alike: They both have four legs.

Different: The unicorn has one horn.

unicorn

cow

A circle and a square

Alike: ______________________________

Different: ______________________________

A castle and an igloo

Alike: ______________________________

Different: ______________________________

A turtle and a seahorse

Alike: ______________________________

Different: ______________________________

How is each pair alike and different?

A bed and a chair

Alike: ______________________________

Different: ______________________________

Milk and soda pop

Alike: ______________________________

Different: ______________________________

Skin and grass

Alike: ______________________________

Different: ______________________________

Crying and laughing

Alike: ______________________________

Different: ______________________________

Read each sentence. Think how the first pair of things go together. Use the word bank to complete the sentence and make the second pair of things go together **in the same way** as the first pair. The first one is done for you.

1. Boots are to feet as gloves are to hands.
2. Puppy is to dog as kitten is to ____________________ .
3. Finger is to hand as toe is to ____________________ .
4. Bird is to nest as cow is to ____________________ .
5. Thursday is to Friday as May is to ____________________ .
6. Coat is to closet as car is to ____________________ .
7. Apple is to fruit as rose is to ____________________ .
8. Milk is to drink as meat is to ____________________ .

road	June	April	garage
cat	hands	ring	barn
eat	flower	mother	foot

Read each sentence. Think how the first pair of things go together. Use the word bank to complete the sentence and make the second pair of things go together **in the same way** as the first pair.

1. Bee is to sting as cat is to____________________ .

2. Pancakes are to fry as cake is to ____________________ .

3. State is to Ohio as city is to ____________________ .

4. Horse is to colt as bear is to ____________________ .

5. Herd is to sheep as flock is to ____________________ .

6. Hen is to seed as horse is to ____________________ .

7. Walk is to slow as jump is to ____________________ .

8. Tadpole is to frog as caterpillar is to ____________________ .

wolf	Boston	butterfly	high
bake	California	cocoon	birds
hay	cub	barn	scratch

Think about how the first two things in each sentence go together. Then fill in the blanks with two more things that go together **in the same way.**

1. Calf is to cow as ____________________ is to _________________________ .

2. King is to castle as __________________ is to _________________________ .

3. Circle is to round as _________________ is to _________________________ .

4. Eyes are to see as __________________ is to _________________________ .

5. Drive is to car as ___________________ is to _________________________ .

6. Dog is to "woof" as _________________ is to _________________________ .

7. Hat is to head as ___________________ is to _________________________ .

8. Fish is to water as _________________ is to _________________________ .

Match each set of directions to the correct box. Write the letter next to the box. The first one is done for you.

1.

2.

3.

4.

5.

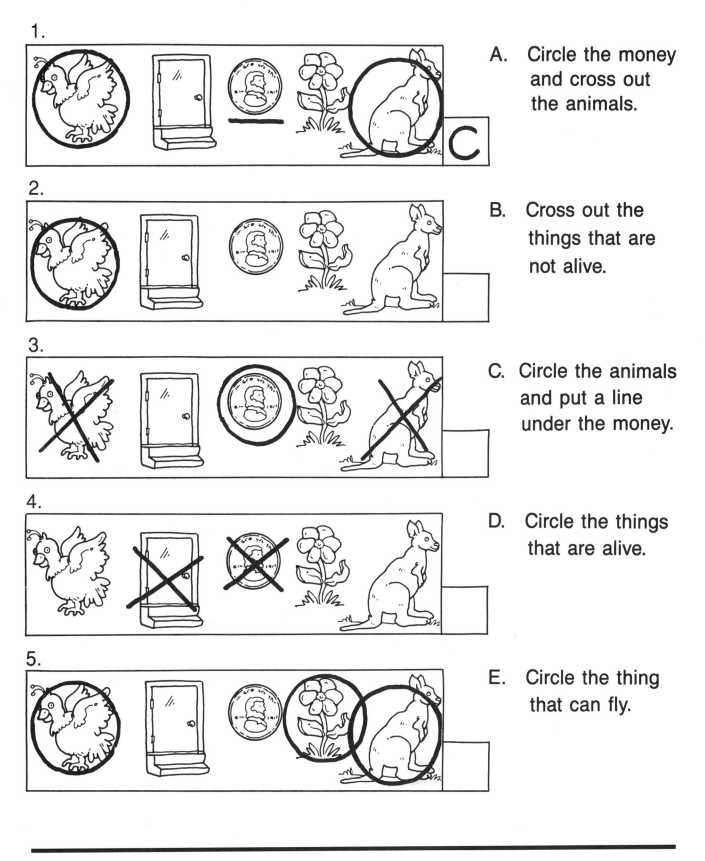

A. Circle the money and cross out the animals.

B. Cross out the things that are not alive.

C. Circle the animals and put a line under the money.

D. Circle the things that are alive.

E. Circle the thing that can fly.

Match each set of directions to the correct box. Write the letter next to the box.

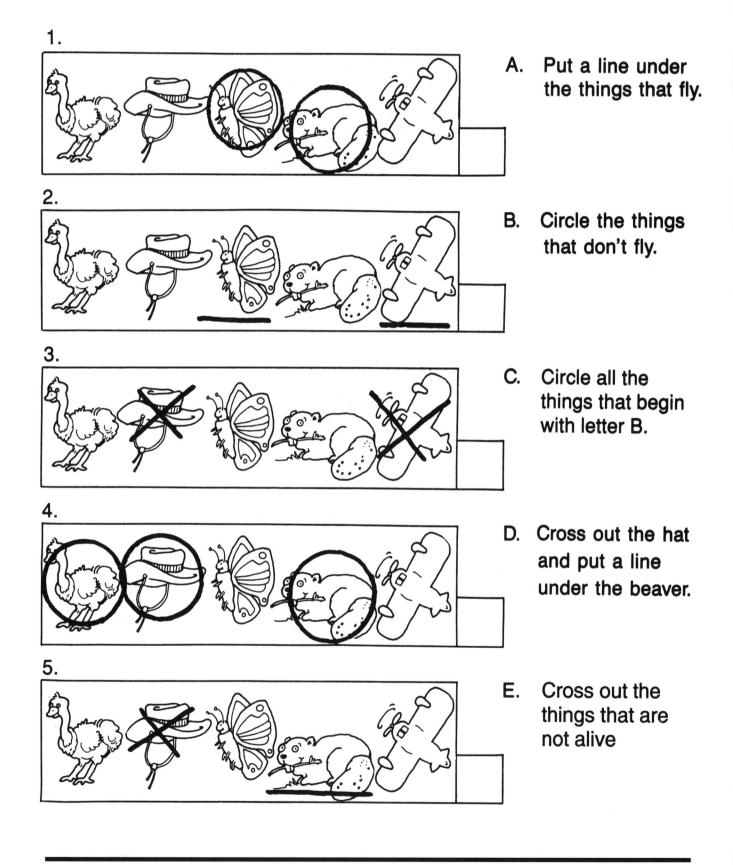

1.

A. Put a line under the things that fly.

2.

B. Circle the things that don't fly.

3.

C. Circle all the things that begin with letter B.

4.

D. Cross out the hat and put a line under the beaver.

5.

E. Cross out the things that are not alive

Read the directions for each row. Have they been followed correctly? Mark yes or no.

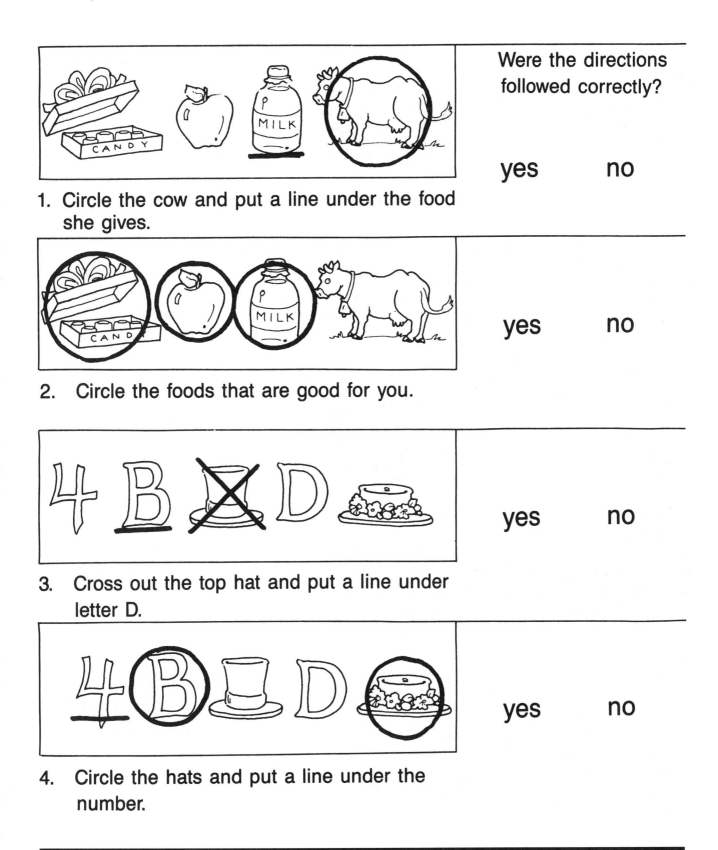

Were the directions followed correctly?

yes no

1. Circle the cow and put a line under the food she gives.

yes no

2. Circle the foods that are good for you.

yes no

3. Cross out the top hat and put a line under letter D.

yes no

4. Circle the hats and put a line under the number.

Read the directions for each row. Have they been followed correctly? Mark yes or no.

Were the directions followed correctly?

yes no

1. Circle the things that begin with letter H.

yes no

2. Put a line under the things that live in water and circle the number.

yes no

3. Cross out the things that rhyme.

yes no

4. Cross out the two things that live in water and put a line under the opposite of thin.

The computer mixed up two stories! Each story is in the right order, but both are tangled together. On the next page copy each story as it should be.

The King loved to cook. Mary was a happy witch. He baked a chocolate cake for the Queen. He began to carry the huge cake into the royal dining room. But Mrs. Noseup, who lived next door, was not happy. Then the King slipped! She did not like living next door to a witch. One night Mary heard Mrs. Noseup scream. The cake fell all over the Queen. A robber was tying up Mrs. Noseup. The Queen just laughed. Mary turned the robber into a toad. Now Mrs. Noseup is happy to have a witch next door. "I love upside-down cake," she said.

When you have finished untangling the stories, write a title for each one.

Story 1: ______________________________

Story 2: ______________________________

Here's a limerick for you:

There was a young lady named May,
Who liked to watch TV all day.
She stayed in her bed,
And sat there like lead,
Till her mom threw the TV away!

Below are two mixed-up limericks. You must sort them out and put them in the right order. Look at the next page. The first line of each one is done for you.

There was an old witch named Elaine,
She washed once a year,
Who thought being a king was a bore.
And put money down
She won't even go out in the rain!
There was a king from Baltimore,
Who thought taking a bath was a pain.
And from what I hear,
He gave up his crown,
To open a grocery store!

There was an old witch named Elaine,

There was a king from Baltimore,

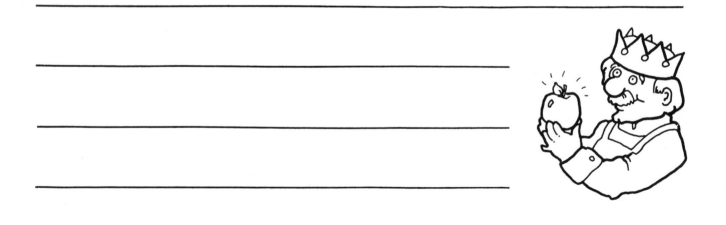

Four friends have pets. Read all the clues. Then mark the chart with X's to match each pet with its owner.

	goldfish	parrot	cat	dog
Luisa				
Tyrone				
Jason				
Jennifer				

1. Luisa likes dogs and cats, but dogs make her mother sneeze.
2. Jennifer and Tyrone have pets that don't go for walks.
3. Jason and Tyrone bought their pets at the same store. One of them bought a dog.
4. Jennifer is teaching her pet to talk.

It's spring cleaning at the Rogers' house! Read all the clues. Then mark the chart with X's to match each person with his or her job.

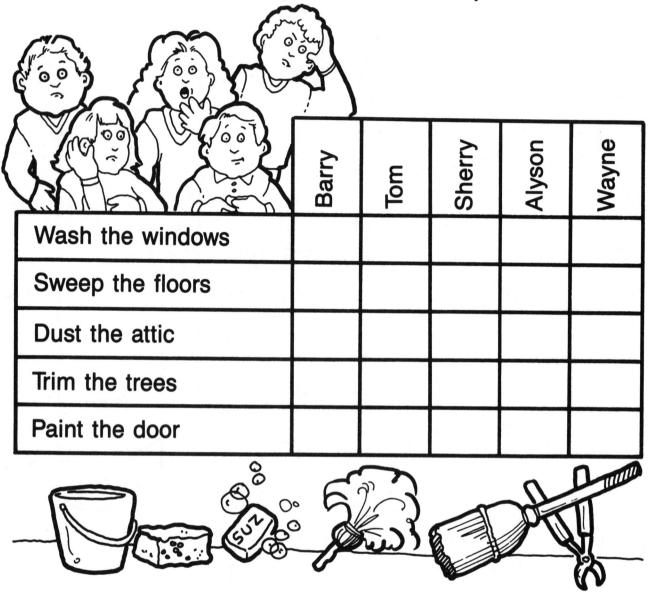

	Barry	Tom	Sherry	Alyson	Wayne
Wash the windows					
Sweep the floors					
Dust the attic					
Trim the trees					
Paint the door					

1. Tom was the only one who used soap and water.

2. Wayne needed a ladder and clippers.

3. Sherry did not dust.

4. Barry swept the floors.

5. Alyson did not paint.

Every hippo helped get ready for Wanda's tea party. Read all the clues. Then mark the chart with X's to show what each hippo did.

	plates	cups	tea	cake
Wanda				
Ellie				
Rex				
Ralph				

1. Wanda brewed the tea.
2. Someone brought the cups.
3. Rex hates to cook, but Ralph loves to bake.
4. Ellie remembered the plates.

Four children went to the park. Read all the clues. Then make X's on the chart to match the children with the things they rode to the park.

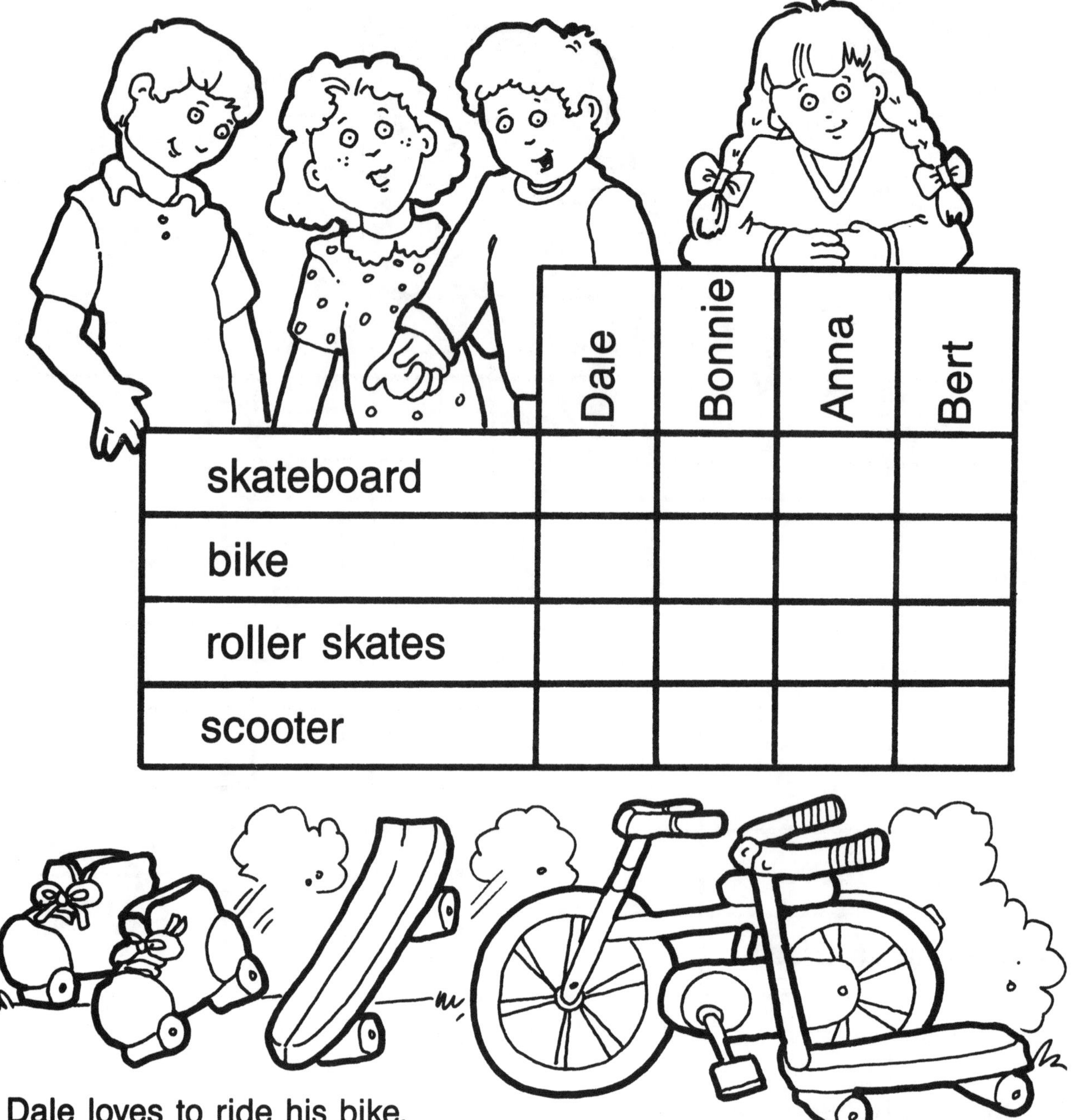

	Dale	Bonnie	Anna	Bert
skateboard				
bike				
roller skates				
scooter				

1. Dale loves to ride his bike.
2. Dale lives across the street from the person with the skateboard.
3. Bert lives next door to Dale.
4. Bonnie just got her new scooter.

Read all the clues. Then fill in the chart to show which candy each person ate.

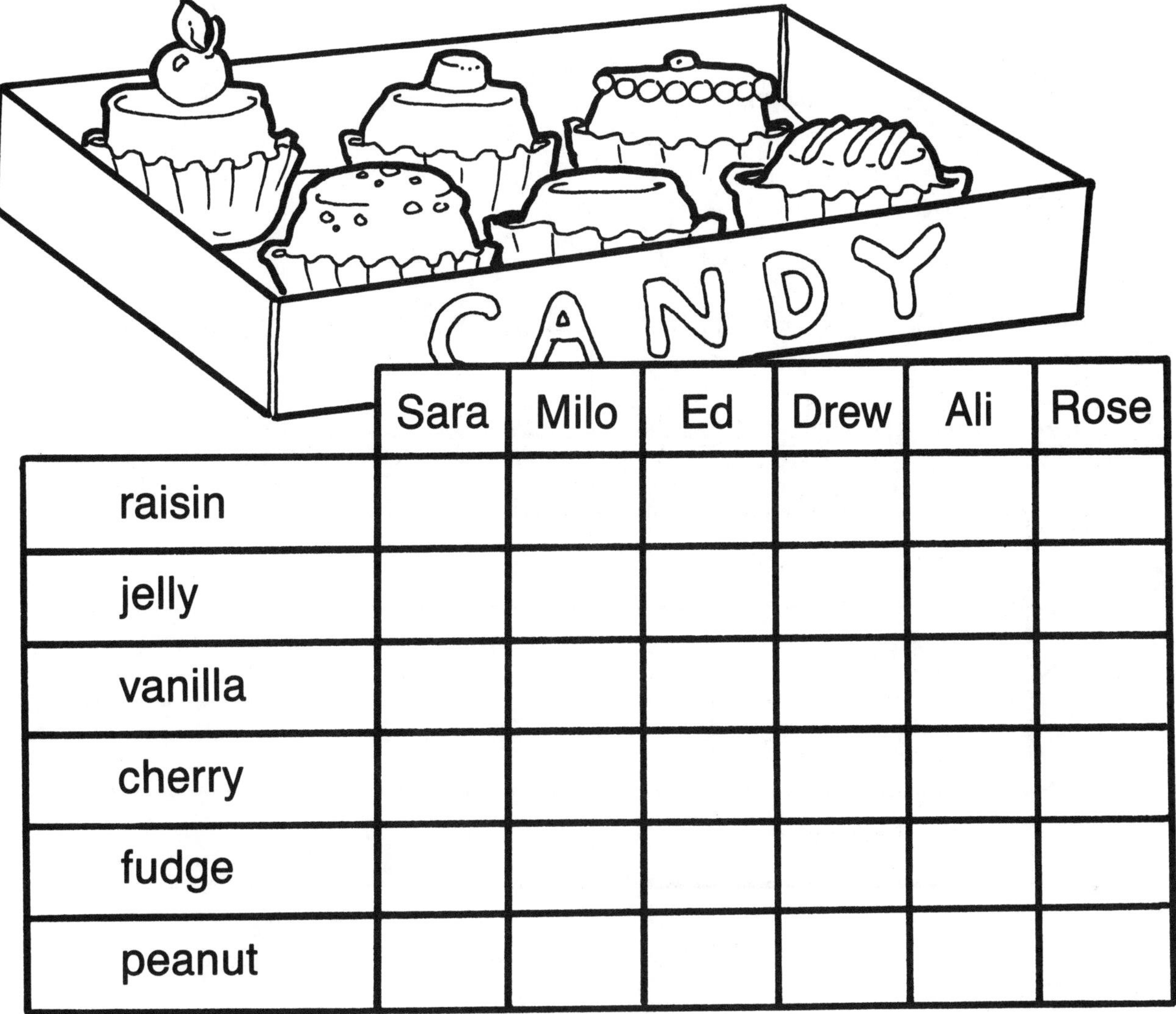

	Sara	Milo	Ed	Drew	Ali	Rose
raisin						
jelly						
vanilla						
cherry						
fudge						
peanut						

1. Sara hates raisins.
2. Milo ate a candy that was white inside.
3. Ed ate the fudge or the peanut.
4. Drew always loves what his sister Sara hates.
5. Ali ate the peanut.
6. Rose loves fruit flavors.

Try to solve this puzzle. Read everything first! Then write your answers.

1. Tony bought toys for his brother and his two sisters.
2. He bought a ball, a game, and a coloring book.
3. Amy does not like games, and Tony did not give her the ball.
4. Mark likes everything, and Tracy doesn't like to play ball.

Amy got the ______________________________.

Mark got the______________________________.

Tracy got the______________________________.

Read all the clues first. Then think carefully and write the answers to this puzzle. What does each parrot say?

1. Luis taught his three parrots to talk.

2. He taught them to say "hello," "wow," and "stop."

3. Sukie cannot say "stop," and Luis did not teach her to say "wow."

4. Luis did not teach Pookie to say "stop."

Sukie Flookie Pookie

Here's a puzzle for experts! Read everything before you answer. Then write the name of each turtle in its correct place.

1. Four turtles had a race.

2. Luke got to the finish line in six days, and Lulu got there sooner.

3. Harry finished behind Lulu and in front of Luke.

4. Jenny got to the finish line before Lulu.

Who won? ______________________________

Who came in last? ______________________________

Which monster is which? Read all the clues carefully. Then write the correct name under each monster.

A. ________________

C. ________________

B. ________________

1. Igor is between Ralph and Bruno.

2. Bruno is wearing a hat.

Who's on top? Read all the clues. Then write the correct name next to each acrobat.

1. Joe is on the bottom.
2. Ed is in the middle.
3. Jack is under Max.
4. Where is Fred?

A. ____________

B. ____________

C. ____________

D. ____________

E. ____________

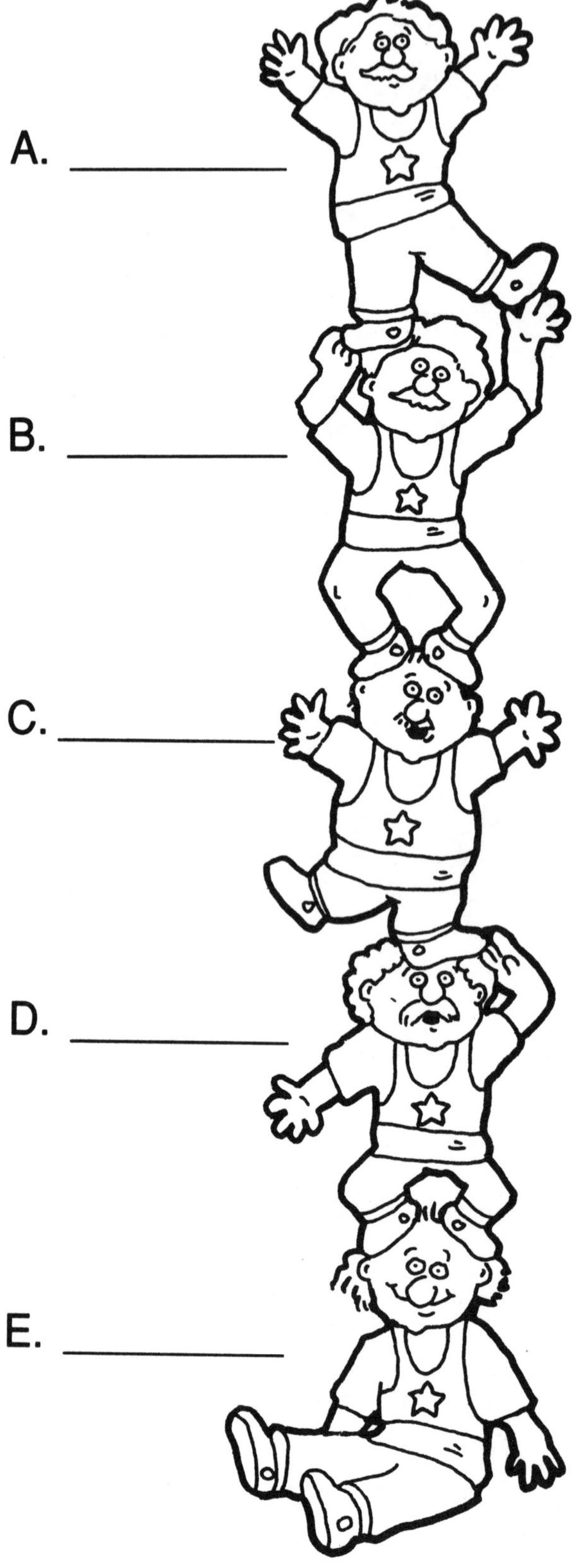

Nurse Noodle mixed up all the babies! Read all the clues and write the correct name on each crib.

A. ________________

B. ________________

C. ________________

D. ________________

E. ________________

1. One baby is named Carlos.

2. Cathy is crying.

3. Yolanda is asleep between Paul and Betty.

4. Paul is not next to Cathy.

Who's behind the books? Read all the clues. Then write the correct name under each book.

A. ____________________

B. ____________________

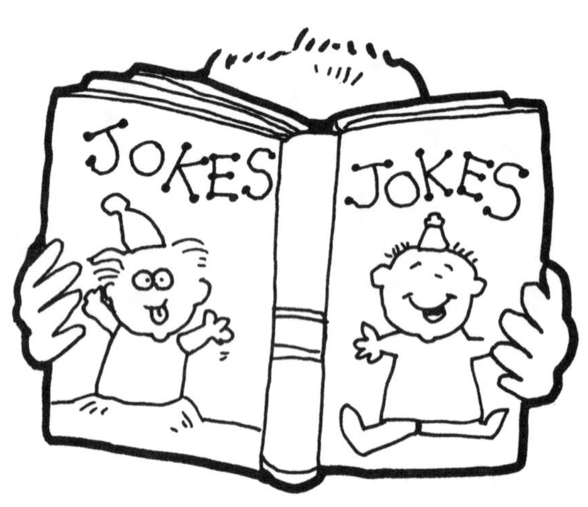

C. ____________________

D. ____________________

1. David does not like scary stories.
2. Danny likes to read about dragons.
3. Sally does not like fairy tales.
4. Luisa loves to tell jokes.

Where do Mike, Jennifer, Mary, Amy, Erik, and Jon sit? Read all the clues. Write the correct name under each desk.

A. ________________ B. ________________ C. ________________

D. ________________ E. ________________ F. ________________

1. Erik sits behind Jennifer.
2. Jennifer has her hand up.
3. Jon and Mary sit in the front of the room.
4. Amy is behind Mike.

Here is the juggling bear. Read all the clues and then color each ball.

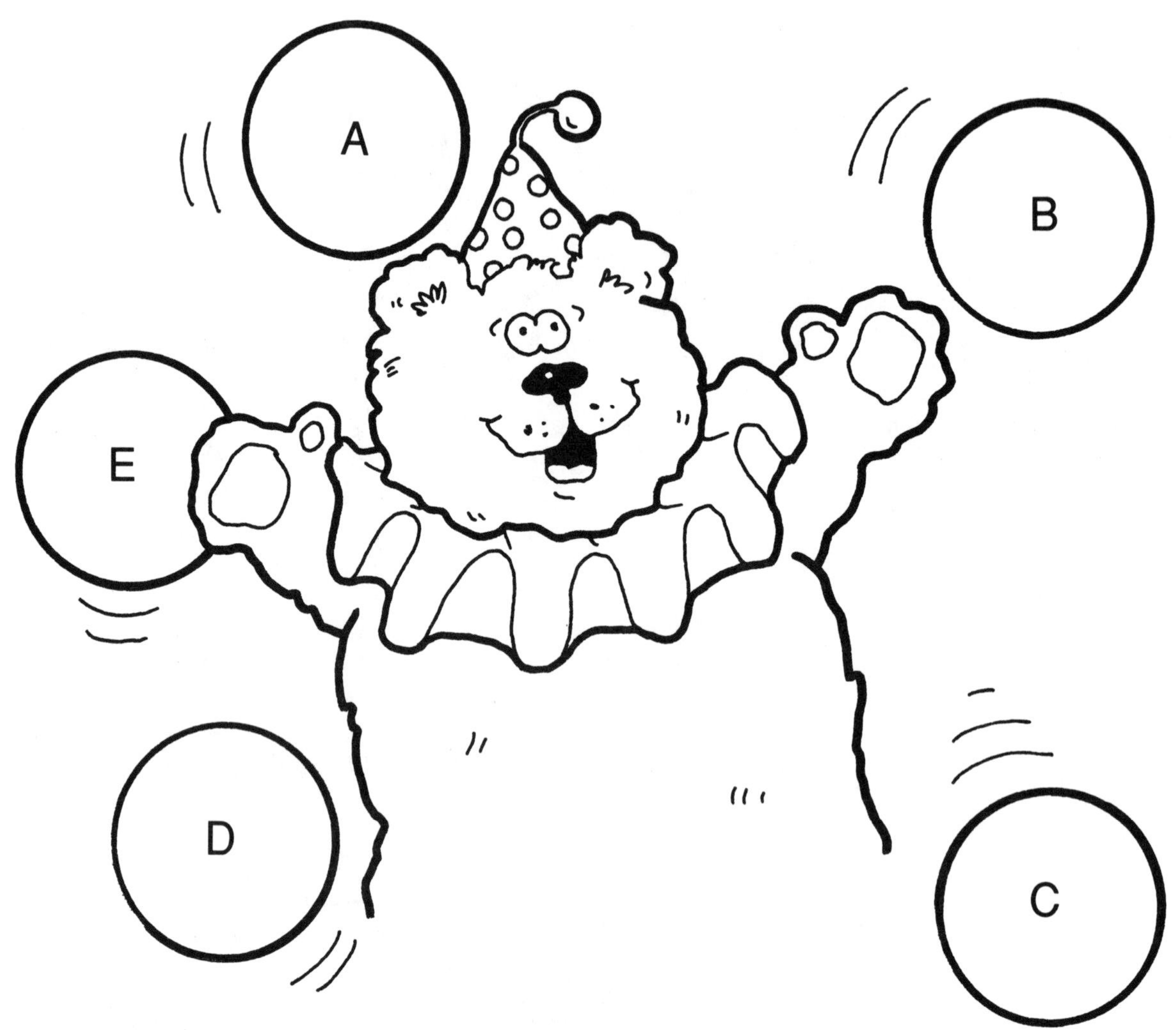

1. The purple ball is lowest.
2. The red ball is highest.
3. The yellow ball is not next to the red ball.
4. The green ball is next to the yellow one.
5. One ball is blue.

The dogs are chasing each other! Read all the clues. Write the correct name under each dog.

1. Fluffy has spots.
2. Fluffy is between Rover and Sam.
3. Sam is chasing Rex.
4. One dog is named Pug.

Five children dressed up for Halloween — and then they switched costumes! Read all the clues. Write the correct name under each costume.

1. Ann wore what Alberto had on before.

2. Scott switched with Kate.

3. Alberto wore something with a long tail.

4. Jill wore the only costume left.

What animal is this? Look at the puzzle and guess which animal the pieces will make. You can cut out the pieces and put them together to see if you were right.

Below are the steps you need to make a birthday cake, but they are all mixed up! Number the steps in order from 1 to 4. There are two steps that you **don't need.** Put an X next to these steps.

_______ A. Pour the batter into the pan.

_______ B. Mix the eggs with flour, sugar, and milk.

_______ C. Blow up the balloons.

_______ D. Crack the eggs into the bowl.

_______ E. Wrap the birthday gift.

_______ F. Put the cake in the oven.

What is this? Look at the puzzle and guess what object the pieces will make. You can cut out the pieces and put them together to see if you were right.

Below are the steps you need to build a doghouse, but they are all mixed up! Number the steps in order from 1 to 5. There are two steps that you **don't need.** Put an X next to these steps.

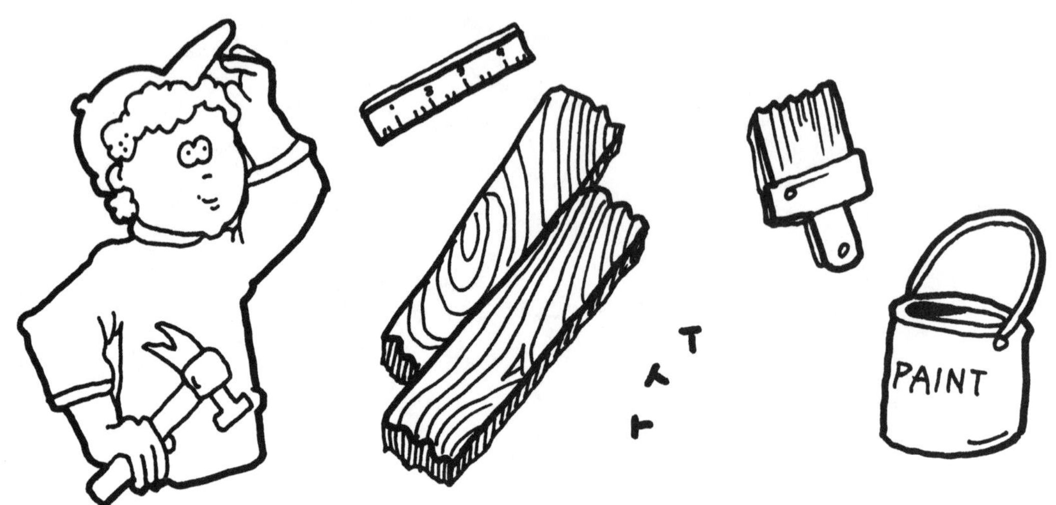

_______ A. Put up the walls.

_______ B. Put the dog food in the dish.

_______ C. Paint the doghouse.

_______ D. Get the tools you need.

_______ E. Give the dog a bath.

_______ F. Measure and cut the wood.

_______ G. Put on the roof.

SAM

Which fairy tale is this? The puzzle pieces make a scene from a fairy tale. Guess which one! Then you can cut out the pieces and put them together to see if you guessed correctly.

Read the sentences below. Circle all the things on the menu that the dragon ate for dinner.

1. He ate all the green vegetables.

2. He ate everything with fruit in it.

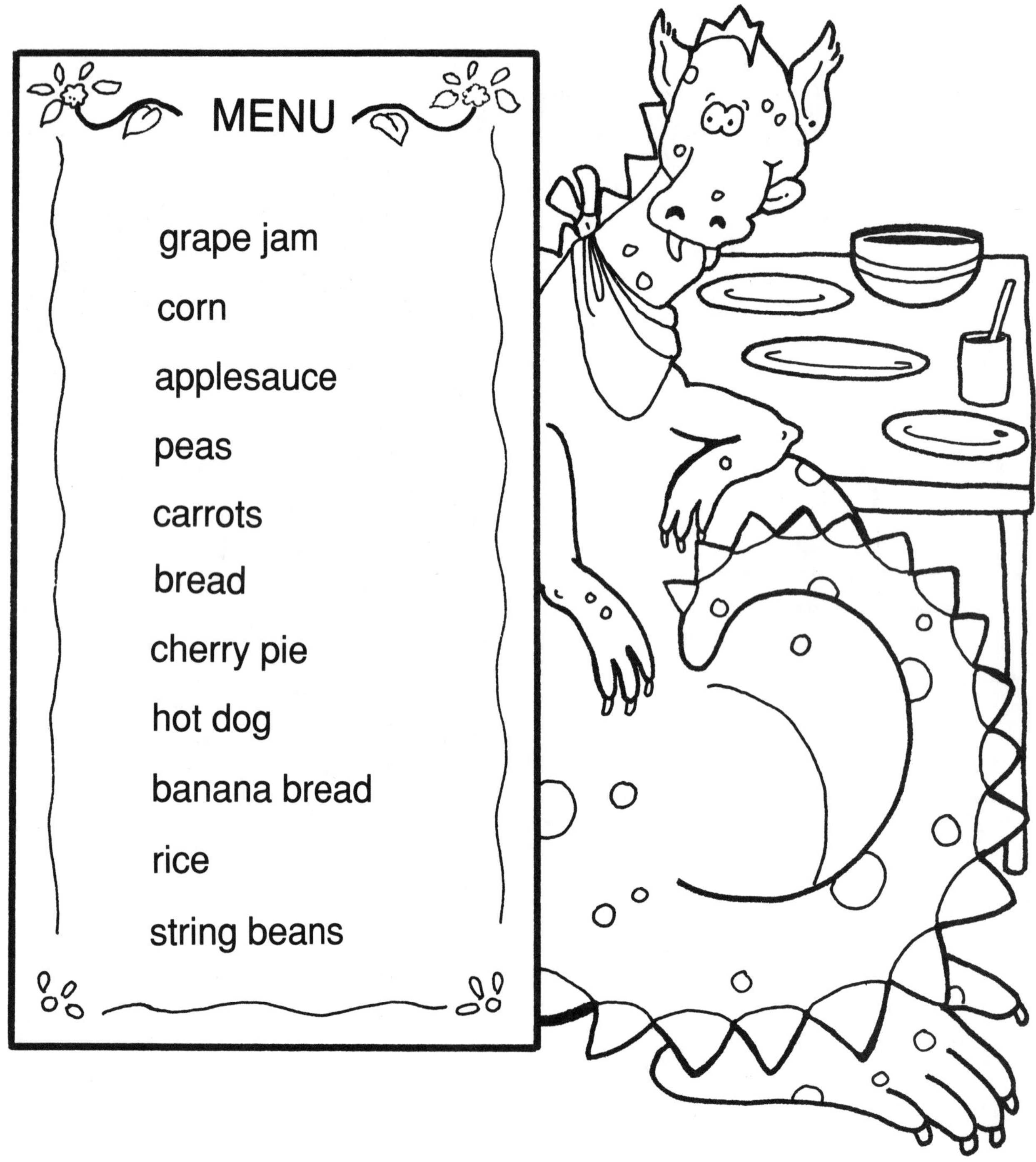

Ann cleaned her room. Read the sentences below and cross out all the things she put away.

1. She put away all her toys.

2. She put away all her clothes.

Ann's mother found one thing left under her bed. What was it?

____

Find 7 people who are in a **family.**

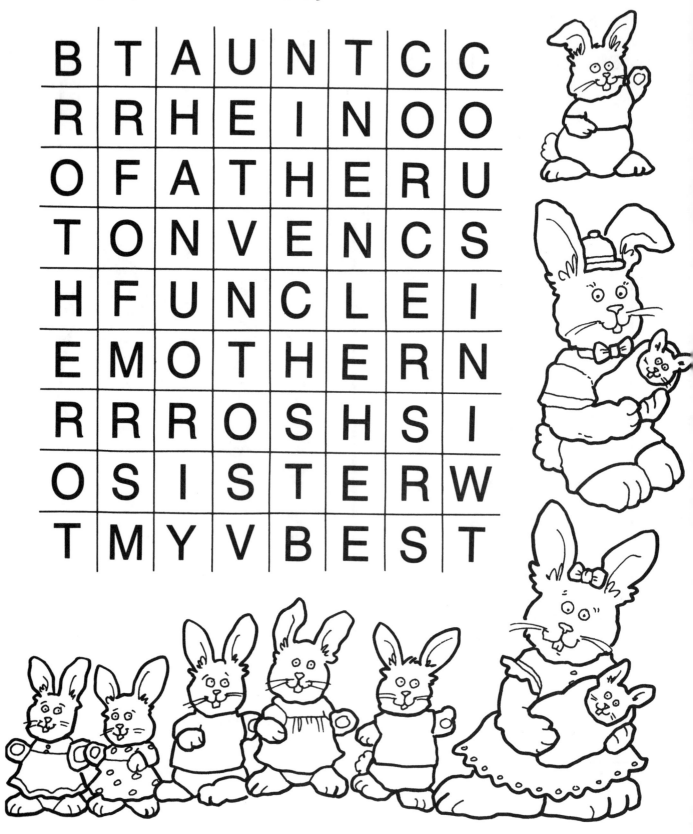

B	T	A	U	N	T	C	C
R	R	H	E	I	N	O	O
O	F	A	T	H	E	R	U
T	O	N	V	E	N	C	S
H	F	U	N	C	L	E	I
E	M	O	T	H	E	R	N
R	R	R	O	S	H	S	I
O	S	I	S	T	E	R	W
T	M	Y	V	B	E	S	T

Find 3 things that are **sharp.**

Find 3 things that are **round.**

Find 3 things made of **glass.**

K	N	I	F	E	I	M	O	L	D
H	E	L	P	O	A	S	G	R	J
A	T	O	M	B	A	L	L	B	A
A	X	K	E	T	O	F	R	O	R
Y	O	W	I	N	D	O	W	E	P
U	R	U	K	E	C	K	T	R	E
A	C	S	U	N	X	S	A	W	O
B	O	T	T	L	E	L	C	L	I
Q	U	A	I	N	I	W	K	U	L
D	F	O	W	H	E	E	L	N	T

Put an X on the one word in each row that does not belong.

1. hat ball coat shoes
2. roof door floor cloud
3. pine oak daisy palm
4. table sheet blanket pillow
5. morning top noon night
6. car taxi boat bus
7. paper ruler pen banana
8. hot sun cold warm
9. sleep jump run hop
10. tall short happy thin

Put an X on the one word in each row that does not belong.

1. bag nail basket suitcase
2. cow goose gorilla hen
3. bee jet frog kite
4. aunt uncle teacher sister
5. steel pillow cotton silk
6. arm box air ax
7. windmill record kite Ferris wheel
8. zebra newspaper panda sun
9. iron oven ice dryer
10. father aunt son uncle

Which animals are small enough to fit into a car? Think of as many as you can and write their names on this page.

Write words that start with the letters given for each category.

	Food	Names	Colors
S			
M			
A			
R			
T			

Draw a line from the box to the word that best describes the things in the box.

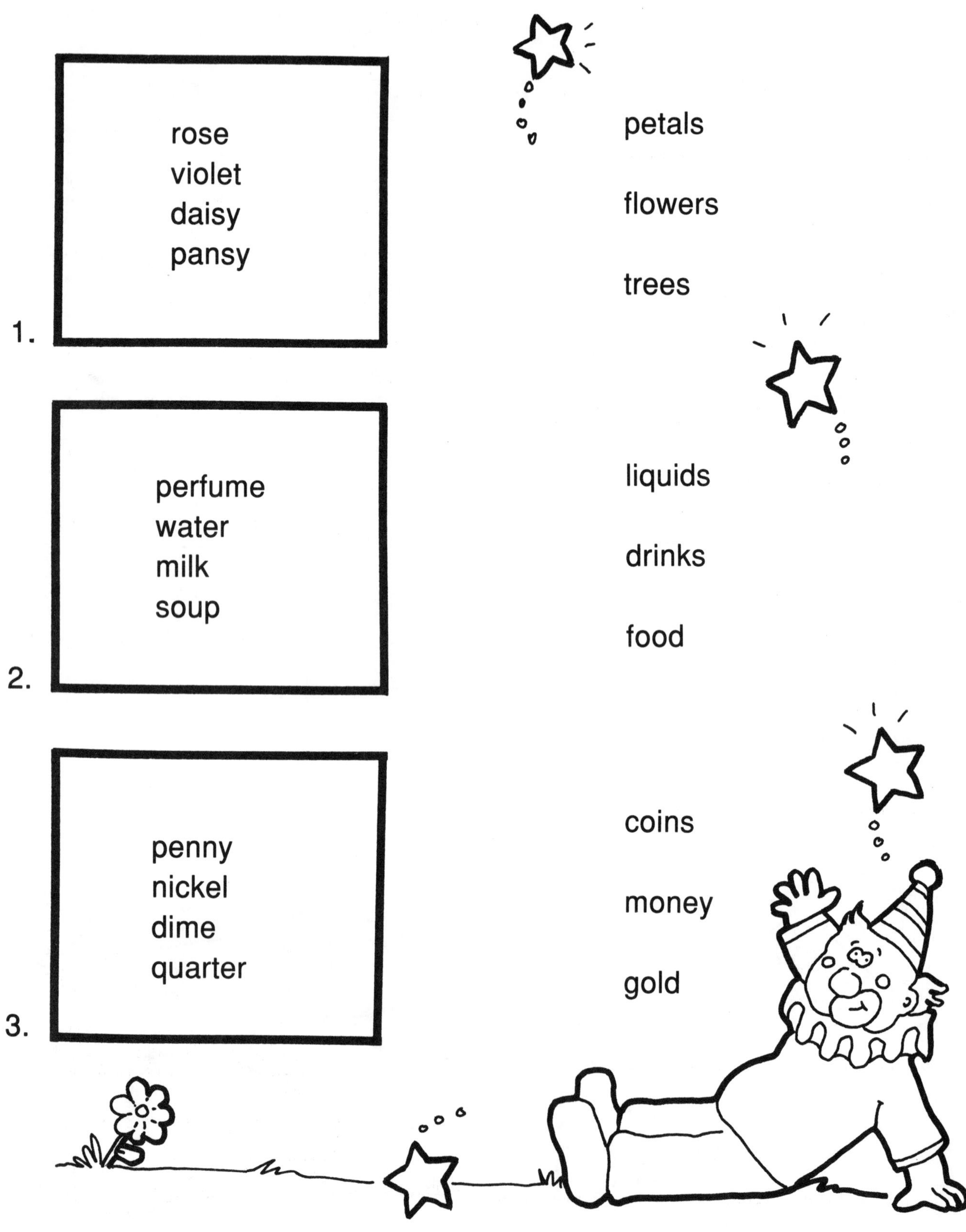

1.
rose
violet
daisy
pansy
petals
flowers
trees
2.
perfume
water
milk
soup
liquids
drinks
food
3.
penny
nickel
dime
quarter
coins
money
gold

Draw a line from the box to the word that best describes the things in the box.

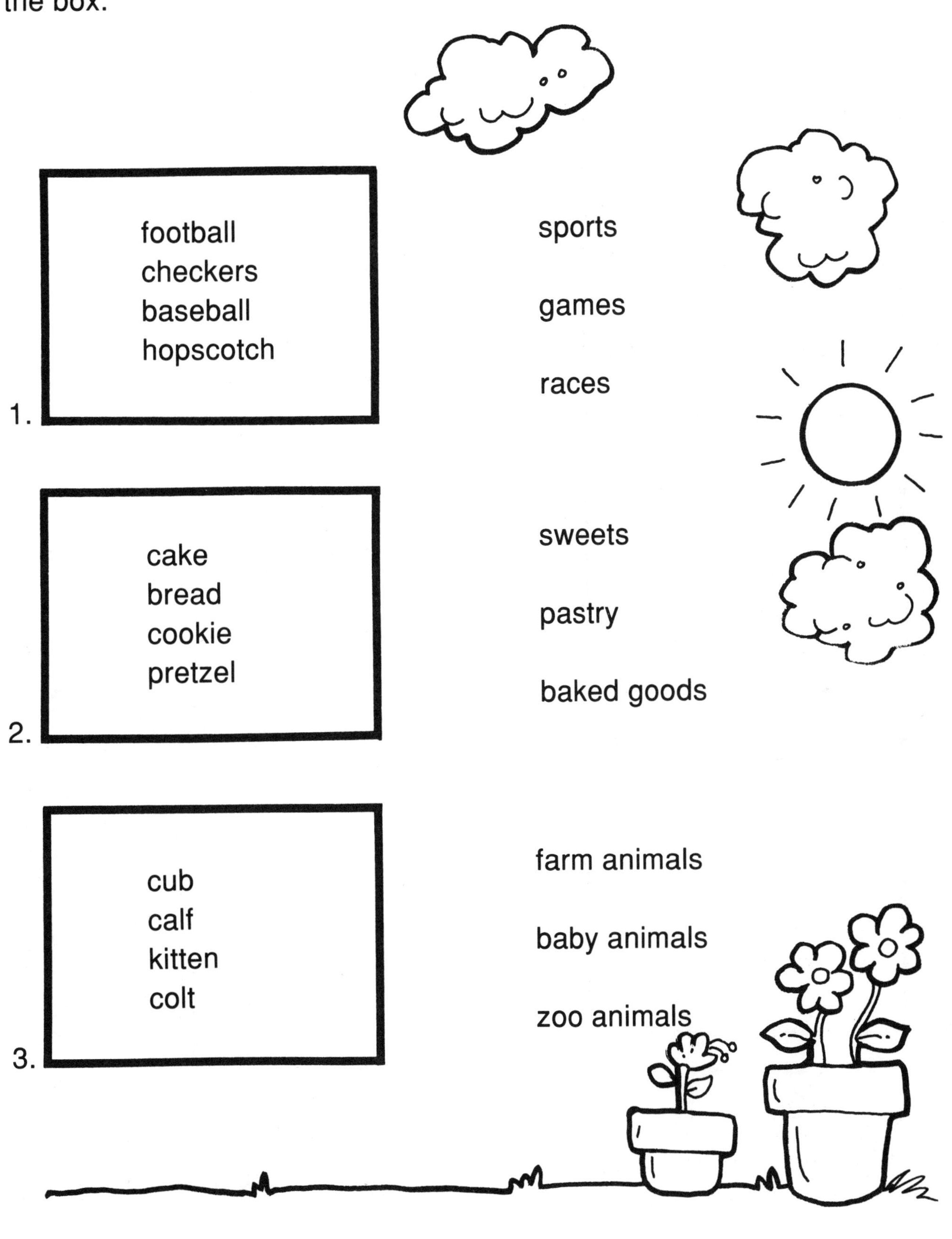

1.

football
checkers
baseball
hopscotch

sports

games

races

2.

cake
bread
cookie
pretzel

sweets

pastry

baked goods

3.

cub
calf
kitten
colt

farm animals

baby animals

zoo animals

Draw a line from the box to the word that best describes the things in the box.

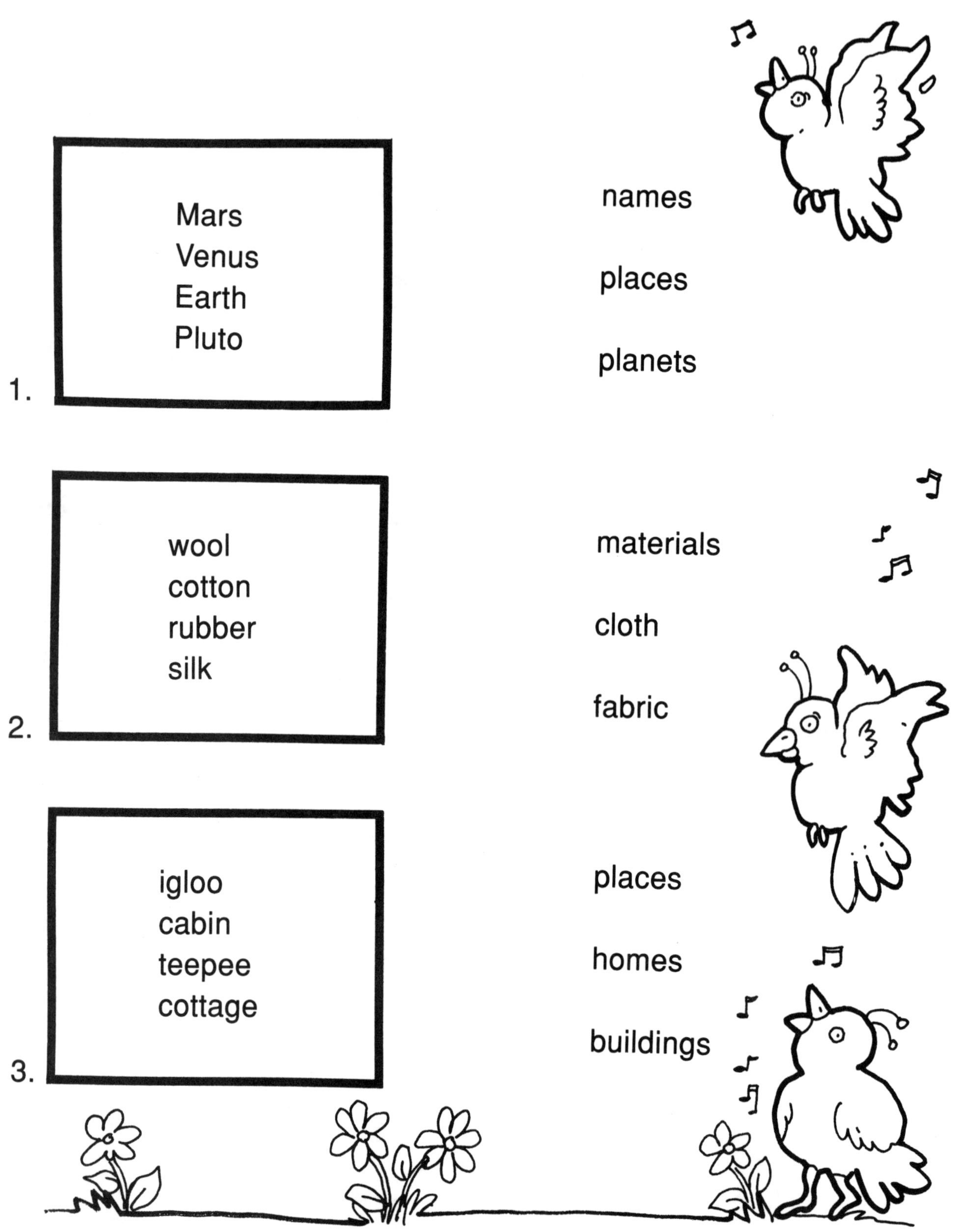

1.
Mars
Venus
Earth
Pluto
names
places
planets
2.
wool
cotton
rubber
silk
materials
cloth
fabric
3.
igloo
cabin
teepee
cottage
places
homes
buildings

Follow the footprints of the princess. Then number the sentences below in order from 1 to 4.

A. ________ She goes into the dragon's cave.

B. ________ She eats her lunch.

C. ________ She jumps over the water.

D. ________ She steps on the dragon.

Follow the pirate's footprints. Then number the sentences below in order from 1 to 4.

A. ________ He goes over the bridge.

B. ________ He finds the treasure map.

C. ________ He finds the treasure!

D. ________ He goes around the hill.

Follow the monster's footprints. Then number the sentences below in order from 1 to 4. Cross out the one sentence that does **not** belong.

A. ________ He buys a hat.

B. ________ He mails a letter.

C. ________ He gets a haircut.

D. ________ He eats dinner.

E. ________ He crosses the street.

Follow the footprints of the farmer and the duck. Then number the places that they went in order from 1 to 3.

_____ pond

_____ tree

_____ barn

_____ pond

_____ tree

_____ barn

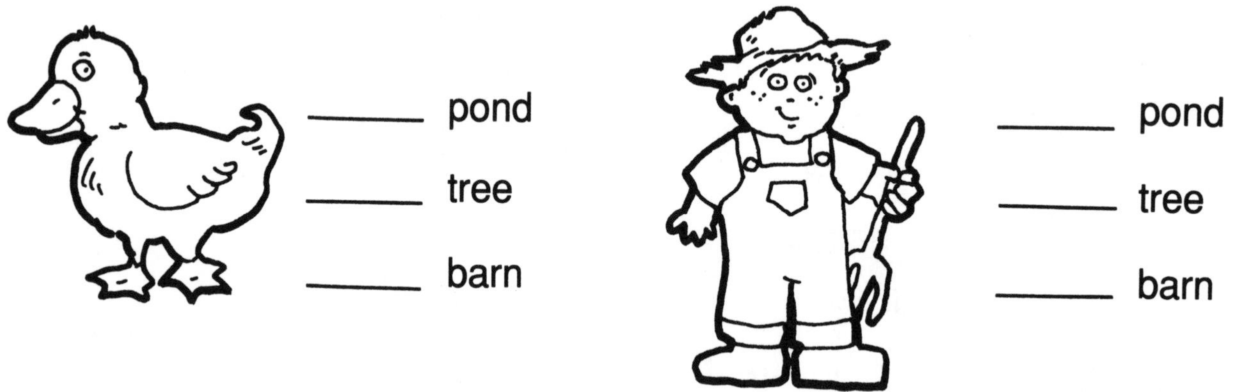

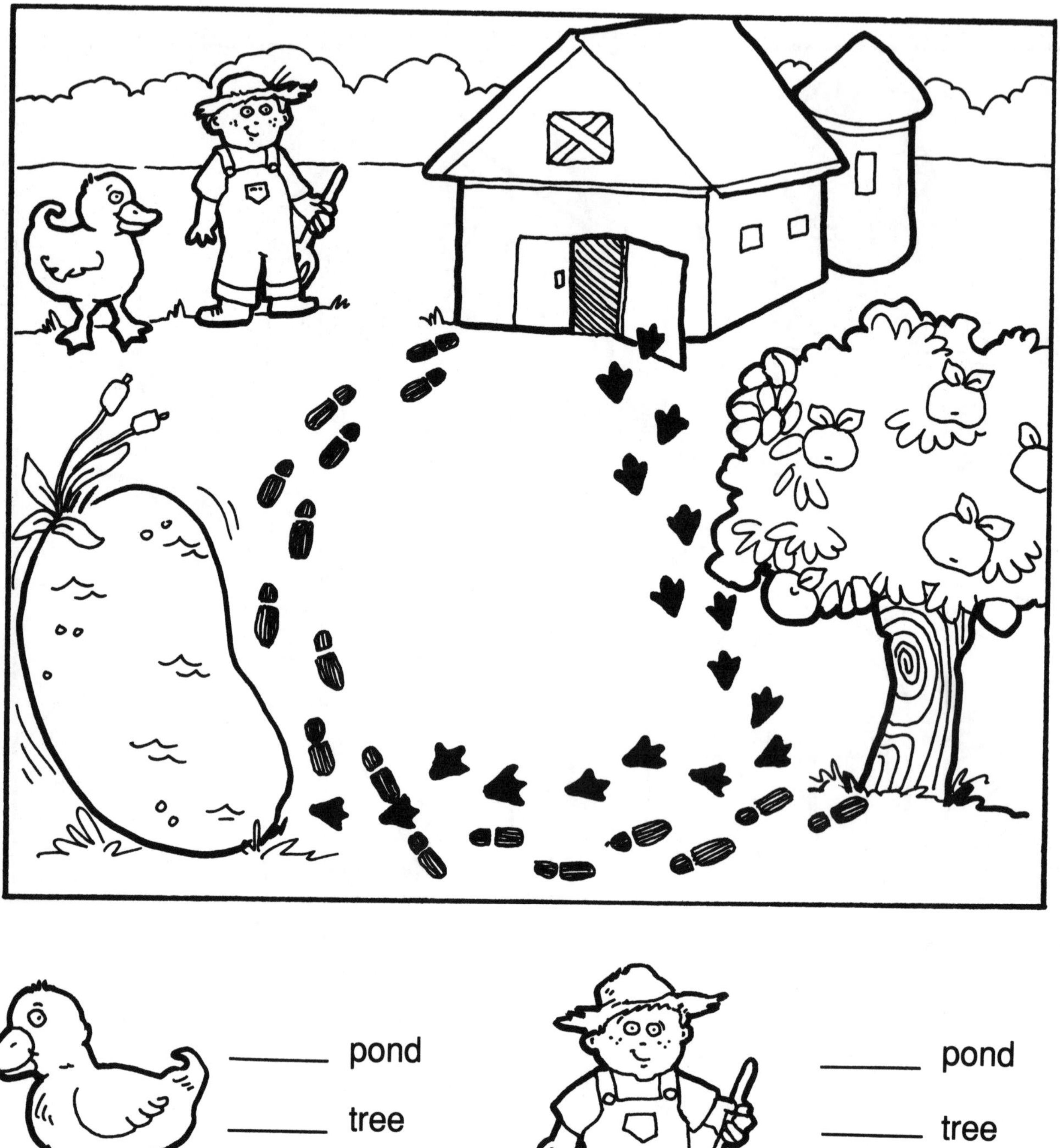

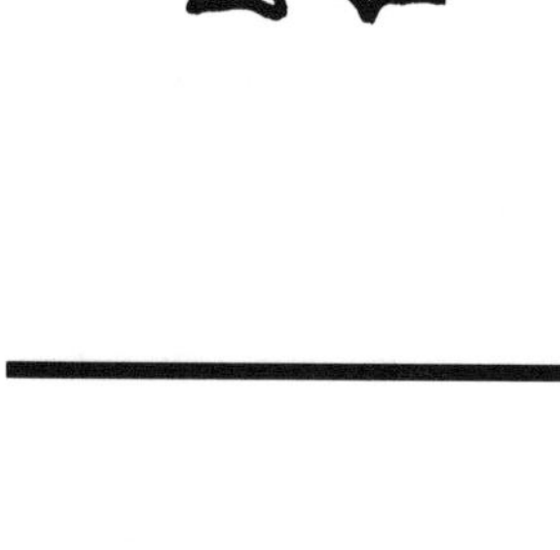

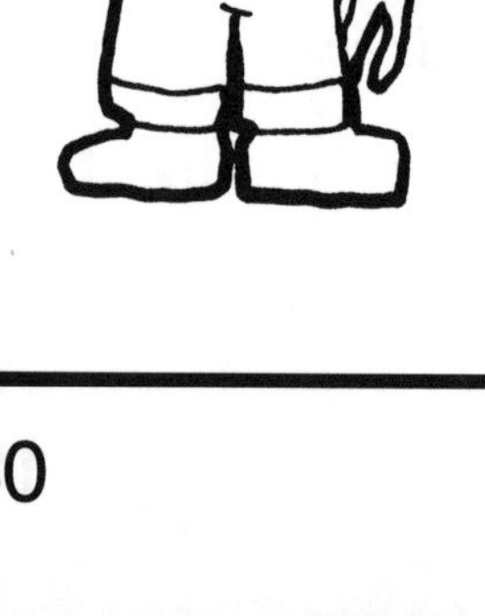

Follow the footprints of Peg-Leg Pete and Pirate Sam. Then number the places that they went in order from 1 to 3. On each pirate's list there is one place that does not belong. Cross it out.

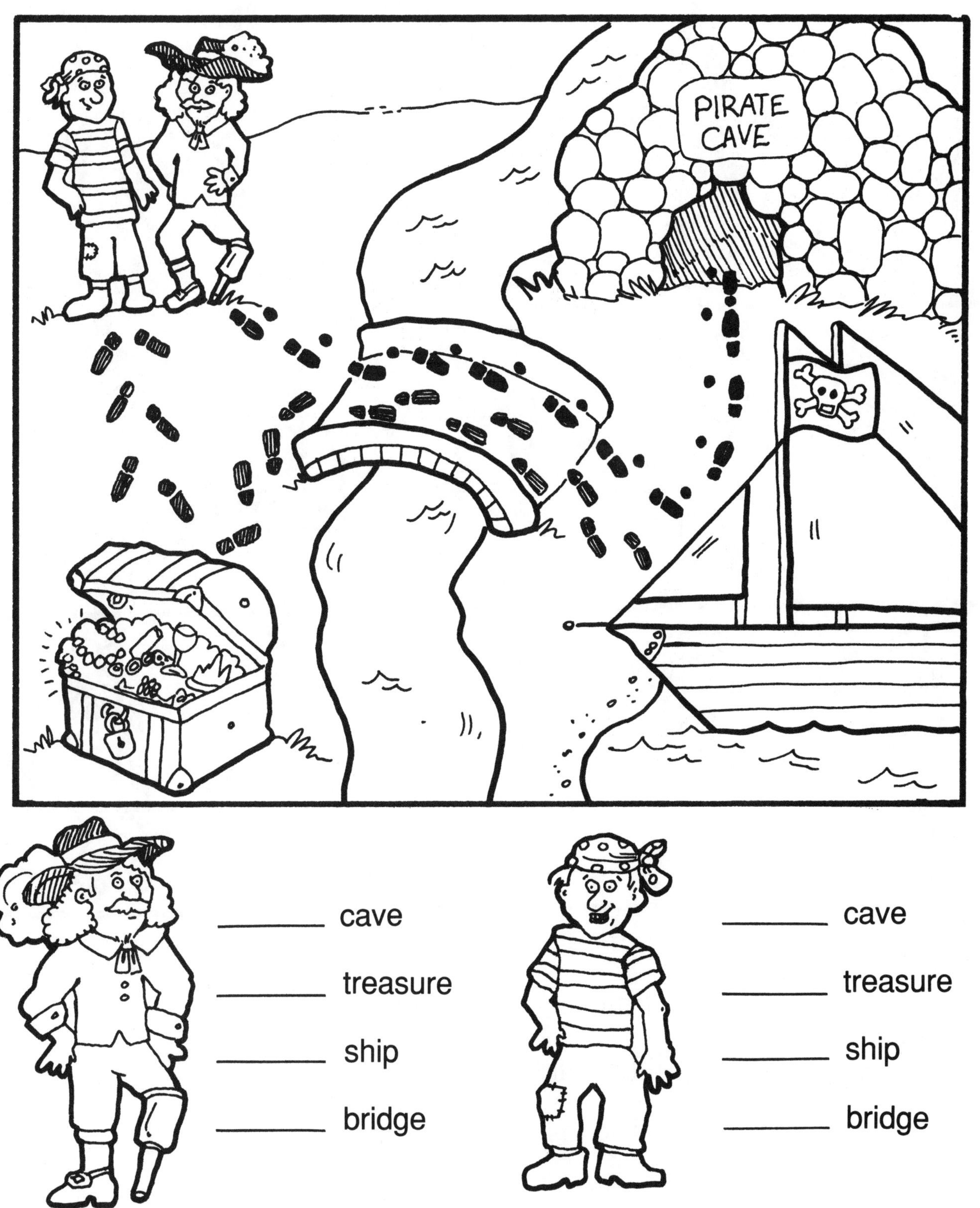

_______ cave

_______ treasure

_______ ship

_______ bridge

_______ cave

_______ treasure

_______ ship

_______ bridge

Look carefully at each row. Circle the one sentence below that tells what is the same about **all** the rows.

The first clown is happy.

The middle clown is fat.

The last clown is thin.

Look carefully at each row. Circle the one sentence below that tells what is the same about **all** the rows.

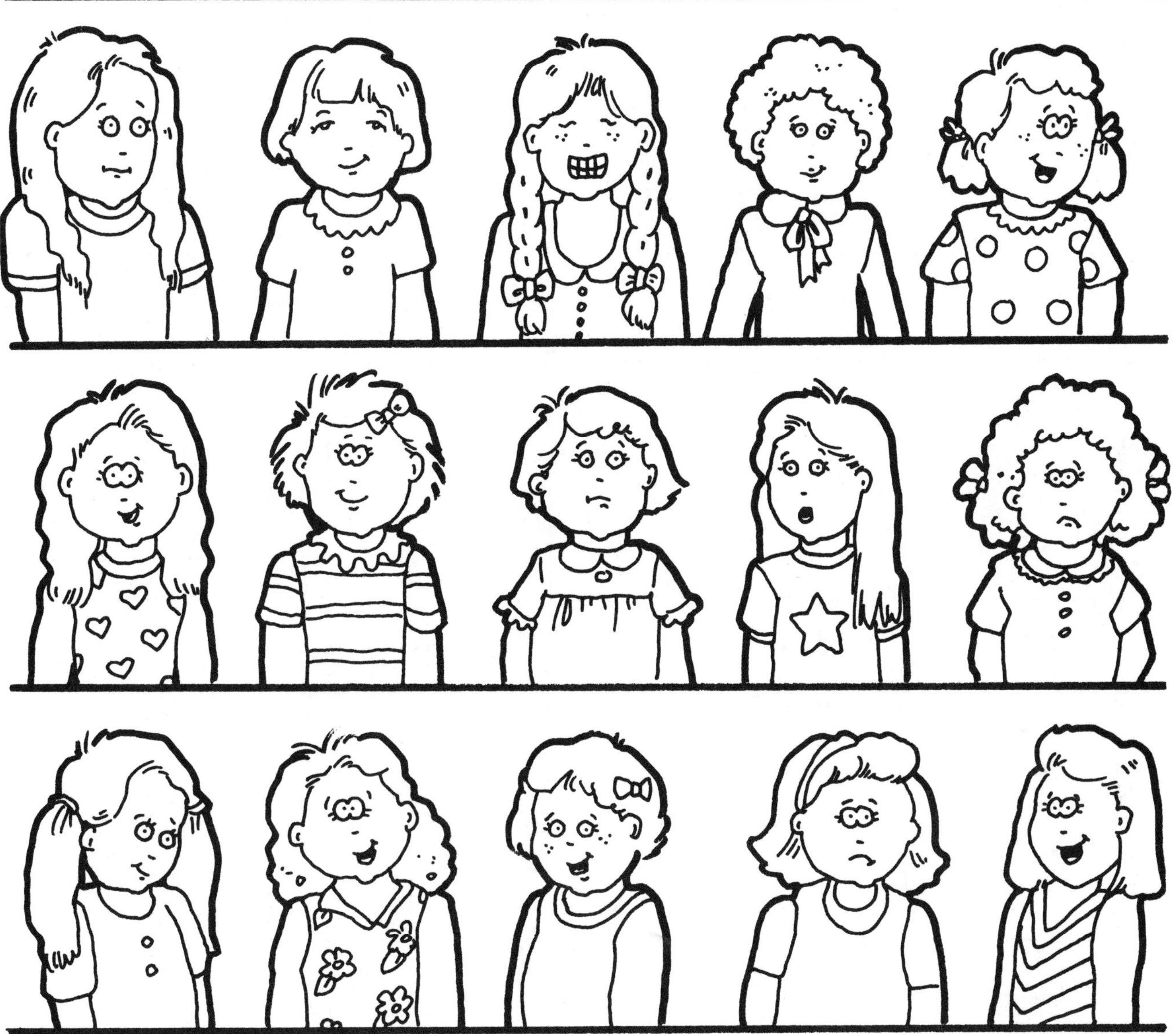

The first girl has long hair.

The middle girl has short hair.

The last girl is sad.

Look carefully at each row. Circle the one sentence below that tells what is the same about **all** the rows.

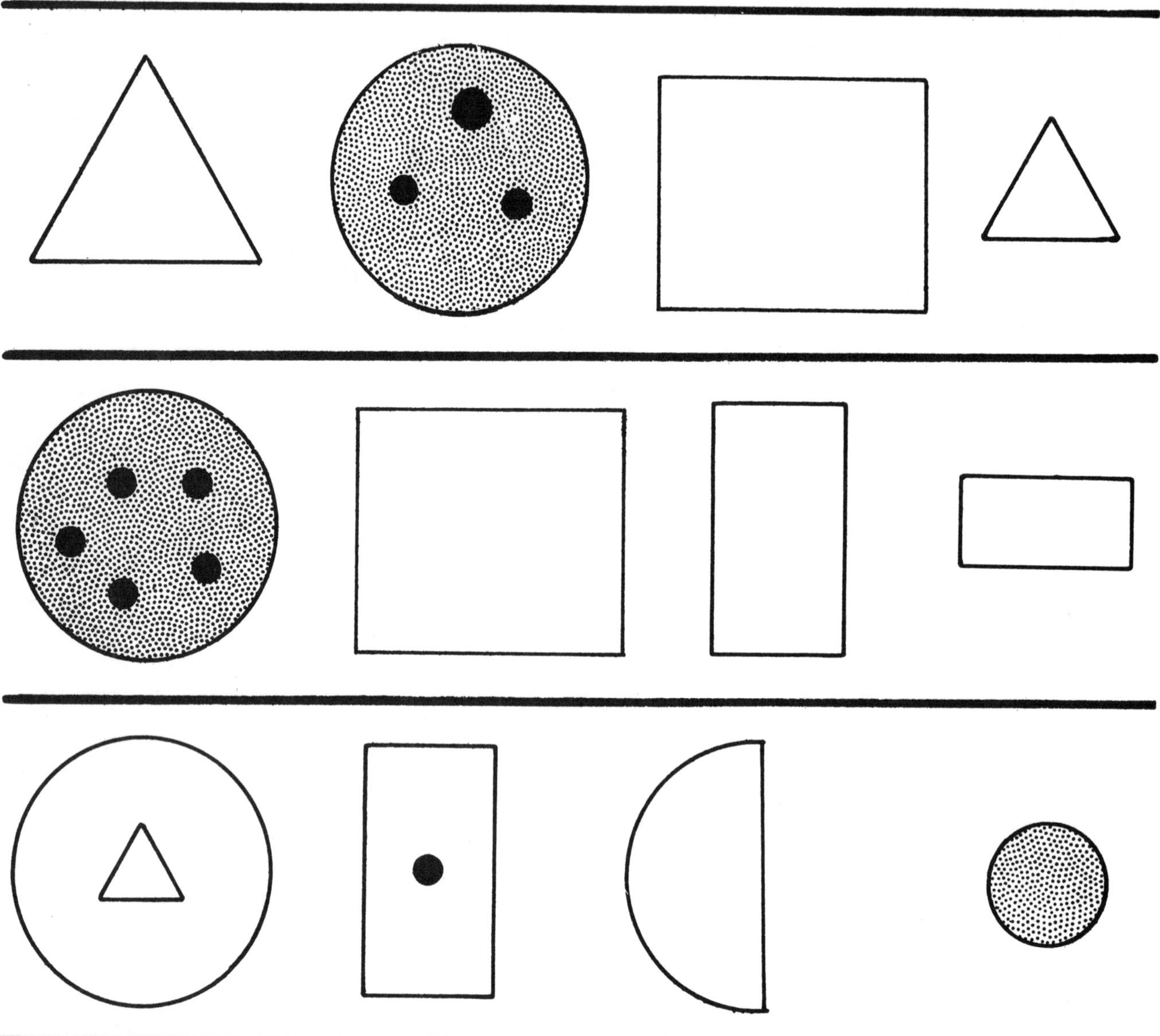

The first shape is a circle.

The circles have spots.

The last shape is small.

The police officer wants to know where these people were last night when the Queen's crown was stolen. Which one is **not** telling the truth? How do you know?

Witch Princess Pirate

Three students do not have their homework. They each tell the teacher what happened. Which one is **not** telling the truth? How do you know?

I dropped it on
my way to school.
My baby sister
ripped it up.
I lost it at my
violin lesson.
Shelly
Joshua
Nora

The Littleton Store was robbed on the night of January 12. The alarm sounded, but the robber still got away. The police are sure that someone must have seen the robber. They question three people. One is not telling the truth. Which one?

Pete: "I didn't see or hear anything. I was asleep."

Paul: "All my window shades were down."

Pat: "I couldn't see. The leaves from the oak tree block my window."

There is $1,000 missing from the safe of the Tuckabuckaway Bank. The safe locks automatically every night at 8:15. The thief must have arrived before that time. The police talk to three people who worked at the bank last night. Write the time each person arrived. Which worker may have taken the money?

Mr. Troy: "I got to the bank at 8:45."

Mr. Bond: "I got to work 30 minutes before Ms. Rollo."

Ms. Rollo: "I got to work 15 minutes before Mr. Troy."

While Mr. Rodney Rich was having a party, someone stole his gold watch. The police know that the thief was the last person to leave the party. Write the time each person left. Who stole the watch?

Miss Gold left at 6:15. __________

Mr. Simon left 15 minutes after Ms. Jones. __________

Ms. Jones left 30 minutes after Mr. Smith. __________

Mr. Smith left 15 minutes before Miss Gold. __________

Look at all the pictures one at a time. When you think you can remember them all, look at the next page.

Now circle only the pictures you saw on the page before.
Did you remember them all?

Look at all the pictures one at a time. When you think you can remember them all, look at the next page.

Now circle only the words that describe the pictures you saw on the page before.

man

cake

boy

tree

car

toy

hat

pen

dog

girl

Did you remember them all?

Look at the words one at a time. When you think you can remember them all, look at the next page.

house **window**

jar **boat**

baby **cat**

flag **hat**

Now circle only the pictures of the words you saw on the page before.

Did you remember them all?

LANGUAGE ARTS

The following activities help youngsters to practice their basic language skills. Children will become familiar with the various parts of speech, such as nouns and verbs, as well as learn about rhyming words, compound words, and homonyms. This section also focuses on improving and developing your child's vocabulary. It is helpful to keep a dictionary handy so you and your child can look up new and unfamiliar words.

Read all the clues. Write the correct letter on each pancake.
Hint: Make sure you read all the clues before you start.

1. **J** is on top.
2. **P** is under **M**.
3. **U** is under **J**.

What word did you spell? ____________________

Read all the clues. Write the correct letter on each drum.

1. The first drum in the line is **H**.
2. **R** is behind **C**.
3. **M** is last.
4. **A** is between **R** and **M**.

What word did you spell? ______________________________

Read all the clues. Write the correct letter in each space.

1. **H** is on the bottom.

2. **P** is not on top.

3. **S** is between **H** and **A**.

4. **L** is under **P**.

5. There is one more **S**.

What word did you spell? ______________________

Read all the clues. Write the correct letter on each hatbox.

1. One box is **A**.
2. **P** is the highest box.
3. **I** is between **P** and **R**.
4. **T** is not next to **R**.
5. **E** is on the bottom.

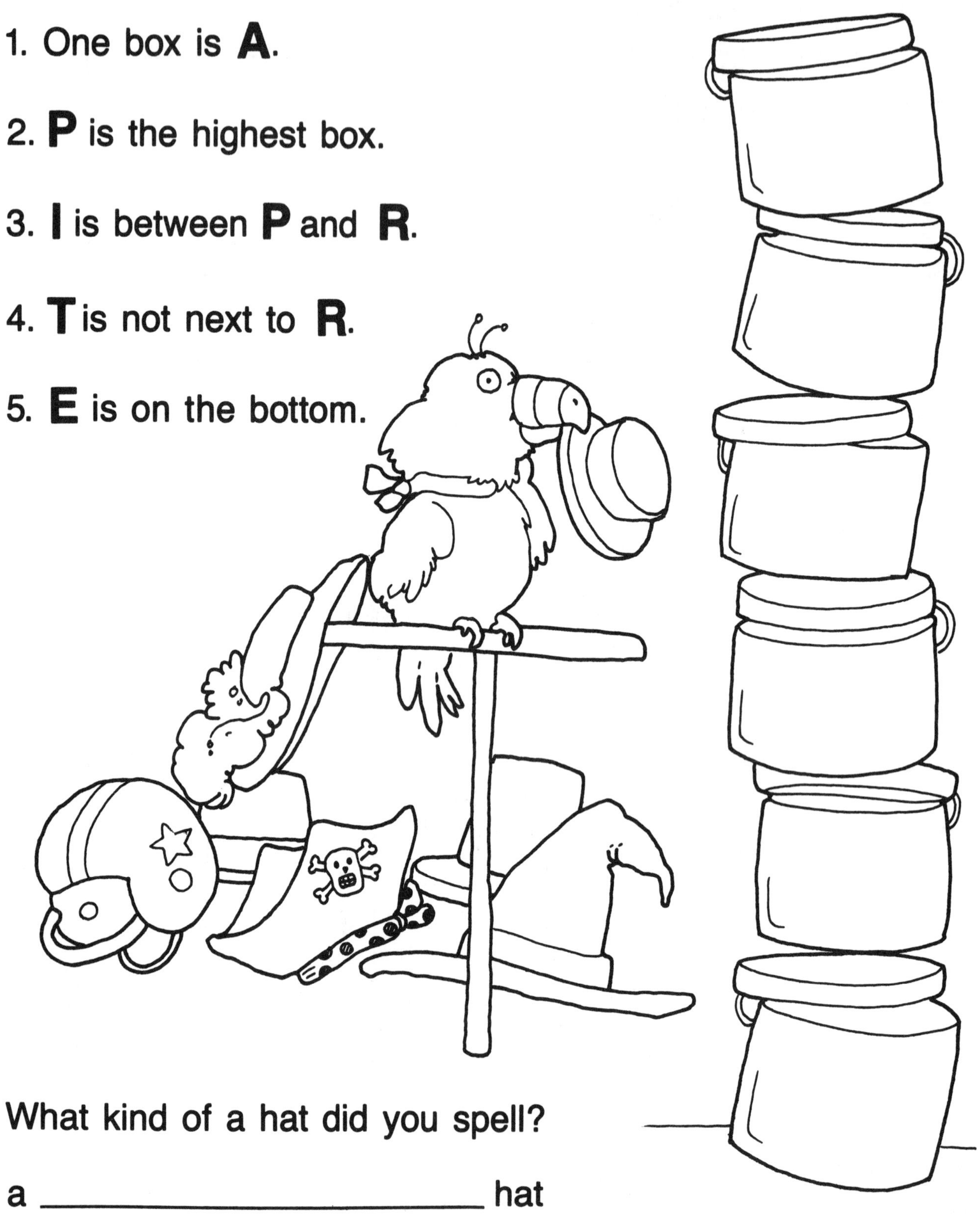

What kind of a hat did you spell?

a ____________________ hat

Read all the clues. Write the correct letter in each box.

1. The biggest box is **C**.
2. **C** is across from **Y**.
3. **A** is **not** next to **D**.
4. **A** is next to **N**.
5. **C** is **not** next to **D**.

What word did you spell? ______________________
(It's what Rosie Rhino loves most.)

Read all the clues. Write the correct letter in each car.

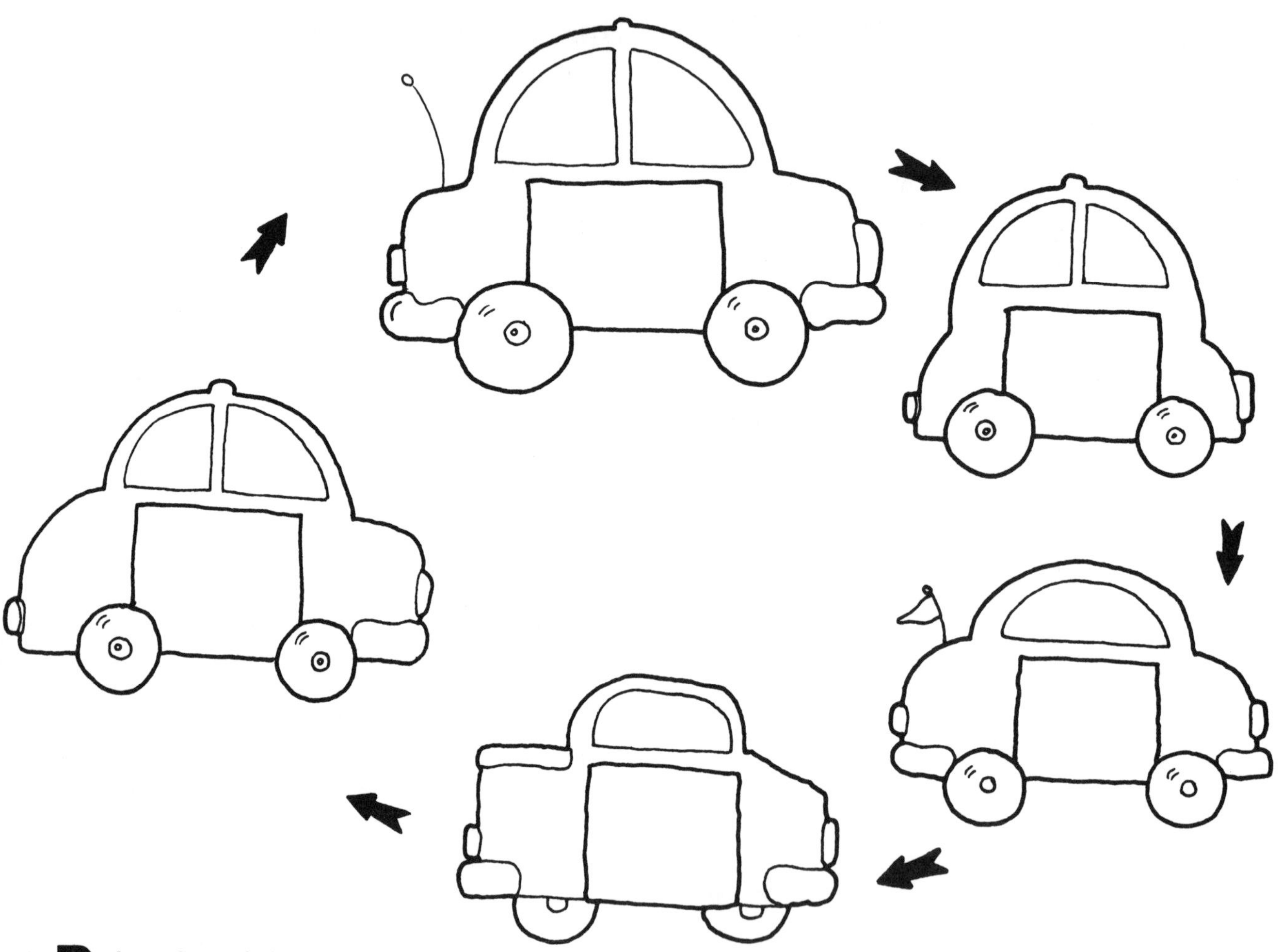

1. **D** is the biggest car.

2. **D** is between **E** and **R**.

3. **R** is behind **I**.

4. One car is **V**.

What word did you spell? (Start with the letter on the biggest car.) ______________________________

Long ago Indians drew pictures to tell stories or send messages. Look at the Indian pictures below. Read the message in the box. Write the message on the lines.

These lines || mean the end of a sentence.

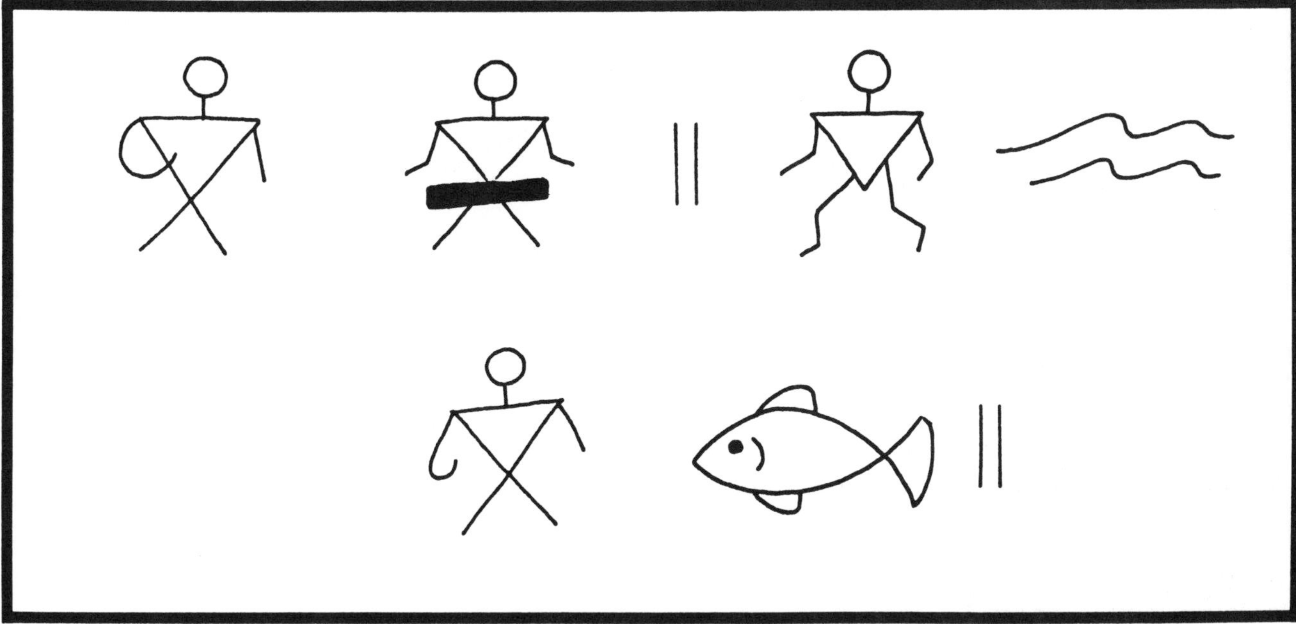

The message is: ______________________________

____

____

Here are more Indian picture symbols. Use these – and the ones on the page before this one – to draw your own message. Write your message on the lines.

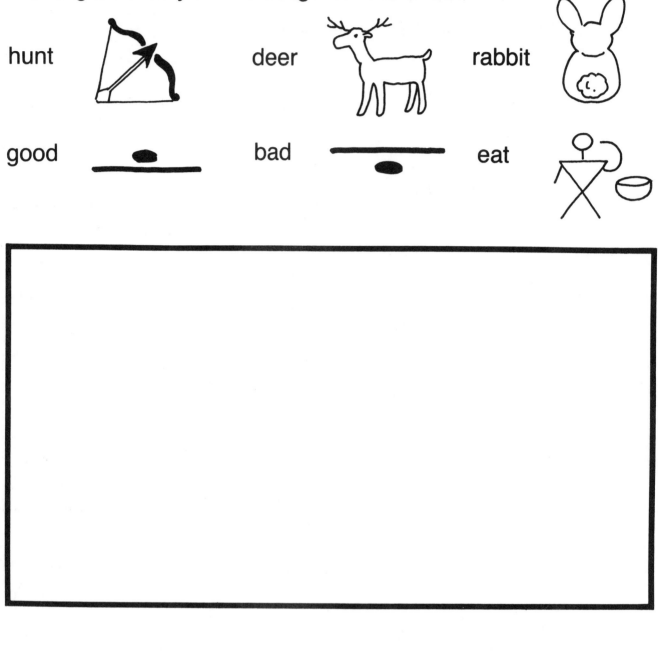

hunt

deer

rabbit

good

bad

eat

Here are more Indian picture symbols. Use them to read the story on the next page. You can also use them to write your own story on another piece of paper. Remember that these lines || mean the end of a sentence.

Read the picture story. Write the story in words on another sheet of paper. Then use another piece of paper to draw your own story. Give it to a friend and have the friend read your story.

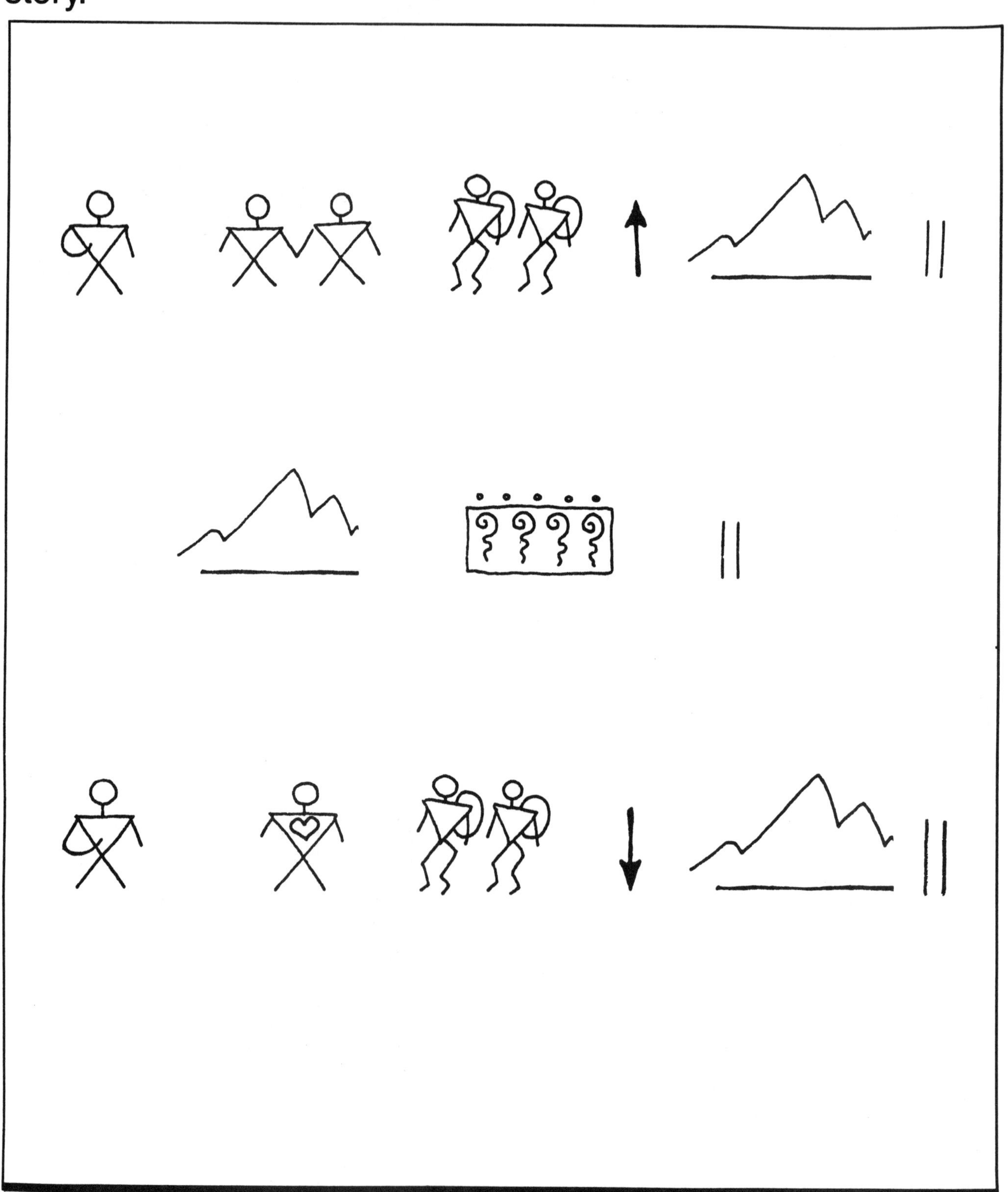

Indians drew picture symbols of the moon to show the time of year.

January: the snow moon

March: the month of the crow

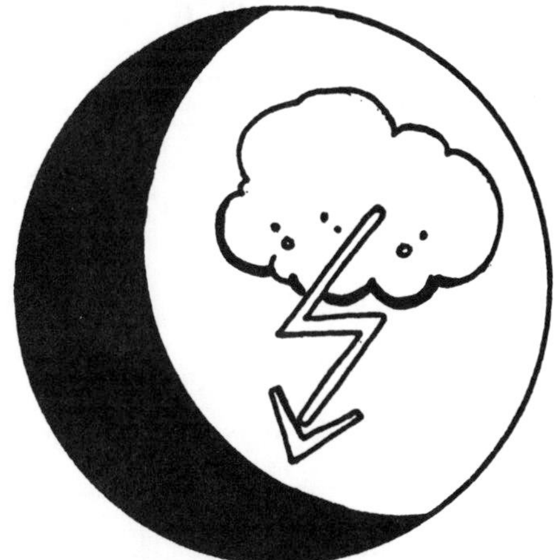

July: the thunder moon

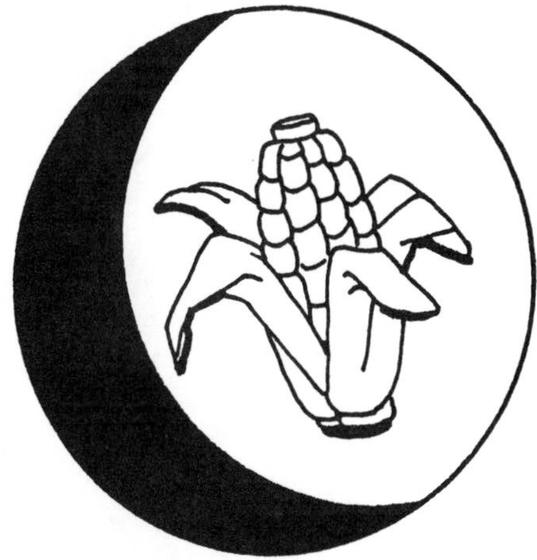

August: the corn moon

November: good month to hunt

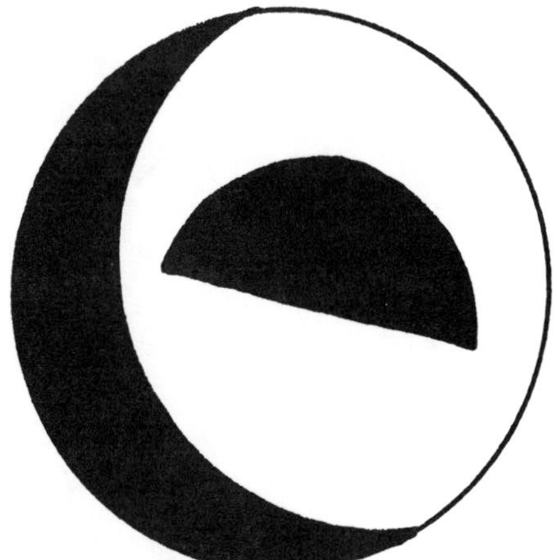

December: the month of long nights

Draw your own picture symbols to stand for the other months of the year.

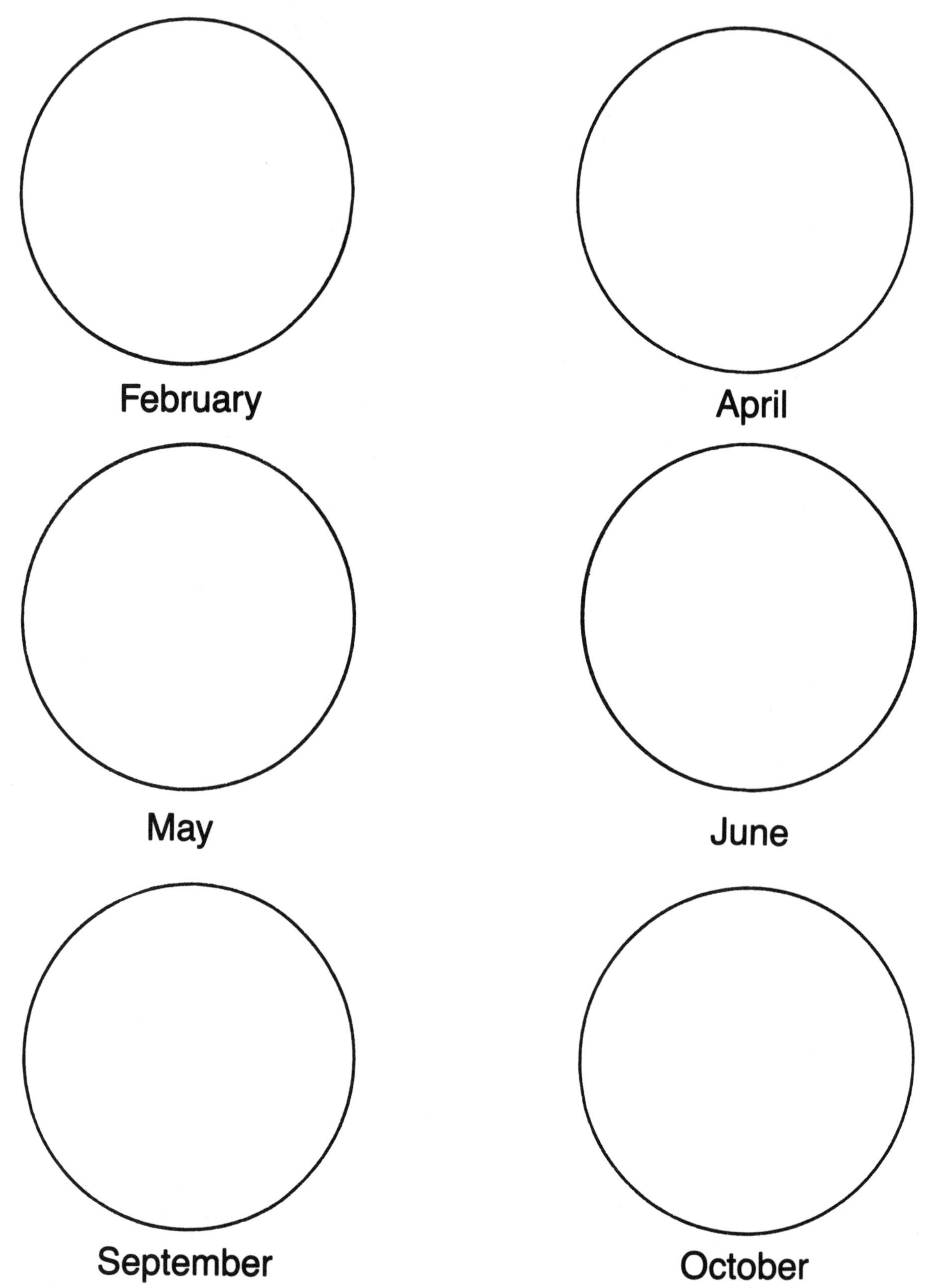

Spell as many words as you can by drawing lines from one letter to another. Do not draw a line through a letter unless it is in the word. Use each letter once. Two are done for you.

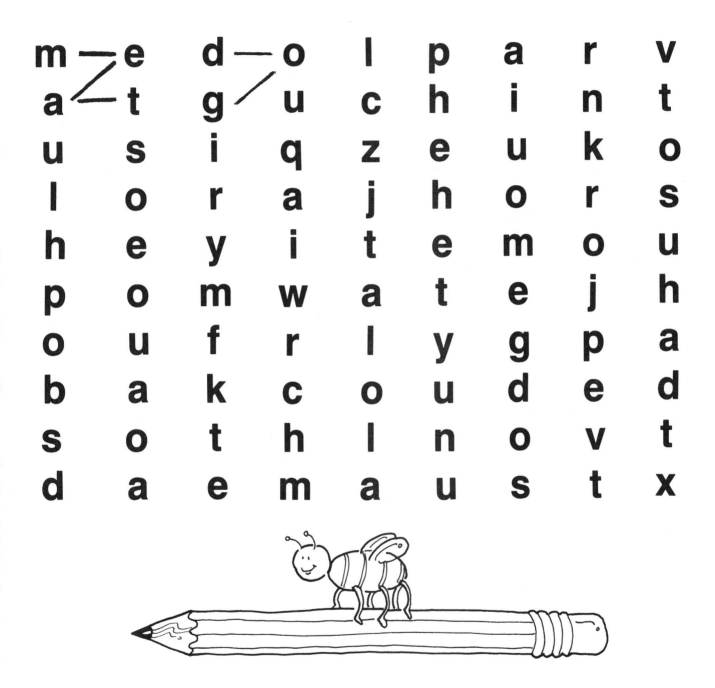

m	e	d	o	l	p	a	r	v
a	t	g	u	c	h	i	n	t
u	s	i	q	z	e	u	k	o
l	o	r	a	j	h	o	r	s
h	e	y	i	t	e	m	o	u
p	o	m	w	a	t	e	j	h
o	u	f	r	l	y	g	p	a
b	a	k	c	o	u	d	e	d
s	o	t	h	l	n	o	v	t
d	a	e	m	a	u	s	t	x

How many words did you find? ____________________

Spell as many words as you can by drawing lines from one letter to another. Do not draw a line through a letter unless it is in the word. Use each letter once.

x	o	y	e	p	u	s	t	e
r	t	j	o	y	a	l	k	u
i	q	t	e	i	c	m	a	r
z	u	a	o	k	h	e	i	w
b	e	d	s	a	z	i	o	c
m	a	r	p	n	u	e	d	i
o	f	h	r	o	s	t	a	l
k	x	a	u	p	v	i	n	d
n	o	b	y	q	g	a	t	e
i	t	a	e	u	a	c	k	n

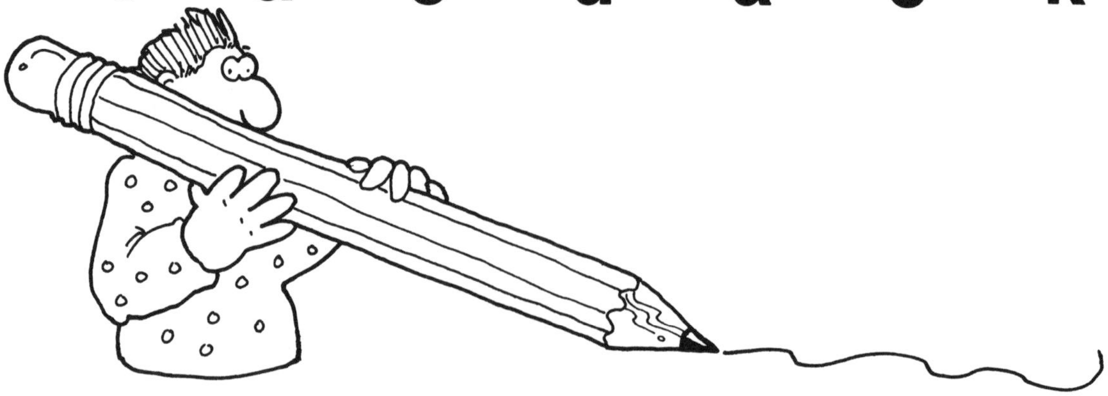

How many words did you find? ____________________

Rapunzel got tired of staying in the castle all day. She opened a new shop in town.

Draw a picture of what you think the witch will look like after Rapunzel fixes her hair!

Imagine that another fairy-tale or nursery-rhyme character gets a job or opens a store. What would the job be? What would the store sell? Draw a picture in the box.

It's fun to add a new verse to an old rhyme. Here is the old rhyme:

Little Miss Muffet
Sat on a tuffet,
Eating her curds and whey.
Along came a spider,
Who sat down beside her,
And frightened Miss Muffet away!

Here is the new rhyme:

Spidey thought he was lucky,
But the curds were so yucky,
He soon began to cry,
"Come back here, Miss Muffet,
You can keep your old tuffet.
I'd rather eat burgers and fries!"

Here's another old rhyme:

Jack and Jill went up the hill,
To fetch a pail of water.
Jack fell down and broke his crown,
And Jill came tumbling after.

Write a new verse to add to the old one. Then draw a picture of it.

Get another piece of paper and try this with some other rhymes!

When two small words fit together to make a bigger word, the new word is called a compound word. Use the words below to make as many compound words as you can. You can use the words more than once. One is done for you.

light	basket	lip	dog
house	candle	foot	boat
broom	moon	stick	ball

basketball

Put the words below together to make compound words. You can use each word more than once.

fire	gold	rain	star
coat	man	bird	bath
snow	bed	fish	room

Use the words below to make as many compound words as you can. You can use each word more than once.

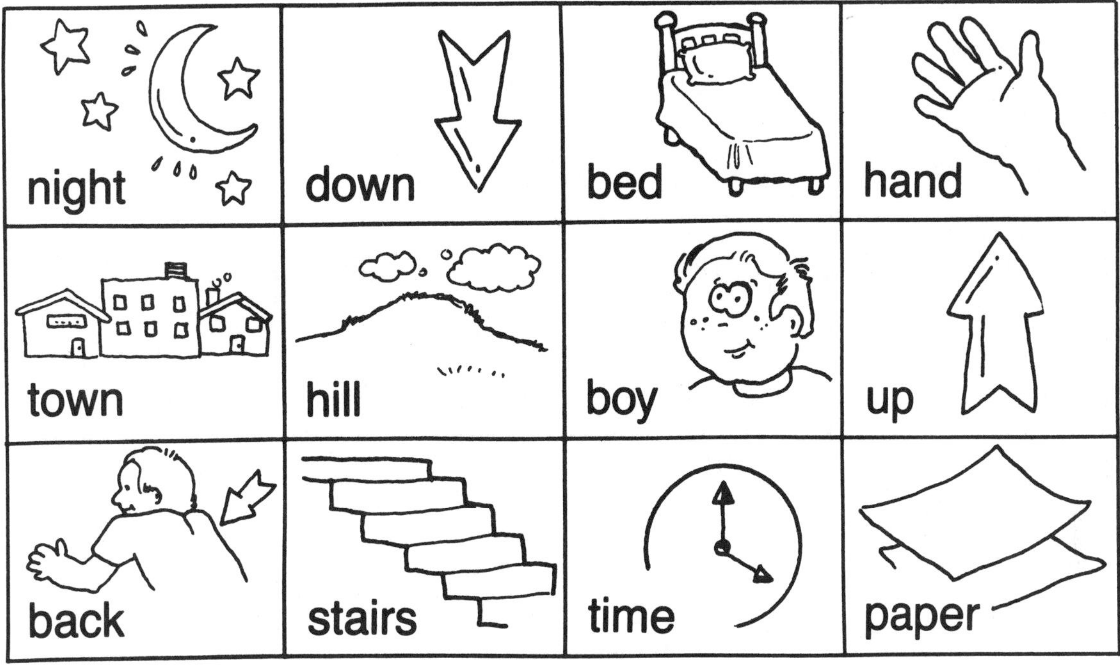

It's fun to draw words and make them look like what they mean.

zoo

cloud

Choose one of the words below and draw it.

run	basket	happy	bump
hill	hair	bed	fat

Use another sheet of paper to draw some of the other words.

Choose three of the words below and draw them in the boxes. One is done for you.

circle sad train pie

rope dance turn jump

wave hop snake people

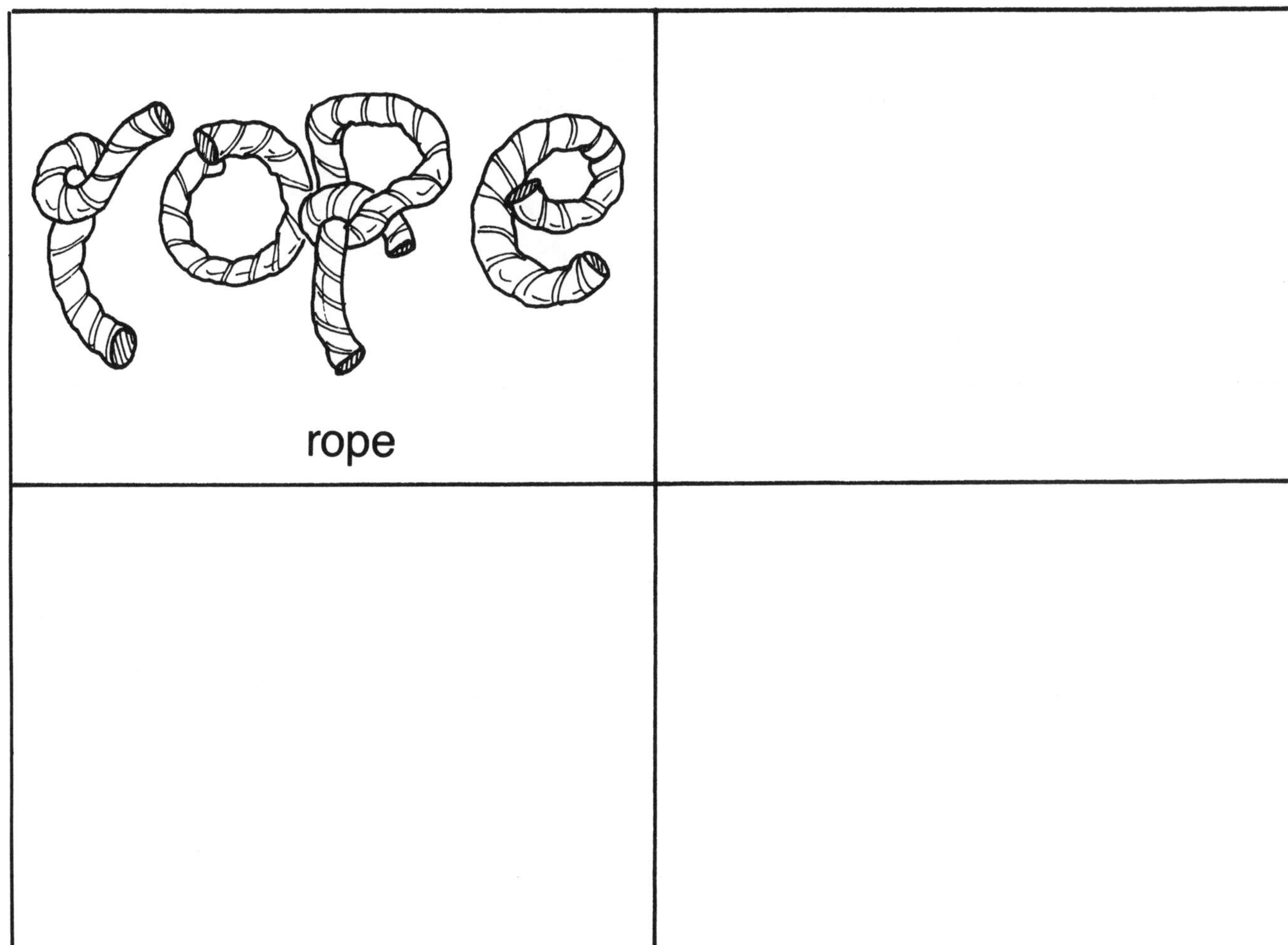

rope

On another sheet of paper draw some more words. Use your own words, too!

A verb is an action word. It tells what someone or something does. A noun is a person, place, or thing. First, list all the verbs you can think of that tell what this dragon might do. Then go back and list nouns to go together with the verbs. The first two are done for you.

Verbs	Nouns
eat	bugs
scare	king

List all the verbs you can think of that tell what this robot might do. Then list nouns that go with the verbs. The first two are done for you.

Verbs	Nouns
clean	house
fix	cars

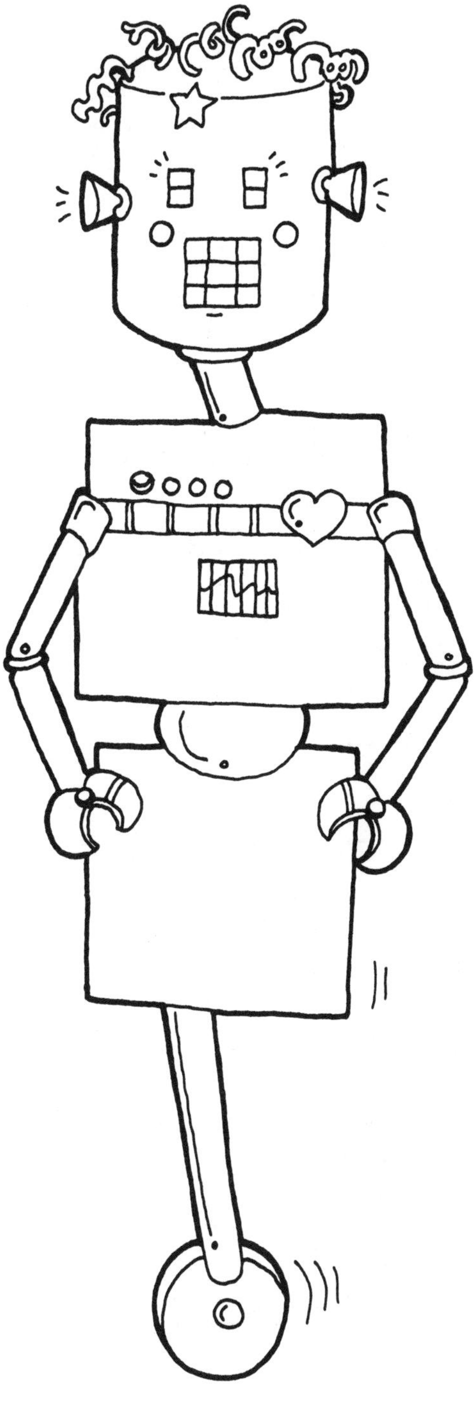

Remember that a noun is a person, place, or thing. List all the nouns that you might find inside Prince Dwayne's castle.

List all the nouns you might find inside Witch Margaret's cauldron.

Which letter is missing from each group of words? One is done for you. Fill in the letters to solve the riddle at the bottom of the page.

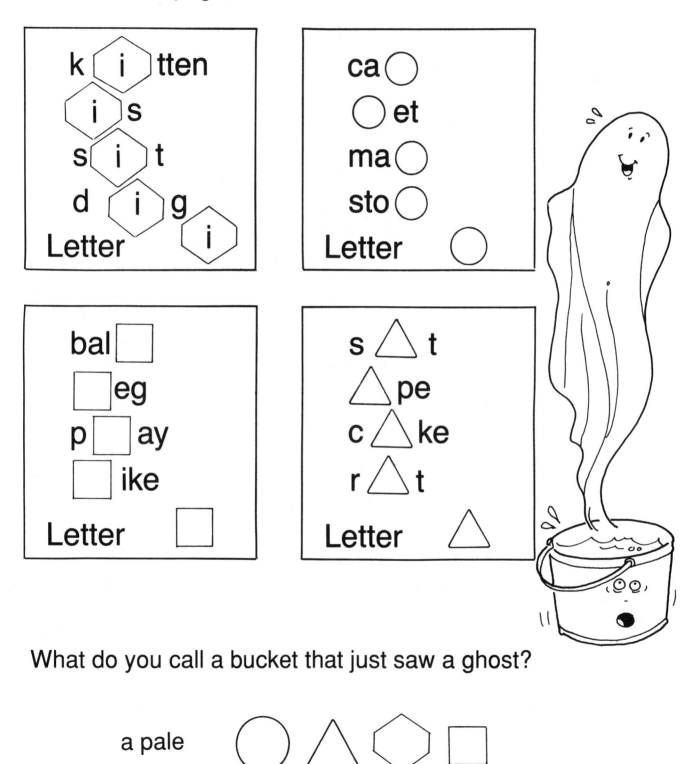

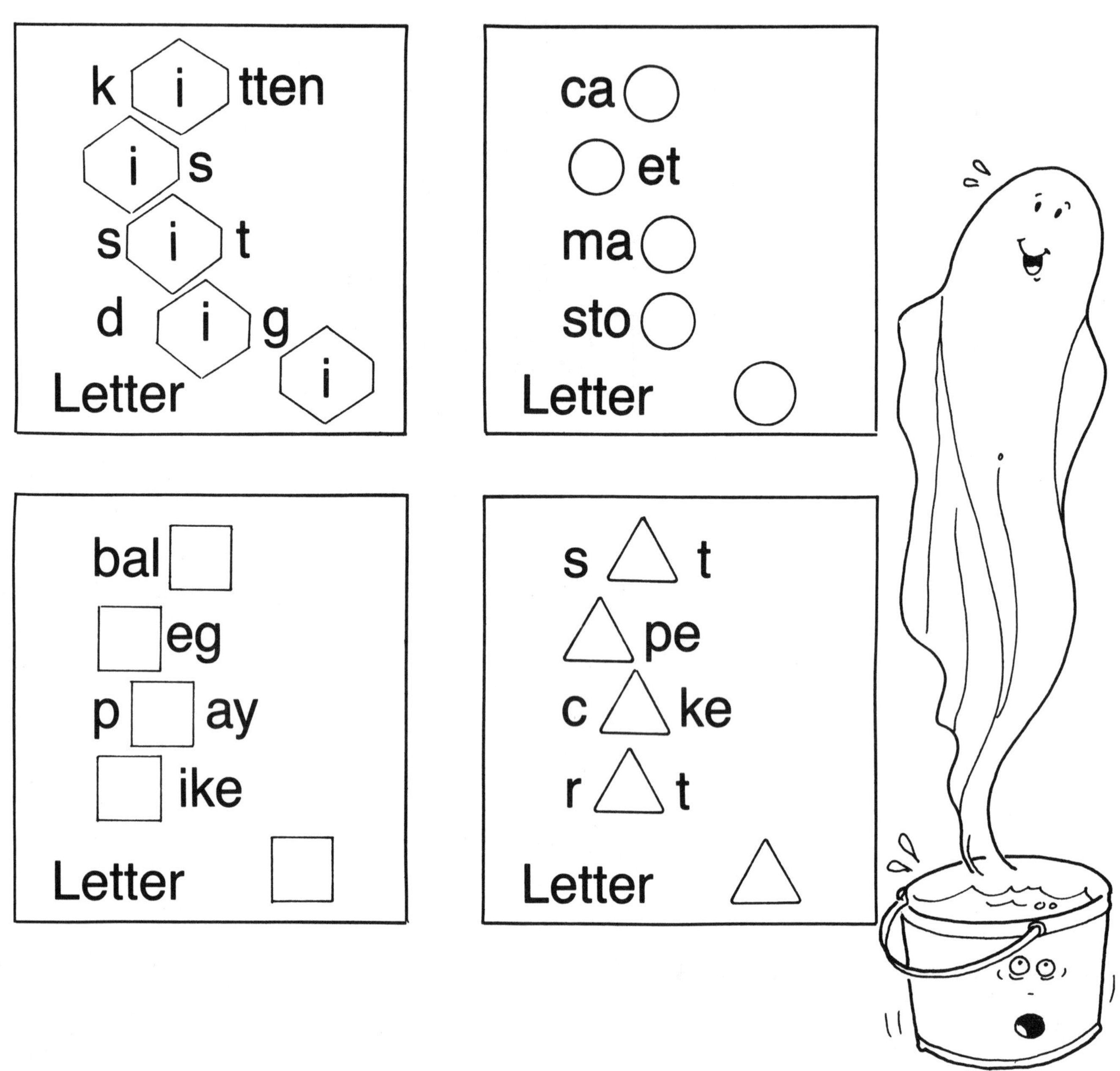

k i tten
i s
s i t
d i g
Letter i
ca
et
ma
sto
Letter
bal
eg
p ay
ike
Letter
s t
pe
c ke
r t
Letter

What do you call a bucket that just saw a ghost?

a pale

Find the letter that is missing from each group of words. Then fill in the spaces and solve the riddle.

What do you call a damp dog?

a wet

Find the letter that is missing from each group of words. Then fill in the spaces and solve the riddle.

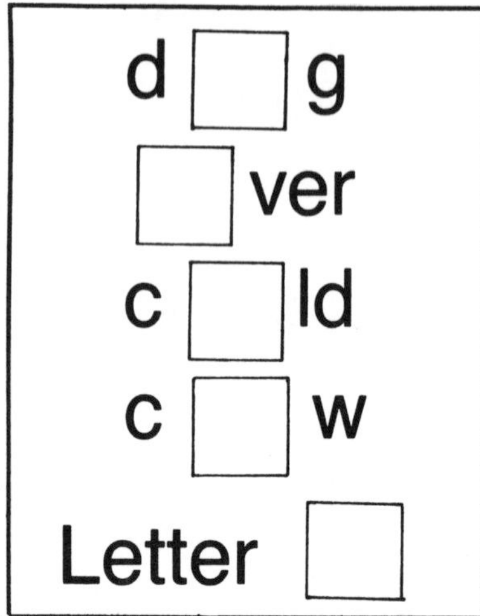

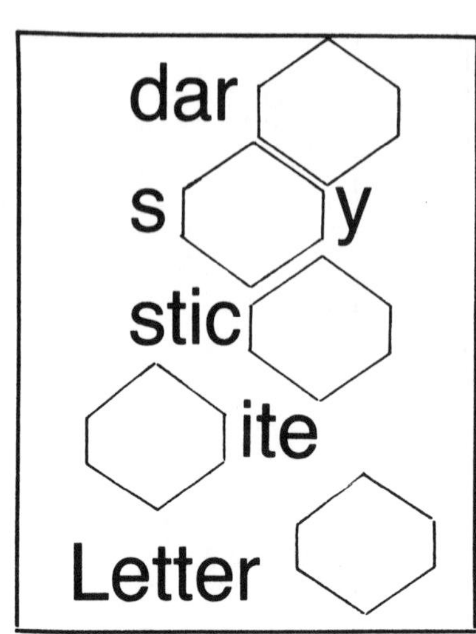

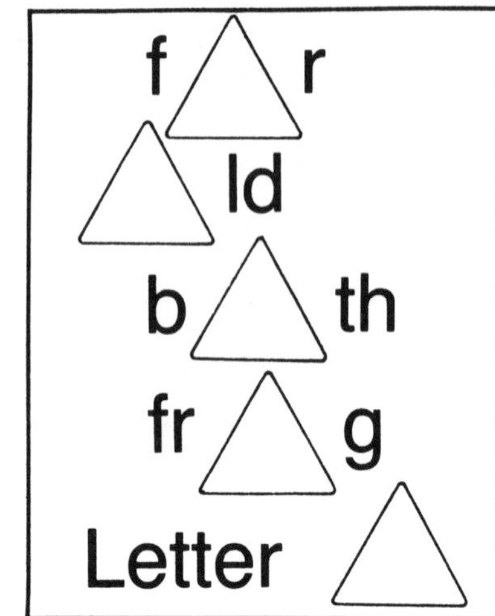

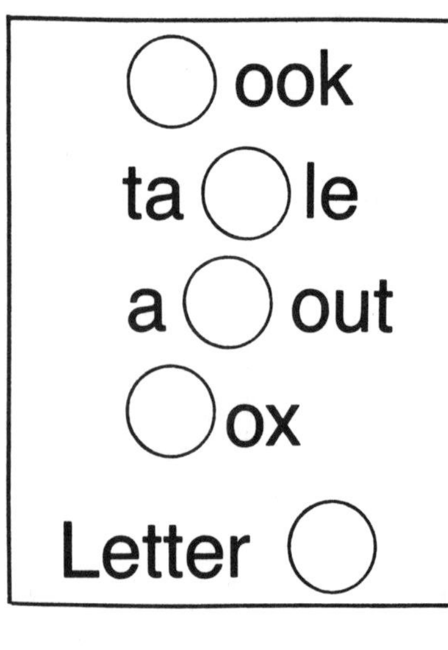

What do you call a person who steals stories?

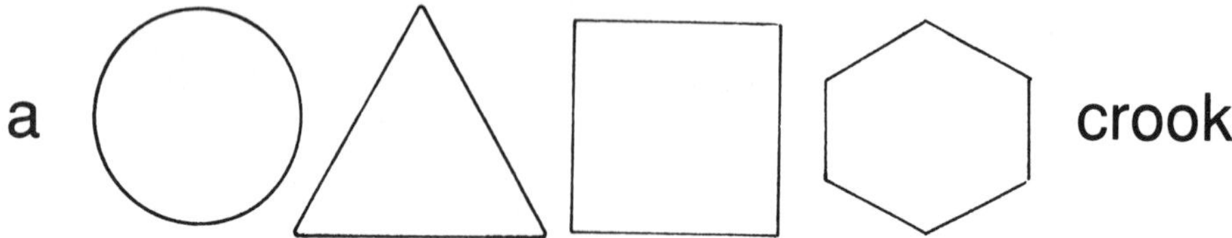

Find the letter that is missing from each group of words. Then fill in the spaces and solve the riddle.

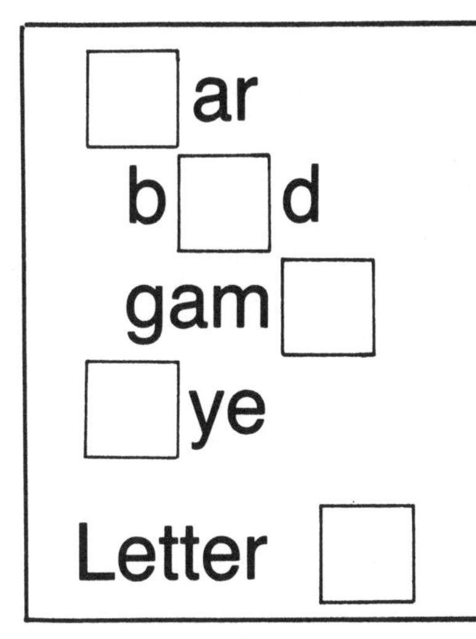

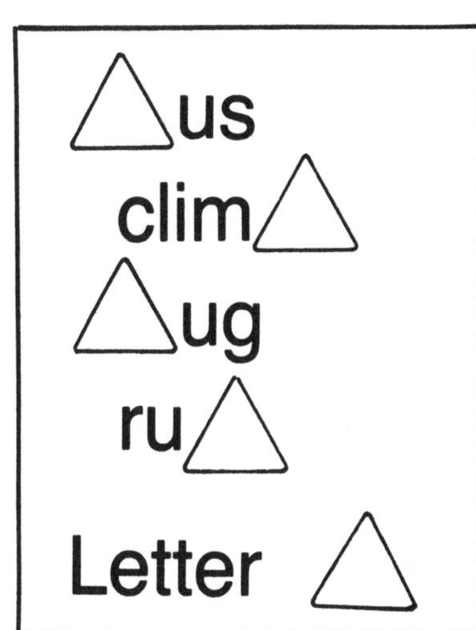

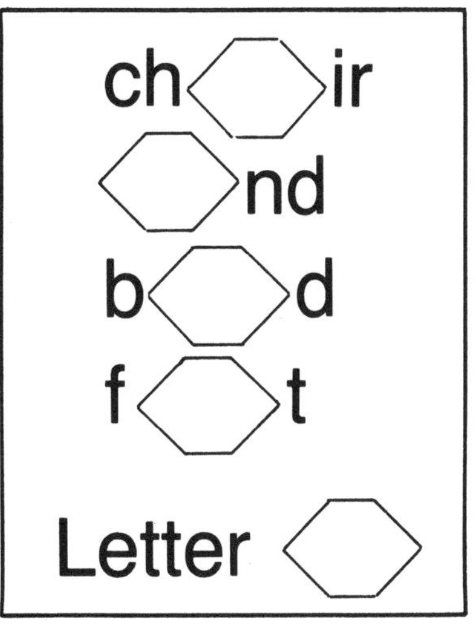

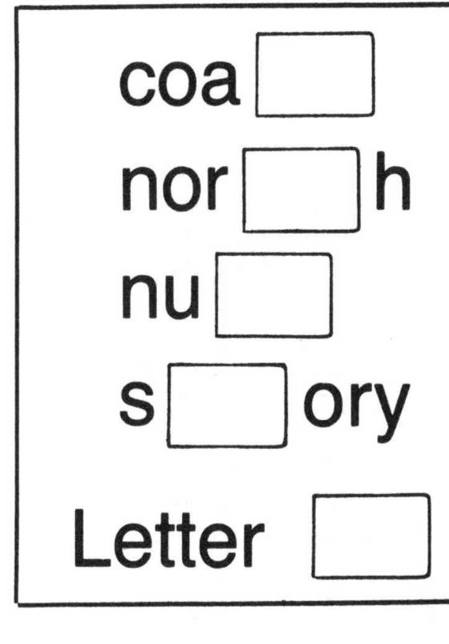

What do you call a monster's dinner?

a △ □ ⬡ ○ □ feast

Solve these word puzzles. The first one is done for you.

– o + =

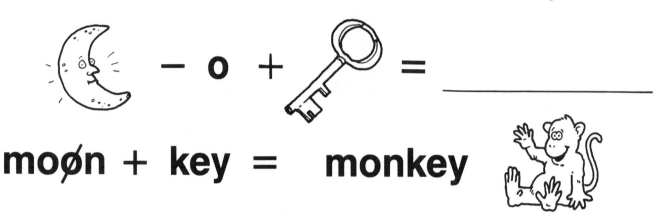

mo~~o~~n + key = monkey

1. 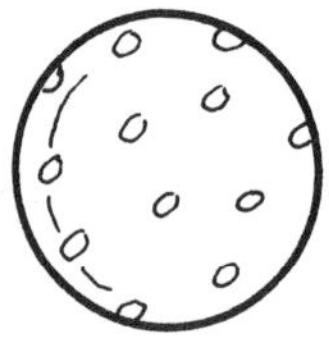 + – m =

2.  – p + loo =

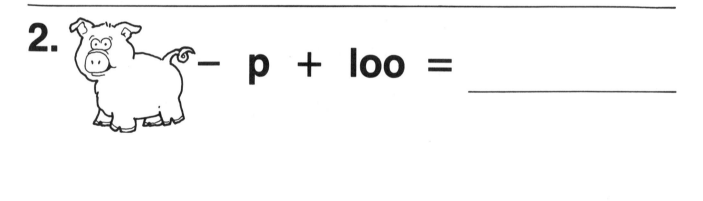

3.  – ie + =

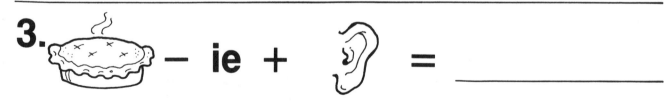

Solve these word puzzles.

1.

g + [house] – use + [star] – ar = ____________

2.

[camel] – cam + ep + [hand] – d + t = ____________

3.

[robber] – ber + [pot] – p = ____________

4.

[bat] – t + b + [moon] – m = ____________

Make up your own word puzzles for the words below.

= **horse**

= **kangaroo**

= **octopus**

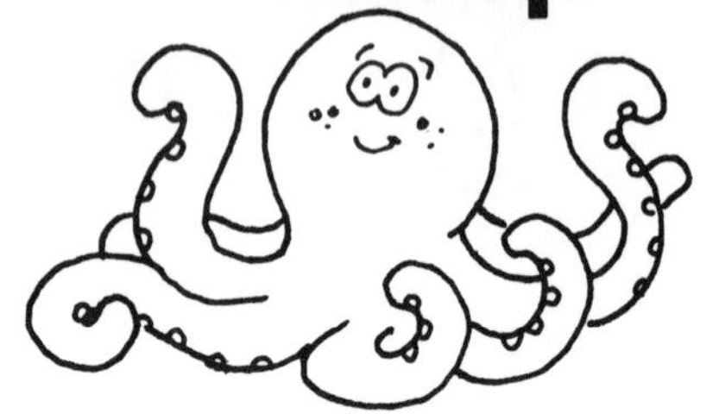

Make up one of your own:

=

Finish the line drawings below. Then write a sentence about each picture. You can be silly or serious. With a little imagination, you can turn a line into anything! Two are done for you.

A
loves to eat leaves.
An
is good if it's chocolate.

Finish the line drawings below. Then write a sentence about each picture.

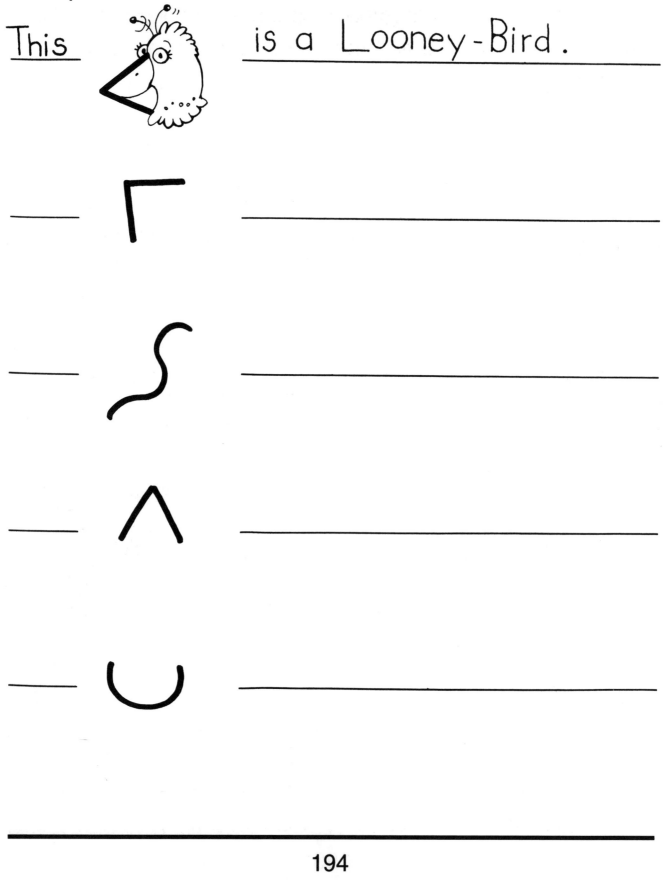

This  is a Looney-Bird.

Homonyms are words that sound the same, but mean different things. Usually they are spelled differently, too. It's fun to put homonyms together and make funny pictures. Use the word box below to find the homonyms. Write each one under the correct picture.

meet - ________

________ - won

bury - ________

________ - prints

one	prince	meat	win	berry	mate

Draw your own silly homonym pictures.

pear - pair

eight - ate

flower - flour

Add as many words as you can to each list – by changing only one letter at a time. The first list has been started for you.

cat	ball
hat	
hot	
hop	

Add as many words as you can to each list by changing only one letter at a time.

get

hand

The answer to the riddle is written in code. To read it you must cross out every other letter in each word. Write the answer on the lines below.

What did Jack's mother think when Jack told her what he got for selling their cow?

She thought Jack was:

fauolel opf bmeharnes

____

____

The answer to the riddle is written in code. To read it you must replace each letter with the letter that comes before it in the alphabet. That means that C changes to B, G changes to F, and so on. Write the answer on the lines below.

What did Daddy Cyclops say to Mommy Cyclops?

"J'mm lffq bo fzf po uif cbcz!"

He said:

"

!"

This code is called the Pig Pen code! Use it to read the answer to the riddle. Write the answer on the lines below.

A
B
C
D
E
F
G
H
I
J
K
L
M
N
O
P
Q
R
S
T
U
V
W
X
Y
Z

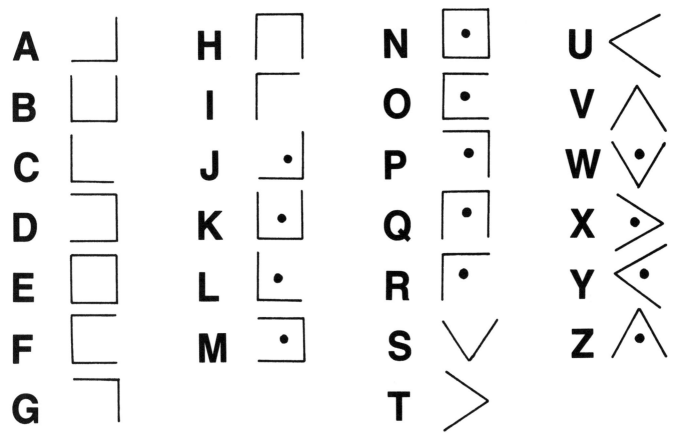

How did the firefighter feel when her husband forgot her birthday?

She was:

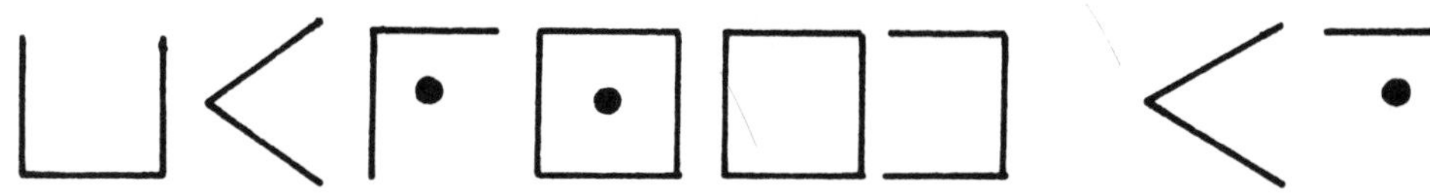

Choose one of the three codes that you used on pages 199, 200, and 201. Write your own coded message in the box. Get a friend to try to read it and write the message below.

The message is: ______________________________

____

____

Match each car to the correct storybook character. One is done for you.

NO FAT

FIDLR3

NO YOLK

ZZZZZZ

Old King Cole

Sleeping Beauty

Jack Sprat

Humpty Dumpty

Match each car to the correct storybook character.

Captain Hook

Old Woman in a Shoe

Little Boy Blue

Georgie Porgie

Choose a storybook character or a real person. Make up a license plate for him or her. Use no more than 8 letters and numbers. Write the person's name on the line at the bottom of the page.

This car belongs to ______________________________.

Dr. Dippo must write four names in her appointment book.
Read **all** the clues below. Write each name in the correct place.

Monday: ____________

Tuesday: ____________

Wednesday: ____________

Thursday: ____________

Friday: ____________

Saturday: ____________

1. Susie's appointment is on Friday.
2. Gary's appointment is one day after Fred's.
3. Fred's appointment is two days before Don's.
4. Don's appointment is two days before Susie's.

Four children signed up for swimming lessons. Read all the clues below. Write each name in the correct place.

Monday: ______________

Tuesday: ______________

Wednesday: ____________

Thursday: ____________

Friday: ______________

Saturday: ____________

1. Angela swims on Thursday.
2. Jim swims three days before Lisa.
3. Rick swims two days after Angela.
4. Lisa swims the day before Rick.

Read the clues below. Fill in the schedule for the shows at Sea Park. Draw the clock hands, too!

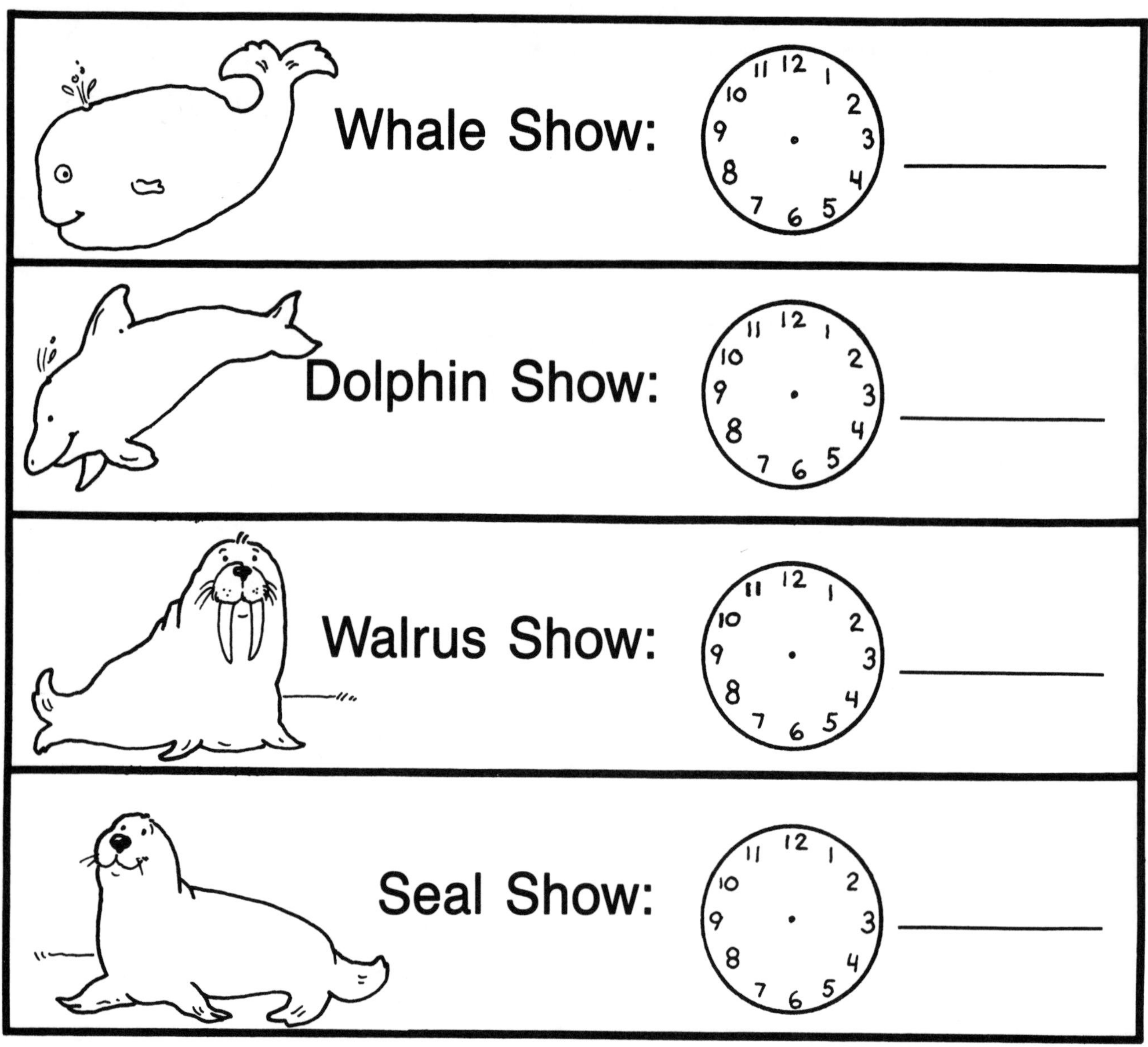

1. The Walrus Show is at 3:30 P.M.
2. The whales perform 1 hour before the seals.
3. The Seal Show is 4 hours before the Walrus Show.
4. The dolphins perform 2½ hours after the seals.

Mix up compound words to make silly new ones! Use the word box below. Write your "crazy compounds" on the lines below and draw a picture of each one. One is done for you.

goldfish	mailbox	cheeseburger
eggshell	broomstick	treetop
hairbrush	junkyard	popcorn
snowman	seaweed	dishpan

goldfish + broomstick

broomfish

Make more crazy compounds! Use the compound words in the box below. You can also use the word box on page 209.

horseshoe	bedroom	rattlesnake
farmhouse	butterfly	moonlight
football	bathtub	scarecrow
arrowhead	starfish	spaceship

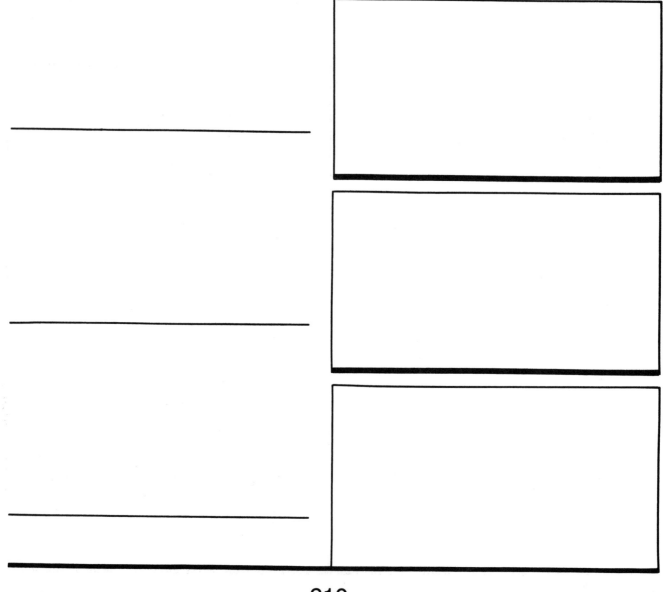

Read this Good Luck — Bad Luck story.

1. What good luck!
   The bears were out.

2. What bad luck!
   One bear went out too far.

3. What good luck!
   He was friendly.

4. What bad luck!
   He was **too** friendly.

5. What good luck!
   He was ticklish.

Write your own Good Luck — Bad Luck story. Draw pictures for it.

1. What good luck!

2. What bad luck!

3. What good luck!

4. What bad luck!

5. What good luck!

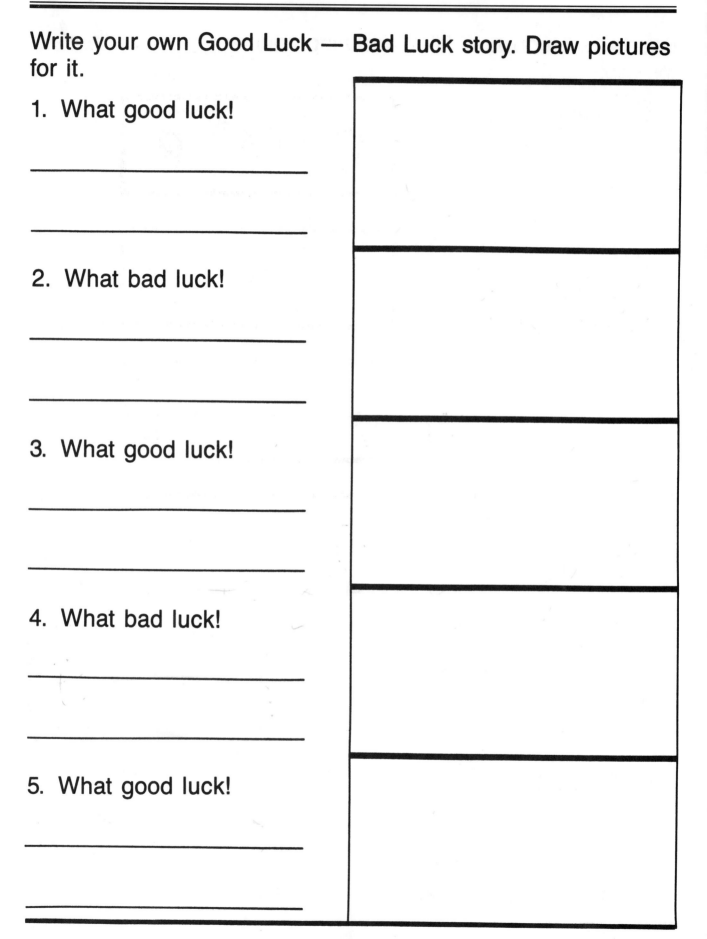

Use the word box to fill in the empty squares. One is done for you.

Word Box

flag	thing	ring	roll
top	want	thin	stop
water	cake	sled	cap

Use the word box to fill in the empty squares. Make words that go across and down. One is done for you.

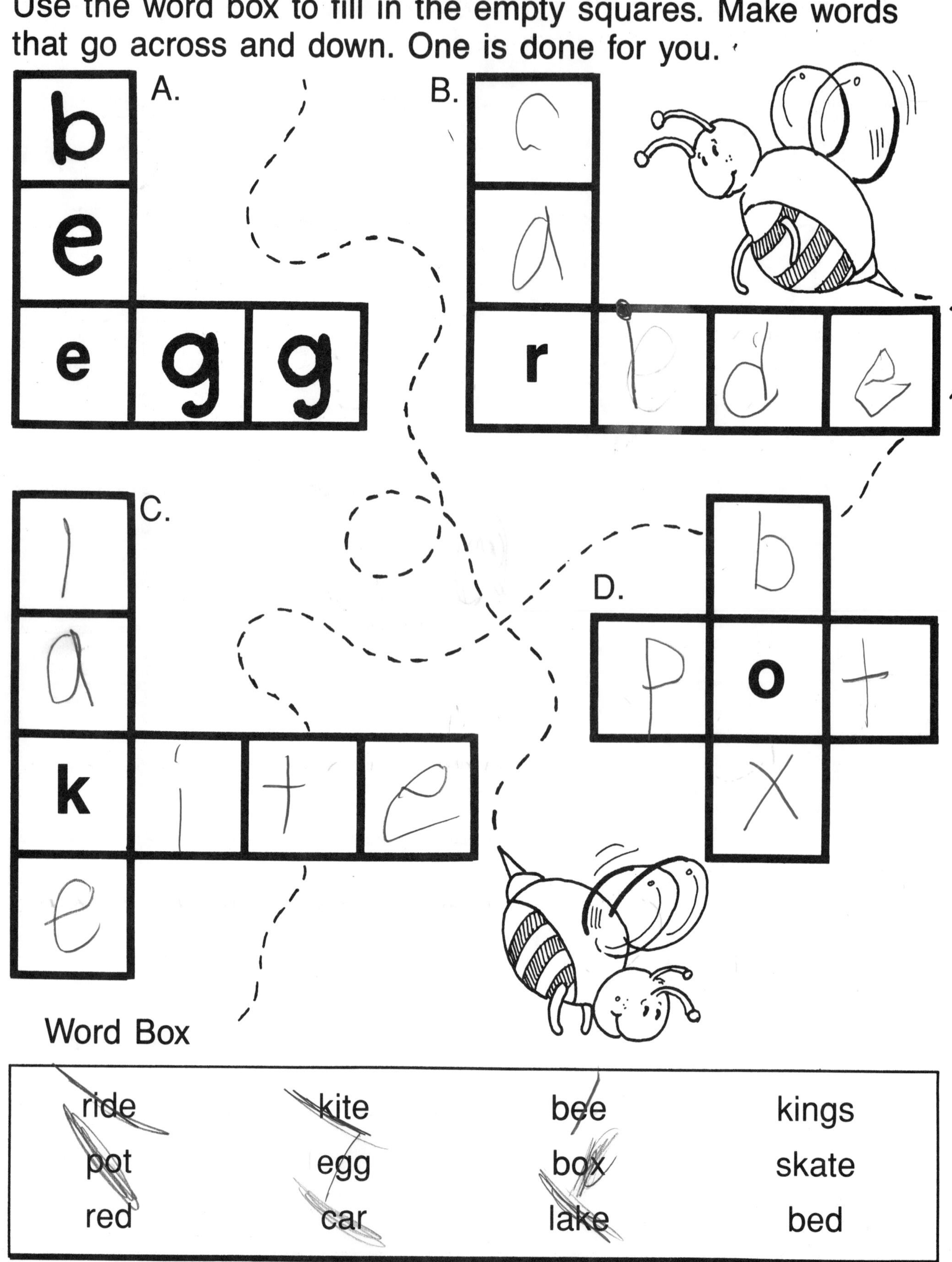

Word Box

ride	kite	bee	kings
pot	egg	box	skate
red	car	lake	bed

Use the word box to fill in the word grid. The words must go across and down. One is done for you.

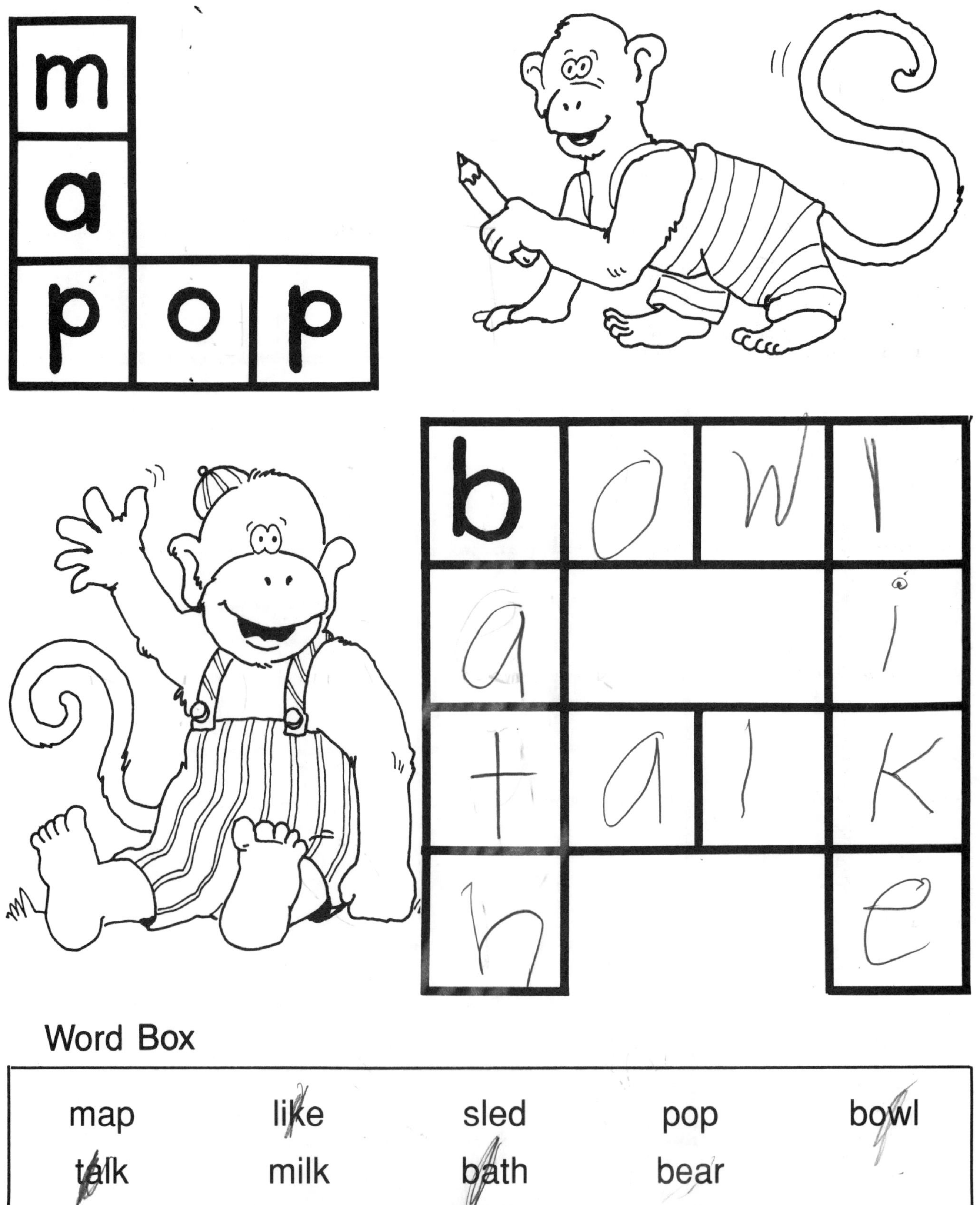

Word Box

map	like	sled	pop	bowl
talk	milk	bath	bear	

Fill in the empty squares to make words. You may use another piece of paper for practice.

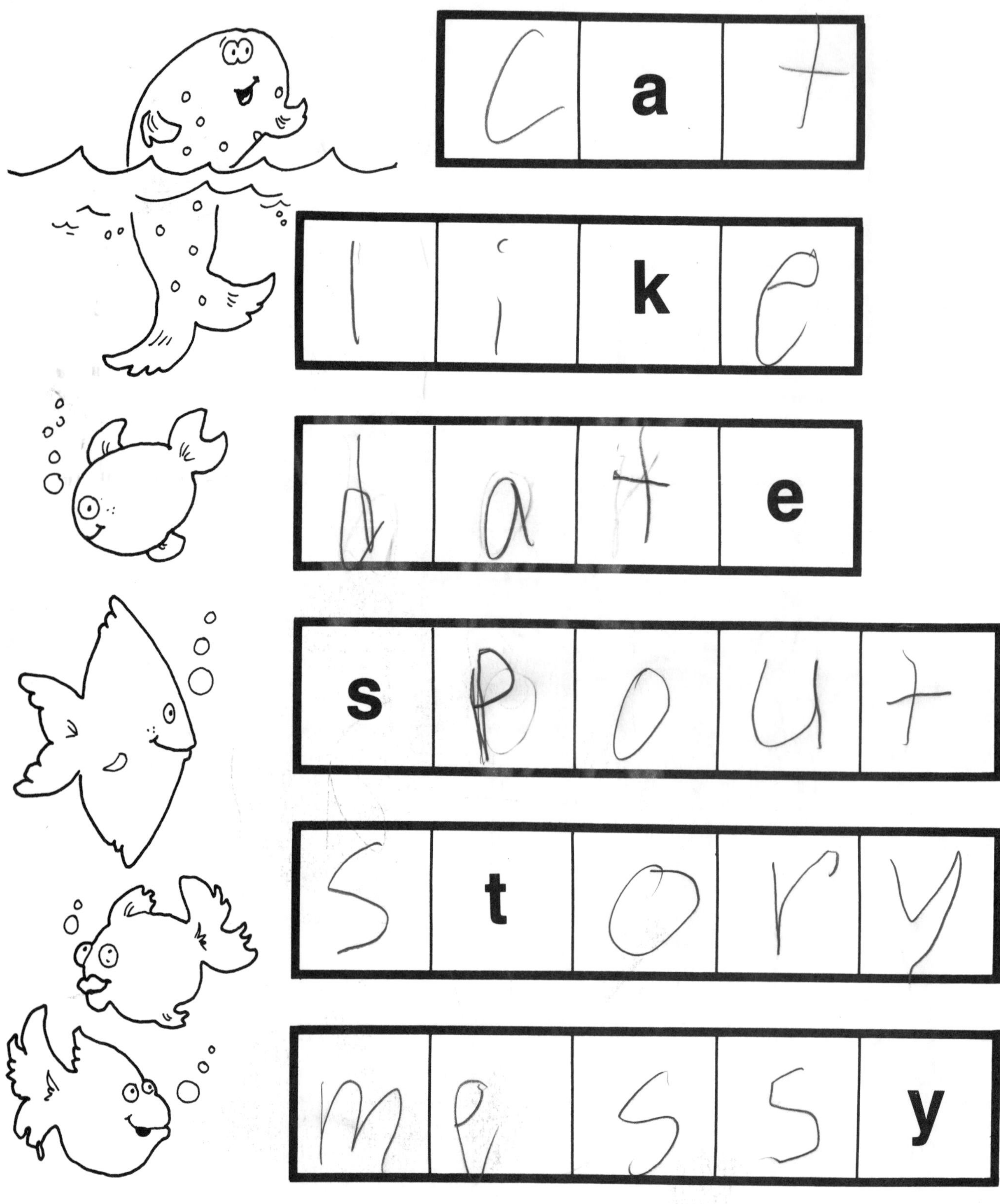

Fill in the empty squares to make words that go across and down. It's a good idea to try out your words on another piece of paper.

Fill in the word grids with words that go across and down. Don't use any word more than once.

Fill in the word grids with words that go across and down. Don't use any word more than once.

Use the letters in this square to make as many words as you can. Two are done for you. You may need to use more paper.

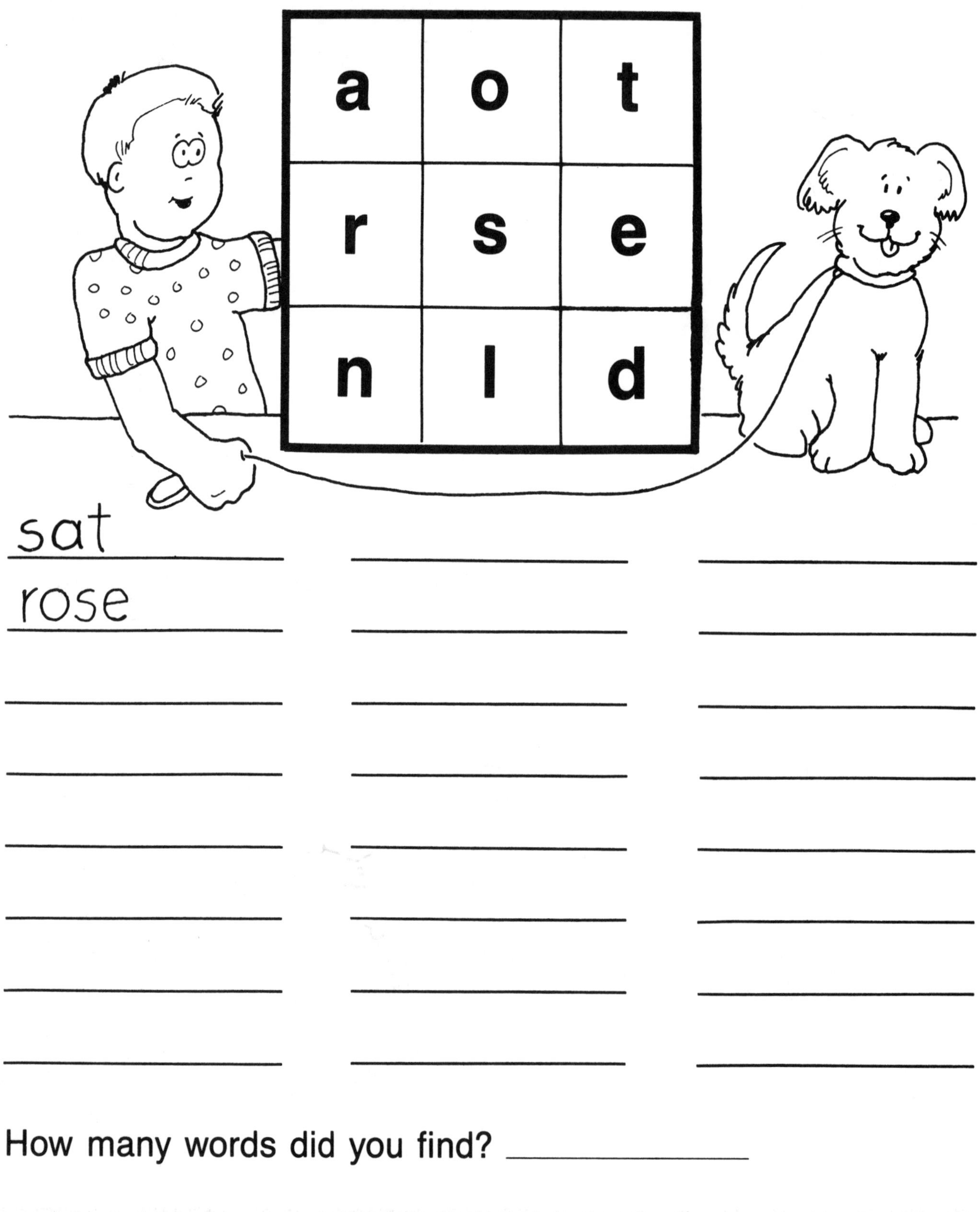

How many words did you find? ____________

Read this "Recipe for a Fall Day."

Ingredients:

24 cups of sunshine

2 small clouds

3 lumps of fresh air

10 tons of falling leaves

1 bunch of children

Directions:

1. Paint leaves red, yellow, orange, and brown.
2. Bake leaves in sunshine until they are dry and crunchy.
3. Add children to leaves. Stir.

Write a recipe for something you **don't** eat — a party, a rainbow, a summer vacation, or anything you can think of!

My Recipe for ____________________

Ingredients: ____________________

____

____

____

Directions: ____________________

____

____

____

____

Draw a picture of what it looks like when it's all done.

Use the words below to write as many sentences as you can. Be silly or serious! You may need more paper. One is done for you.

I	dog	want
monster to		big
a	have	and

I have a dog. I want a dog. I want to have a dog and a big monster. I have a monster and a big, big dog.

How many sentences did you write? 3

Use the words below to write as many sentences as you can. You may need more paper.

and	**to**	**come**	**tree**
we	**robot**	**she**	**was**
the	**fast**	**a**	**not**
over	**will**	**apple**	**eat**

How many sentences did you write? ________

Everything is always **wrong** in Looneyville. The Loonies like it that way! Today the mayor is upset because there are some things that are **right** in Looneyville! Find and circle 10 things that are **right** on this page and page 226.

If one storybook character sent a valentine to another character, it might look like this:

Dear Tink,
You are the light of my life.
Love,
Peter

Here is another make-believe valentine from a real person who lived a long time ago:

Dear Martha,
I cannot tell a lie.
I love you.
Love,
George

Write a valentine from a storybook character or a person who lived long ago.

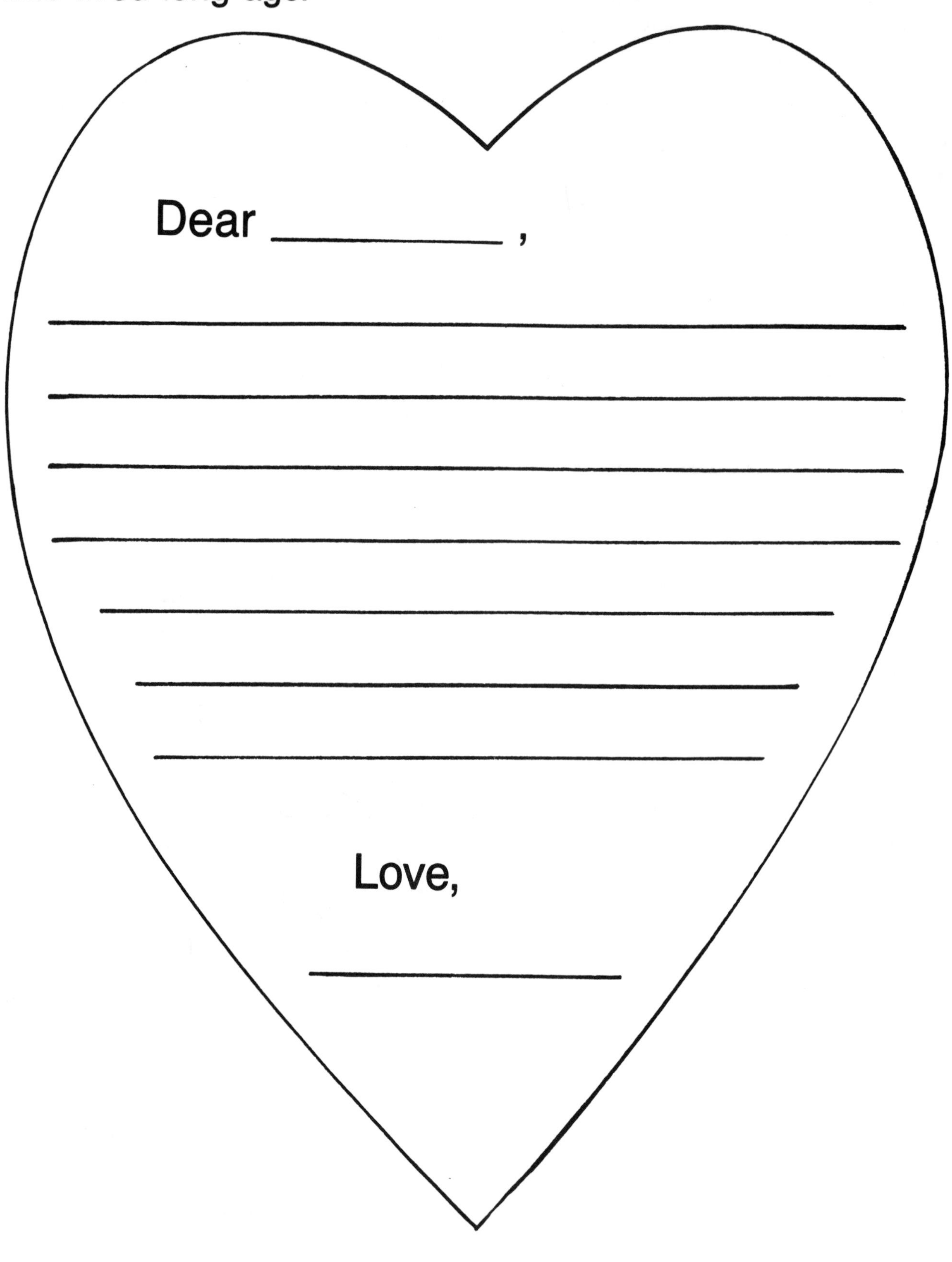

Samuel Morse invented this famous code. Use the Morse Code to find the answer to the riddle below. Write the answer on the line at the bottom of the page.

Morse Code

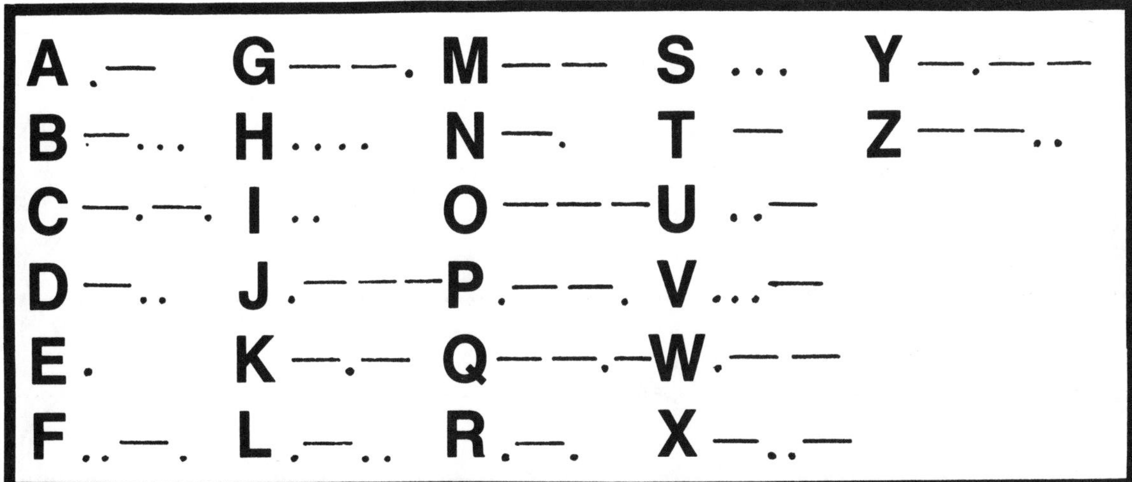

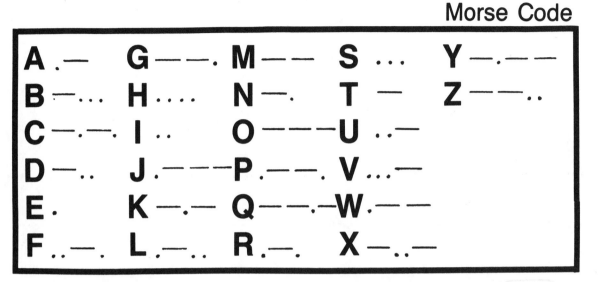

A	.—	G	——.	M	——	S	...	Y	—.——
B	—...	H	....	N	—.	T	—	Z	——..
C	—.—.	I	..	O	———	U	..—		
D	—..	J	.———	P	.——.	V	...—		
E	.	K	—.—	Q	——.—	W	.——		
F	..—.	L	.—..	R	.—.	X	—..—		

What does the Gingerbread Boy use to make his bed?

—.—. ——— ——— —.— .. . . —

He uses a ______________________________.

Use the Morse Code to decode the answer to this riddle:

What did the mommy skunk say to the baby skunk?

—.—— ——— ..— .— .—. .

——— —.. ——— .—. .— —... .—.. .

She said: "______________________________________

______________________________________!"

This code is called Trevanion's Code. To find the secret message in this letter, you must circle every **third** word after a **punctuation** mark. The first word is done for you.

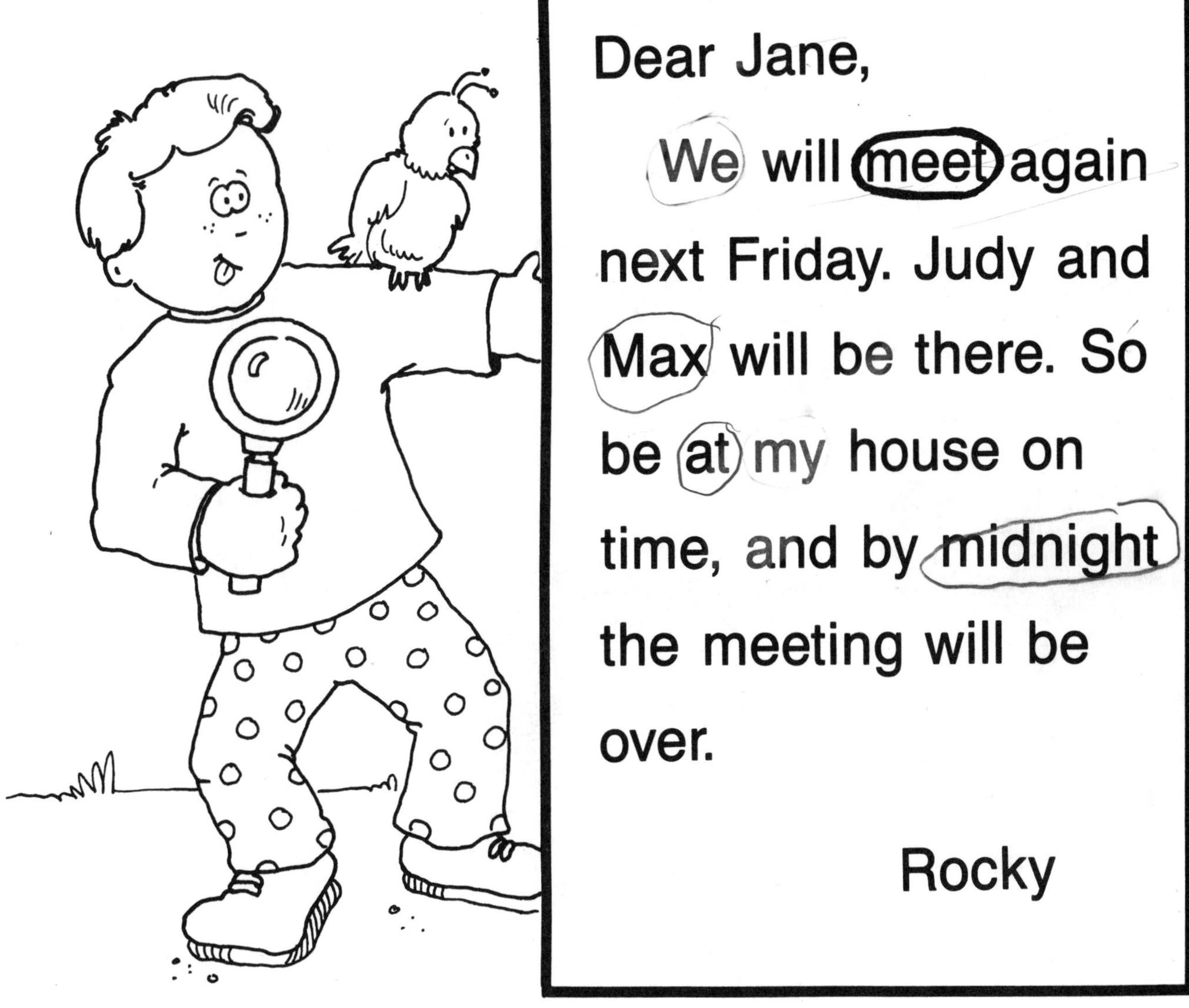

Dear Jane,

We will meet again next Friday. Judy and Max will be there. So be at my house on time, and by midnight the meeting will be over.

Rocky

The secret message is:

Meet Max at midnight

To read the answer to the riddle below, you must replace **each letter with the letter that comes after it in the alphabet. C becomes D, S becomes T, and so on. Write the answer on the line.**

What do penguins like to ride?

Answer: h b d b x b k d r

They ride on ______________________________.

Here is a Box Code. To decode the message, you must read the letters in the box from left to right. The first one is done for you.

M	y	d	o
g	h	a	s
t	e	n	f
l	e	a	s

The message is:

My dog has ten fleas.

Find the message below. Write it on the lines.

T	h	r	e	e
m	o	n	s	t
e	r	s	a	r
e	b	e	h	i
n	d	y	o	u

Make up a message in Box Code. Your message must have 36 letters. Write it in the box below. Give it to a friend and see if he or she can decode it!

The secret message is: ______________________________

____

____

____

This is the Typewriter Code. Use it to find the answer to the riddle. Write the answer on the line below.

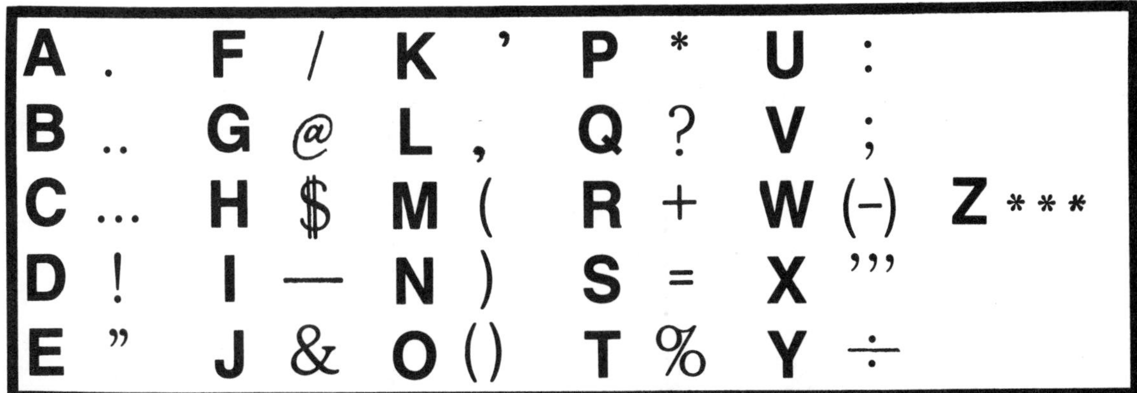

A	.	F	/	K	’	P	*	U	:		
B	..	G	@	L	,	Q	?	V	;		
C	...	H	$	M	(	R	+	W	(-)	Z	***
D	!	I	—	N	)	S	=	X	’’’		
E	”	J	&	O	()	T	%	Y	÷		

What do you get when you cross a chicken with a bell?

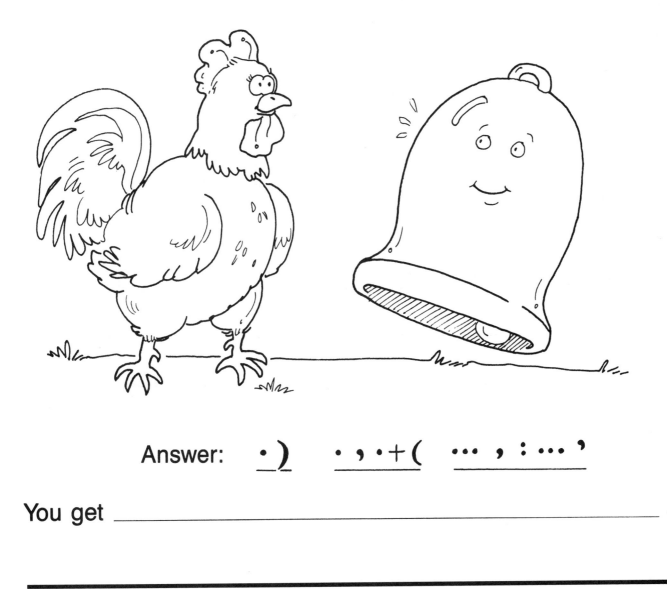

Answer: .)   . , . + (... , : ... ’

You get ______________________________.

Use the word box to help you fill in the word pyramid. One word is done for you.

Word Box

star	so	saw	story	was
lions	best	is	stones	

Use the word box to help you fill in the word pyramid.

Word Box

window	look	on	over	socks
most	no	outside	box	

Fill in the word pyramid with 5 words.

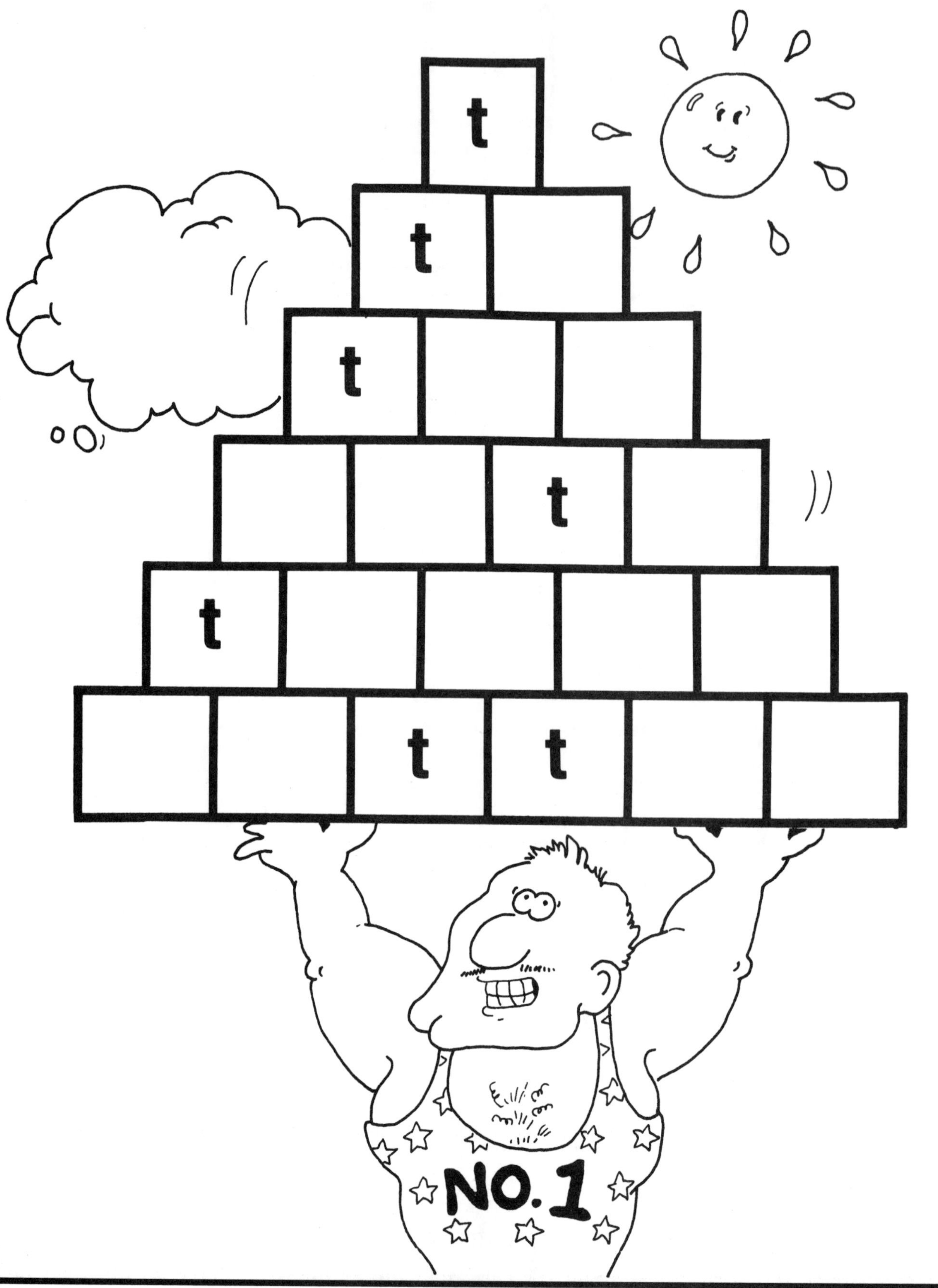

You need 10 words to fill in this big word pyramid!

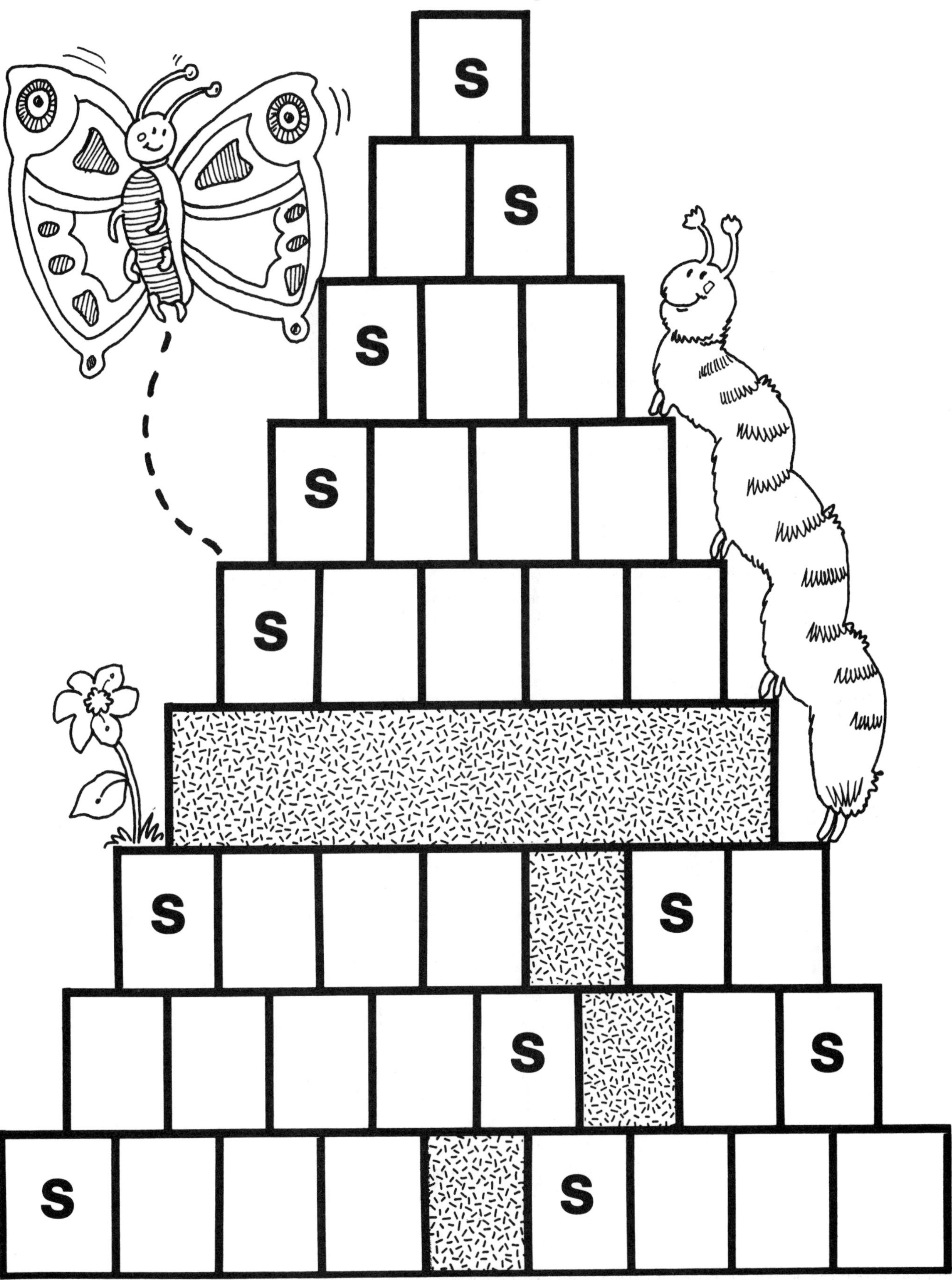

Fill in this word pyramid with 10 words. Use as many letter a's as you can.

a

How many a's are in your pyramid? ________

Look at the words on the dial. Close your eyes. Move your finger around the dial. Stop. Open your eyes. Write the word you stopped on. Do it again. Draw a picture of one thing that your two words tell about. On this page one is done for you.

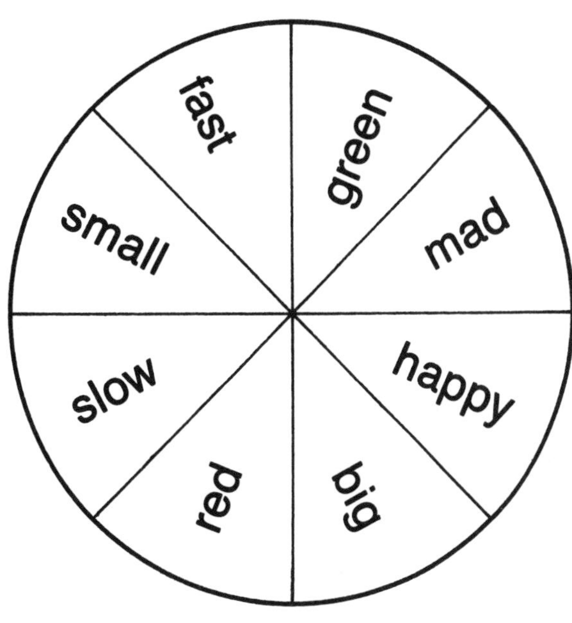

Here is something fast and green.

It is a pickle on his way to a picnic..

Use the dial on the page before. Write your words below. Draw your pictures.

1. Here is something ____________ and ____________ .

It is a ____ .

2. Here is something ____________ and ____________ .

It is a ____ .

Draw a picture in each box. The first one is done for you.

Did you ever see . . .

. . . a hot dog?

. . . a home run?

. . . a soda pop?

. . . time fly?

Draw a picture in each box.

Did you ever see . . .

. . . a banana split?	. . . a hat box?
. . . a wrist watch?	. . . a jelly roll?

List things you can change by making them bigger. Two are done for you.

Make it bigger and change a . . .

coffee cup into a swimming pool

fork into a rake

__________ into __________

__________ into __________

__________ into __________

__________ into __________

__________ into __________

__________ into __________

__________ into __________

List things you can change by making them smaller. Two are done for you.

Make it smaller and change a . . .

helicopter into a fan

blanket into a napkin

__________ into __________

__________ into __________

__________ into __________

__________ into __________

__________ into __________

__________ into __________

__________ into __________

MATH

This section focuses on building fundamental math skills using critical and creative thinking. Not only will youngsters practice addition and subtraction, they will also be introduced to basic geometry and word problems. These exercises concentrate heavily on deductive reasoning, inference, sequencing, and creative problem solving.

Sassy Hen lost her eggs. Her eggs are marked with numbers that are:

more than 5
less than 12

Circle the eggs that belong to Sassy.

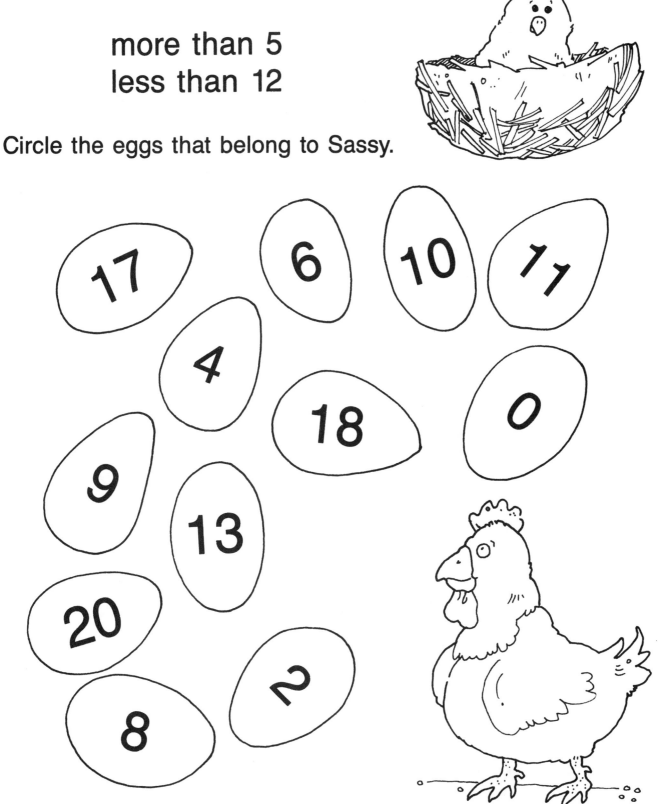

Catch the king's butterflies. His butterflies are marked with numbers that are:

even numbers
less than 14

Circle the butterflies that belong to the king.

Geraldo Giraffe eats leaves with numbers that are:

odd numbers
more than 9

Circle the leaves that Geraldo will eat.

Can you find food for the Sneekle? Sneekles eat numbers that are:

even numbers
more than 8
less than 20

Circle the things that the Sneekle will eat.

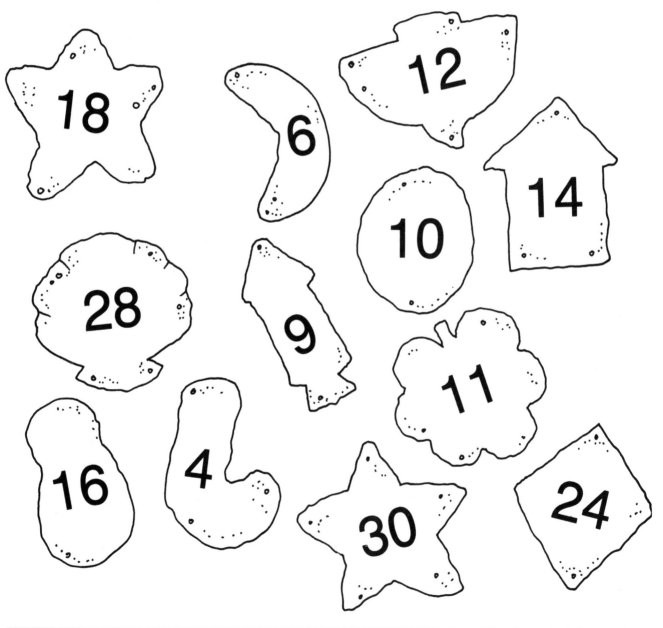

18 6 12

14 10

28 9 11

16 4 30 24

Can you find the Meecher's footprints? A Meecher's footprint is a number that is:

an odd number
more than 70
less than 100

Circle the Meecher's footprints.

93 99 87 75 63 74 81 86 101 72 98 79

Can you find the hats for this Blicking? A Blicking is a monster who only wears hats with numbers that are:

divisible by 3
less than 36
even numbers

Make a number puzzle for a friend.

Can you find the Numberoos? Numberoos have numbers that are:

Color this design, but use only **three** colors — and make sure that no shapes of the same color touch each other. Think before you color!

Color this design, but use only **four** colors — and make sure that no shapes of the same color touch each other. (It's a good idea to start by coloring the shapes that touch a lot of others.)

One of the numbers fell into the math contraption. Which one was it? Write the number on the empty ball.

Which number fell into the math contraption? Write the number on the empty circle.

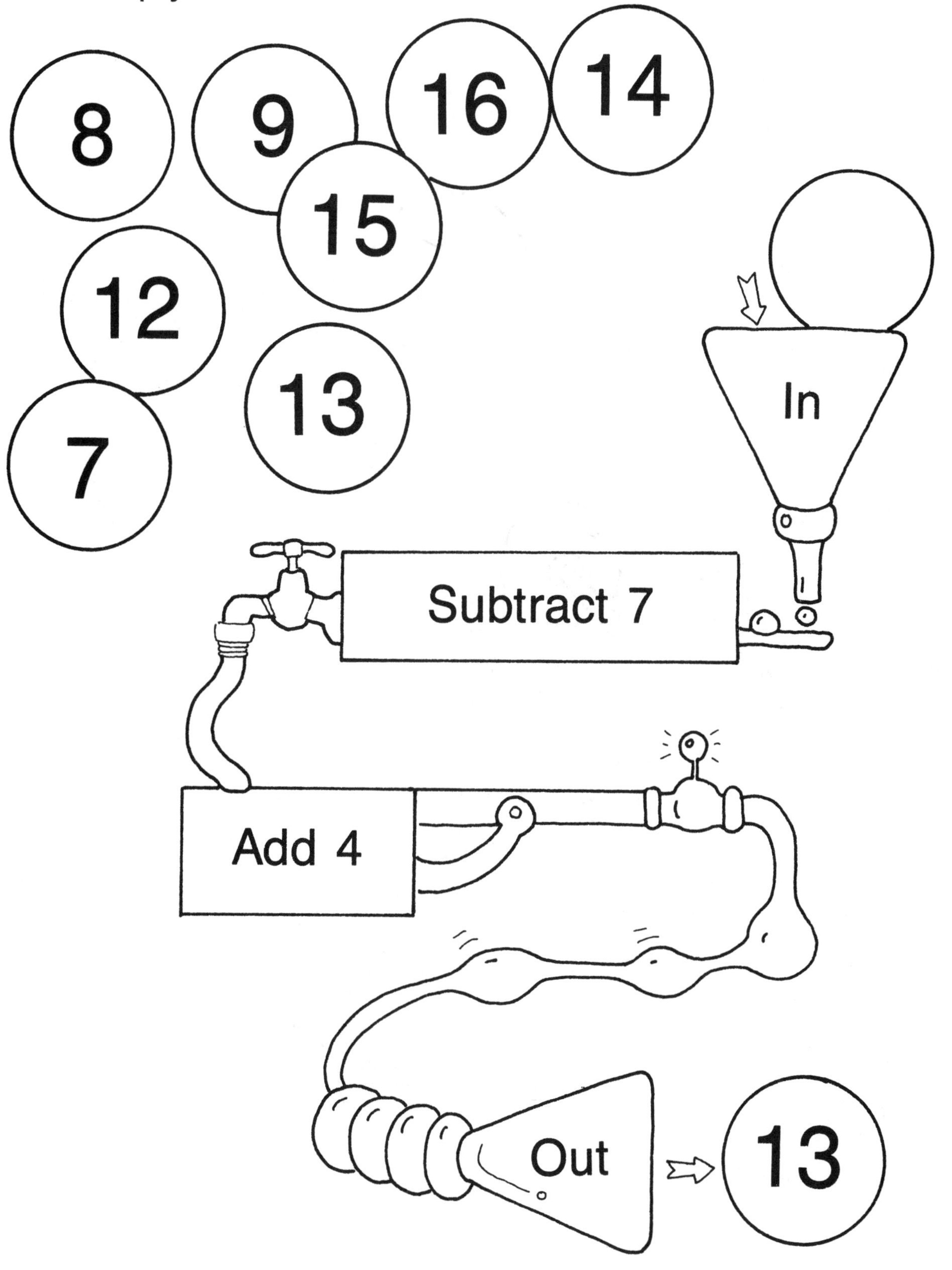

Which two numbers fell into the math contraption? Write the numbers on the empty circles.

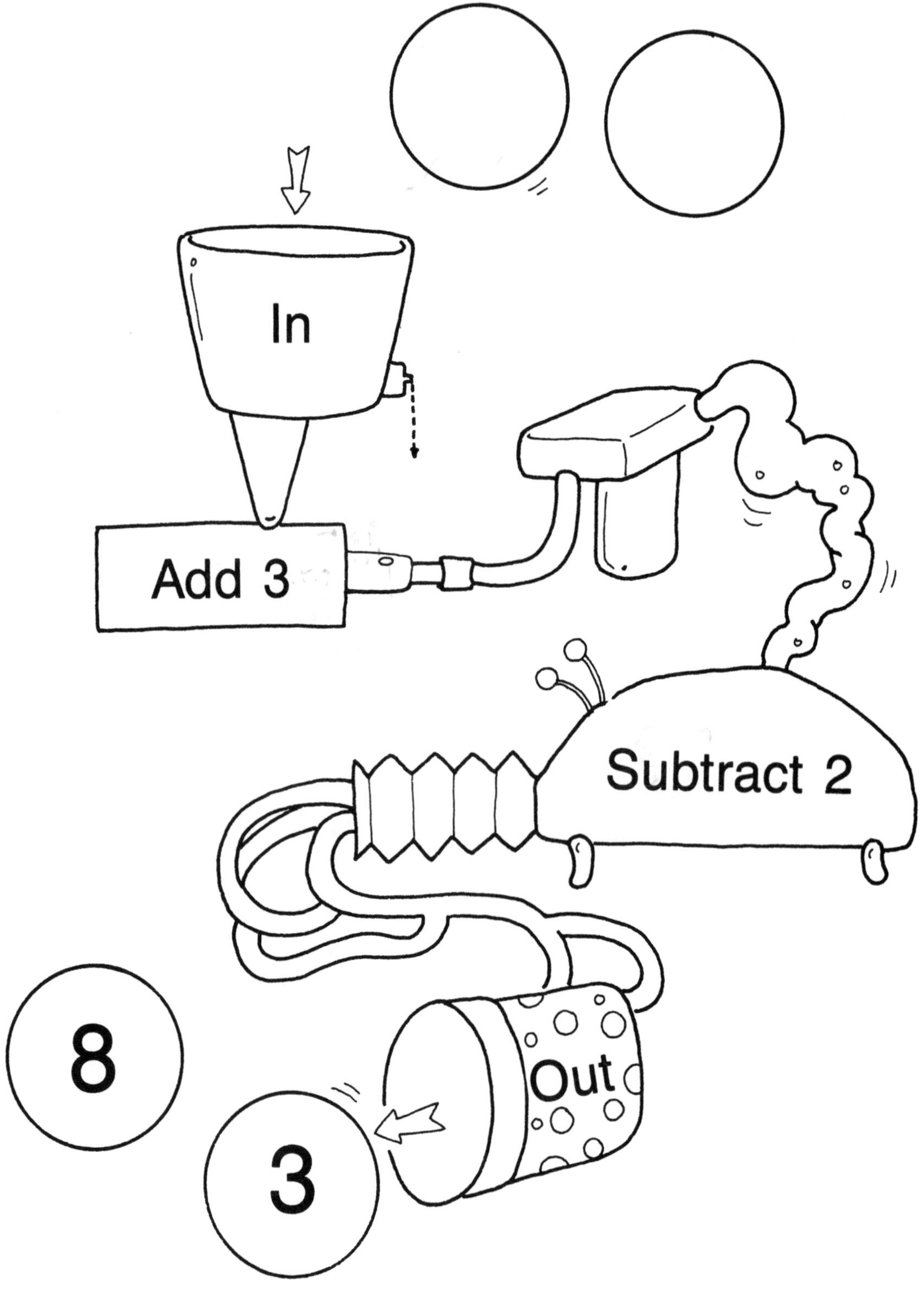

Which numbers fell into the math contraption? Write the numbers on the empty circles.

14 13 9 11

Make your own math contraption, and get a friend to try to solve it.

Redwood School held an apple-eating contest. Read all the clues. Then write the correct names next to the number of apples he or she ate.

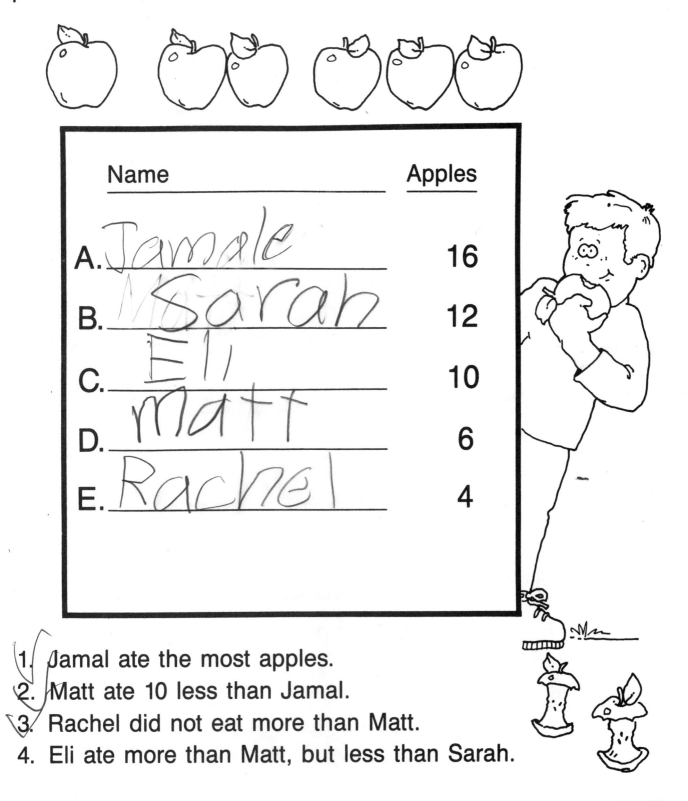

	Name	Apples
A.	Jamale	16
B.	Sarah	12
C.	Eli	10
D.	Matt	6
E.	Rachel	4

1. Jamal ate the most apples.
2. Matt ate 10 less than Jamal.
3. Rachel did not eat more than Matt.
4. Eli ate more than Matt, but less than Sarah.

Michele, Kevin, Daniel, and Amanda played Space Pirates. Read all the clues and write the correct name next to each score.

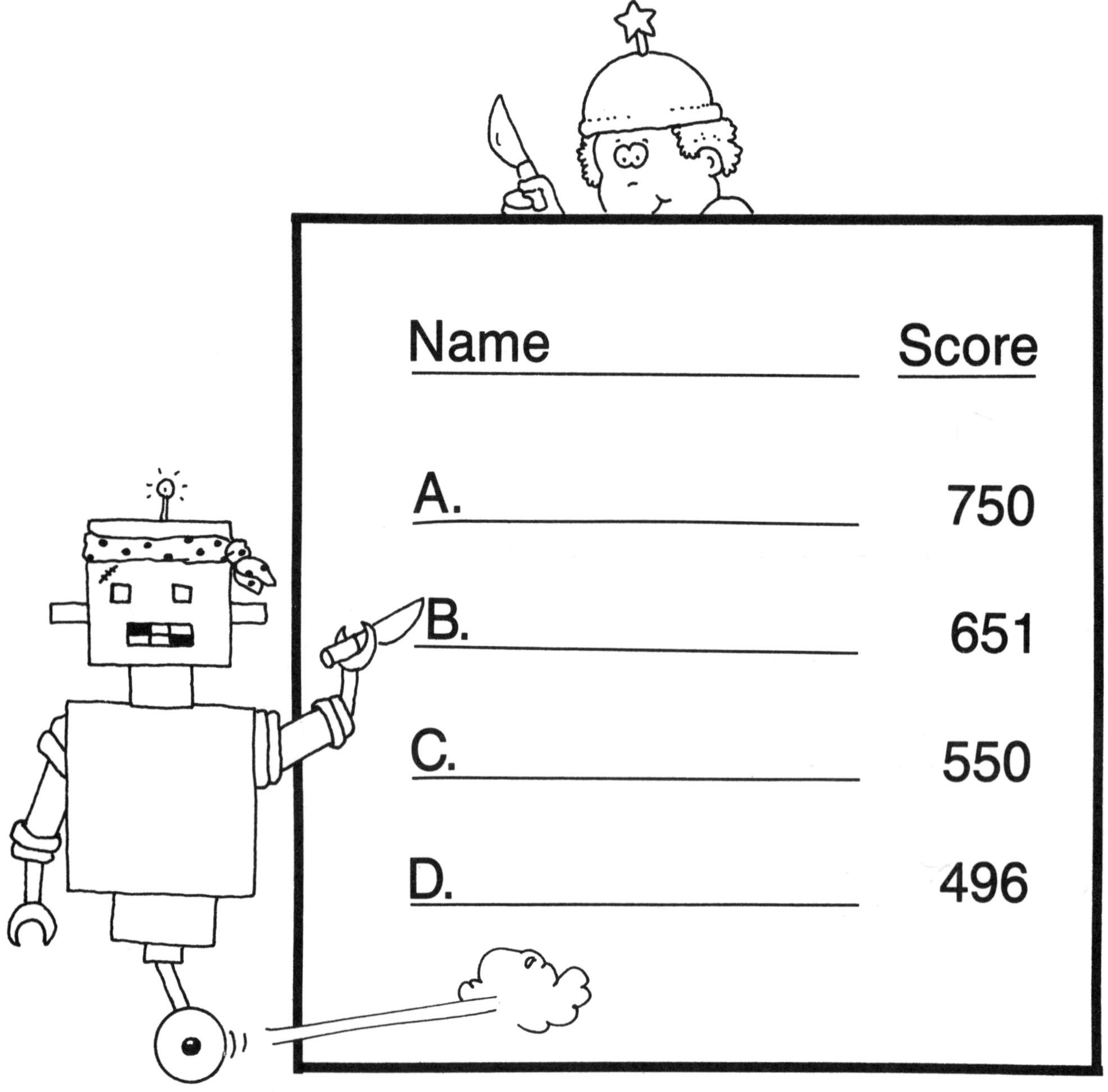

Name	Score
A. ________	750
B. ________	651
C. ________	550
D. ________	496

1. If Kevin had scored 100 more points, he would have had the highest score.
2. Amanda scored the highest.
3. Michele scored 200 points less than Amanda.
4. What was Daniel's score?

Megan, Tyrone, Brittany, and Teddy have their birthdays in November. Read all the clues. Then write each name next to the correct date.

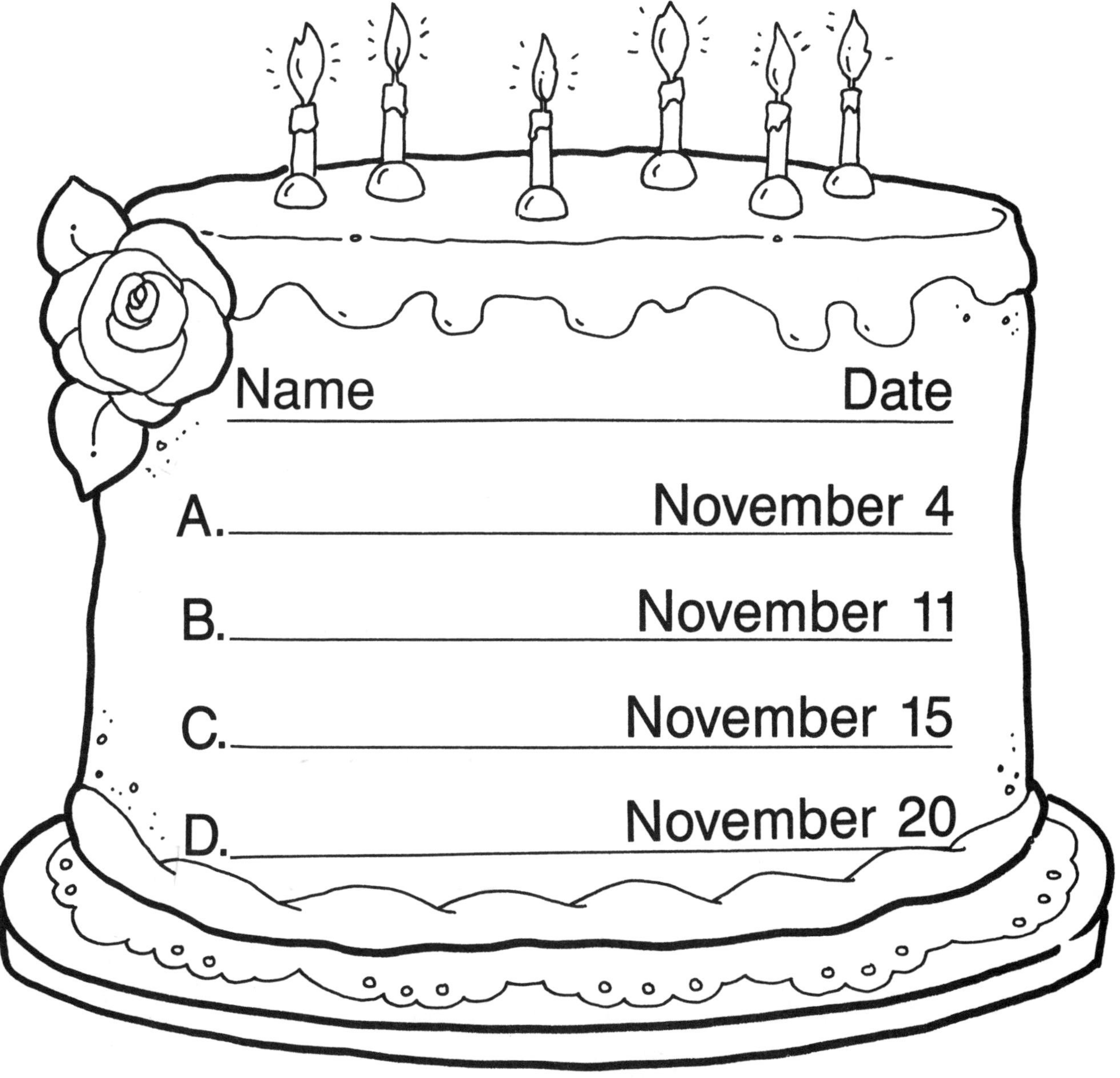

1. Megan's birthday is one week after Teddy's.
2. Teddy's birthday comes first.
3. 7 + 8 equals Brittany's birthdate.
4. When is Tyrone's birthday?

Tara, Michael, Timmy, Nicky, and Soraya have marble collections. Read all the clues and write each name next to the correct number of marbles.

Name	Marbles
A.____________	20
B.____________	12
C.____________	8
D.____________	7
E.____________	5

1. Nicky has only green and blue marbles.
   He has 3 green marbles and 2 blue ones.
2. Soraya has 3 more marbles than Nicky.
3. Timmy has the most marbles.
4. Michael and Soraya together have the same number of marbles as Timmy.
5. How big is Tara's collection?

Courtney, Josh, Sean, Erin, and Damon have piggy banks. Read all the clues. Then write each name next to the correct amount in the piggy bank.

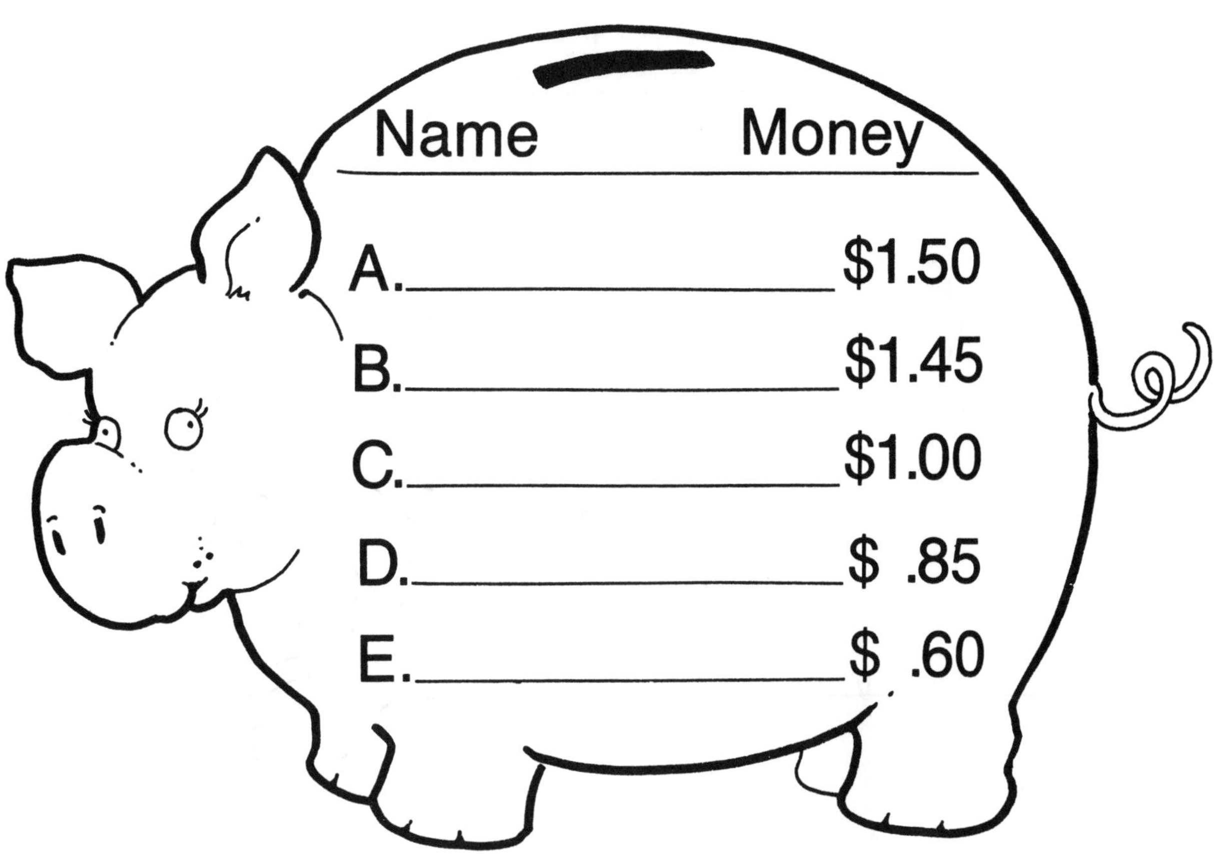

1. Courtney has 3 quarters and 1 dime.
2. Sean has 25 cents less than Courtney.
3. Erin has 6 quarters.
4. Sean and Courtney together have the same amount as Damon.
5. How much money is in Josh's bank?

The Hawks and the Eagles play soccer. Each player wears a different number on his or her shirt. The numbers are listed in the box. Read all the clues. Then write the correct number on each shirt.

4	7	9	11	12	19

1. All the Hawks wear numbers less than 10.
2. The tallest Eagle has the lowest number on his team.
3. The girls are wearing the even numbers.
4. The tallest Hawk does not have the highest number on his team.

Write the numbers 3, 4, 5, 6, 7, and 8 on the acrobats so that the sum of:

the top row is 4
the middle row is 12
the bottom row is 17

You can only use each number **one** time!

Write the numbers 3, 4, 5, 6, 7, and 8 on the balls so that the sum of:

the top row is 4
the middle row is 14
the bottom row is 15

You can only use each number **one** time!

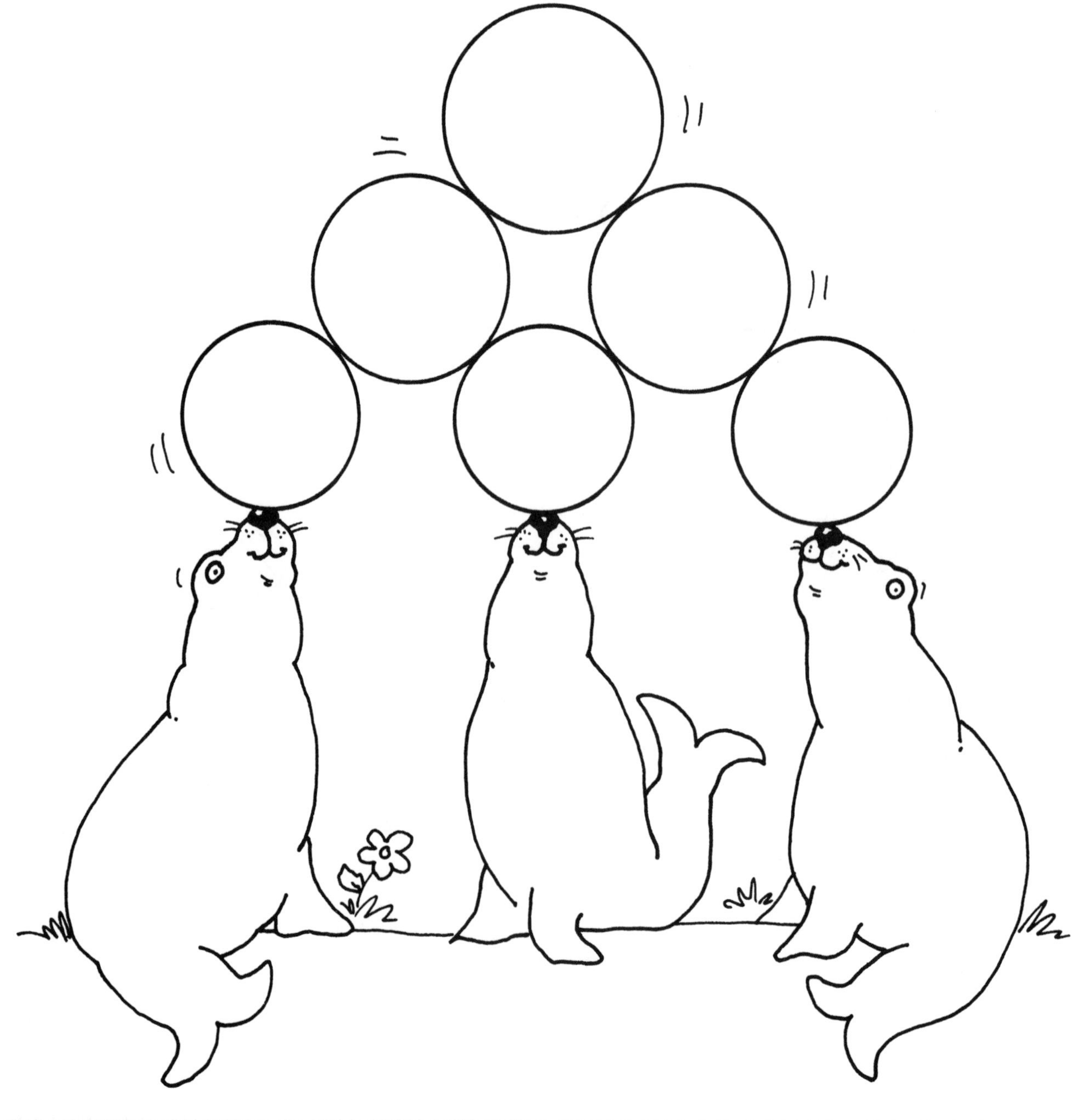

Nicki's phone number begins with the numbers 5, 3, and 7 — but Nicki forgot what order the numbers are in. Arrange the numbers 5, 3, and 7 in as many different ways as you can. Write your combinations in the spaces below.

Jessica forgot her score on the Space Man video game. She does remember that the numbers 1, 6, and 8 were in it. Write all the possible scores that Jessica could have had.

What is the lowest score Jessica could have had? ____________

Which score could have been her highest? ____________

A whistle in a vending machine costs 15¢. The machine only takes dimes, nickels, and pennies. Fill in the chart below with all the different combinations of coins that you could use to buy the 15¢ whistle. The first two are done for you.

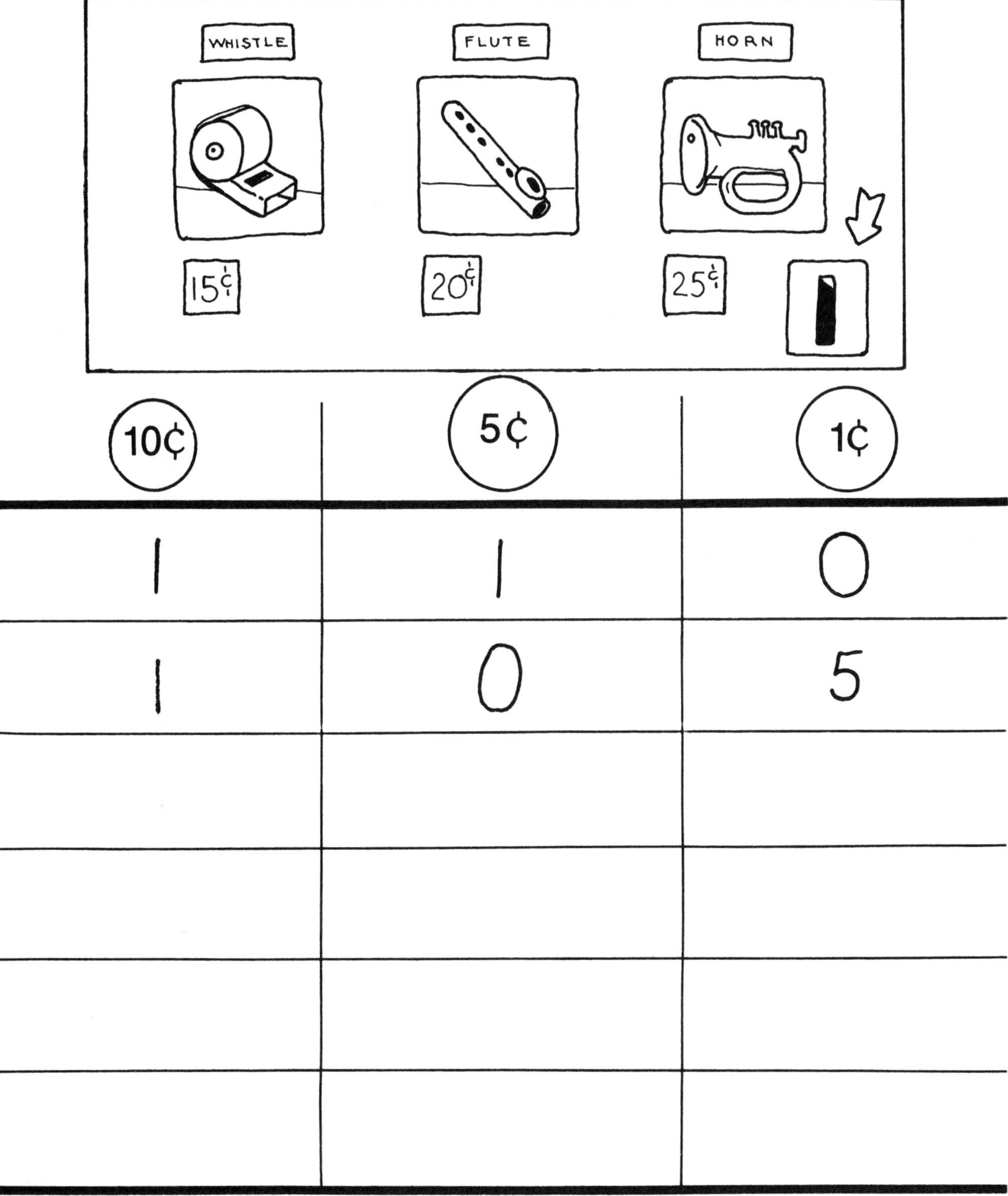

10¢	5¢	1¢
1	1	0
1	0	5

A toy robot in a vending machine costs 50¢. The machine only takes quarters, nickels, and dimes. Fill in the chart with all the different combinations of coins that you could use to buy a robot.

25¢	10¢	5¢

BEAR

5¢

CAR

10¢

ROBOT

50¢

Heather's piggy bank had only nickels and quarters in it. There were 2 less nickels than quarters. The total amount in the bank was $2.60.

Fill in the chart with combinations of nickels and quarters until you find the one that adds up to $2.60.

Hint: There are less than 50¢ worth of nickels in the bank!

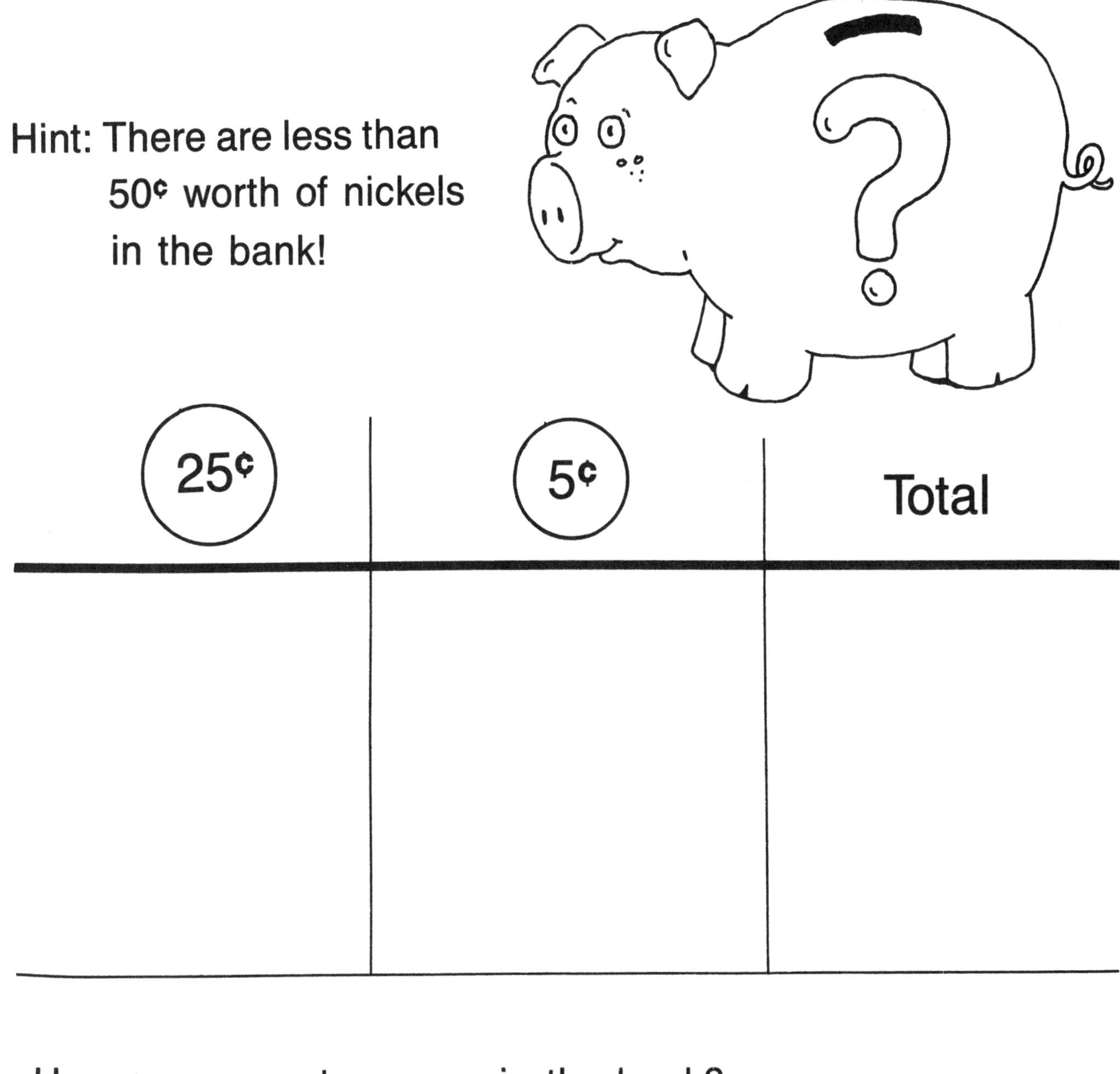

25¢	5¢	Total

How many quarters were in the bank? ______________

How many nickels were in it? ______________

Read these clues:

Breanna is 2 years older than Ryan.
Alisha is 4 years older than Ryan.
If you add up all their ages, the total is 15.
Ryan is less than 6 years old.

Use the chart below to help you figure out the ages of Breanna, Ryan, and Alisha. Start by making a good **guess** about Ryan. Keep making guesses and filling in the chart — until you get the right combination.

Ryan	Breanna	Alisha	Total
Make a guess.	Add 2 to Ryan.	Add 4 to Ryan.	Is it 15?

Read all the clues:

Henry is 4 years older than Luis.
Jimmy is 5 years older than Luis.
If you add up all their ages, the total is 24.
Luis is less than 8 years old.

How old is Luis? ______ Henry? ______ Jimmy? ______

Luis	Henry	Jimmy	Total
Guess	Add 4 to Luis.	Add 5 to Luis.	Is it 24?

Read all the clues. Then use the chart to figure out the answers.

Hilary has read 2 more mystery books than Erica.
Morgan has read 5 more mystery books than Hilary.
If you add up all the mystery books they have read, the total is 18.

How many mystery books has Erica read? ________
Hilary? ____________ Morgan? ____________

Erica	Hilary	Morgan	Total
Guess	Add 2	Add ________	

Read all the clues. Then use the chart to figure out the correct answers.

Josh has 8 less Halloween candies than Adam.
Teddy has 6 less candies than Adam.
Adam has more than 10 candies.
If you add up their candies, the total is 31.

Adam	Josh	Teddy	Total

How many does Adam have? ____________

Josh? ____________ Teddy? ____________

Make your own math puzzle. See if a friend can figure it out.

____________ ate ______ more apples than ______________ .

____________ ate ______ more apples than ______________ .

If you add up the apples they ate, the total is ____________ .

Use the chart to help you.

			Total
Guess	Add __________	Add __________	

How many apples did ____________ eat? ______

__________ ? ______ __________ ? ______

Think carefully (and use scrap paper if you need it) to answer the questions about the Art Attic.

Art Attic Prices	
Watercolors	7¢
Markers	3¢
Crayons	2¢
Paper	5¢

1. Janna bought 2 items and spent 9¢. What items did she buy?

____

____

2. Carrie bought 2 items for 5¢. What items did she buy?

____

____

3. Jeremy bought 3 items and spent 10¢. Which items did he buy?

____

____

Think carefully and answer the questions about the Merry Mart.

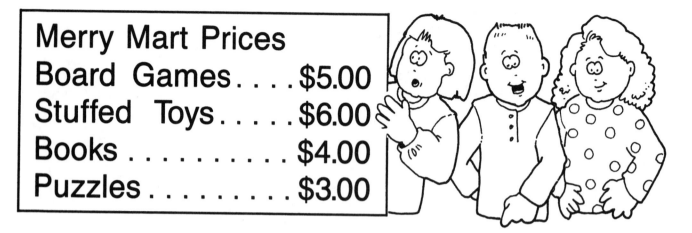

Merry Mart Prices	
Board Games	$5.00
Stuffed Toys	$6.00
Books	$4.00
Puzzles	$3.00

1. Alison bought 2 different items and spent $8.00. Which items did she buy?

2. Brett spent $10.00 for 2 of the **same** items. What did he buy?

3. Jamie bought 2 gifts for his brother. He spent $9.00. What did he buy? (Hint: His brother doesn't like puzzles.)

Read carefully before you answer the questions.

Fast Food Place Prices	
Hot dog	$ .50
Hamburger	$ .75
Milk	$ .25
French fries	$ .50
Apples	$1.00

1. Drew bought 3 different items for lunch and spent $1.50. What did he buy? (Hint: He doesn't like hot dogs.)

   ____

2. Cheryl spent $1.50 on 2 different items. What did she buy? (Hint: Cheryl doesn't like french fries.) ______________

   ______________ ______________

3. Dara spent $1.25 for 3 items. (She doesn't like french fries, either.) What did she buy? ______________

   ______________ ______________

4. Chris spent $2.00 at Fast Food Place. He bought 4 different items. What did he buy? ______________________________

____

5. Erica wants a hamburger, a piece of fruit, and a drink. How much money does she need? ______________________________

6. Heather had 4 items from the menu and spent $2.25. What did she have? (Hint: She doesn't eat apples or hot dogs.)

______________ ______________

______________ ______________

7. Matt bought 2 hamburgers, an order of french fries, and an apple. The cashier gave him $7.00 change. What bill did Matt give the cashier? ______________________________

8. If you had $2.00 for lunch at Fast Food Place, what would you buy? ______________________________

____

____

Make up some tough questions of your own. Find a friend to figure out the answers.

1. ____________ bought 2 items and spent ____________.
   What did ________________ buy?
2. ____________ spent ________ on 3 different items.
   What did ____________ buy?
3. ____________ bought a ____________ and a ____________.
   The cashier gave (him or her) __________ change.
   What did ____________ give the cashier?

Jenny shot 3 arrows in archery class. Each arrow hit the target. Her total score was 10. What targets did she hit?

She could have hit ________ , ________ , and ________ .
She might have hit ________ , ________ , and ________ .
She may have hit ________ , ________ , and ________ .

(Hint: Use each number more than once.)

Eric zapped 3 space ships on the video game. His total score was 15. Circle the space ships he zapped.

Can you solve this puzzle? It isn't easy!
Here are the clues:

The sum of each side must equal 12.
You can only use whole numbers less than 9.
A number can't be used more than **once** on each side.

It's a good idea to start by listing all the combinations of 3 numbers that can add up to 12, such as 8 + 3 + 1 and 4 + 2 + 6.

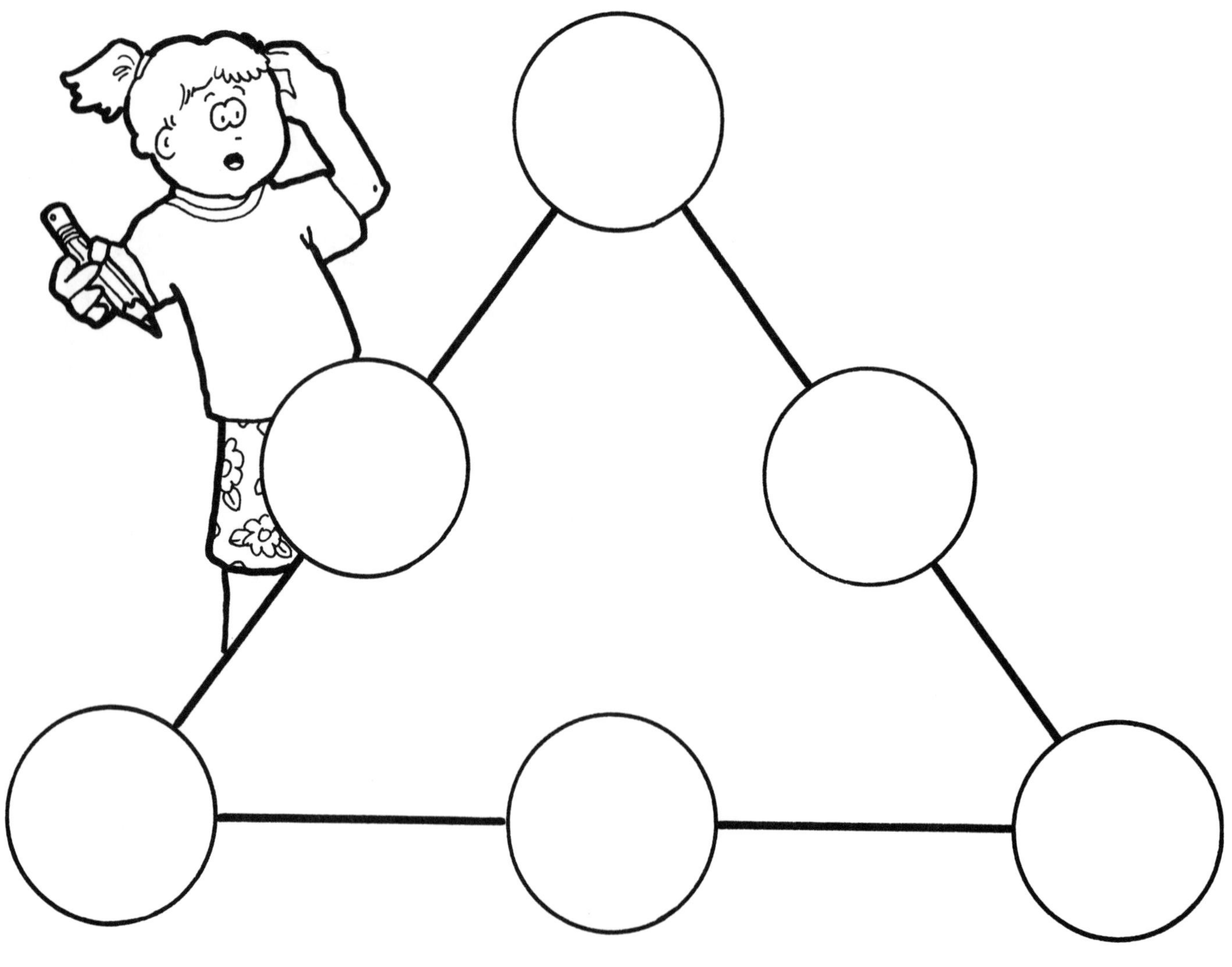

Think how the first two numbers in each box relate to each other. Which number will make the **last** two numbers relate to each other in the same way? Circle that number and write it on the line. The first one is done for you.

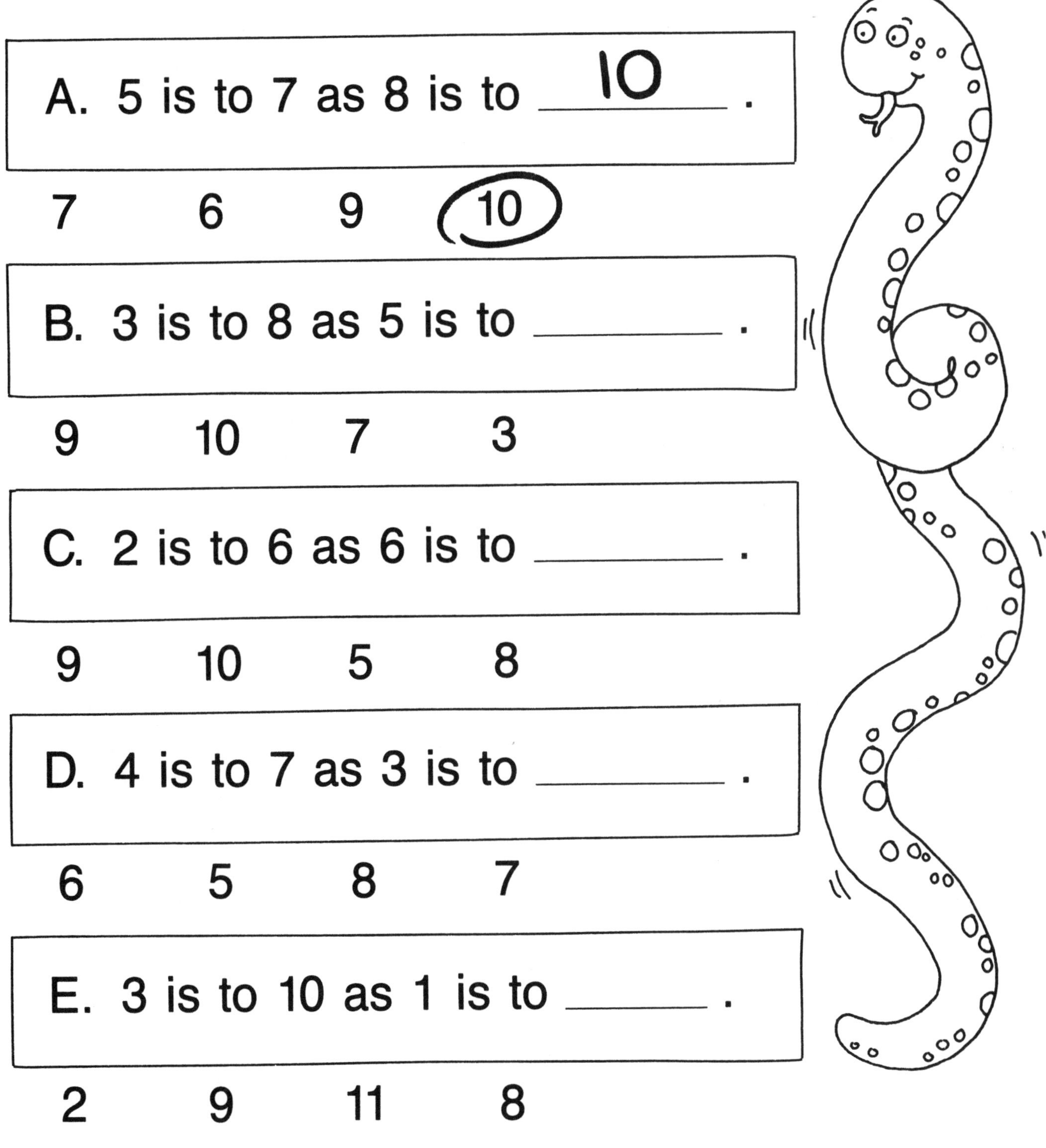

A. 5 is to 7 as 8 is to ___10___ .

7 6 9 (10)

B. 3 is to 8 as 5 is to ________ .

9 10 7 3

C. 2 is to 6 as 6 is to ________ .

9 10 5 8

D. 4 is to 7 as 3 is to ________ .

6 5 8 7

E. 3 is to 10 as 1 is to ________ .

2 9 11 8

Which number will make the last two numbers relate in the same way as the first two? Circle the number and write it on the line.

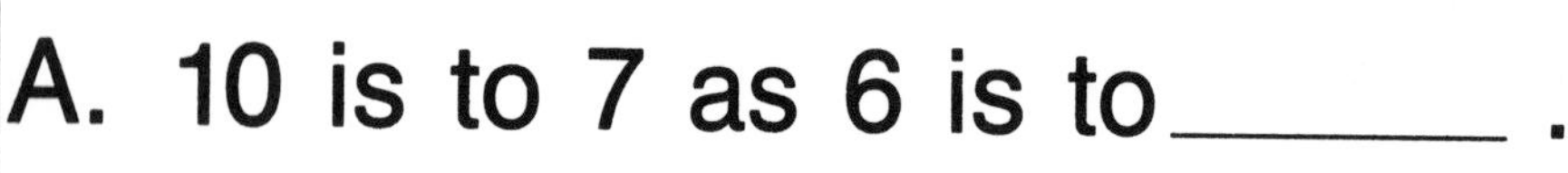

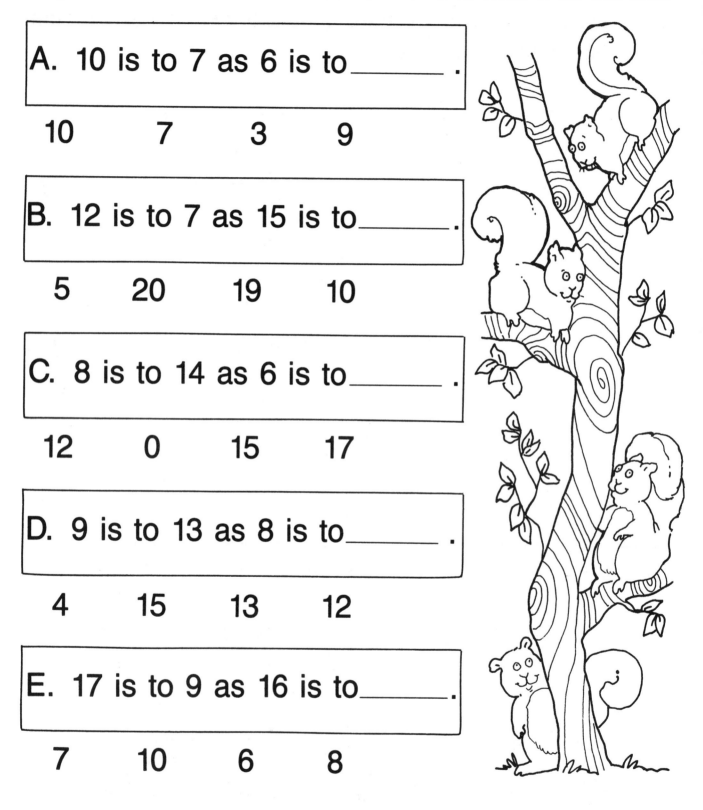

A. 10 is to 7 as 6 is to ______ .

10 7 3 9

B. 12 is to 7 as 15 is to ______ .

5 20 19 10

C. 8 is to 14 as 6 is to ______ .

12 0 15 17

D. 9 is to 13 as 8 is to ______ .

4 15 13 12

E. 17 is to 9 as 16 is to ______ .

7 10 6 8

See if your friends can finish your number sentences. You fill in the first two blanks with two numbers that relate in a special way. Have a friend fill in the blanks with two more numbers that relate in the same way.

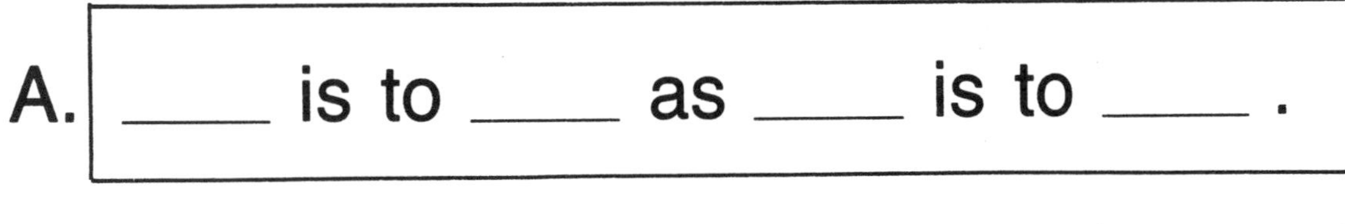
A. ____ is to ____ as ____ is to ____ .

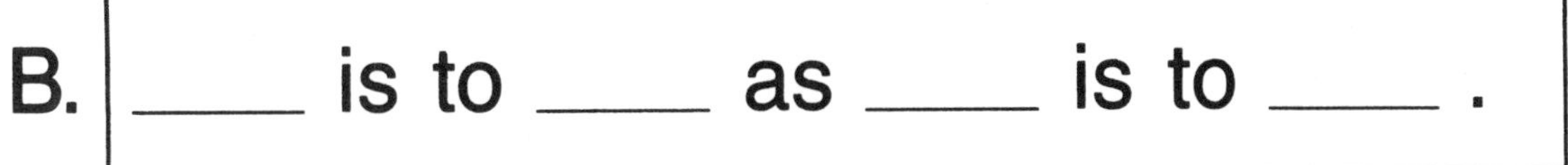
B. ____ is to ____ as ____ is to ____ .

C. ____ is to ____ as ____ is to ____ .

D. ____ is to ____ as ____ is to ____ .

E. ____ is to ____ as ____ is to ____ .

F. ____ is to ____ as ____ is to ____ .

Help the chef. Write each number below on the correct pizza.

Help the monster finish the sign. Write each number in the correct circle.

Help the robot fix the computer. Write each number in the correct circle.

Now make up your own puzzle for a friend.

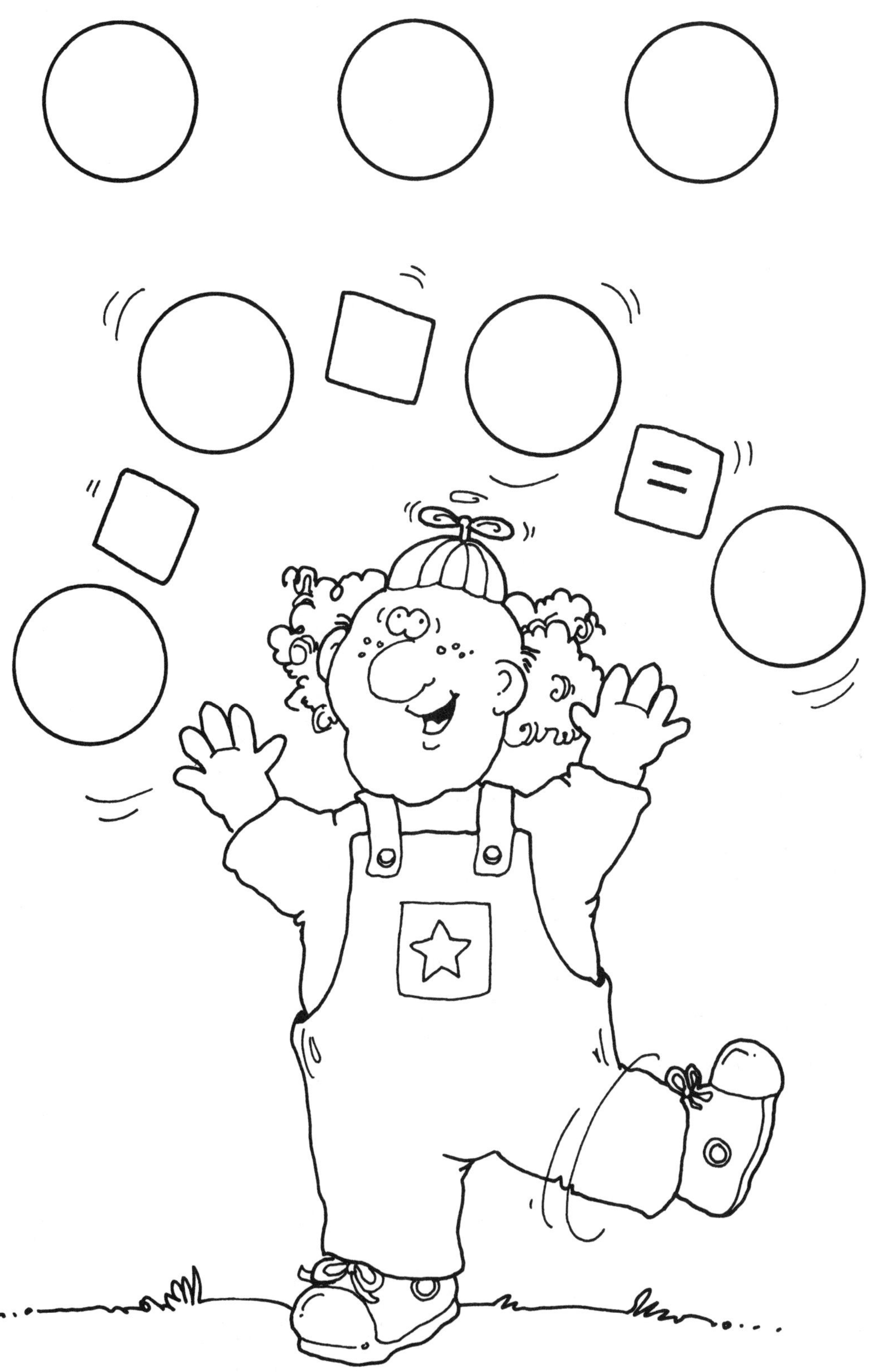

Count the squares in the picture below.

How many squares do you see?

______

Did you see

4 of these?

But that's not all! Look again. The smaller squares are **inside** another square!

There are 5 squares in the picture.

Count all the squares in the picture below. Remember: some squares are **inside** other squares.

Hint: There are more than 10 squares.

How many squares did you find?

____

Count the squares in the picture below. Remember to look for squares inside of other squares!

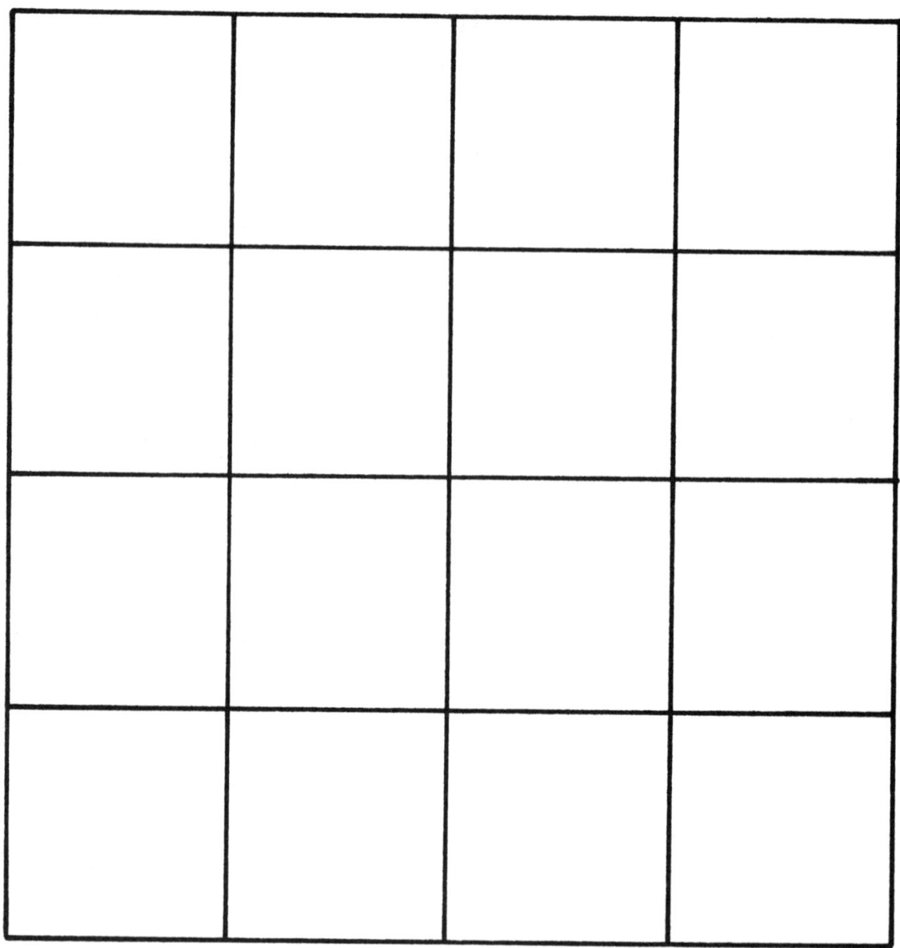

How many squares did you find? ______________

Count the triangles in the picture. Don't forget: some triangles are inside other triangles!

How many triangles did you find? ____________

Count the rectangles in the picture. Hint: a square is also a rectangle.

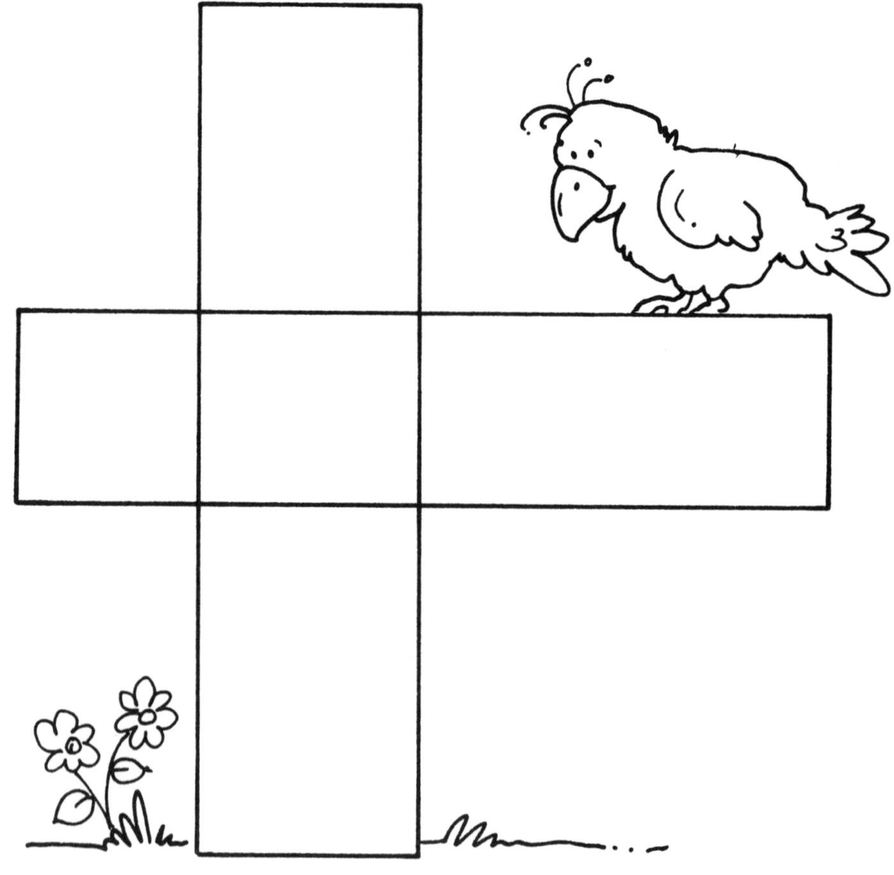

How many rectangles did you find? ____________

Fill in the schedule below so that you can see all the shows at the neighborhood circus **before** lunch. One has been filled in for you.

Shows start at:

Mike's Magic Show
(45 minutes)

10:30 A.M.

1:00 P.M.

Carlos the Clown
(30 minutes)

10:00 A.M.

12:30 P.M.

Denise and Her Dancing Dogs
(30 minutes)

10:15 A.M.

11:30 A.M.

SCHEDULE	
SHOW	TIME
1. ____________	
2. Magic Show	10:30 A.M.
3. ____________	
4. Lunch	12:00 P.M.

Fill in the schedule below so that you can see all the zoo shows in one day. One has been done for you. And don't forget lunch!

Shows start at:

Bird Show (30 minutes)

1:30 P.M.

2:30 P.M.

Seal Show (30 minutes)

10:30 A.M.

1:30 P.M.

Elephant Show (45 minutes)

11:00 A.M.

2:00 P.M.

Monkey Show (45 minutes)

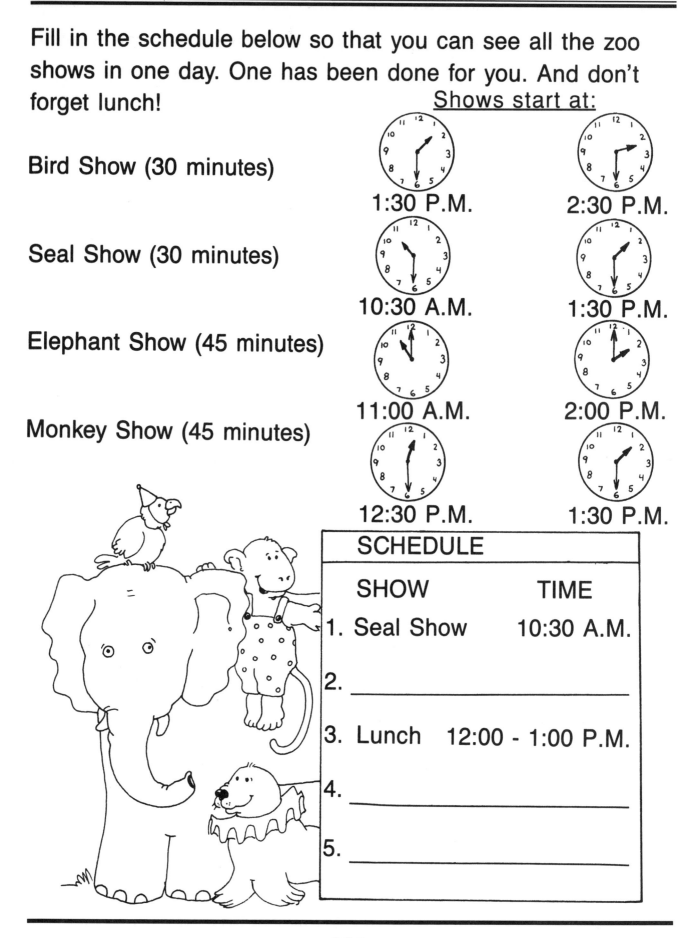

12:30 P.M.

1:30 P.M.

SCHEDULE

	SHOW	TIME
1.	Seal Show	10:30 A.M.
2.	______	______
3.	Lunch	12:00 - 1:00 P.M.
4.	______	______
5.	______	______

At the Fairy Tale Festival, shows are performed outdoors. Plan your day so that you can see all the shows.

	Shows start at:	
Beauty and the Beast (1 hour)	10:30 A.M.	11:30 A.M.
Jack and the Beanstalk (1 hour)	10:00 A.M.	11:00 A.M.
Hansel and Gretel (30 minutes)	10:00 A.M.	11:00 A.M.
Red Riding Hood (1 hour)	12:00 P.M.	2:00 P.M.

ACT 1.

SCHEDULE

SHOW	TIME
1. ______________	
2. Hansel/Gretel	11:00 A.M.
3. ______________	
4. Lunch	12:30 - 1:30 P.M.
5. ______________	

Break the number code. Use the numbers 0, 2, and 4. Each letter stands for one of these numbers. One has been done for you. Figure out the rest.

Figure out this code. Use the numbers 1, 2, 3, 4, and 5. One letter stands for each number. One has been done for you.

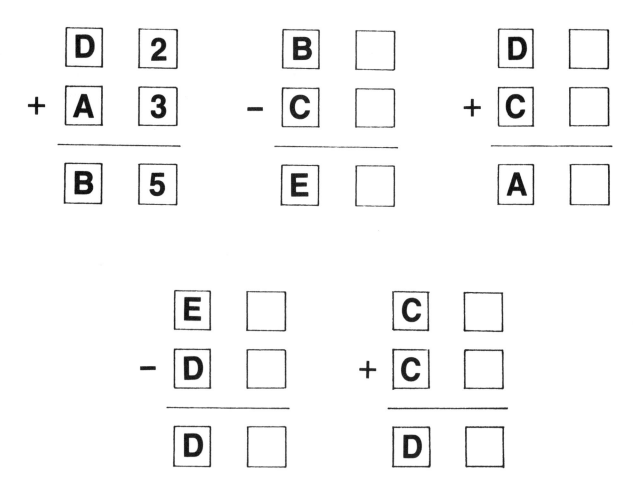

	D	2
+	A	3
	B	5

	B	☐
−	C	☐
	E	☐

	D	☐
+	C	☐
	A	☐

	E	☐
−	D	☐
	D	☐

	C	☐
+	C	☐
	D	☐

Write the correct numbers in the code box.

CODE

A = ☐ C = ☐

B = ☐ D = ☐

E = ☐

Solve the code. Use the numbers 2, 4, 5, 6, and 10. Fill in the code box with the correct numbers.

A		
+	C	
E		

B		
−	D	
D		

E		
+	A	
B		

B		
−	E	
A		

E + E = B + C

☐ + ☐ = ☐ + ☐

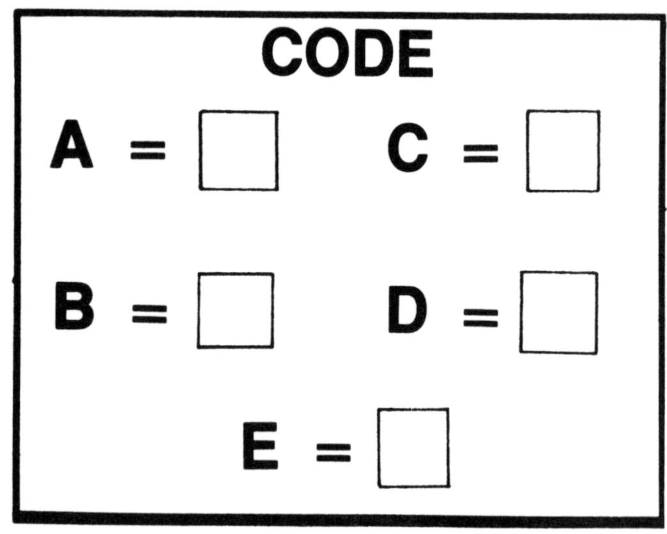

Solve this puzzle. Here are the rules:

1. The sum of each line must equal 10.
2. You can only use the numbers 1, 2, 3, 4, or 5.
3. You can only use each number once.

See how many solutions you can find to this puzzle. Here are the rules:

1. The sum of each line must equal 10.
2. You can only use the numbers 1, 2, 3, 4, 5, 6, or 7.
3. A number can be used only once in each solution.

There are many different answers. How many did you find?

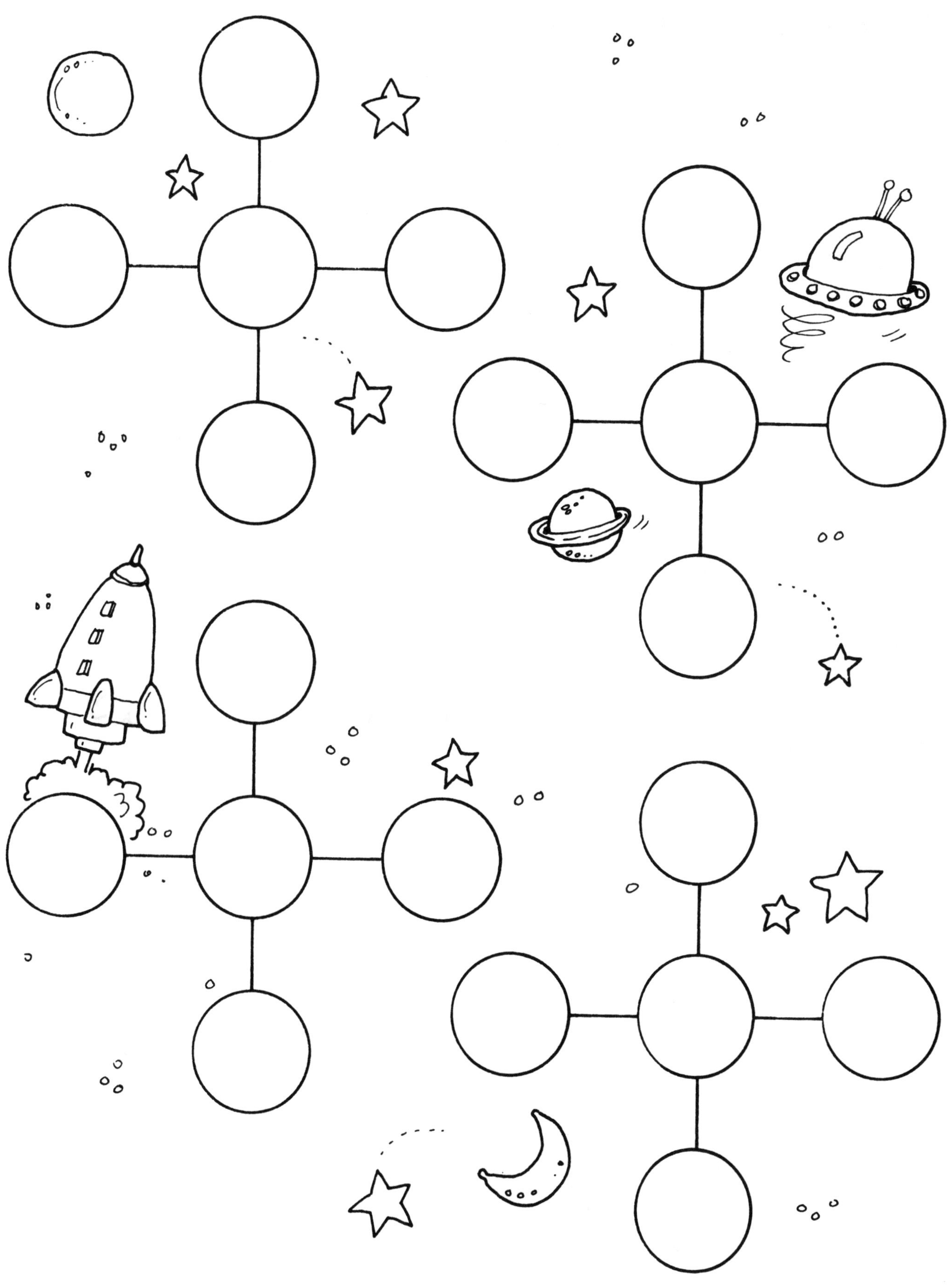

Here are the rules for this puzzle:

1. The sum of each line must equal 12.
2. You may only use the numbers 1, 2, 3, 4, 5, 6, 7, and 8.
3. A number can only be used once.

Hint: Start by listing all the combinations of 3 numbers that can make 12.

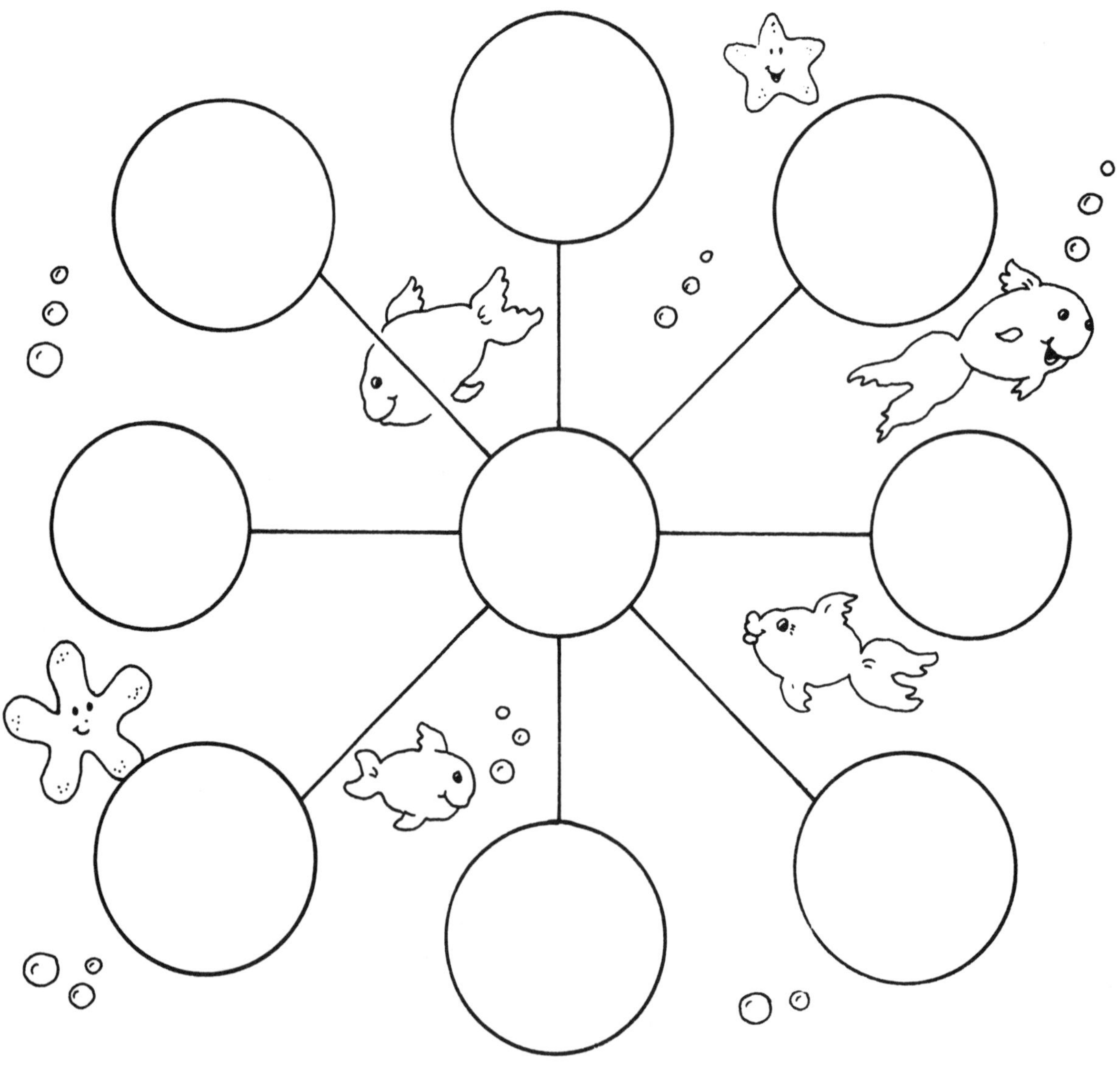

Try this puzzle. Here are the rules:

1. The sum of each side must equal 15.
2. You may only use the numbers 1, 2, 3, 4, 5, 6, 7, and 8.
3. A number can only be used once.

Hint: Think of all the combinations of 3 numbers that can make 15.

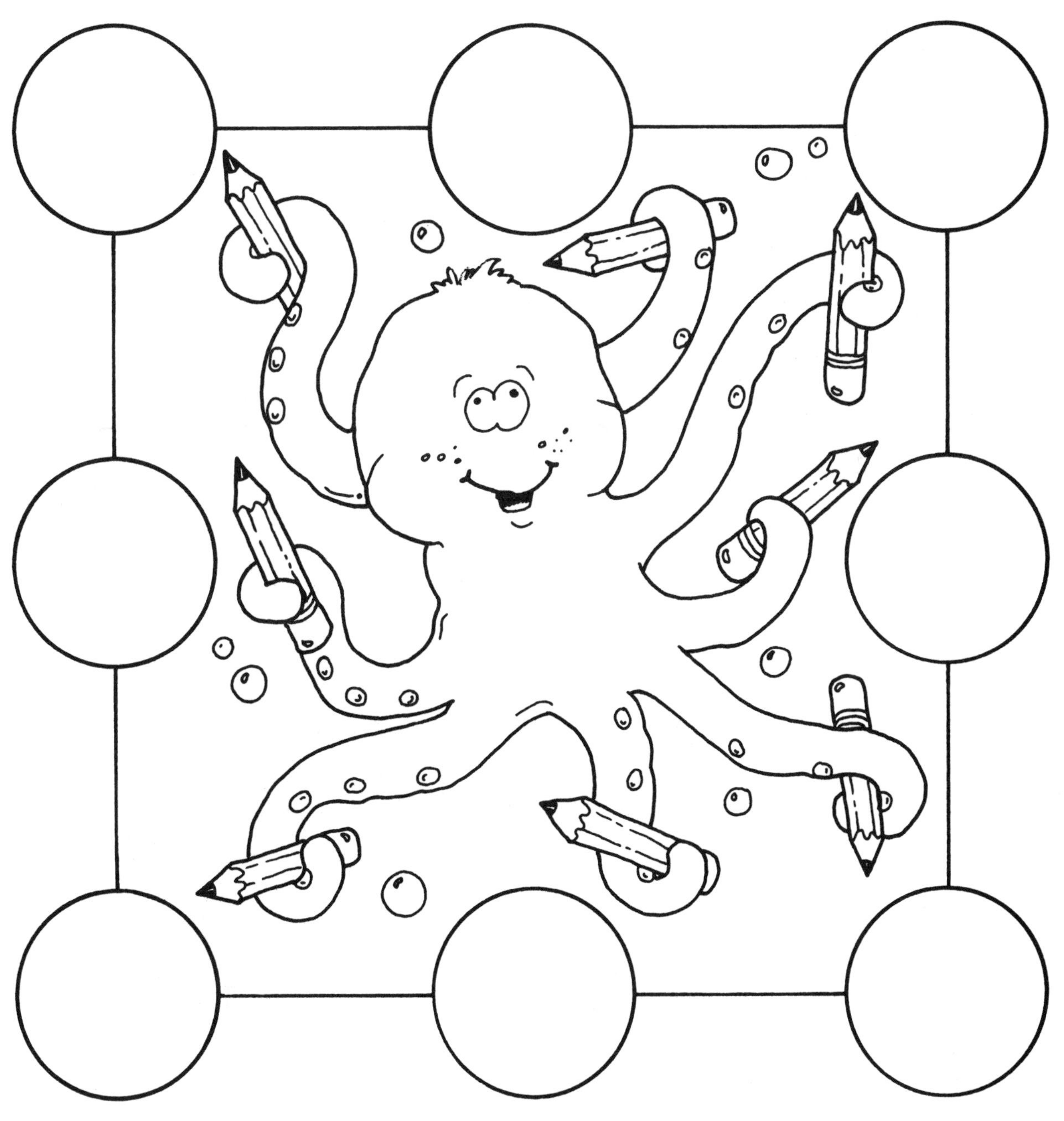

Make a puzzle for a friend. Be careful! Make sure you know the answer!

Can you solve this puzzle? Here are the rules:

1. The sum of each line must equal ________ .
2. You can only use numbers ________________ .
3. You can only use a number once.

This machine is called COMBO. It combines the qualities of each set of objects to make a new set. For example, if we put in TRIANGLES and THINGS THAT ARE BLUE, we will end up with BLUE TRIANGLES!

List the objects that will come out of COMBO when we put in the two sets below. One has been done for you. Use extra paper if you need it!

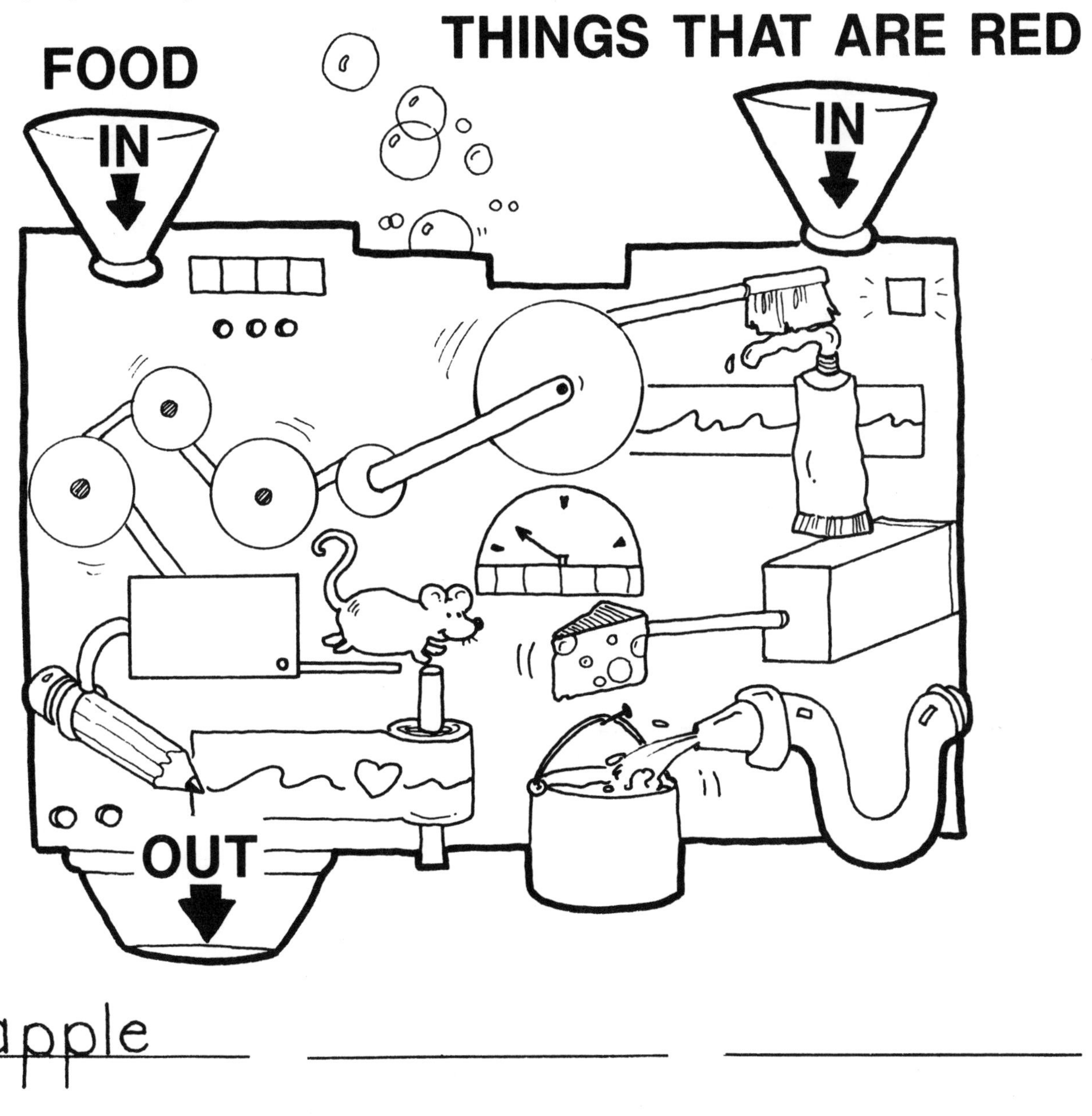

apple

List the things that will come out of COMBO.

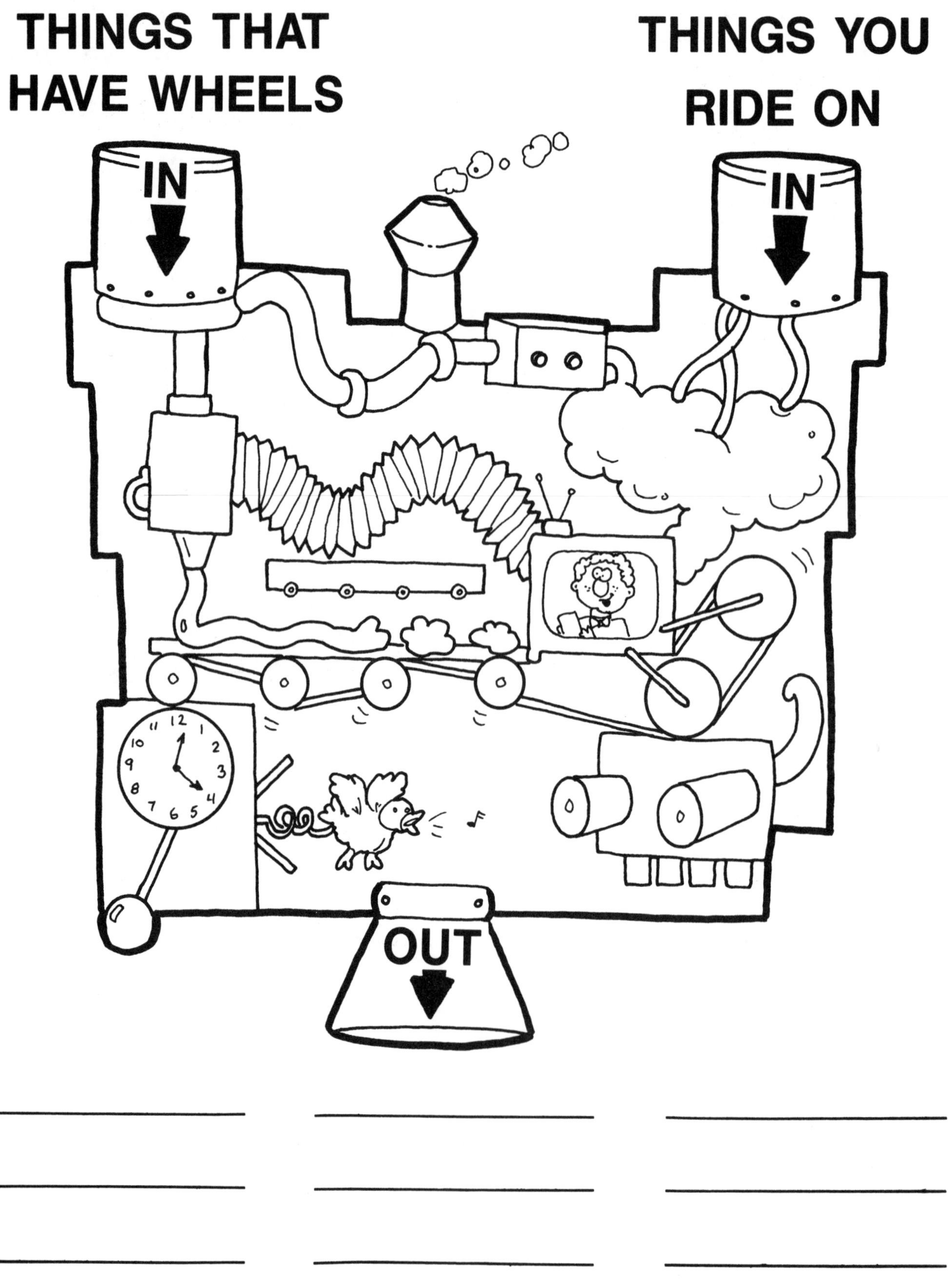

List the numbers that will come out of COMBO.

WHOLE NUMBERS LESS THAN 20 AND GREATER THAN 0

ODD NUMBERS

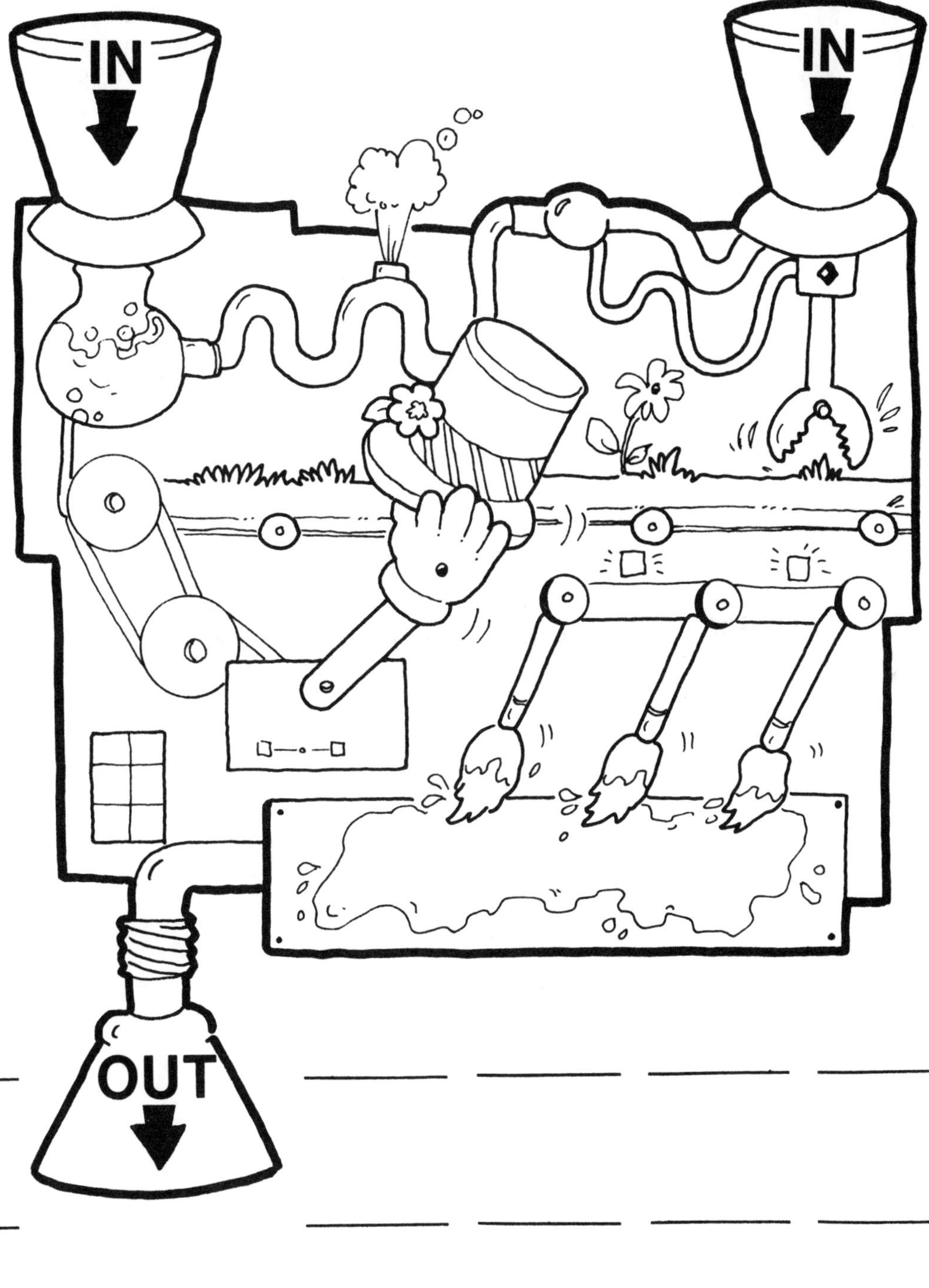

IN

IN

OUT

______ ______ ______ ______ ______

______ ______ ______ ______ ______

List the numbers that will come out of COMBO.

EVEN NUMBERS

WHOLE NUMBERS BETWEEN 40 AND 50

Make this page for a friend.

This machine is called COMBO. It combines the sets of objects going in to form a new set of objects. List the things that will come out of COMBO.

Valerie, Stephen, Hilary, and Casey are having pizza. Where is each one sitting? Read all the clues below. Then write each name on the correct line.

Clues:

1. Stephen is sitting to the right of Hilary.
2. Valerie is sitting to the right of Casey.
3. Casey is wearing a baseball hat.

Keith, Sean, Courtney, and Max are eating dinner. Where is each one sitting? Read all the clues below. Then write each name on the correct line.

Clues:

1. Keith, Sean, and Courtney are eating spaghetti.
2. Sean is sitting to the left of Courtney.
3. Courtney is opposite someone eating a hamburger.
4. Max doesn't like spaghetti.

Matthew lives in West End. He went to see his grandmother in East End. He drove 8 miles to get there and stopped in one city along the way. Where did he stop?

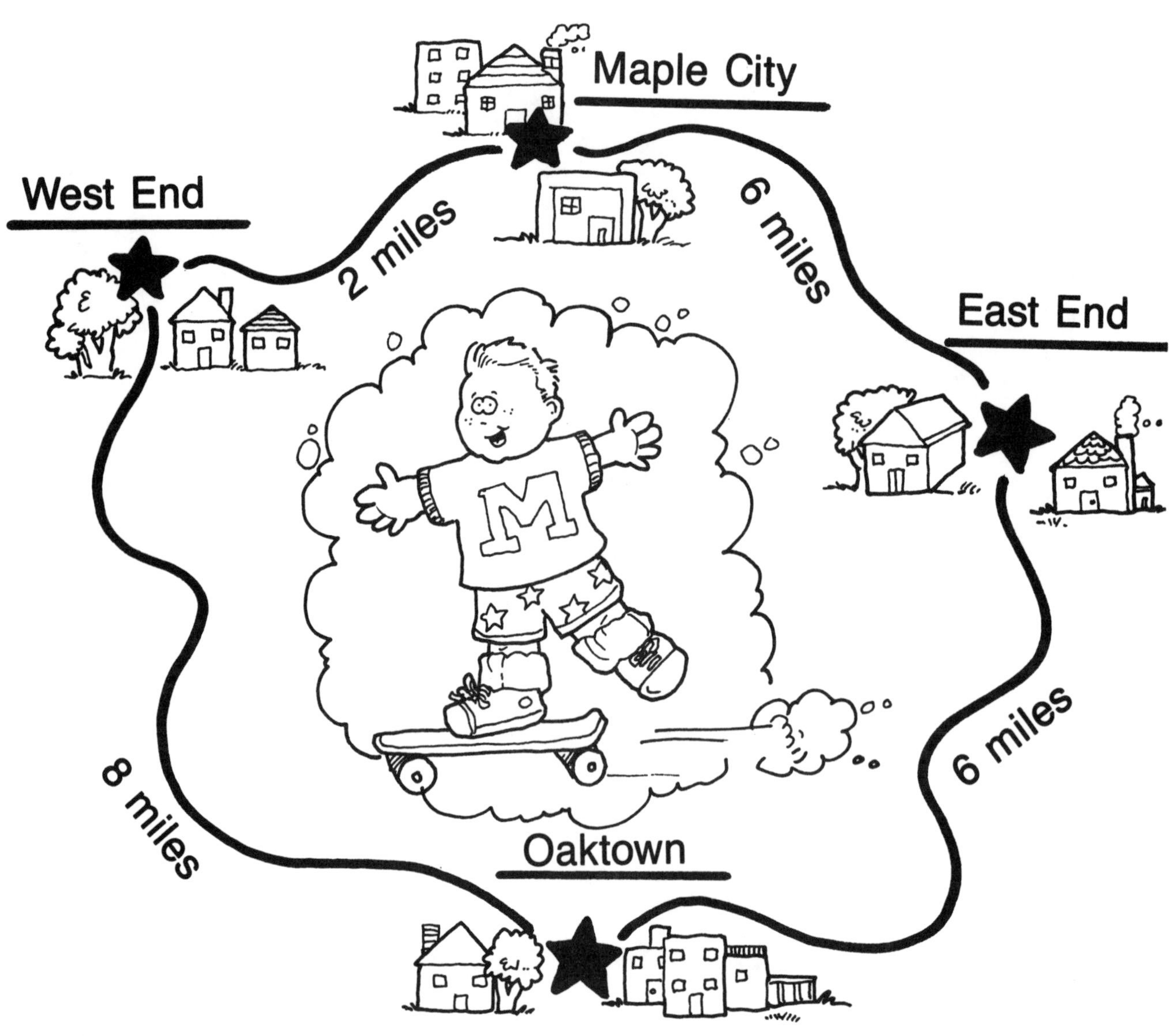

Matthew stopped in ______________________________ .

Andrea lives in Oak Grove. She went to visit her friend in Elm City. She took the shortest route and stopped in 2 cities. Where did she stop?

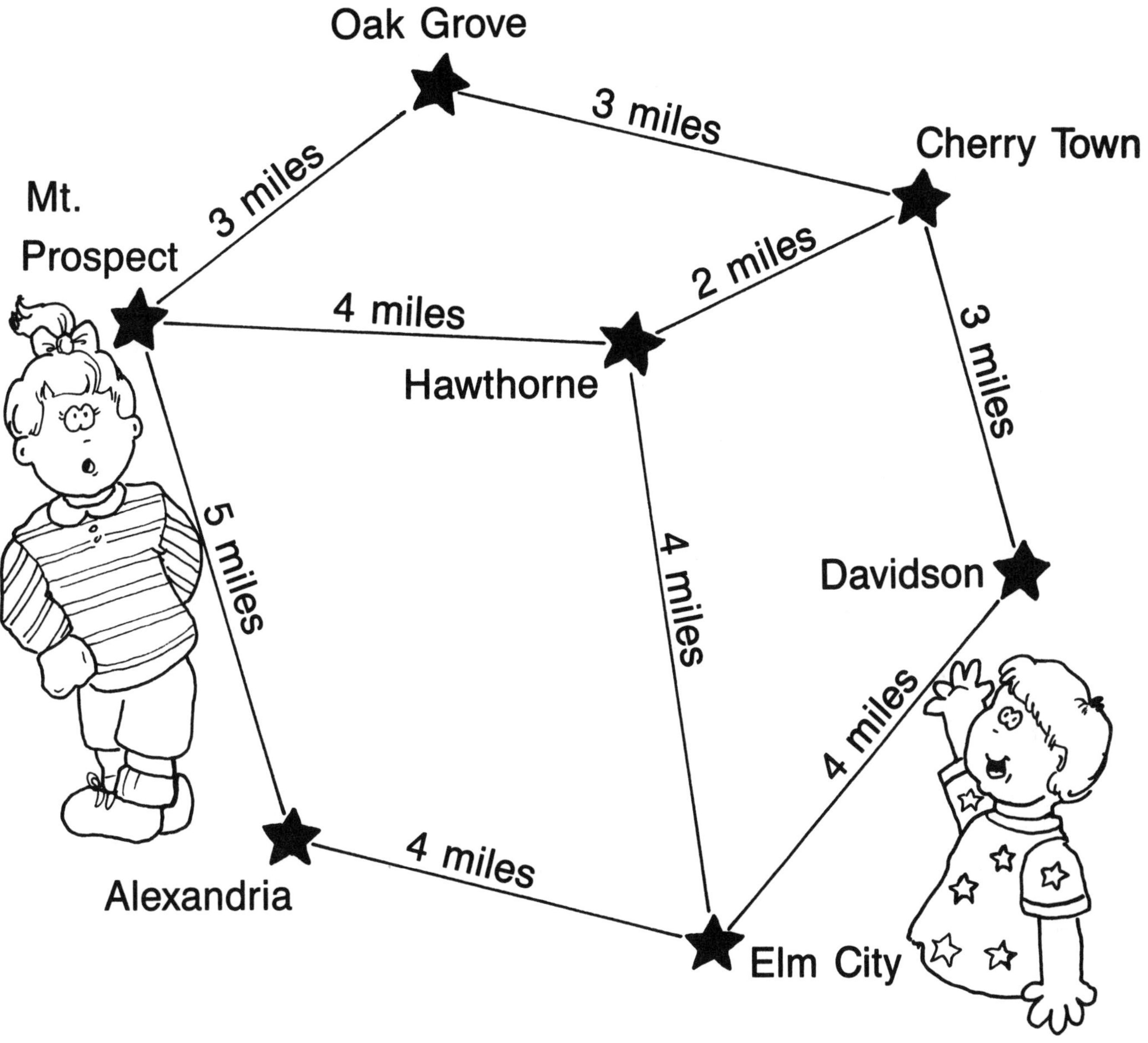

Andrea stopped in ________________ and ________________.

Niliphants come from the star Protozo. On Protozo money looks like this:

Loonies are worth 3¢.
Roonies are worth 6¢.
Zoonies are worth 9¢.

How much money is in each box?

A.
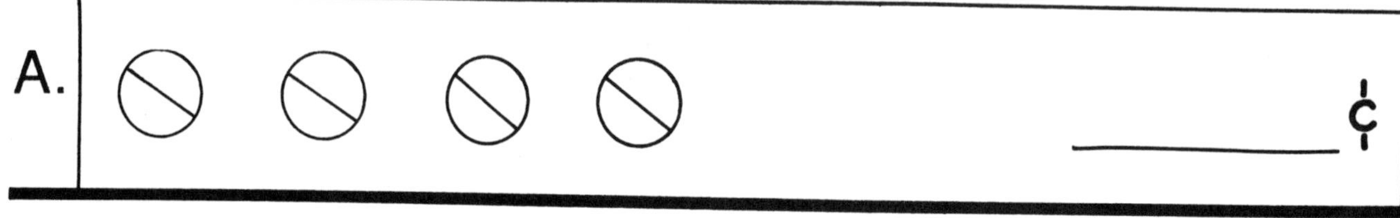

B.
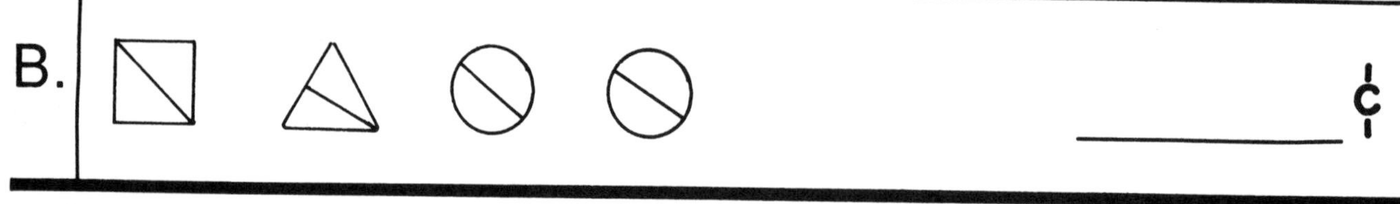

C.
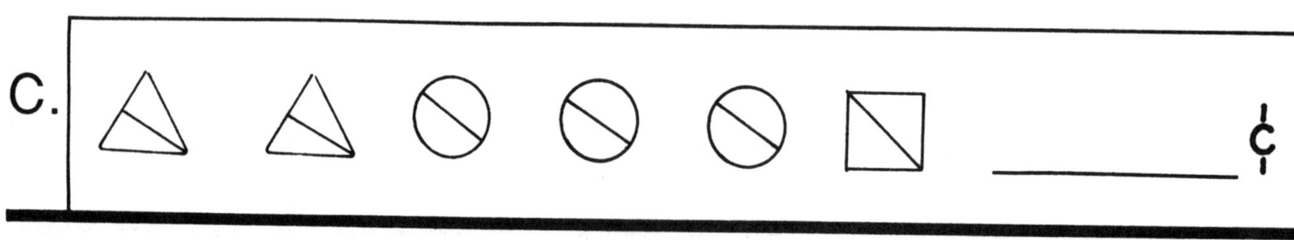

A space vehicle on Protozo costs 18¢. List all the possible combinations of coins that a Niliphant could use to pay for the space vehicle. Two are done for you. Fill in the rest of the chart.

Zoonies	Roonies	Loonies
2	0	0
1	1	1

Pinkums come from another galaxy. Their money system is different from ours. Their system looks like this:

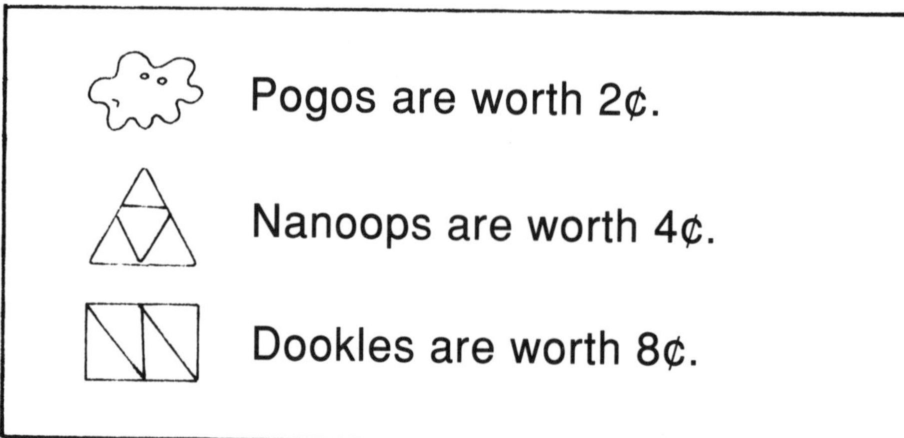
Pogos are worth 2¢.
Nanoops are worth 4¢.
Dookles are worth 8¢.

Write the answers to these questions:

A. How many Nanoops make one Dookle? ____________

B. How many Pogos make one Dookle? ____________

C. How many Pogos make one Nanoop? ____________

A Pinkum has 20 cents. What are all the possible combinations of coins the Pinkum could have? Write the combinations in the chart below.

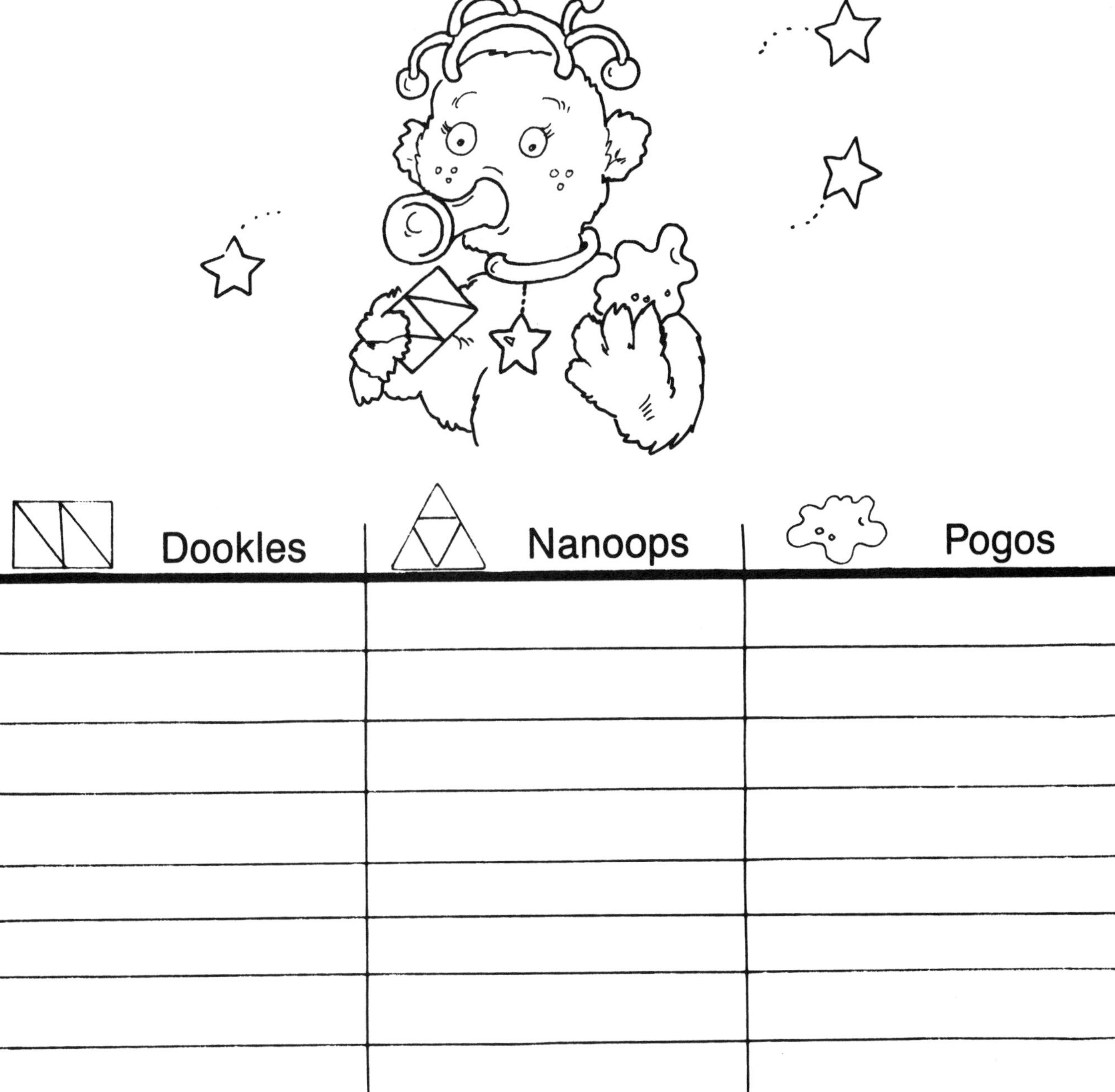

Dookles	Nanoops	Pogos

Heather ordered a pizza to feed 7 people. Draw lines to show how she should cut the pizza using only 3 straight lines.

Hint: The pieces do **not** have to be the same size.

Super Hint: All the lines do **not** have to go through the center!

Draw lines to show how to cut these cakes — following these rules:

1. There must be 8 pieces on each cake.
2. Each piece must be the same size.
3. You must use straight lines.
4. You must cut each cake in a different way.

Hint: There are 3 possible ways to cut the cakes.

Look in the box to find the shape that comes next. Circle the shape.

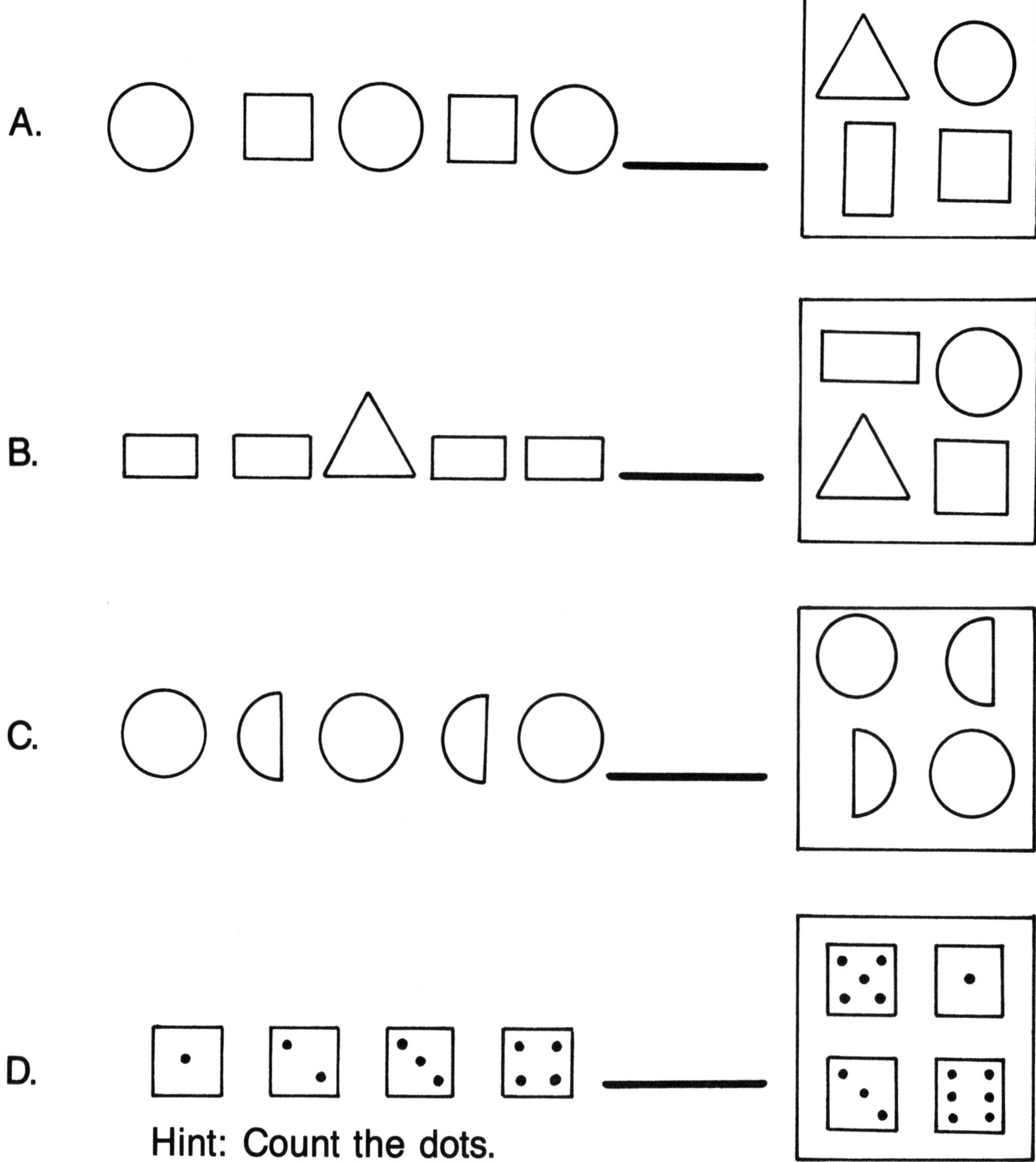

Circle the shape that comes next.

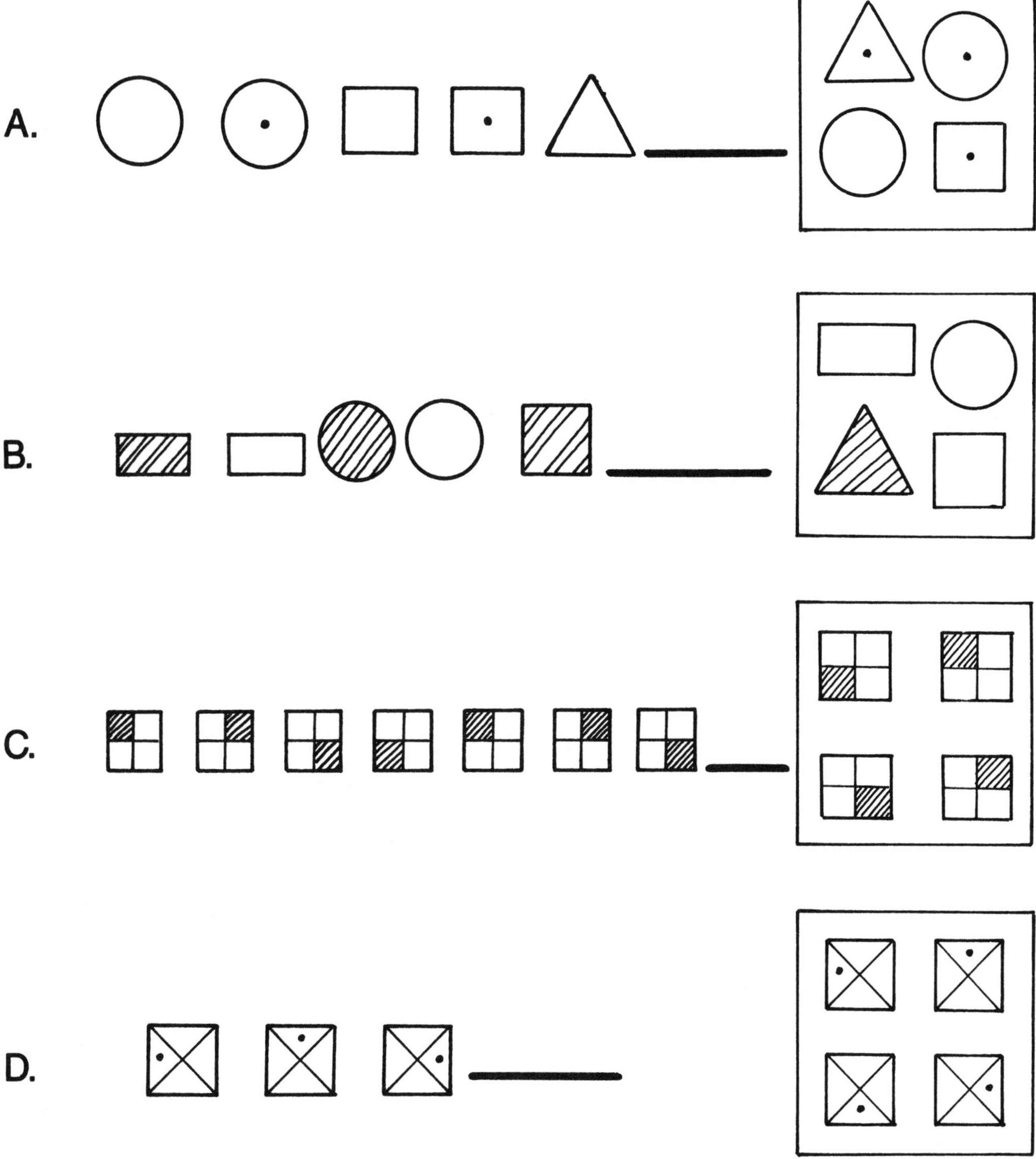

Circle the shape that comes next.

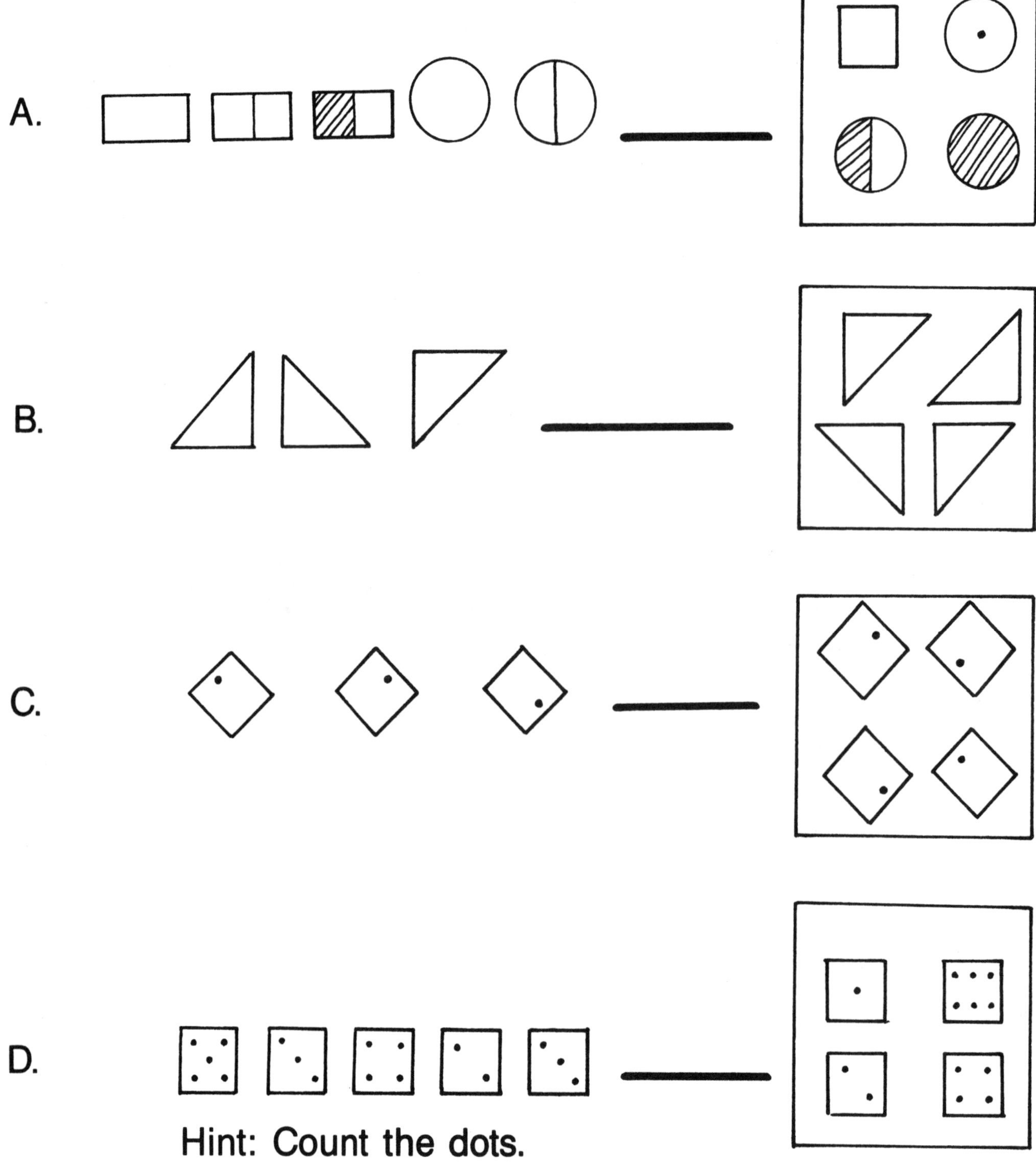

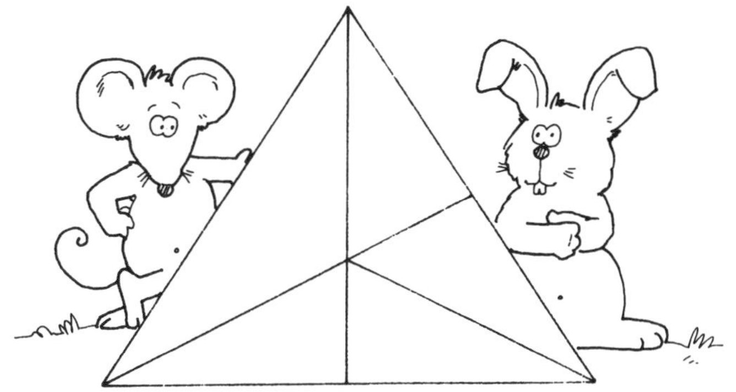

PUZZLES AND GAMES

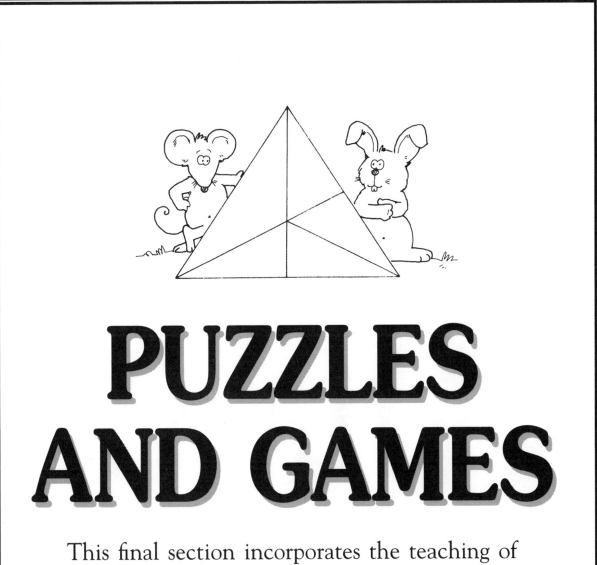

This final section incorporates the teaching of reading and math skills for grades 1–2 with entertaining puzzles and games. Kids will have so much fun doing these activities, they'll hardly realize how much they're learning!

Legend says that a magic square brings good luck. A magic square is a square where all sides have the same sum. Use the numbers 1, 2, 3, 4, 5, 6 to make this into a magic square.

Hint: The sum of each side is 15.
The sum of the diagonals is also 15.

Try this game with a friend.

Game Play: Players take turns.

A player may cross off either 1, 2, or 3 ships in the **same** row on each turn.

The player who crosses off the last ship loses.

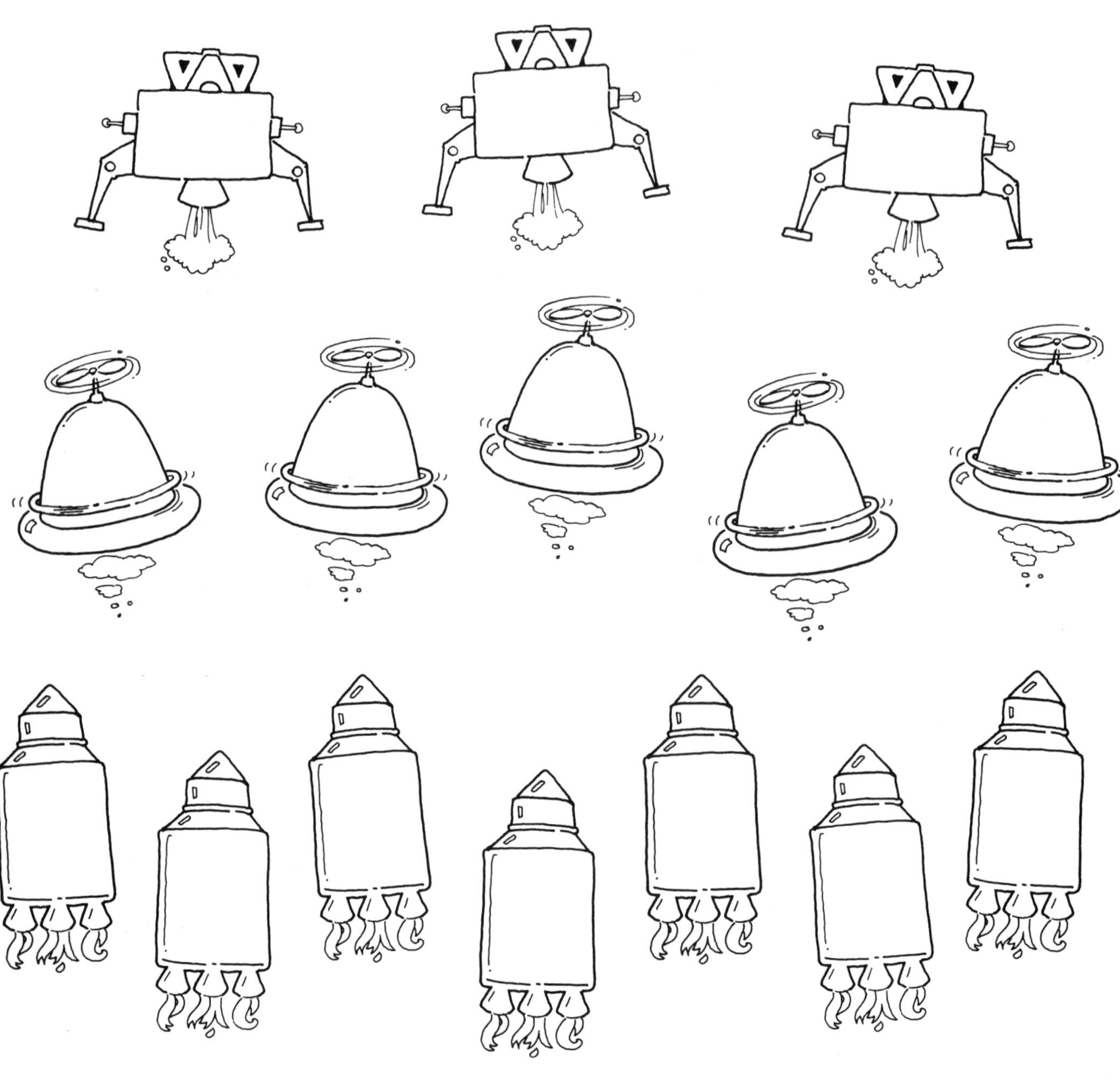

The Fronians are trying to return to the planet Fronia. In order to break through the power shield, they must collect 10 points.

Can you find the way to Fronia by following the arrows?

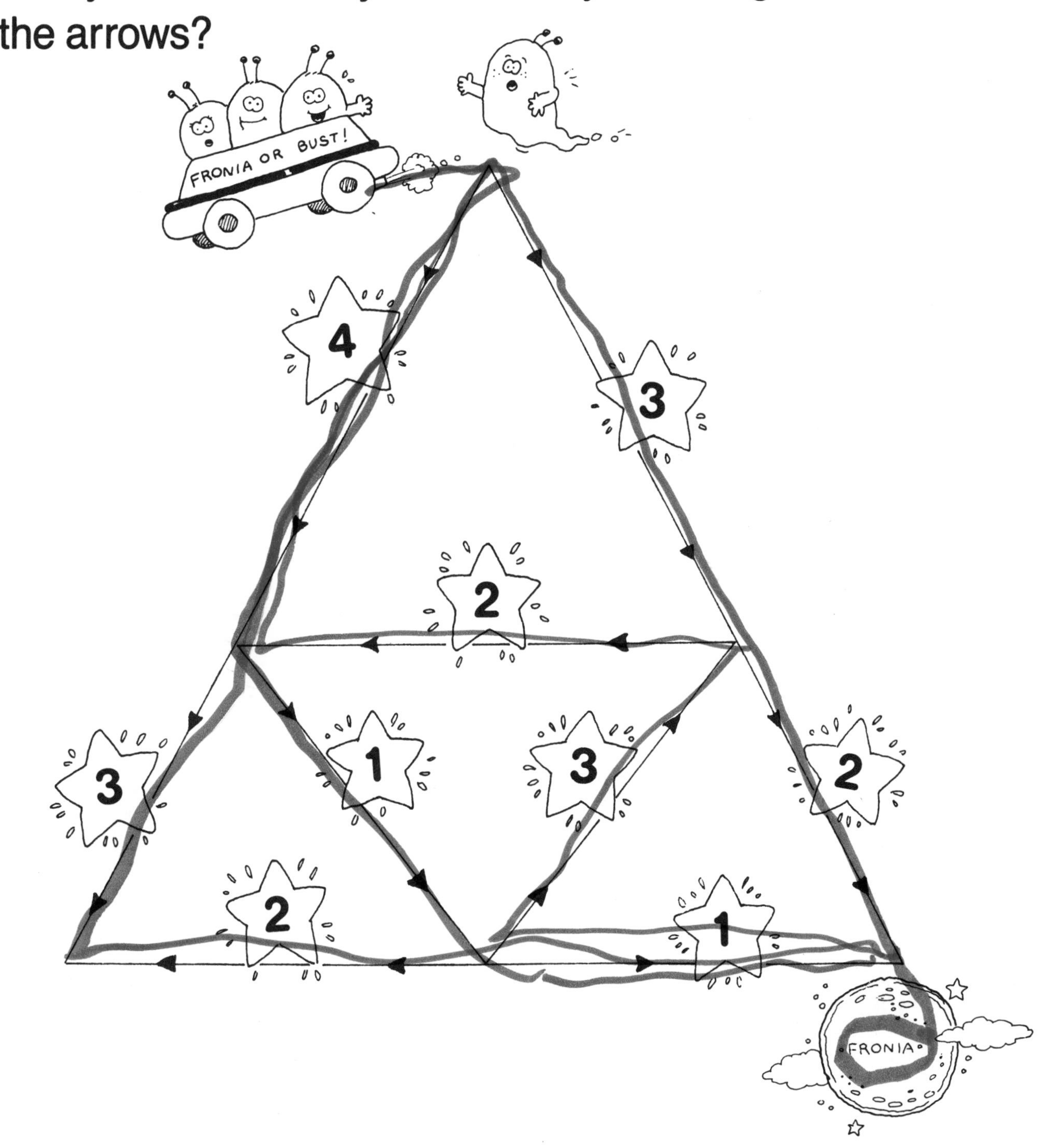

Help the witch complete her spell.

Circle the numbers inside each kettle whose sum is the same as the number on top of the kettle.

The first one is done for you.

Rule: The numbers must be next to, above, or below each other.

Try this game of tic-tac-toe.

Instead of using X or O, players choose either the odd numbers 1, 3, 5, 7, 9 or the even numbers 2, 4, 6, 8, 10.

The object of the game is to be the first person to make a row (up and down, across or diagonally) whose sum is 13. Hint: You can use the same number more than once.

Play this game with a friend.

The object of the game is to win the most squares.

Game Play: Make a 4-by-4 dot grid as shown to the left.

Players take turns drawing a line between two dots. Lines must be up and down or across.

The first player to close a square (see picture) puts his or her initial in the square.

The game continues until there is no place left to move.

The player with the most squares wins.

Help Heather get to the carnival.

Start where Heather is and go through the boxes until you reach the carnival.

Find the path that equals 10.
Find the path that equals 14.
Find the path that equals 19. *
Find the path that equals 22. * *

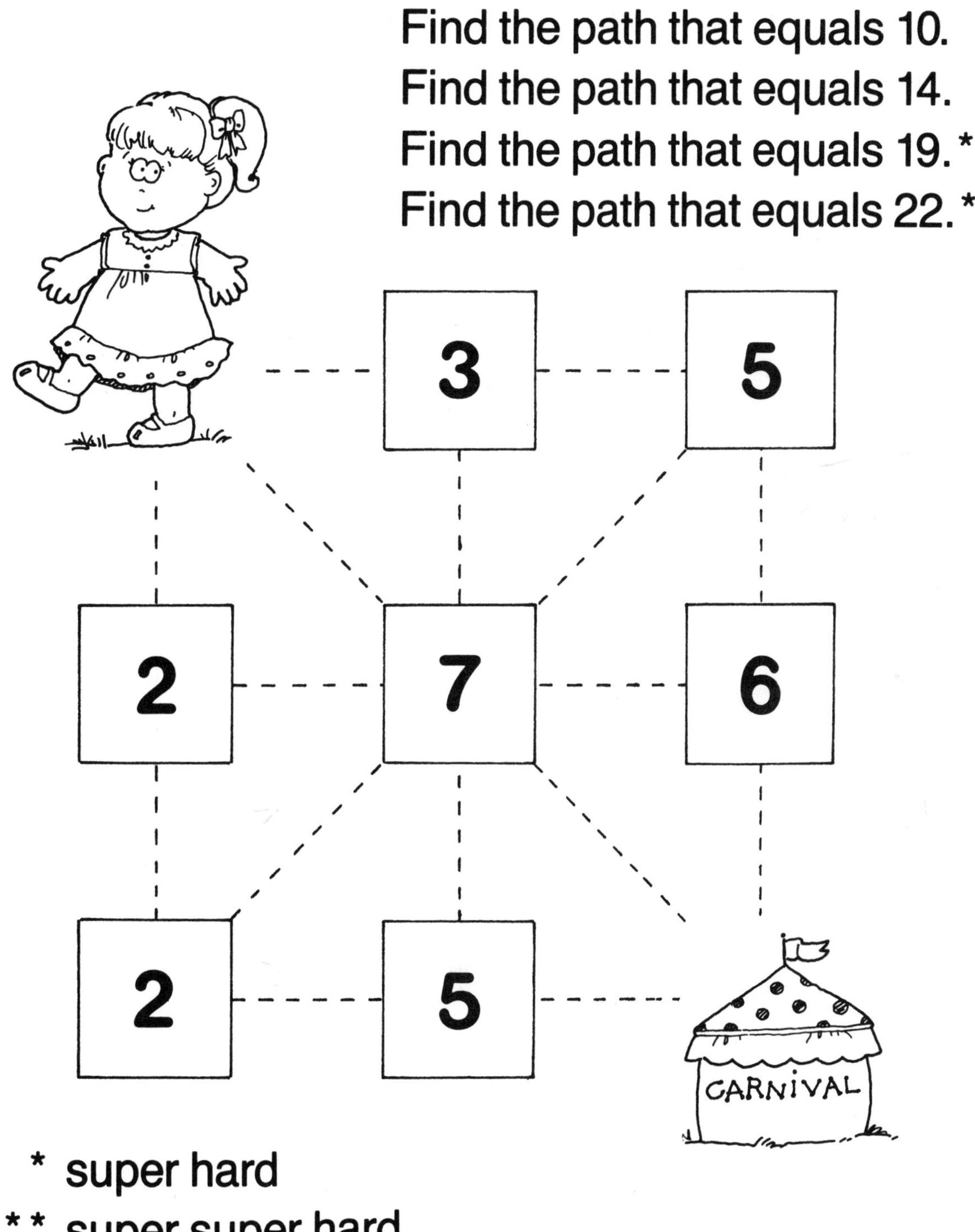

* super hard
* * super super hard

The king's pie is filled with blackbirds numbered from 1 to 20.

Can you find which numbers are missing?

___ and ___.

Which numbers are used more than once?

___ ___ ___

Which number is greater than 20? ___

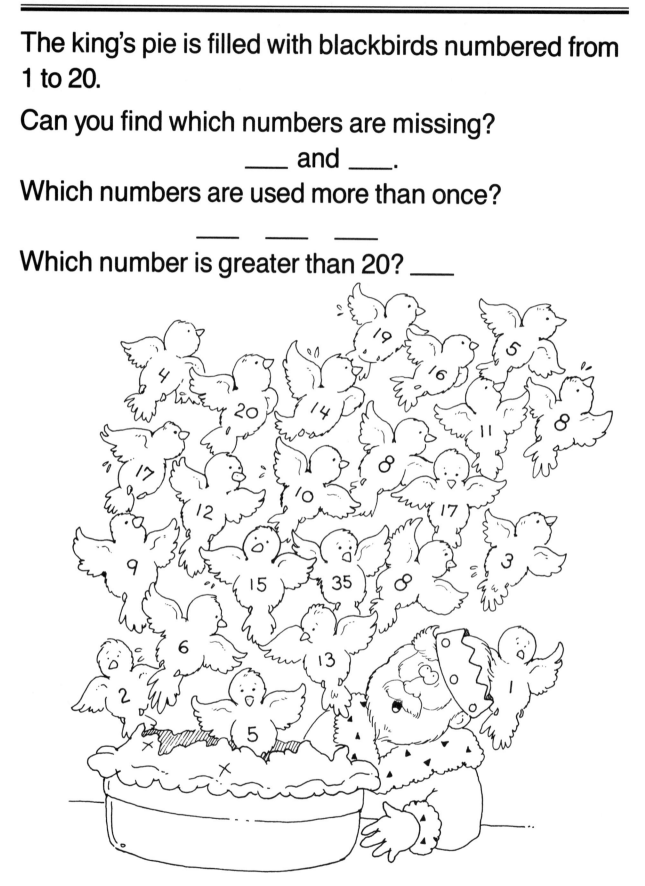

Help Katie find the toys in this shop.

Be sure to start where it says START. The first one has been done for you.

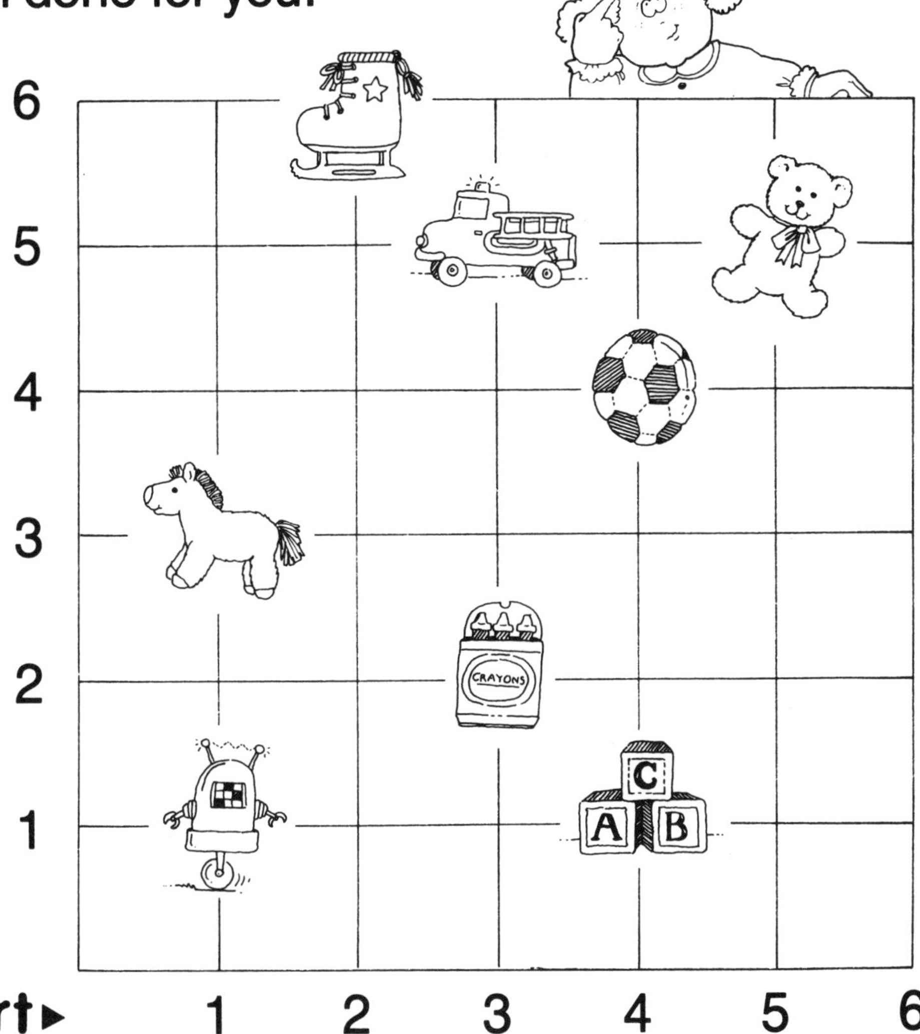

start ▸

	over ▸	up ▴
	3	2

	over ▸	up ▴

At Jon's birthday party everyone played video games, but they forgot to put their names on the score cards. Can you write the correct name on each score card? Be sure to read the clues at the bottom of the page.

SCORES:
Jon 222
Erica ?
Adam 264
Marta 178
Samantha ?
Casey 332
Benjie ?
Michael 249
1. Name
567 − 235
2. Name
172 + 215
3. Name
362 − 140
4. Name
234 + 45
5. Name
117 + 132
6. Name
296 − 32
7. Name
45 + 133
8. Name
724 − 403

Samantha's score was the highest.
The sum of the numbers in Erica's score is 6.
Benjie's score was higher than Adam's.

Help Jana solve this puzzle.

Put a box around the numbers that make 10.

Put a circle around the numbers that make 7.

The numbers must be next to each other or above and below each other like this:

(5)	[3	7]
(2)	1	2

5	8	2	6	4
2	1	9	3	4
7	6	3	8	4
3	5	5	2	3

Hint: It's okay if a number is in both a box and a circle.

Score: 3 circles 4 boxes = GREAT!

4 circles 5 boxes = SUPER!

5 circles 6 boxes = FANTASTIC!

Erica is trying to find out how much her name is worth. Can you help? Look at the chart below to see how much each letter is worth.

E R I C A

4¢ ___ ___ ___ ___

Write your name. How much is it worth?

____

___ ___ ___ ___ ___ ___ ___ ___ ___ ___ ________ ¢

Write 2 friends' names. What are they worth?

____

___ ___ ___ ___ ___ ___ ___ ___ ___ ___ ________ ¢

____

___ ___ ___ ___ ___ ___ ___ ___ ___ ___ ________ ¢

Try this with a friend. See who can write the most expensive sentence.

A	B	C	D	E	F	G	H	I	J	K	L	M
2¢	1¢	3¢	1¢	4¢	2¢	3¢	5¢	2¢	3¢	1¢	4¢	5¢
N	**O**	**P**	**Q**	**R**	**S**	**T**	**U**	**V**	**W**	**X**	**Y**	**Z**
2¢	1¢	2¢	3¢	4¢	1¢	5¢	2¢	3¢	1¢	4¢	3¢	5¢

Use this code to solve the puzzle:

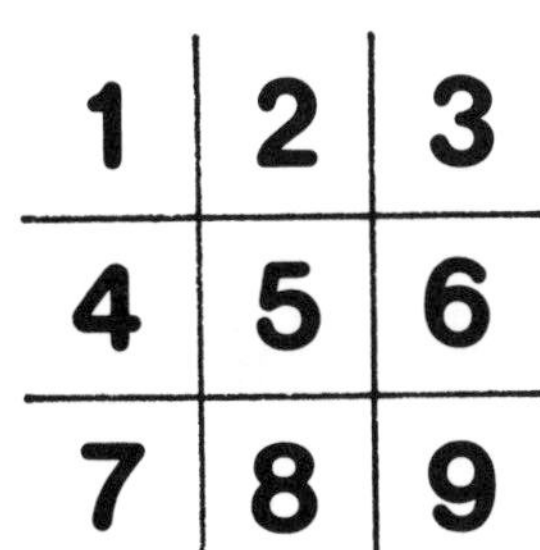

1 + 6 = 　　　　 + =

9 - 5 = 　　　　 - =

\+ = 　　　　 + =

\- = 　　　　 + =

Make some puzzles for a friend.

___ + ___ = ___

___ – ___ = ___

Little Red Riding Hood is going to visit her grandmother. Color the road she should take to get there. Be sure she does not go down the road that equals 6, because the Big Bad Wolf is hiding there.

The road that equals 8 is the fastest way there.

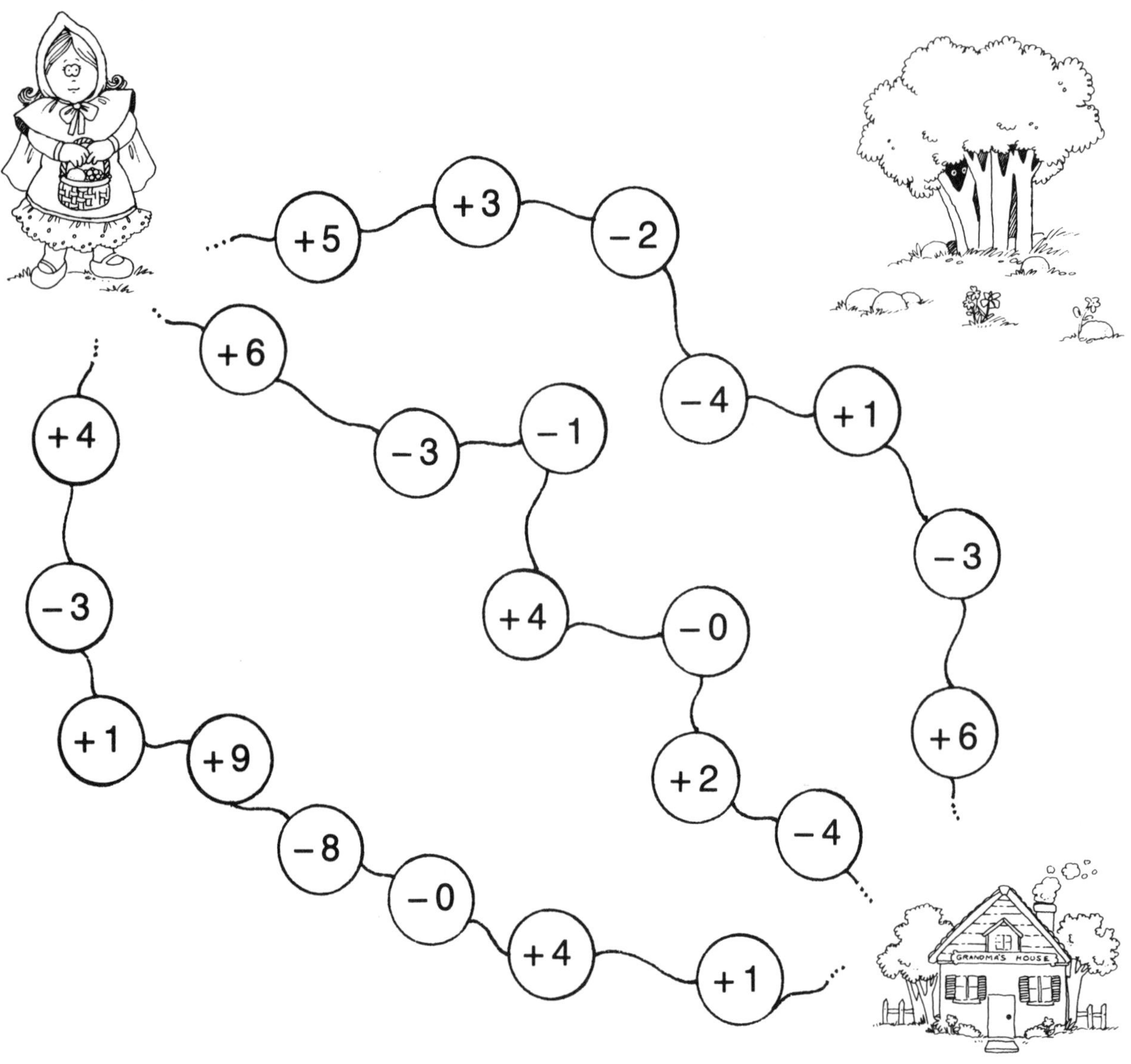

Did you take the fastest road? ____

Can you solve the Tigers' baseball puzzle?

Place all the objects below in the squares.

Rule: Only one of each object may be in each row, column, or diagonal.

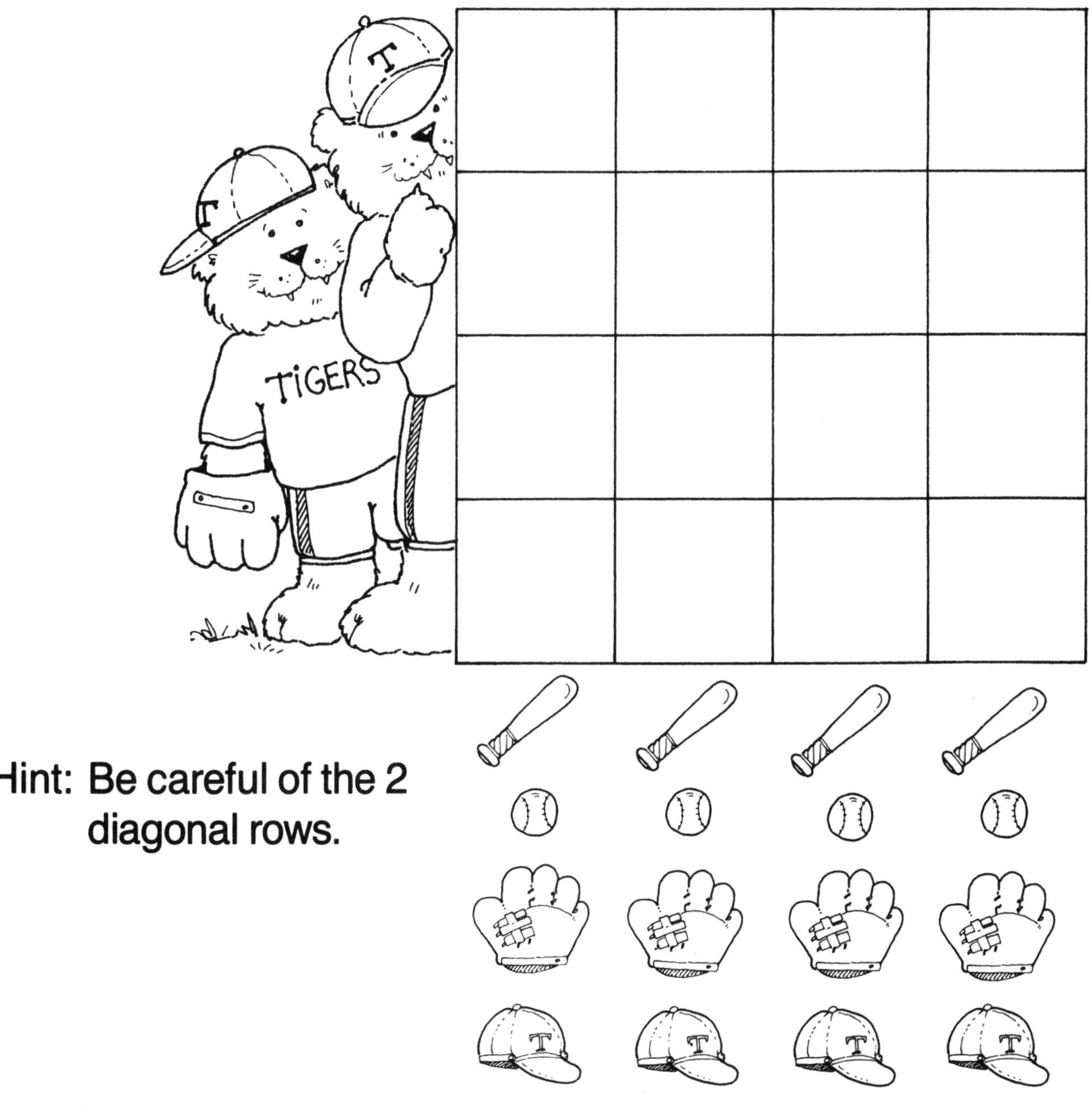

Hint: Be careful of the 2 diagonal rows.

Suggestion: Draw the pictures on little squares of paper so that you can move them around until you solve the puzzle.

A tangram is an old Chinese puzzle. There are hundreds of pictures that can be made with a tangram.

Cut out the 7 pieces and try the puzzles on the next 3 pages.

Can you make this picture using all 7 tangram pieces?

Hint: You need to turn the ▱ upside down.

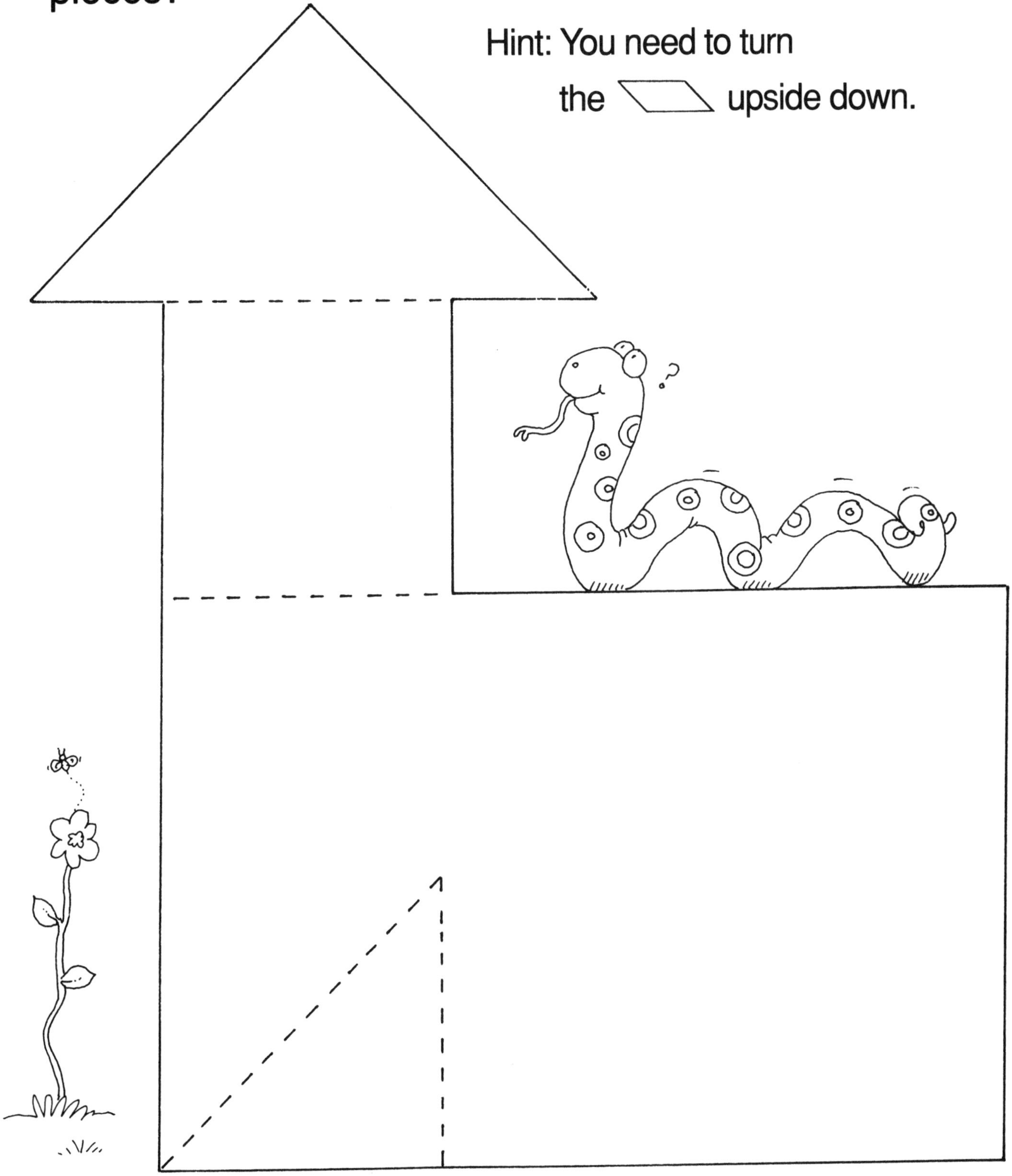

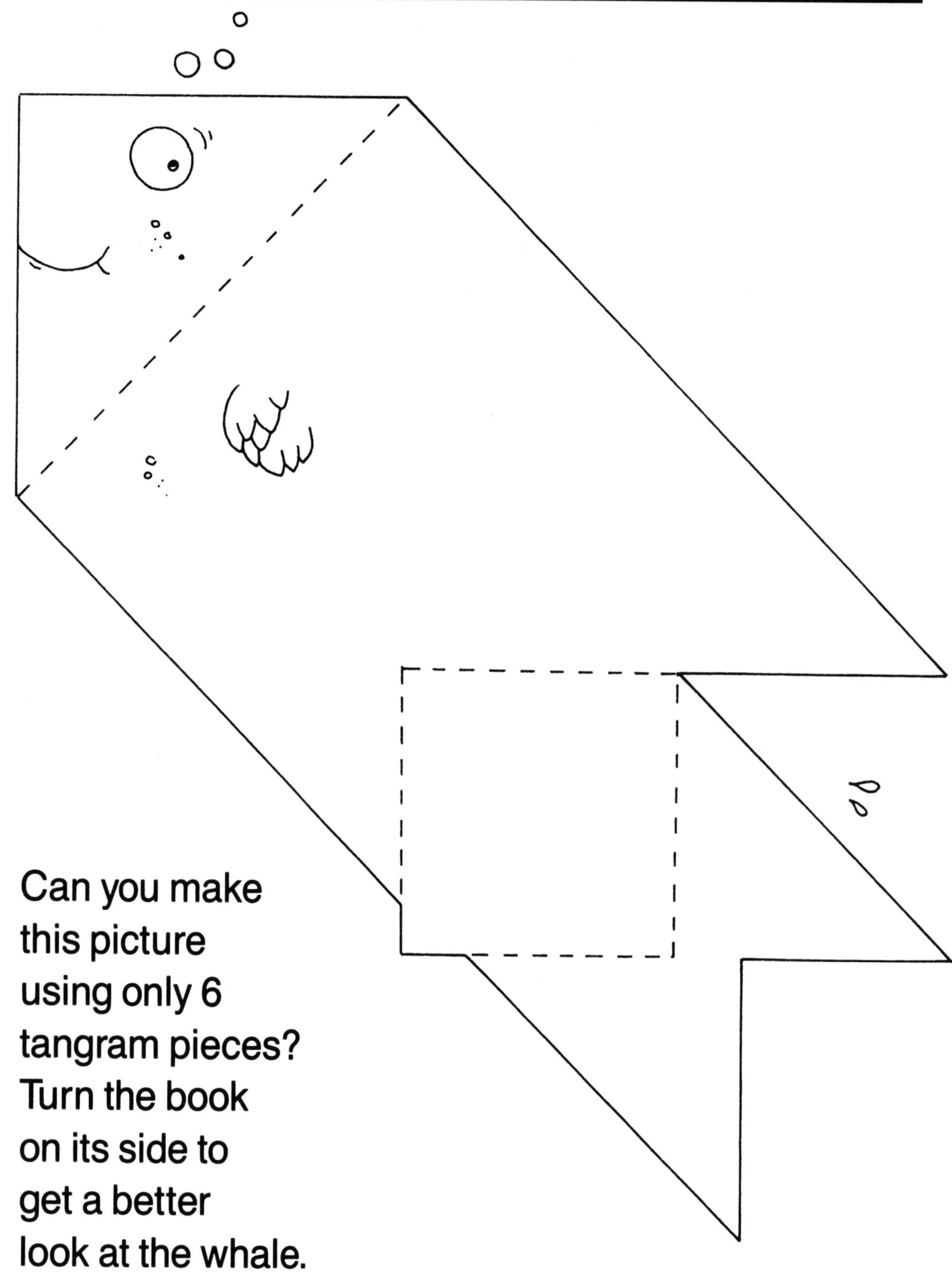

Can you make this picture using only 6 tangram pieces? Turn the book on its side to get a better look at the whale.

Try these puzzles with your tangram.

Can you make a boat?

Pick an animal and try to make it.

Hint: Many people have made cats or ducks.

Try making some numbers or letters.

Can you make a chair?

Make a design for a friend to try.

Help Jason with this puzzle.

Look at the pieces below to find the right answer.

In the town of Backwards, people play tic-tac-toe differently. The winner is the person who does **not** put 3 marks in a column, row, or diagonal.

Can you play by the same rules as the people in Backwards?

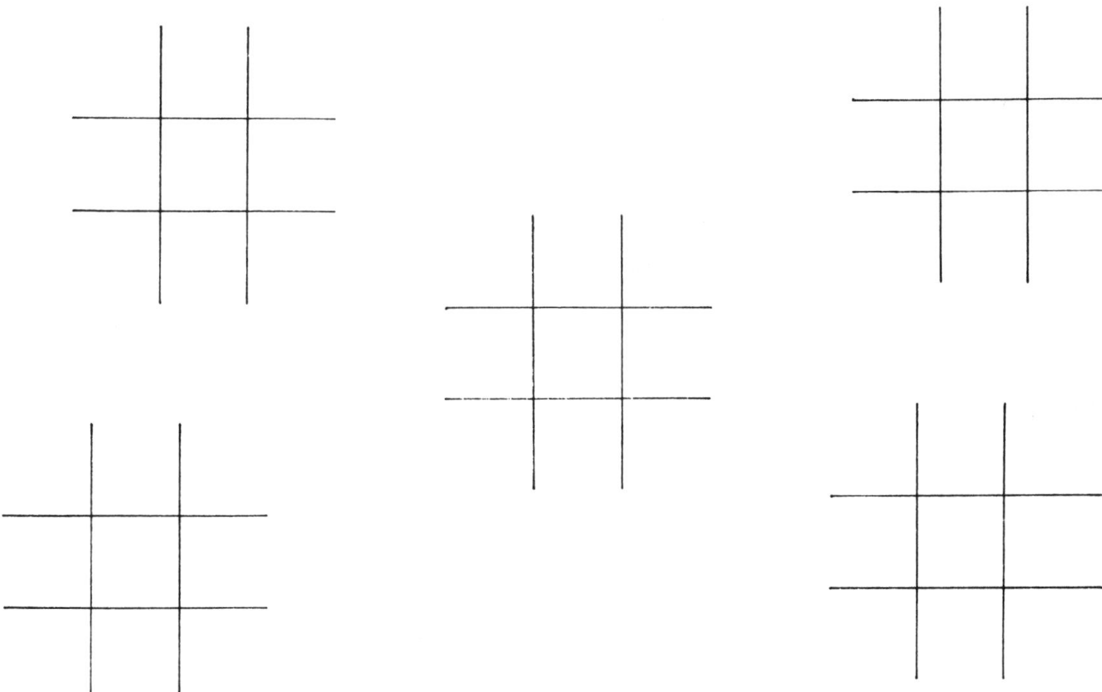

Dara needs a score of 17 to win this video game. What is the greatest amount of objects she can capture to win? _____ Put a red box around these. What is the smallest amount of objects she can capture? _____ Put a blue ring around these.

Help these animals.

Fill in the missing numbers.

Rules: The sum of *each* side must be the same as the number in the animal's mouth.

You can only use the numbers 1, 2, 3, 4, 5, 6, 7, 8, 9.

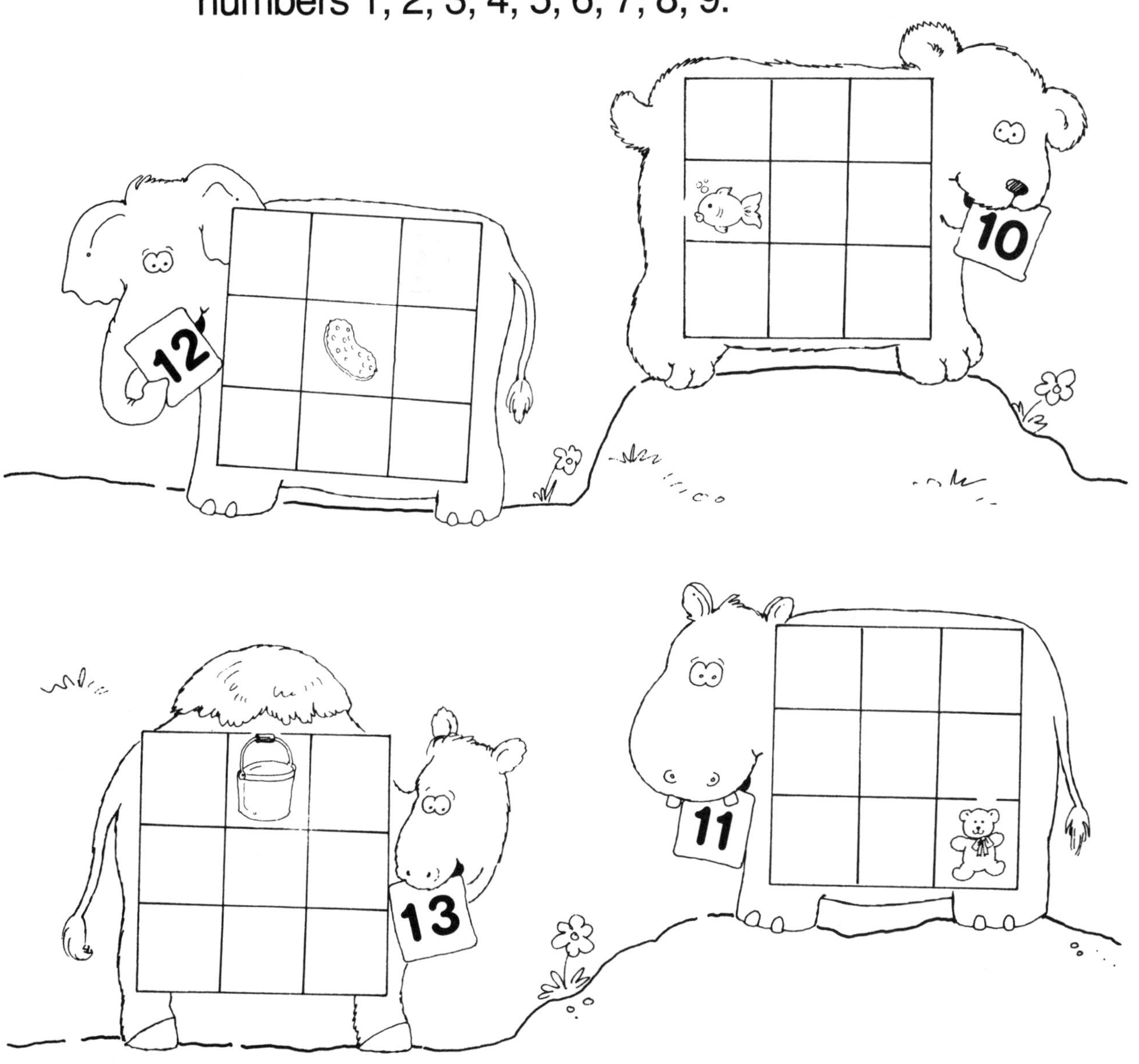

The Gyrosian numbers look different from ours. Here are some numbers from the planet Gyros:

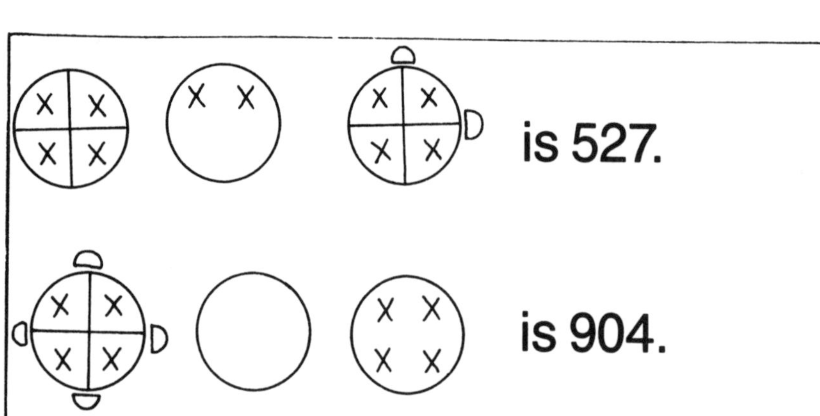

1. Can you tell what this number is?

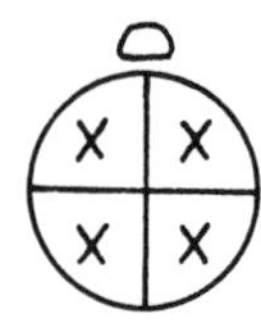 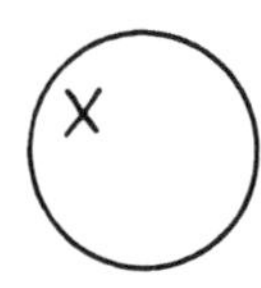 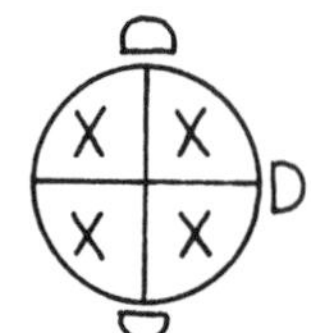 ___ ___ ___

2. Can you write the Gyrosian numbers from 0 to 9?

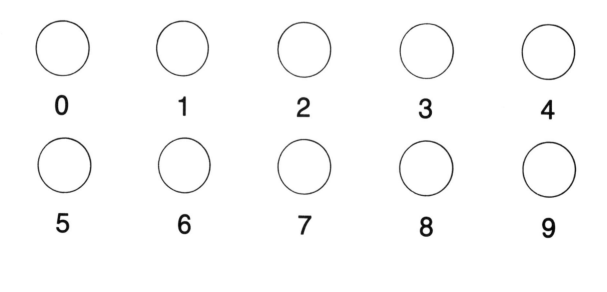

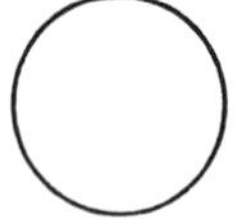 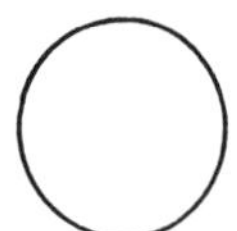 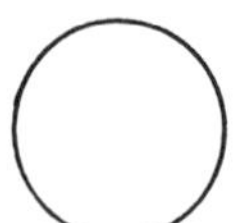 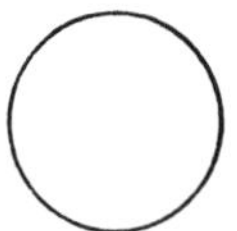 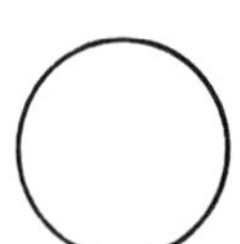

0 1 2 3 4

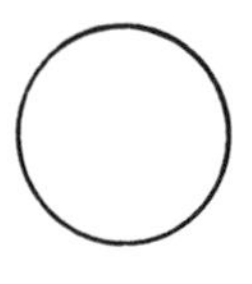 ◯ ◯ ◯ 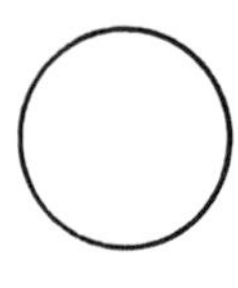

5 6 7 8 9

Try these problems from Gyros.

Be sure to answer in Gyrosian numbers.

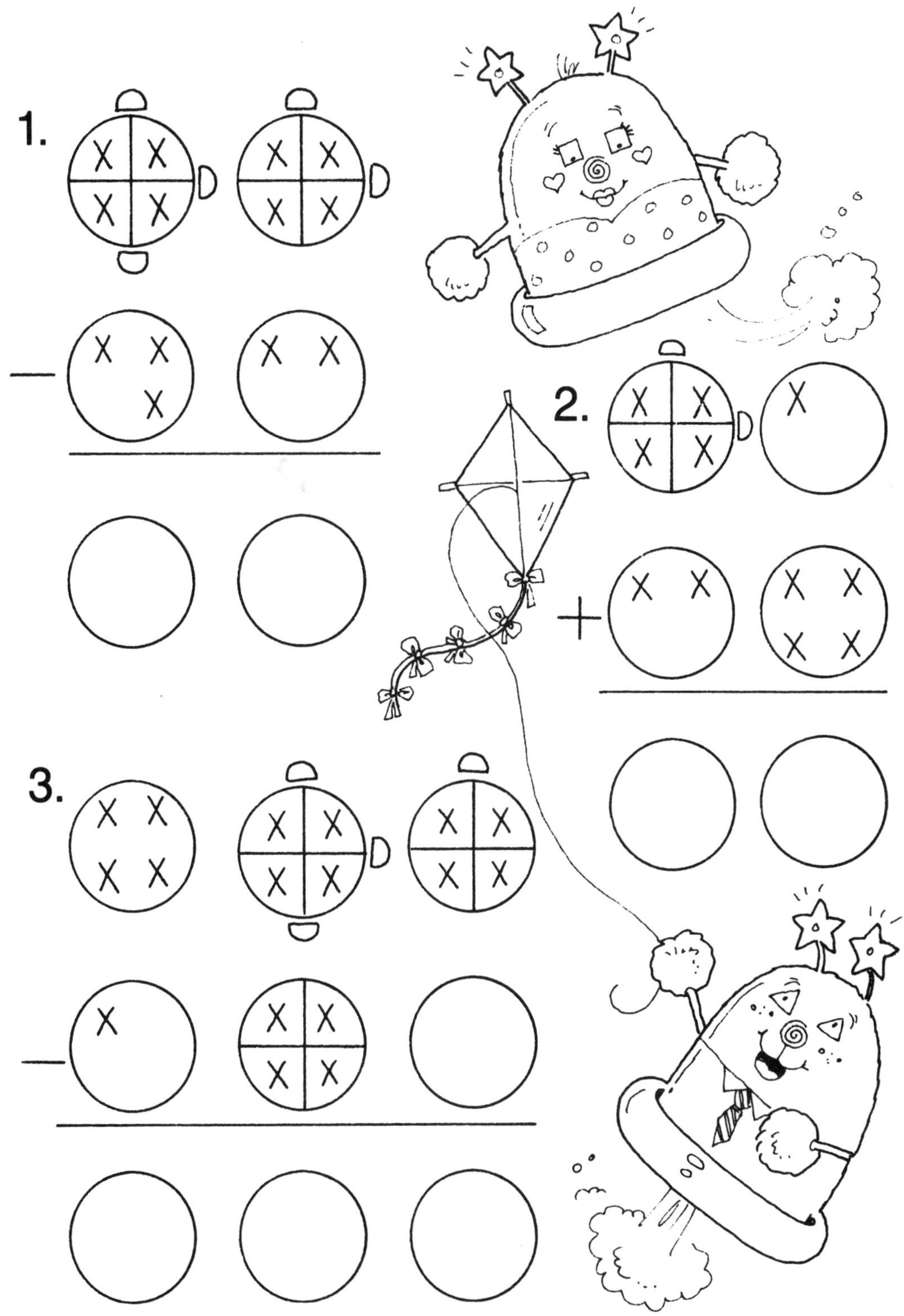

Try this puzzle.

Set 16 toothpicks on a table so they look like the picture on this page.

Can you make 5 squares by moving only 2 toothpicks?

Try this number-search puzzle.

Put a ring around all the numbers that equal 12.

The first one is done for you.

How many did you find?

4 rings = GREAT!

6 rings = SUPER!

9 rings = FANTASTIC!!

Jamie has lost his favorite toy. Help him find it.
Color the numbers *less* than 40 green.
Color the numbers *more* than 40 red.

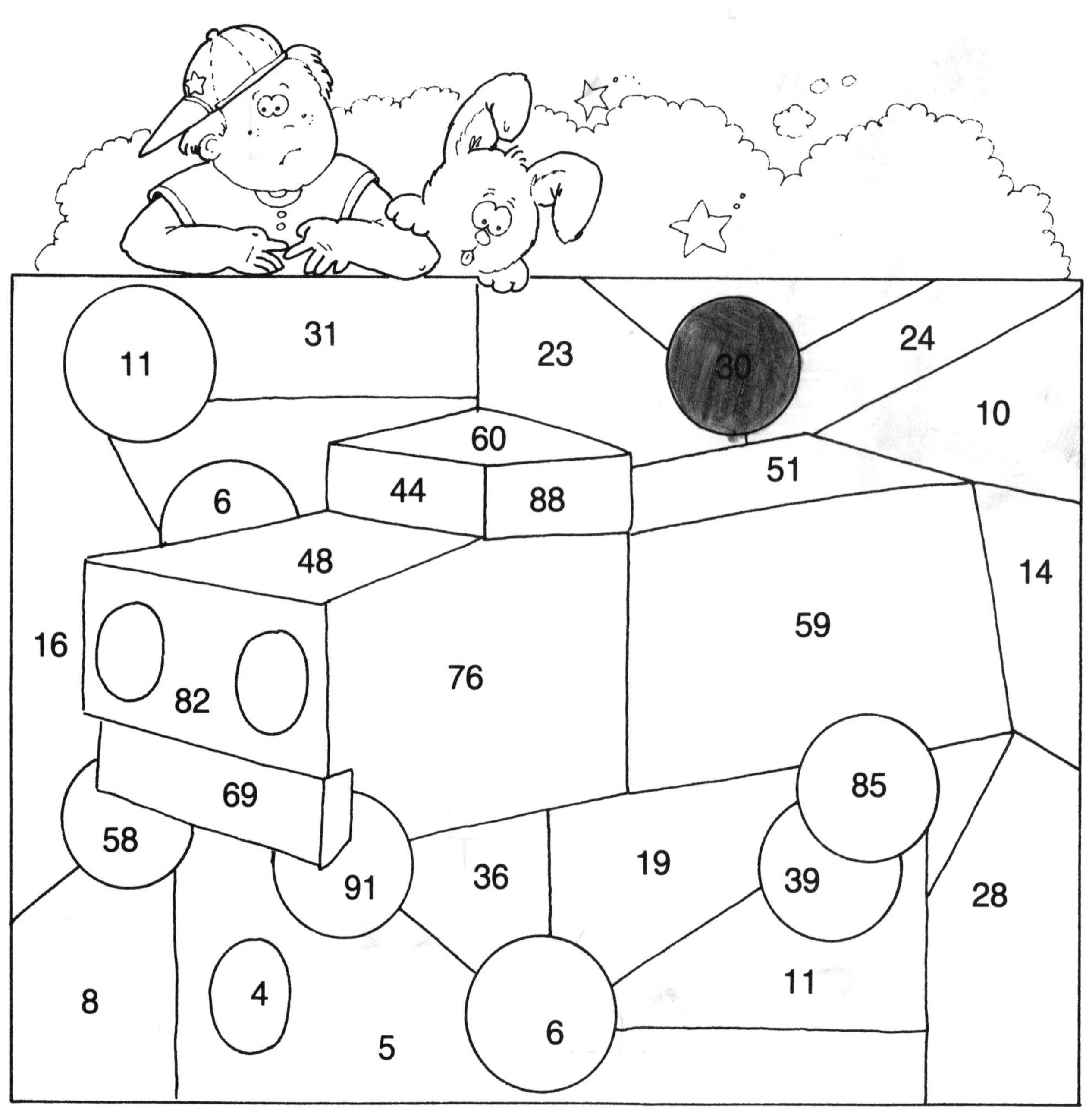

Use the chart below to find out how much this clown is worth.

The clown is worth _____¢.

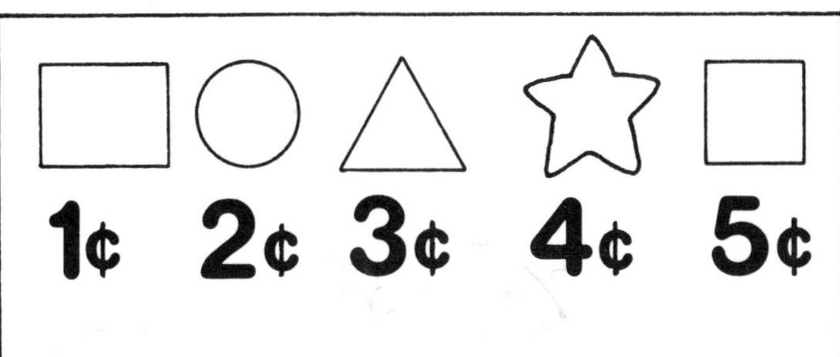

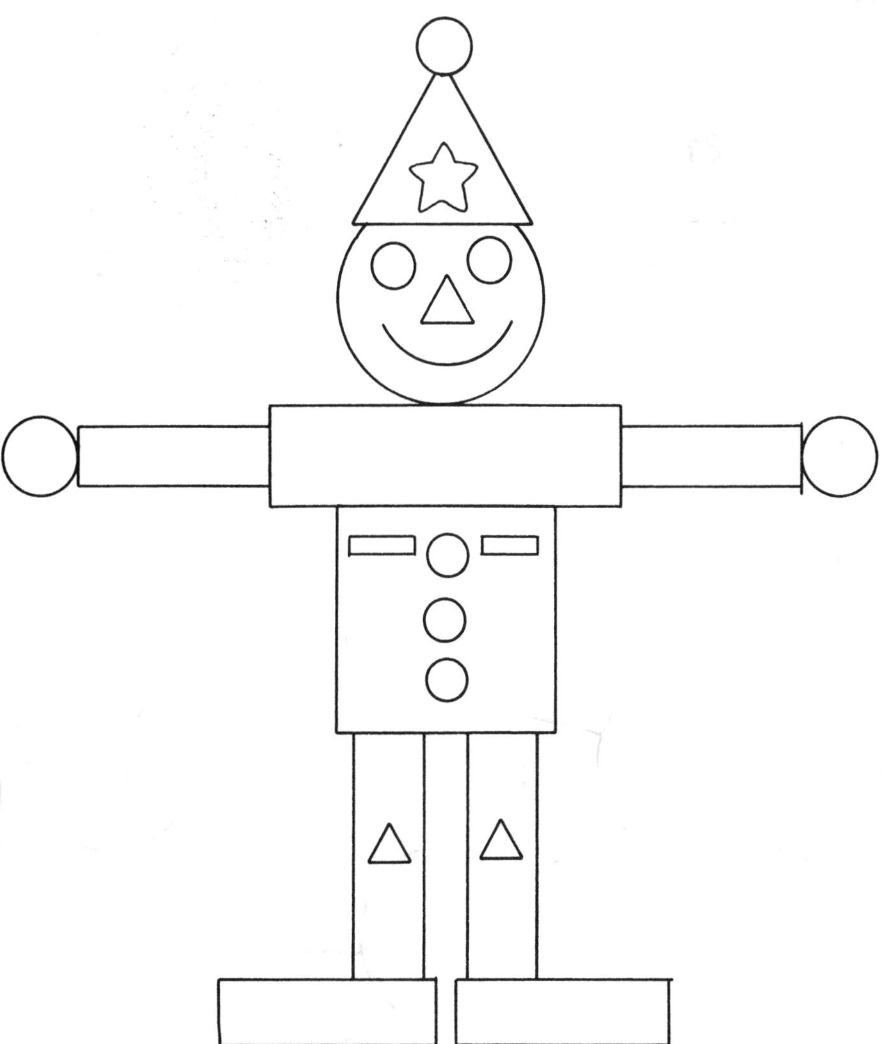

Solve this puzzle.

Use the numbers 4, 5, 6, 7, 8, 9.

Make the sum of the top row = 6.

Make the sum of the middle row = 16.

Make the sum of the bottom row = 17.

Can you color this picture?

Rules: You can only use 4 colors.

No shapes of the same color can touch each other.

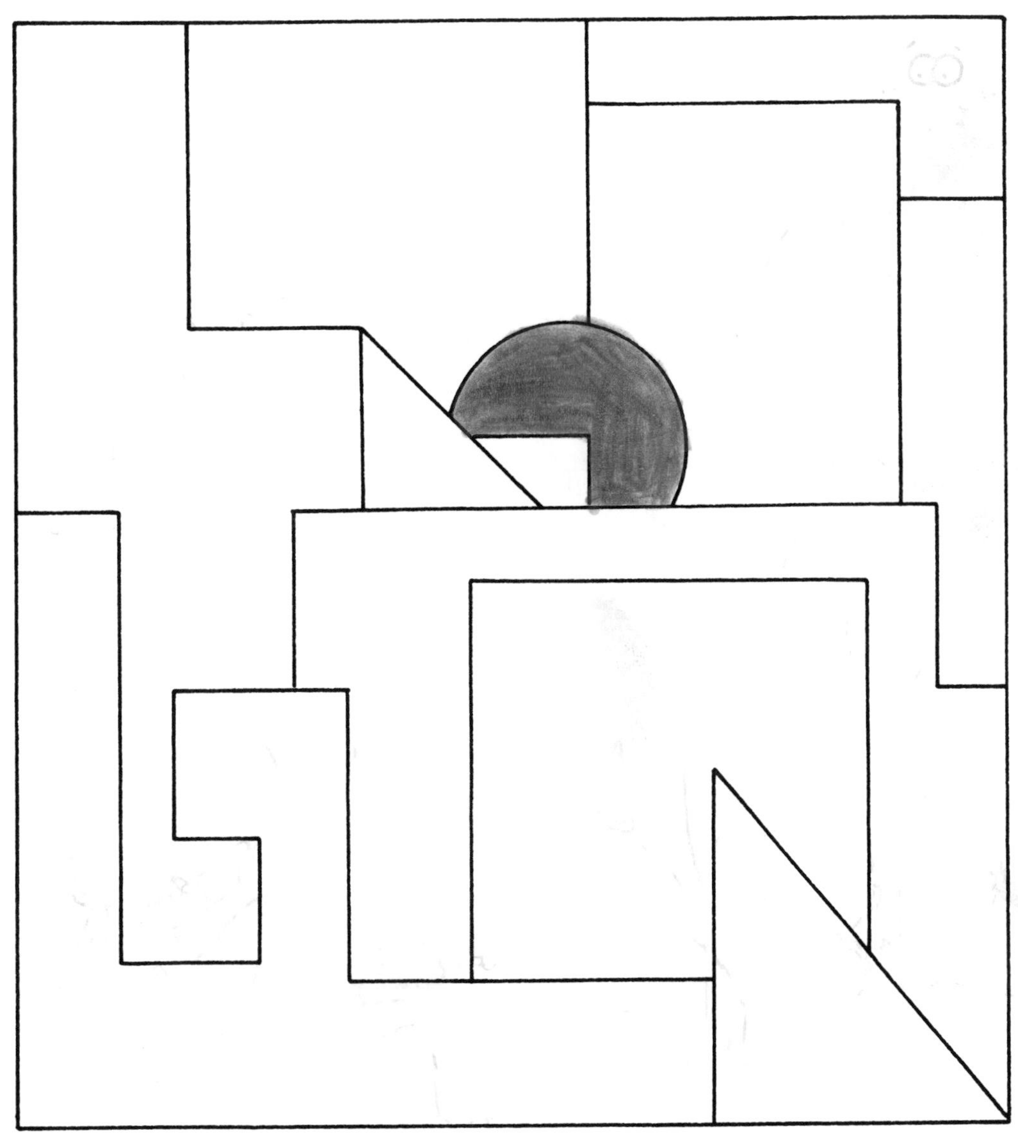

Color the ○ red

□ yellow

△ blue

▭ green

How many △ s did you find? 3

Connect the dots to find out what Amanda would like to be when she grows up. Hint: Count by 2s.

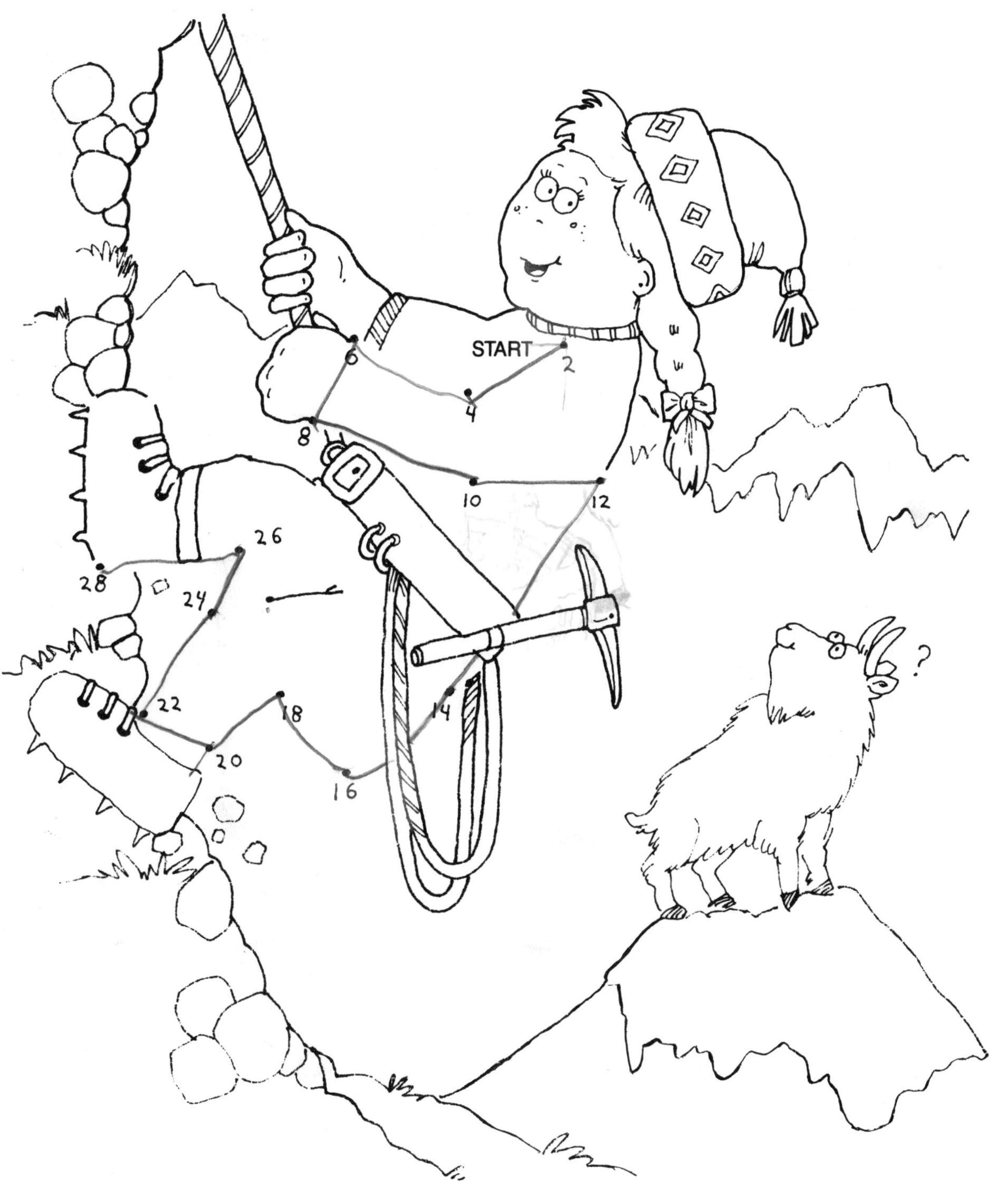

Try these puzzles:

Put 10 pennies on the table just like the circles in this picture. Can you turn the triangle upside down by moving just 3 pennies?

Move these 9 pennies around to make 3 lines with 4 pennies in each line.

Hint: This makes a shape.

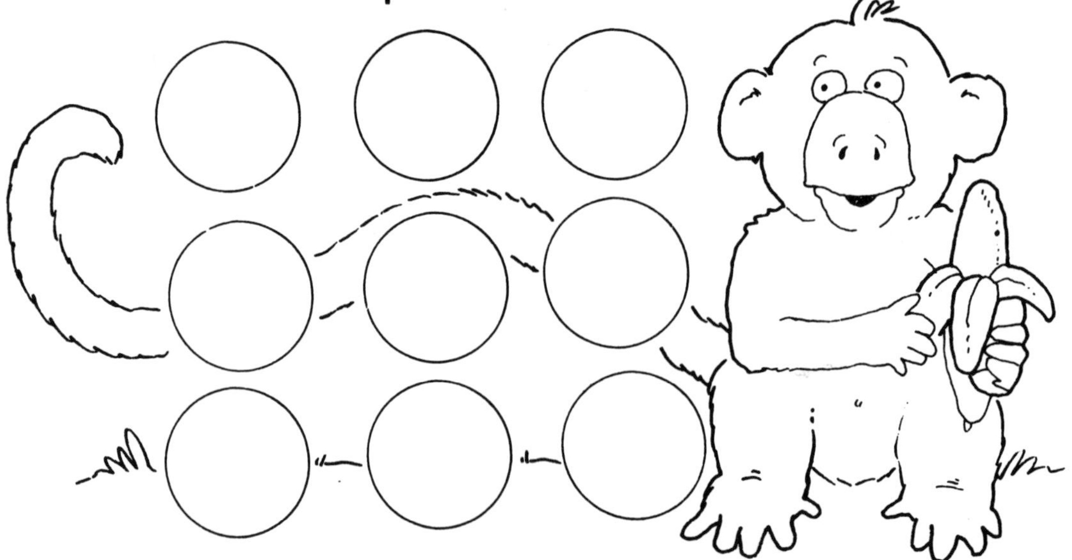

Jose is caught in a giant spiderweb. The only way he can break the spider's spell and get out is by finding the path that equals 12. There are at least two paths that equal 12. The first one is shown. Can you find another?

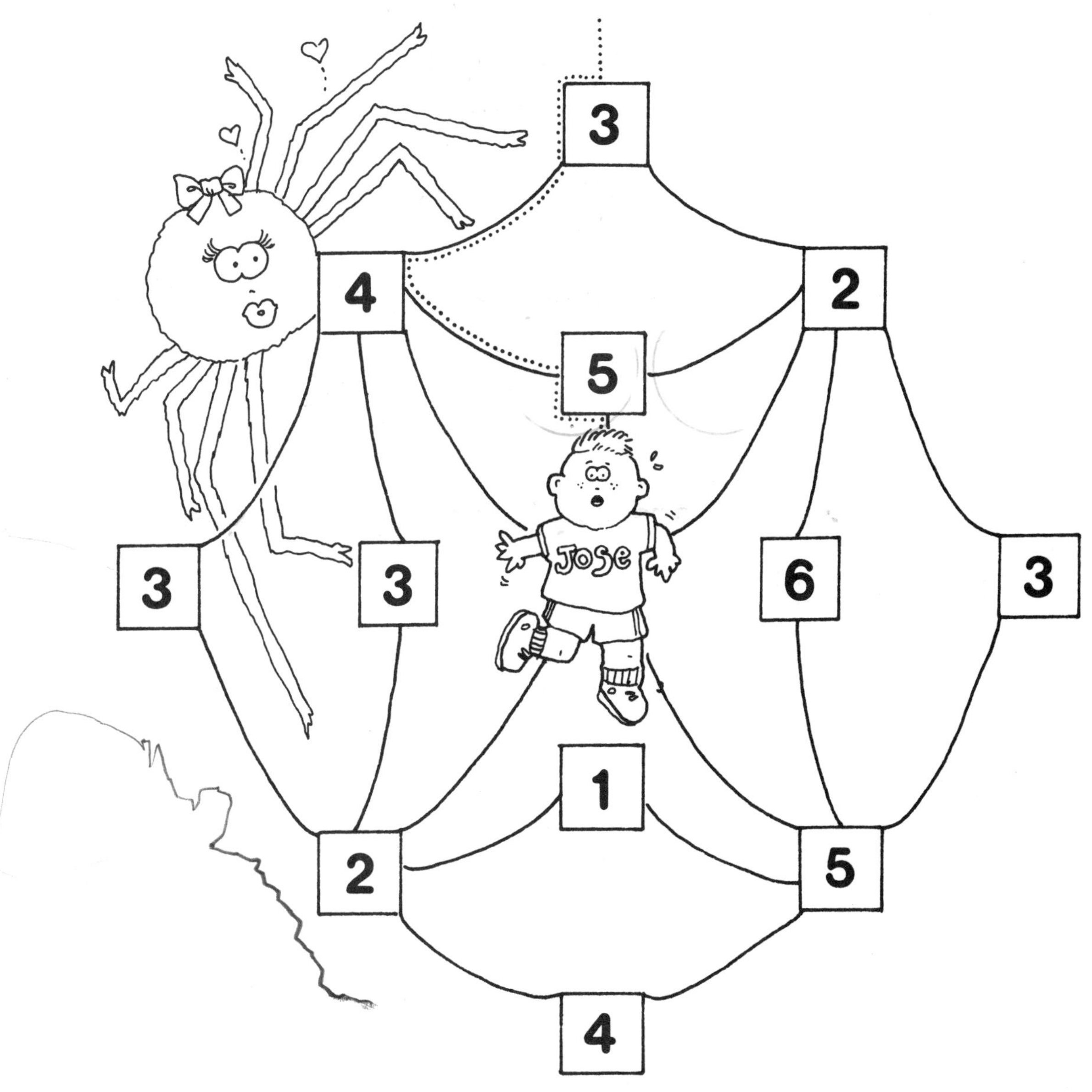

Help Juliana count all the squares in this picture.

_____ squares

Hint: There are more than 10.

How many triangles are in this picture?

_____ triangles

Hint: The triangles are different sizes.

Color all the 7s yellow.
Color all the 8s blue.
Color all the 9s red.

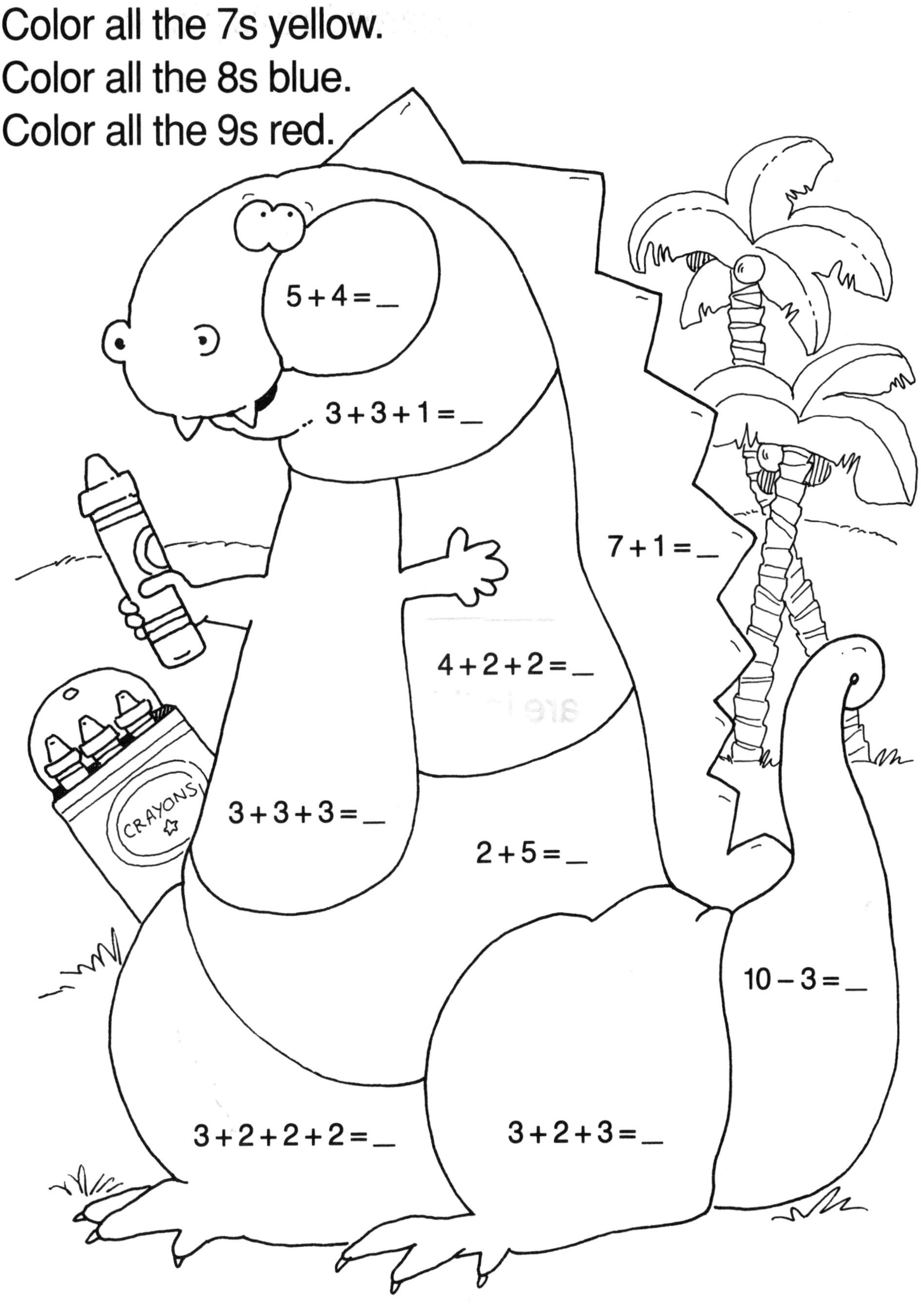

Help this fleet of spaceships get ready for its mission. Number the ships 1, 2, 3, 4, 5, 6, 7, 8.

Rule: Numbers that come before or after each other may not be placed next to one another in *any* direction (even on a diagonal).

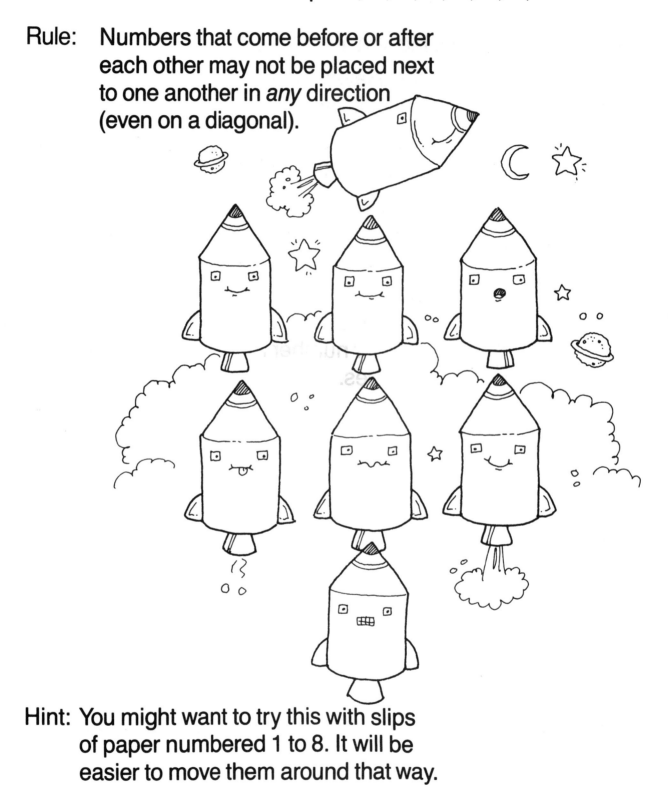

Hint: You might want to try this with slips of paper numbered 1 to 8. It will be easier to move them around that way.

Play this game with a friend.

The object of the game is to score the most points.

Game Play: Make a 4-by-4 grid as shown.

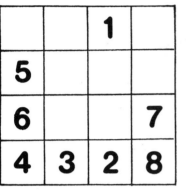

		1	
5			
6			7
4	3	2	8

SCORE

even	odd
8	0

One player chooses odd numbers; the other player chooses even numbers.

The odd number player begins by placing a 1 anywhere on the board.

The next player must put a 2 in the same row either up and down or across.

Rule: No other numbers can come between the two numbers when they are placed. Blank spaces are okay, but another number in between is against the rules.

The player who is able to make the last move wins and scores that number of points (see picture).

Can you solve this puzzle?

Read the clues and fill in the blanks.

ACROSS

2. There are ___ minutes in an hour.
4. There are ___ pennies in a quarter.
5. There are ___ toes on three human feet.
7. In 1987 Heather had her 6th birthday. In what year was she born?

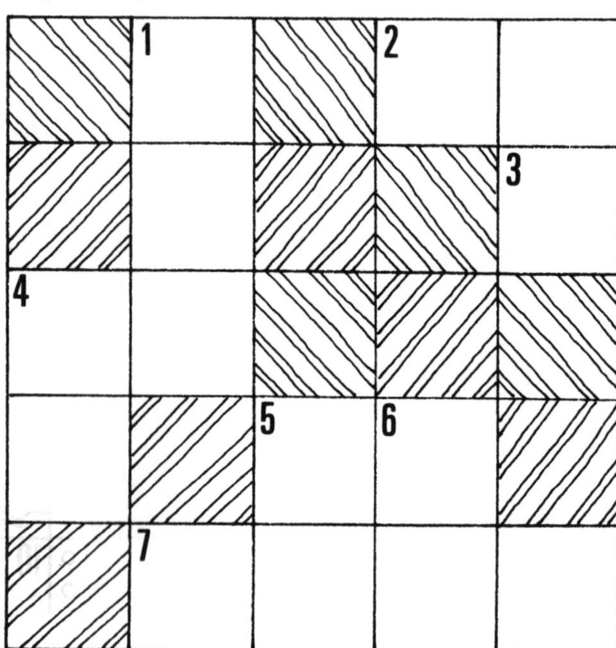

DOWN

1. There are ___ days in a year.
3. There are ___ wheels on a tricycle.
4. There are ___ letters in the alphabet.
5. 16 + 3 = ___
6. The number after 57 is ___.

Can you do this puzzle?

Read the clues and fill in the blanks.

ACROSS

1. 5 + 6 = ___
3. The number before 62.
5. The total number of your fingers and toes.
6. An even number less than 4 but greater than 0.
9. 5 dimes and 2 pennies = ___¢
10. $\begin{array}{r} 988 \\ -536 \\ \hline \end{array}$

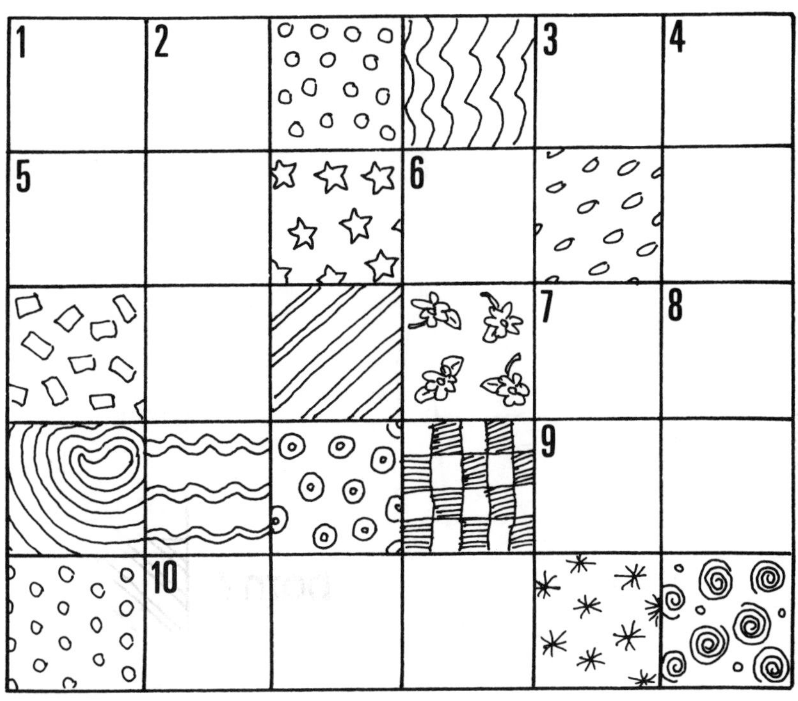

DOWN

1. A dozen cookies is ___ cookies.
2. The number after 99 is ___.
4. $\begin{array}{r} 3743 \\ -2311 \\ \hline \end{array}$
7. The number of fingers on 5 human hands.
8. $\begin{array}{r} 20 \\ +12 \\ \hline \end{array}$

Here's a game to play with a friend.

You will need: 1 egg carton
60 beans (peanuts, popcorn kernels, or raisins work well also)

Object of the Game: To collect the most beans.

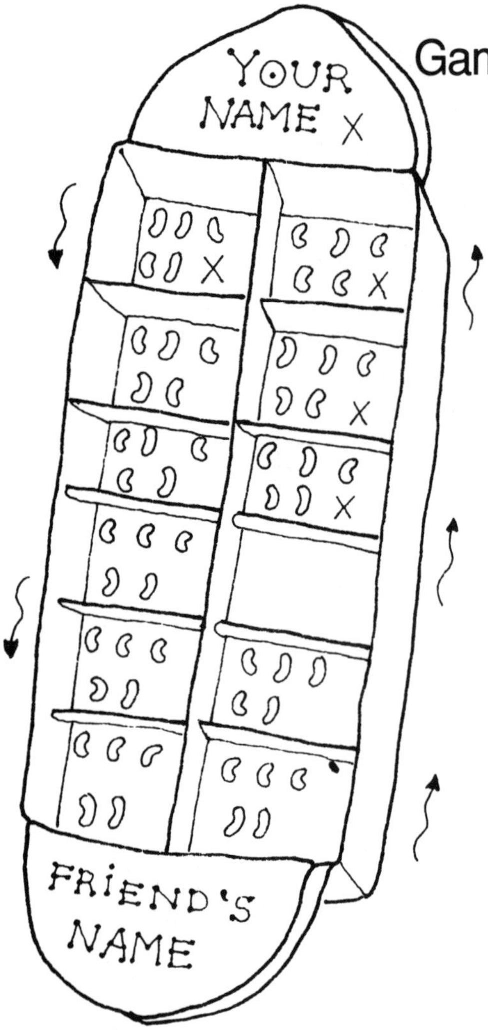

Game Play: Place 5 beans in each of the slots of the egg carton.

Label one end of the egg carton with your name; the other end with your friend's name.

On your turn, pick up all the beans in one of the slots. Starting with the slot above or below (you must move counterclockwise), place one bean into each slot until you run out of beans. If you pass your end of the carton, you may drop a bean there.

(In the picture the Xs show the beans that were moved on the first turn.)

Continue playing until one side of the egg carton is empty. Count your beans. The player with the most beans wins.

Can you answer this riddle?

What do you get when you cross a cow with a duck?

Color all the boxes with *even* numbers.
Read what is left to find the answer.

4 I	6 T	5 M	1 I	3 L	7 K	2 C	8 A	4 N

3 A	1 N	7 D	6 W	2 I	8 L	4 L	2 D	6 O

4 I	1 Q	5 U	7 A	3 C	1 K	5 E	1 R	3 S

Put the underlined letters together to make a new word.

It starts like

car

and ends like

bat

The new word is

___ ___ ___

It starts like

go

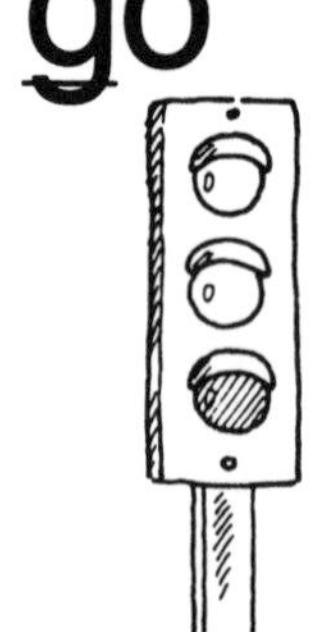

and ends like

name

The new word is

___ ___ ___ ___

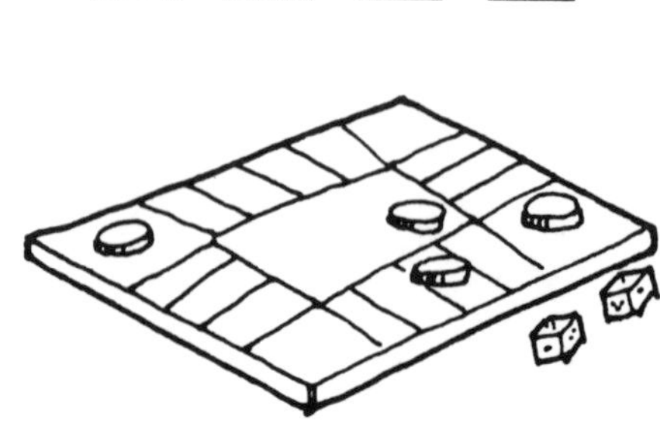

It starts like

bug

and ends like

tag

The new word is

___ ___ ___

Put the underlined letters together to make a new word.

It starts like	and ends like	The new word is
sweets	ring	_ _ _ _ _

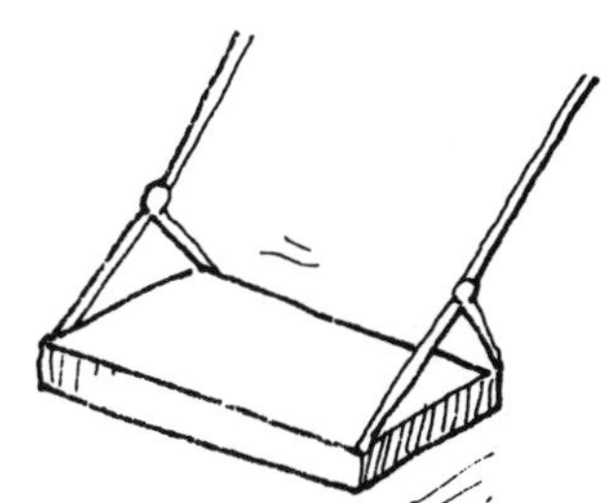

It starts like	and ends like	The new word is
grow	seen	_ _ _ _ _

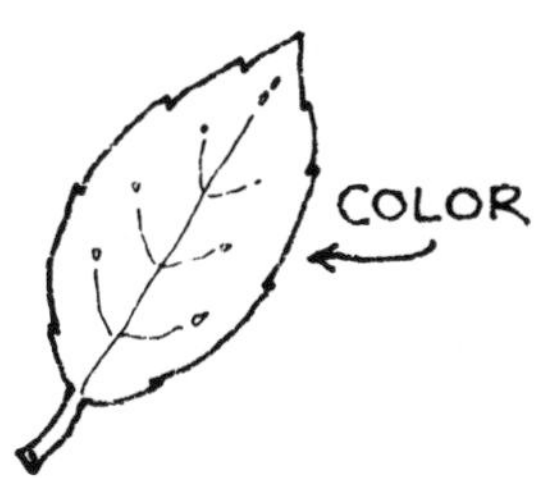

It starts like	and ends like	The new word is
chair	rain	_ _ _ _ _

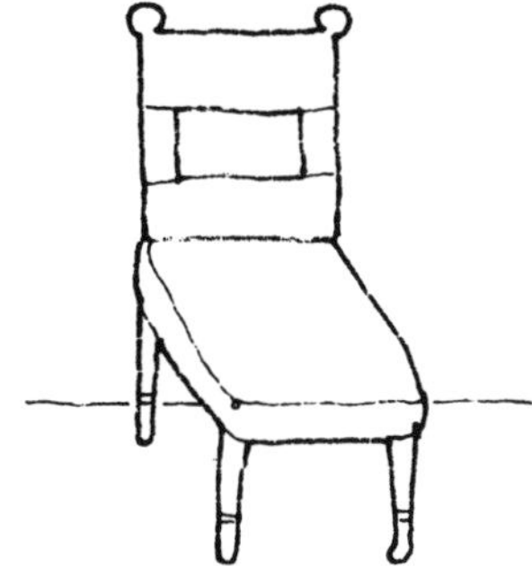

1. Put the underlined letters together to make a new word.
2. Color the picture that shows more than one thing.

1. It starts like **bridge** and ends like **light.**

It's __ __ __ __ __ __

2. It starts like **short** and ends like **tweet.**

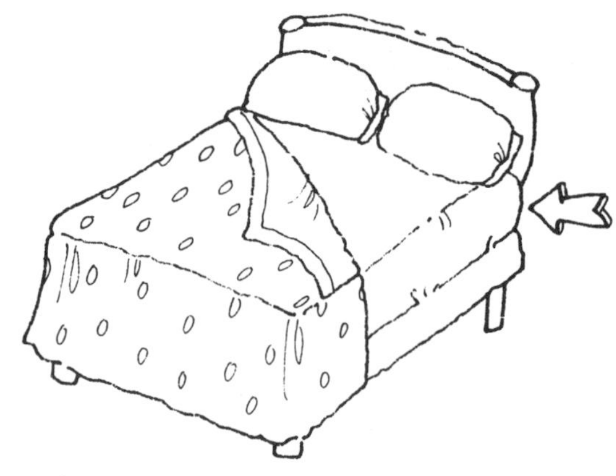

It's __ __ __ __ __

3. It starts like **sleep** ends like **trim.**

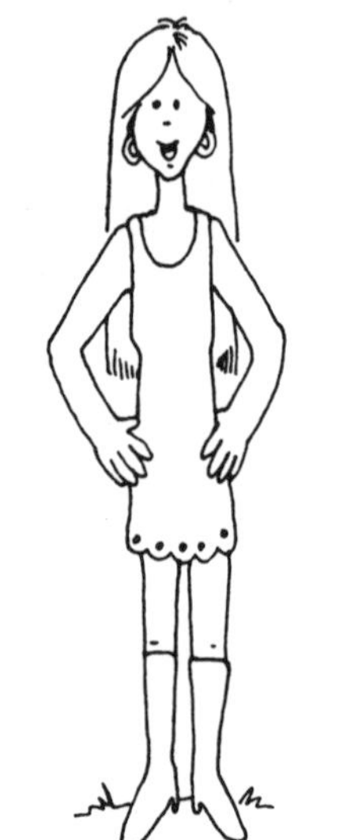

It's __ __ __ __

4. It starts like **ground** and ends like **tapes.**

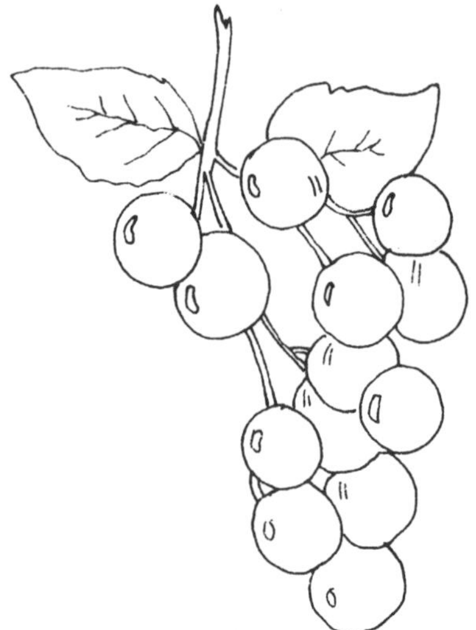

It's __ __ __ __ __ __

1. Use the underlined letters to make new words.
2. Color the picture that shows **someone** doing something.

1. chin → _ _ _ _ _ ← smart

2. drip → _ _ _ _ _ ← sink

3. free → _ _ _ _ _ ← tame

4. pretty → _ _ _ _ _ ← size

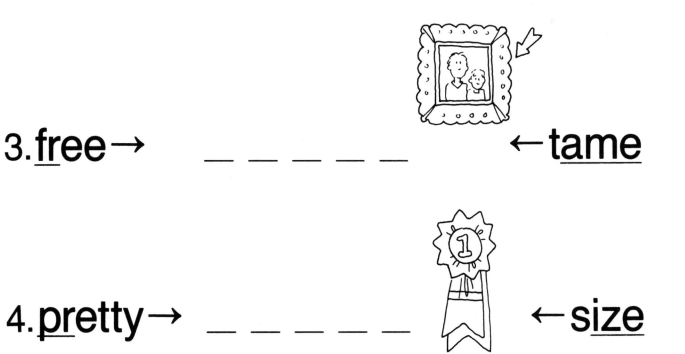

1. Use the underlined letters to make new words.
2. Color the picture that shows a way to travel.

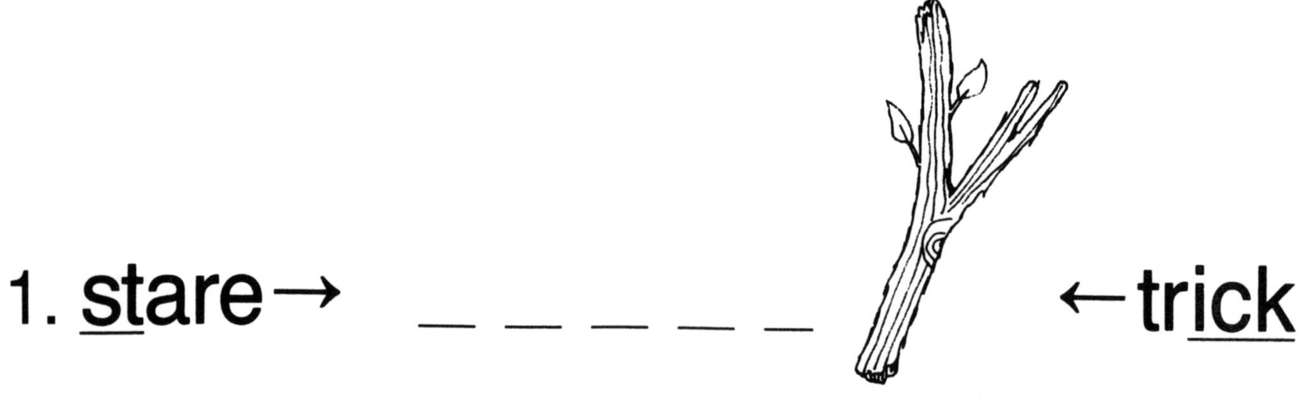

1. stare→ _ _ _ _ _ ←trick

2. share→ _ _ _ _ ←trip

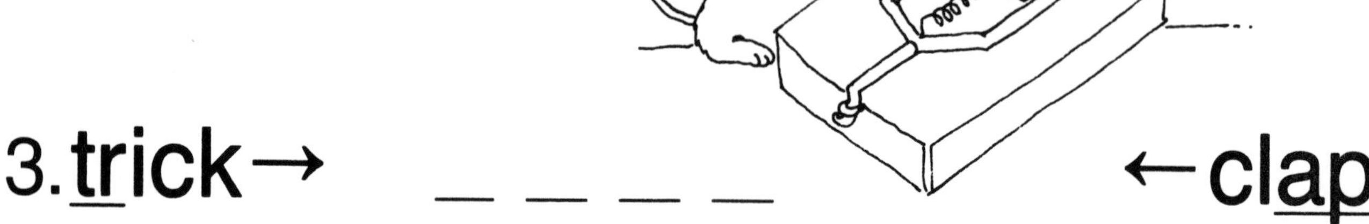

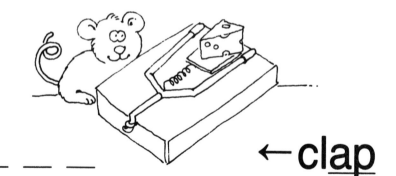

3. trick→ _ _ _ _ ←clap

4. write→ _ _ _ _ ←slap

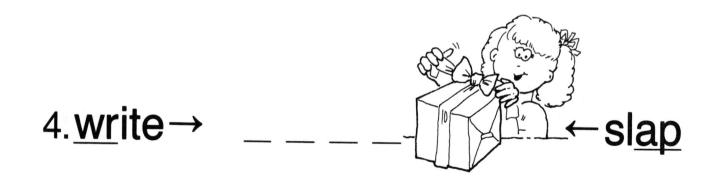

1. Use the underlined letters to make new words.
2. Draw a picture for each word you make.

1. flat _ _ _ _ _ _ shower

2. take _ _ _ _ _ able

3. snack _ _ _ _ _ shake

4. stand _ _ _ _ _ shore

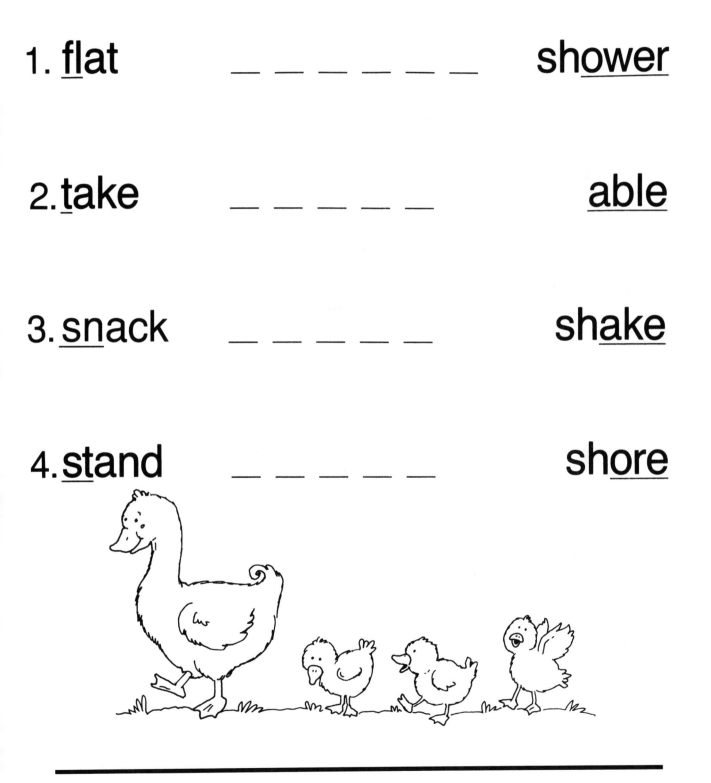

1. Use the underlined letters to make new words.
2. Put the new words in order to make a sentence.

1. lip _ _ _ _ song

2. drip _ _ _ _ _ stove

3. before _ _ _ _ _ _ outside

4. bring _ _ _ _ _ _ ridge

John _ _ _ _ _ _ _ _ _ _ _ _

the _ _ _ _ _ _ _ _ _ _ _ _.

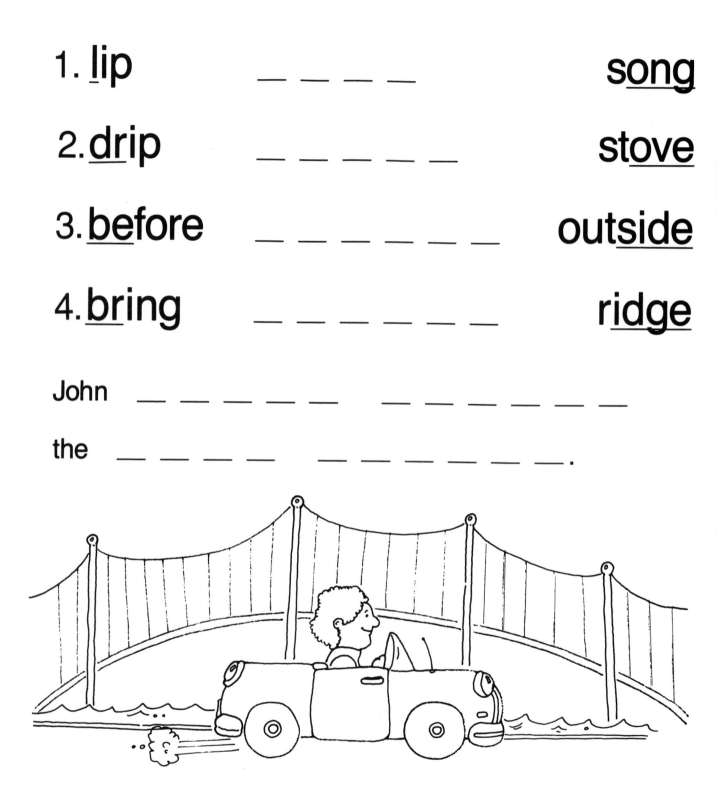

Look at the picture (symbol) for each letter in the secret code. Write the letter for each picture on the lines below.

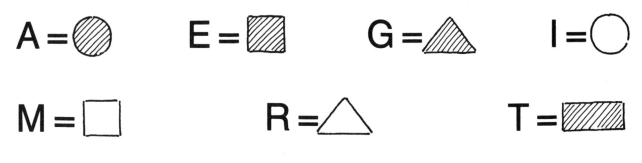

A = ● E = ■ G = ▲ I = ○

M = □ R = △ T = ▬

What are you?

I ___ ___ ___ ___ ___ ___ ___!

1. Use the code to find out what to do.
2. Do what it tells you to do.

A = └   D = ┐   G = ┐•

O = └•   R = ╲   W = ╱

___ ___ ___ ___   ___   ___ ___ ___.

┐ ╲ └ ╱   └   ┐ └• ┐•

1. Decode the secret message.
2. Follow the directions in the message.

A = B = E = F =

G = K = L = M = U =

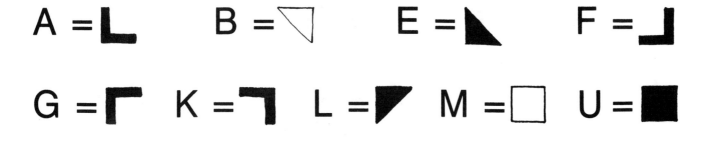

This is called the "Letter Before" code. Can you guess why?

B = A   F = E   I = H   T = S

U = T   X = W   Z = Y

___ ___ ___ ___

U I B U

X B T

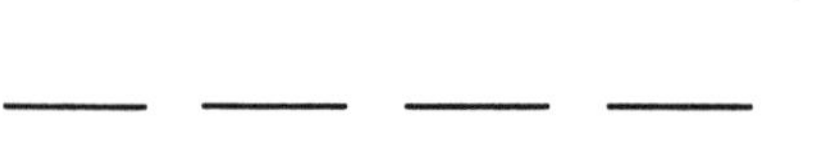

F B T Z

Finish the code by writing the letter that comes before the letter shown.

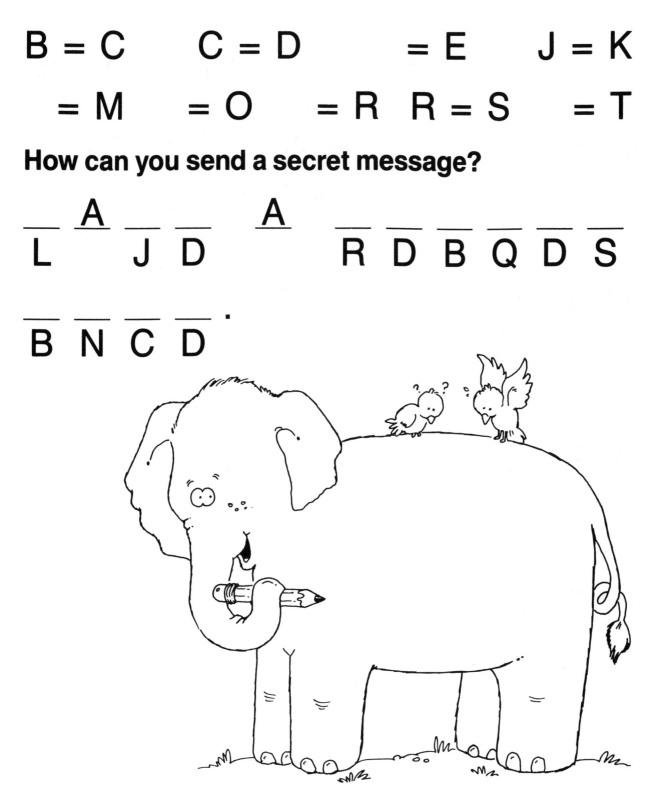

B = C   C = D   __ = E   J = K

__ = M   __ = O   __ = R   R = S   __ = T

How can you send a secret message?

__	A	__	__		A		__	__	__	__	__	__
L		J	D				R	D	B	Q	D	S

__	__	__	__	.
B	N	C	D	

This is the "Game" code. Match the letters with their game symbols.

= C = E = I = M

= N = O = P = R

= S = T

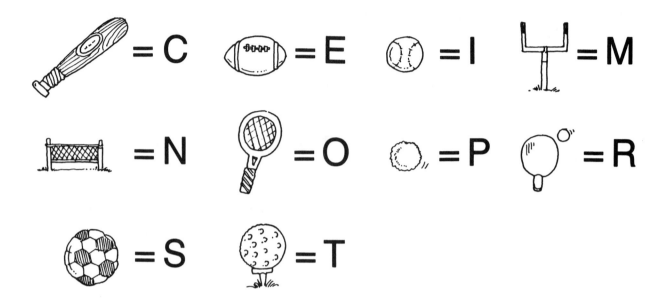

How can your team win?

___ ___ ___ ___ ___ ___ .

This is the "Letter After" code.

D = E   E = F   K = L   N = O

Q = R   R = S   S = T

What comes in the mail?

___ ___ ___ ___   ___ ___

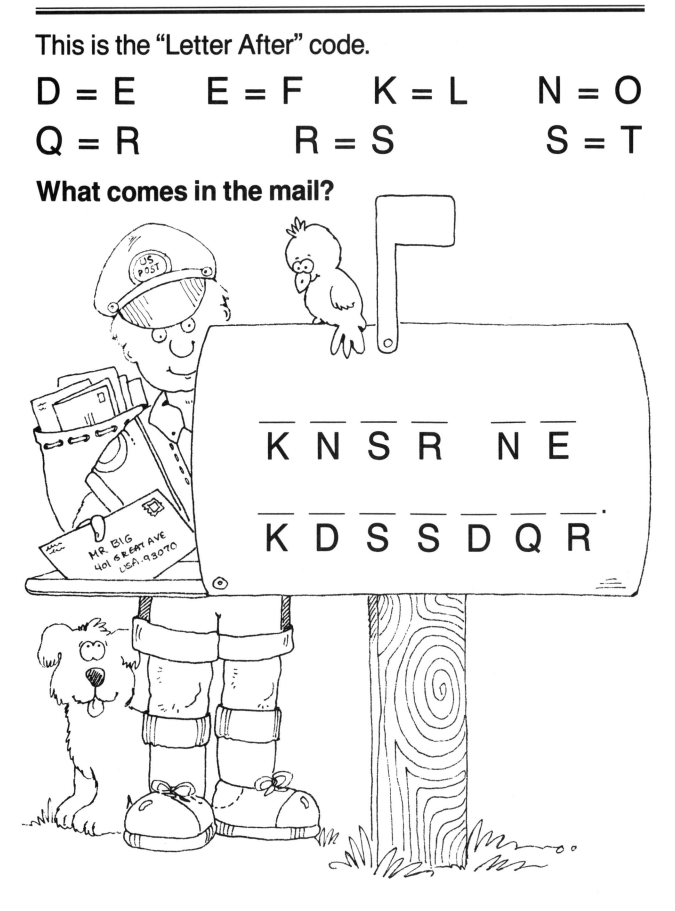

K N S R   N E

___ ___ ___ ___ ___ ___ ___.

K D S S D Q R

This is the "Funny Animal" code.

A =  E =  H =

O =  T =  Z =

Where should you use this code?

___ ___   ___ ___ ___   ___ ___ ___ .

Finish making the "Letter Before" code by writing the ABCs in order in the boxes.

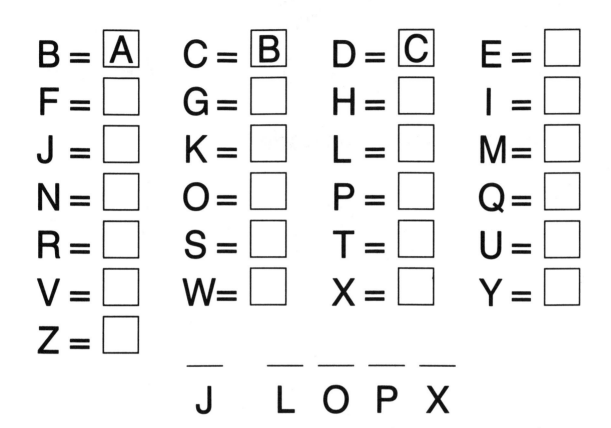

B = A	C = B	D = C	E = ☐
F = ☐	G = ☐	H = ☐	I = ☐
J = ☐	K = ☐	L = ☐	M = ☐
N = ☐	O = ☐	P = ☐	Q = ☐
R = ☐	S = ☐	T = ☐	U = ☐
V = ☐	W = ☐	X = ☐	Y = ☐
Z = ☐			

__ __ __ __ __

J L O P X

__ __ __ __ __ __ __.

U I F B C D T

1. Use the code from page 395 to write a message to your friend.
2. See if your friend can read the message.

Find the letter that is missing from each group of words. Fill in the letters to solve the riddle at the bottom of the page. The first one is done for you.

Find the letter that is missing from each group of words. Fill in the letters to solve the riddle at the bottom of the page.

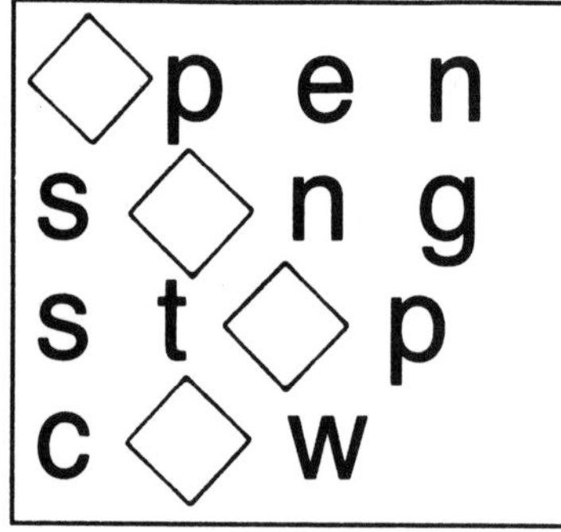

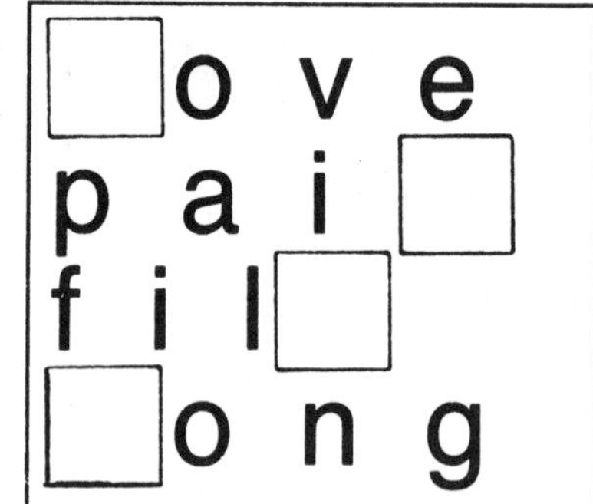

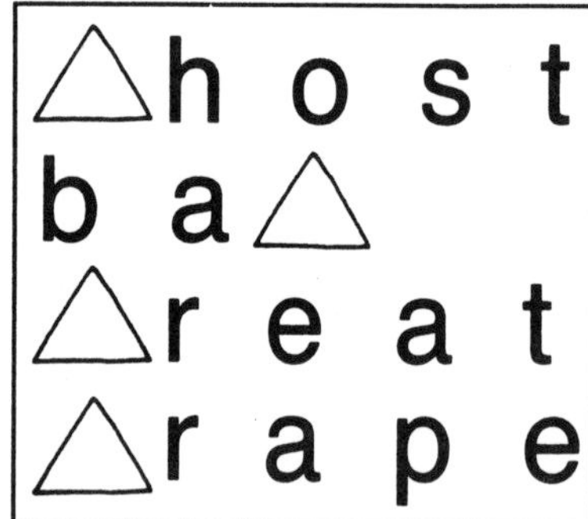

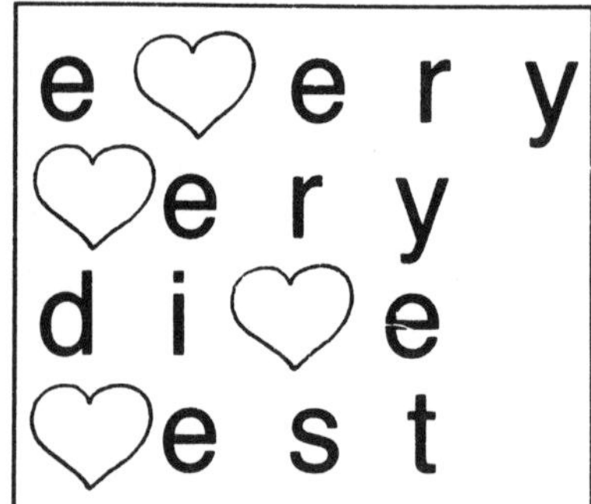

What has fingers but can't use them?

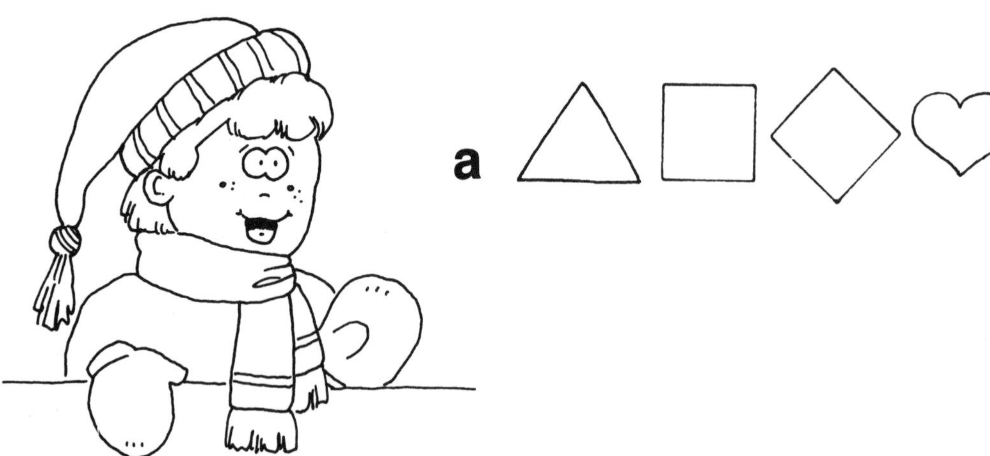

Find the letter that is missing from each group of words. Fill in the letters to solve the riddle at the bottom of the page.

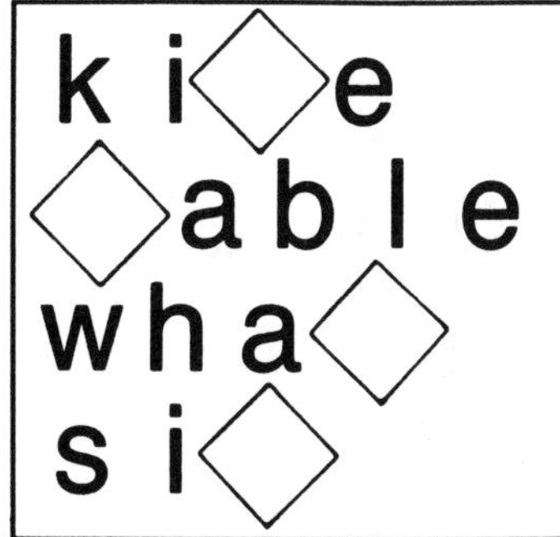

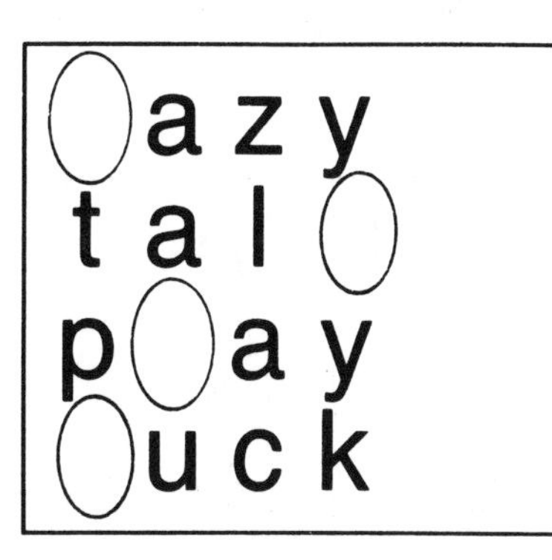

What gets wet when it's drying?

a 

1. Start at the bottom.
2. Climb the ladder by changing one letter on each rung. Use the letters from the box.

i p d

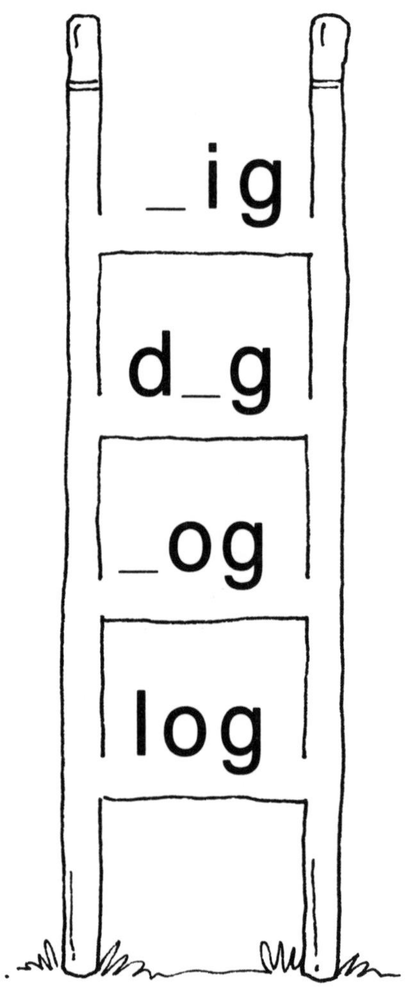

Use the letters from the box to help you make new words as you climb the ladder.

n c o

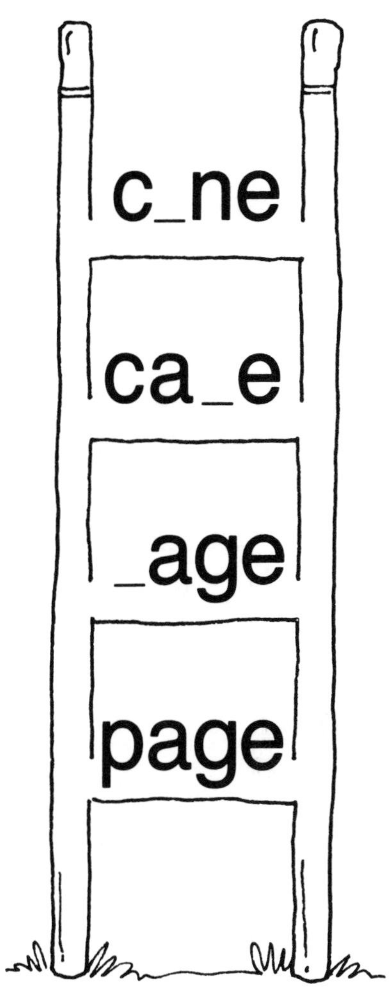

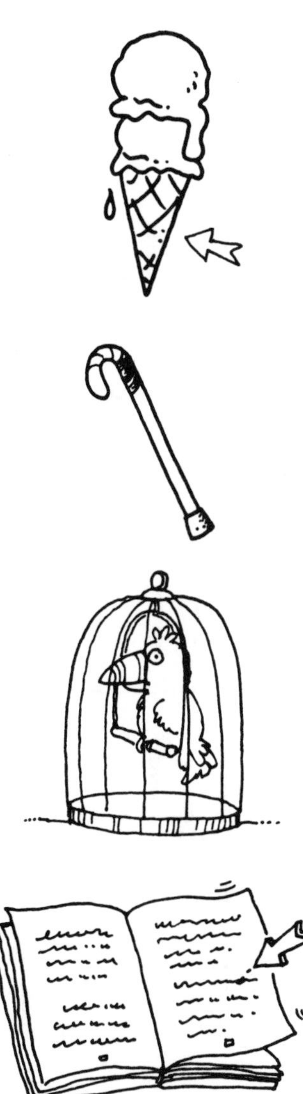

Use the letters from the box to help you make new words as you climb the ladder.

p s c

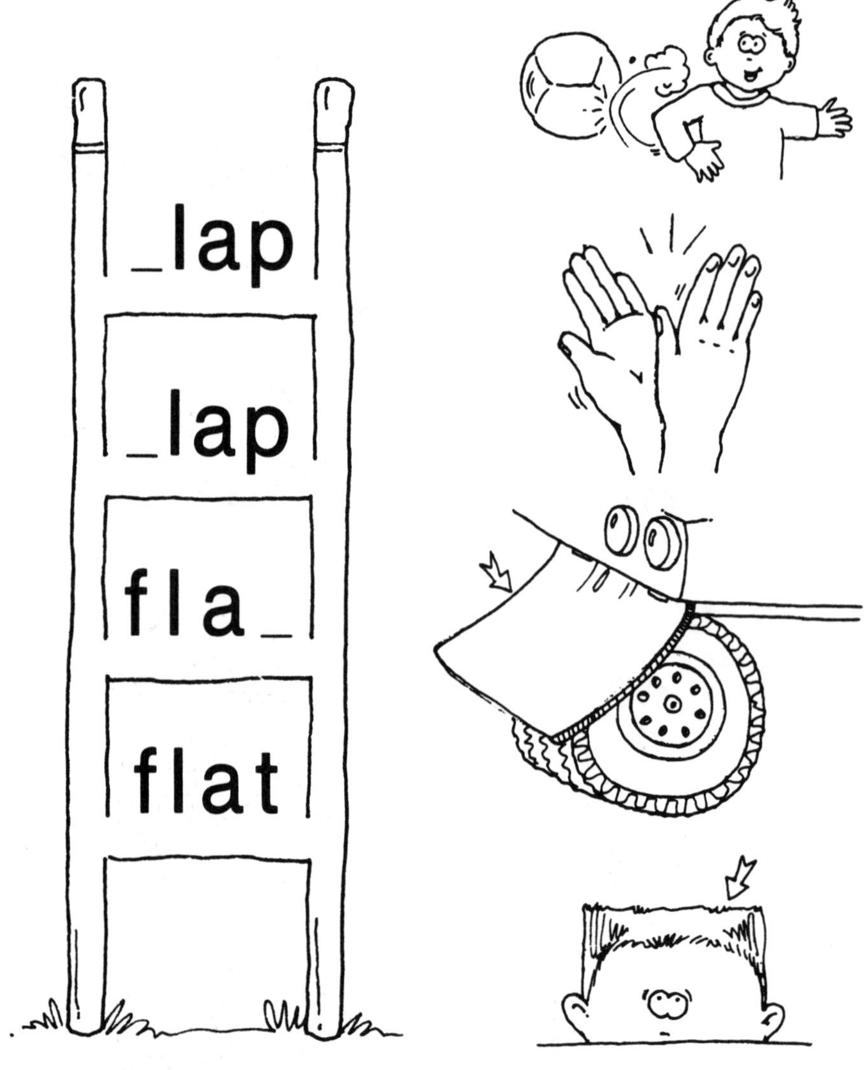

Use the letters from the box to help you make new words as you climb the ladder.

s g m

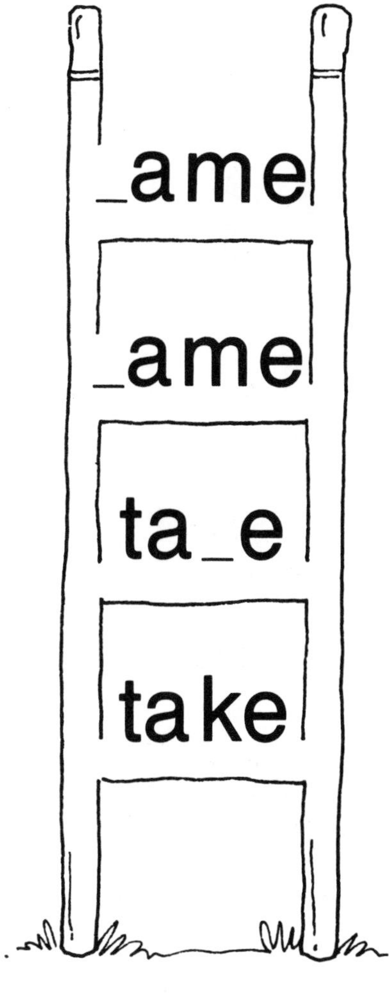

1. Change the vowel to make a new word.
2. You may use any vowel that makes a word:
   a, e, i, o, and **u** are vowels you may use.

1. wit w _ t

2. had h _ d

3. bat b _ t

4. sit s _ t or s _ t

A Silly Square has words that can be read down or across.

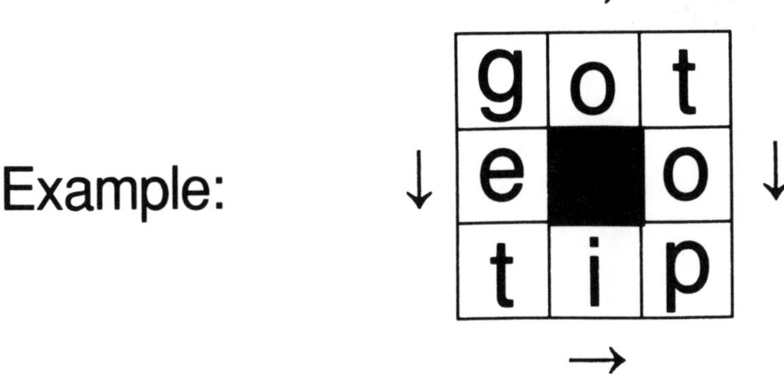

Use a vowel to make a new Silly Square.

The vowels are **a, e, i, o, u,** and sometimes **y.**

1. Write the vowels _, _, _, _, _, and sometimes y.
2. Use the vowels to make a Silly Square.

p		g
	■	
t		g

1. Consonants are all the letters that are not vowels. Cross out the vowels below and you will have the consonants.

a b c d e f g h i j
k l m n o p q r s t
u v w x y z

2. Make a Silly Square. Write a consonant in each blank square.

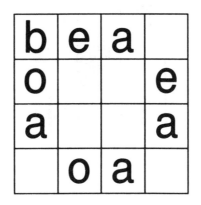

b	e	a	
o			e
a			a
	o	a	

1. Write the missing consonants: b c _ f _ _ j k
   _ _ n p _ r s _ v w _ y _ .
2. Use some of the consonants to finish the Silly Square.

	o	a	
e			i
a			e
	e	e	

Try this Silly Square with only two pictures to help you.

	o	a	
r			o
i			o
	a	i	

1. Make a Silly Square of your own.
2. Draw some pictures to go with your square.

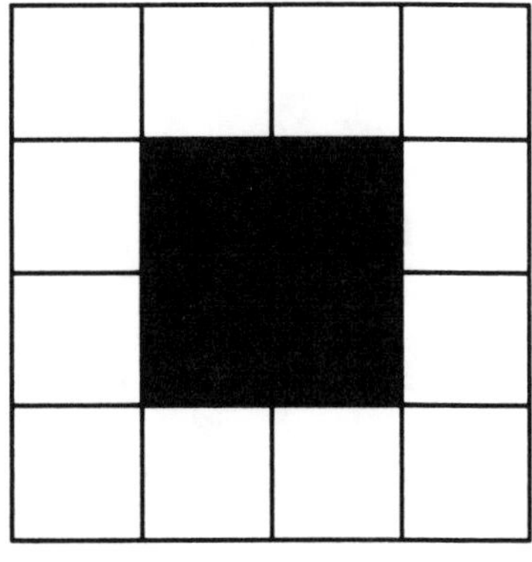

Palindromes are words that are the same when you read them left to right or right to left.

Here are some palindromes:

gag

pop

Fill in the missing letters to make more palindromes.

Try each vowel **(a, e, i, o,** or **u)** until you make a word.

b _ b   d _ d   m _ m

These palindromes need 2 letters. Try vowel pairs **(aa, ee, ii, oo,** or **uu)** to complete these words.

p _ _ p   t _ _ t   n _ _ n

Many names are palindromes.

Try to write these palindrome names.

N _ _ B _ _ E _ _

These people are standing in alphabetical order.

Copy their names on the lines.

________ ________ ________

Here are some longer palindromes. The middle letter will be different when a palindrome has 5 letters.

Example: RADAR

1. Draw a red circle around each R.
2. Draw a blue circle around each A.

Can you use the same pattern to make these palindromes?

k a _ _ _

m a _ _ _

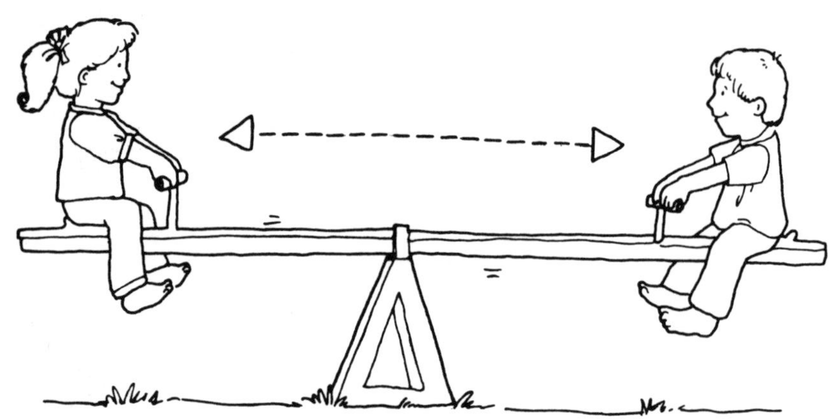

l e _ _ _

Some words spell new words when written backwards.

Example: **pin** backwards spells **nip**

1. Write these words backwards.
2. Draw a line from your new word to its picture.

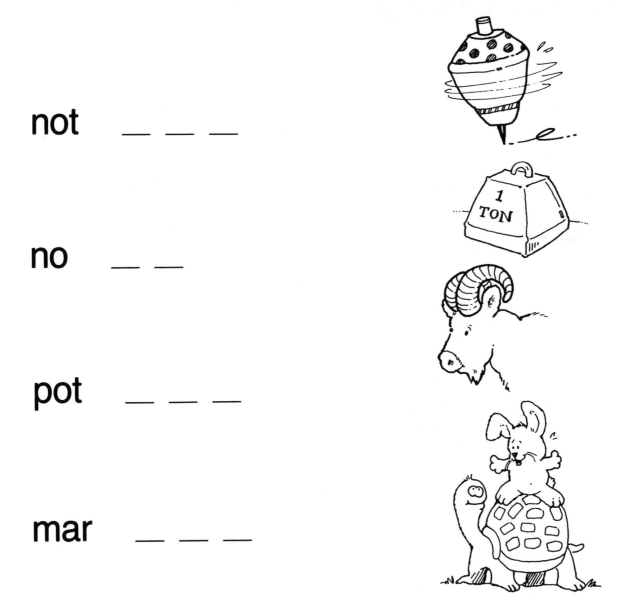

not __ __ __

no __ __

pot __ __ __

mar __ __ __

Anagrams are words whose letters are mixed up.
Unscramble these letters to make words.
Draw a line from your new word to its picture.

atb __ __ __

yob __ __ __

ogd __ __ __

ogl __ __ __

atr __ __ __

Unscramble these anagrams to make words. Use the letters to solve the riddle at the bottom of the page.

geg = △ g g ___

rgil = ___ ___ ___ ◇

nkig = ___ ○ ___ ___

clema = □ ___ ___ ___ ___

What did the penguin ride to work?

an

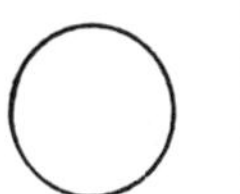

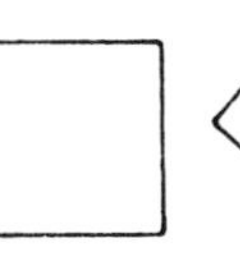

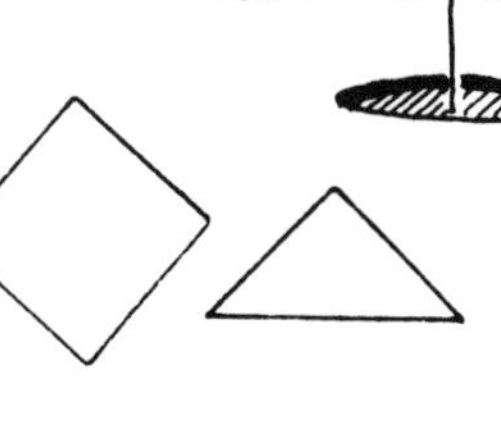

Unscramble these anagrams to make words. Use the letters to solve the riddle at the bottom of the page.

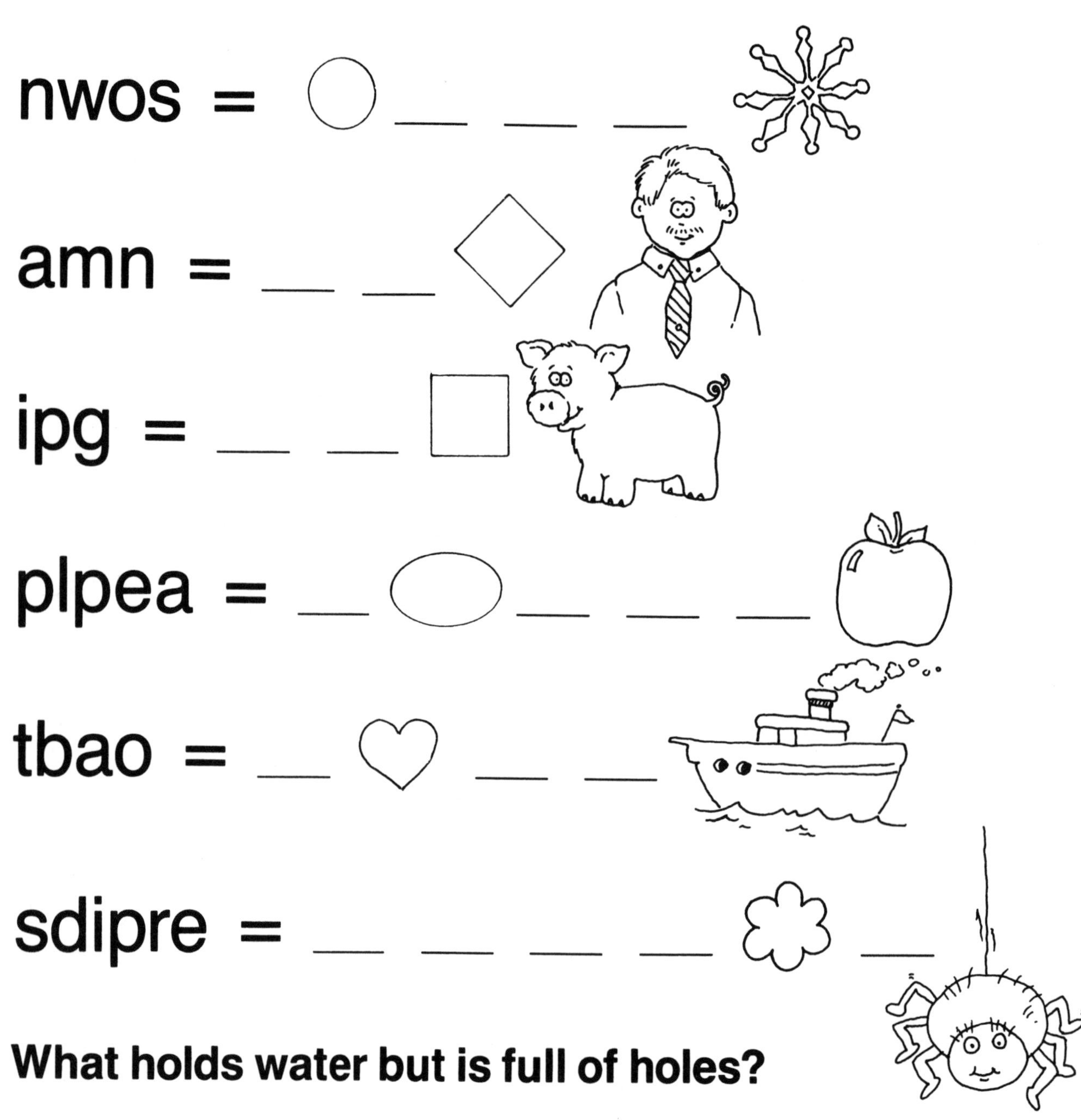

What holds water but is full of holes?

a

Unscramble these anagrams to make words. Use the letters to solve the riddle at the bottom of the page.

eirf = ___ ___ ___ ___

anir = ___ ___ ___ ___

dnha = ___ ___ ___ ___

aktbse = ___ ___ ___ ___ ___ ___

gthin = ___ ___ ___ ___ ___

lcuod = ___ ___ ___ ___ ___

What goes up but never moves?

a

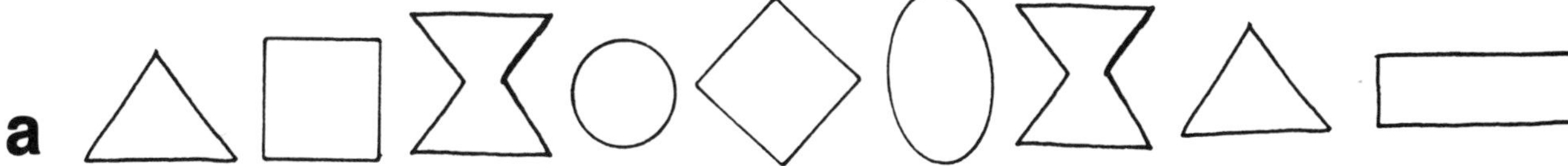

Move the letters in the underlined word around to make a new word.

Make **taco** into something you wear. __ __ __ __

Make **slid** into something to cover jars. __ __ __ __

Change **mean** into what we call someone. __ __ __ __

Make **near** into a way to get money. __ __ __ __

1. Read the clues.
2. Write the answers for the across clues going across → like GO.
3. Write the answers for the down clues ↓ like B
E.
4. Let the pictures help you.

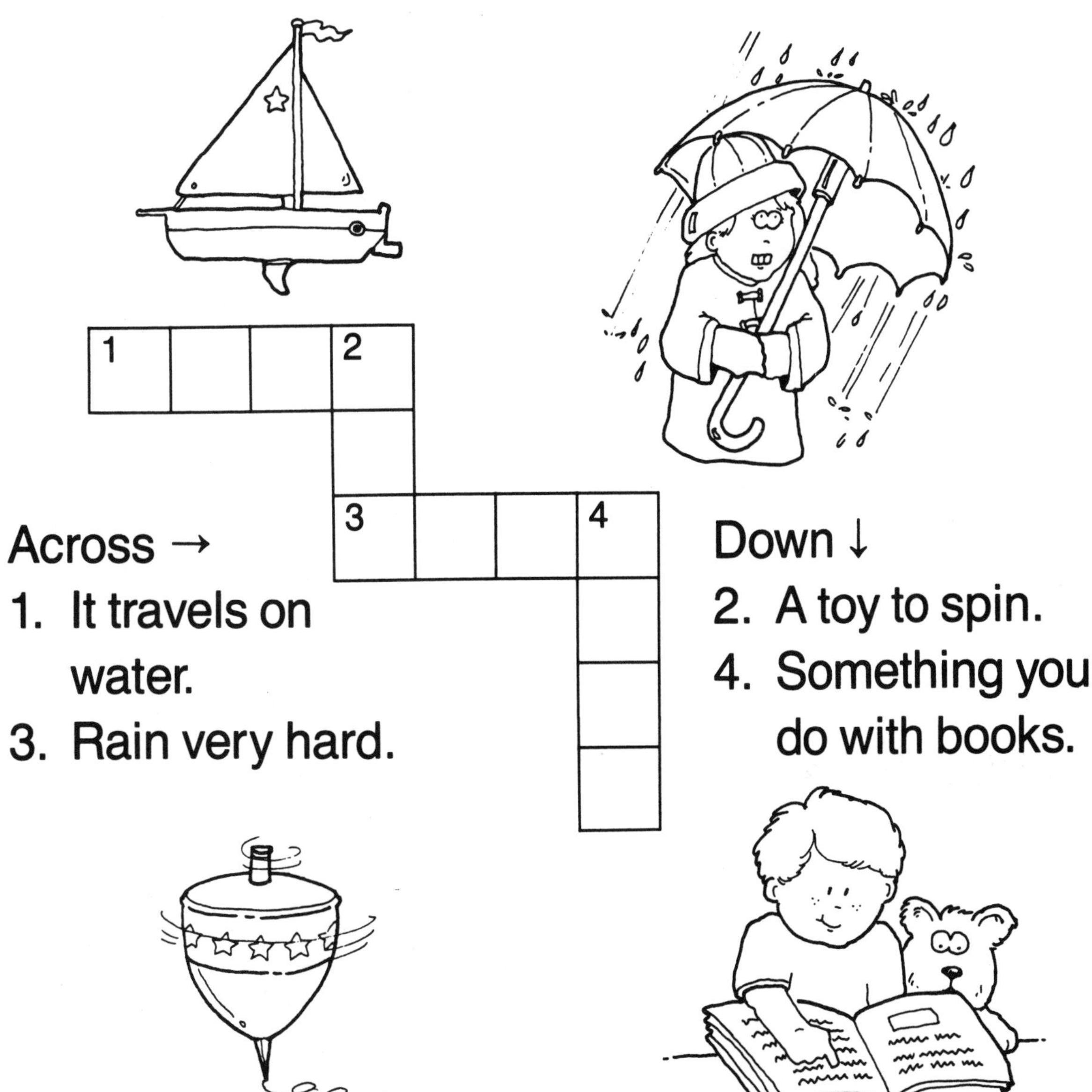

Across →

1. It travels on water.
3. Rain very hard.

Down ↓

2. A toy to spin.
4. Something you do with books.

1. Read the clues.
2. Write the answers.

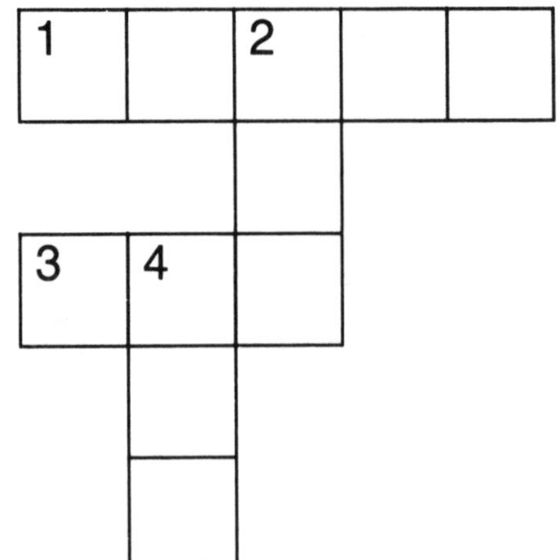

Across →
1. A place to sit and eat.
3. You do it to food.

Down ↓
2. A Halloween animal.
4. A large jungle animal.

1. Read the clues.
2. Write the answers.

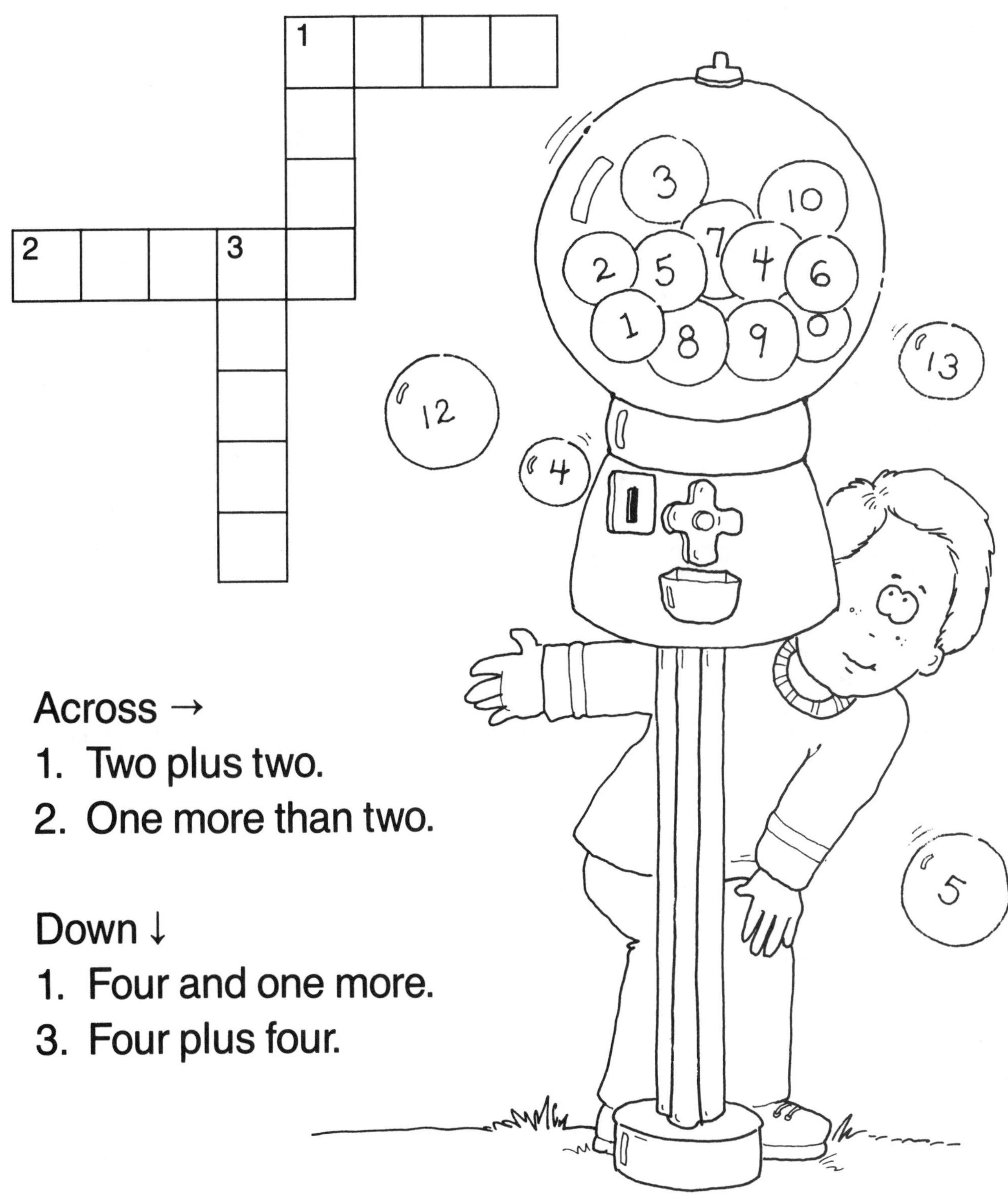

Across →

1. Two plus two.
2. One more than two.

Down ↓

1. Four and one more.
3. Four plus four.

Opposites are words that mean very different things.

Write the opposites. Fill in the letters to solve the riddle at the bottom of the page.

Up and **down** are opposites. **Sit** and **stand** are opposites.

The opposite of **go** is ___ ◇ ___ □

The opposite of **big** is ___ ___ ___ ___ ___ ○

The opposite of **near** is ___ ___ △

The opposite of **play** is ___ ___ ___ ✿

The opposite of **night** is ___ ___ ▭

The opposite of **take** is ___ ☁ ___ ___

What do you call a cat who just washed her hair?

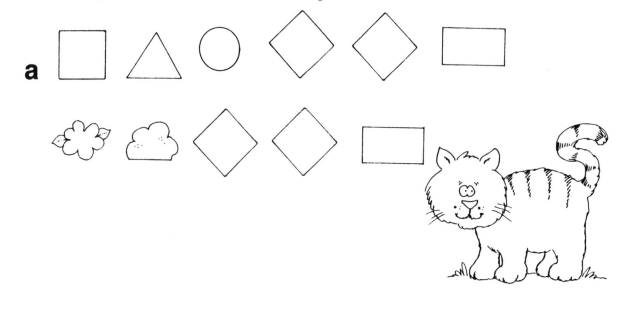

a □ △ ○ ◇ ◇ ▭

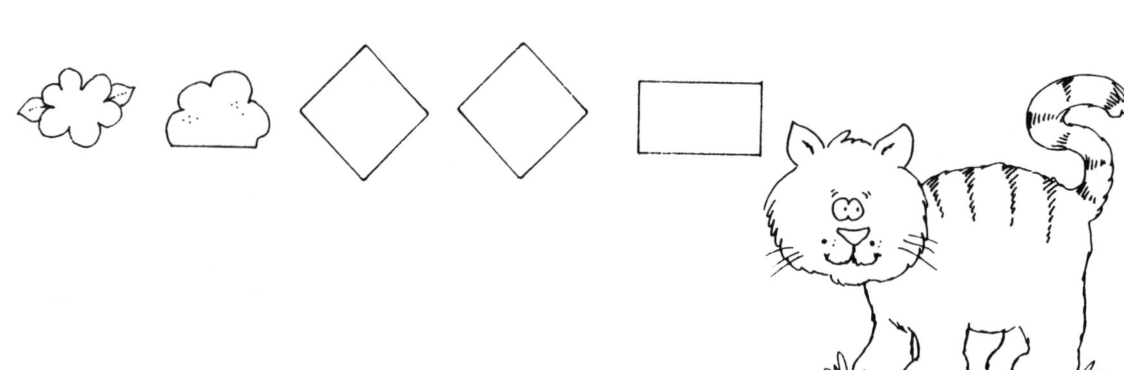

Finish each line with a word that rhymes with the underlined word.

The little **cat** had on a ___ ___ ___.

There was a **tear** in the baby ___ ___ ___ ___.

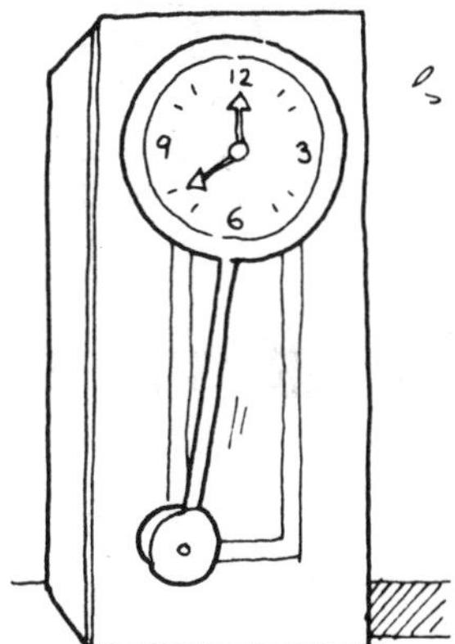

The huge **clock** said tick ___ ___ ___ ___.

She took the **car** out of the ___ ___ ___.

See how many words you can find in the grid below. Words may be formed by using any letter squares that touch each other horizontally, vertically, or diagonally. Each letter square may be used only once in each word.

R	E	P	E
E	D	I	T
H	A	R	Y
S	F	L	G

On the lines below, list the words you find.

Use the letters to fill in the blanks below. Use each letter only once. Read from top to bottom to find the hidden word.

w a o r i n b

Use the letters to fill in the blanks below. Use each letter only once. Read from top to bottom to find out where the animals live.

a e f h m n o r t

Use all the letters in the alphabet to complete the letter ladder. Use each letter only once.

a b c d e f g h i j k l m n o p q r s t u v w x y z

Use all the letters in the alphabet to complete the letter ladder. Use each letter only once.

What's wrong with this picture? Find the parts of the picture that **don't** make sense. Circle them.

Lots of things are wrong with this picture! Find the parts of the picture that **do** make sense. Circle them.

What's wrong with this picture? Find the parts of the picture that **don't** make sense. Circle them.

Hidden in this outer space scene are pictures of foods we eat and drink. Circle all the foods you can find. Write the number below.

How many foods did you find? ______

Hidden in the flower garden are pictures of things that people wear. Circle as many as you can find.

How many did you find? ______

Find 15 schoolroom items hidden in and around this "school" of fish.

On the lines below, write the name of each item you find.

What is in the bag? Draw a picture of your idea in the box below.

What is in the crate? Draw a picture of your idea in the box below.

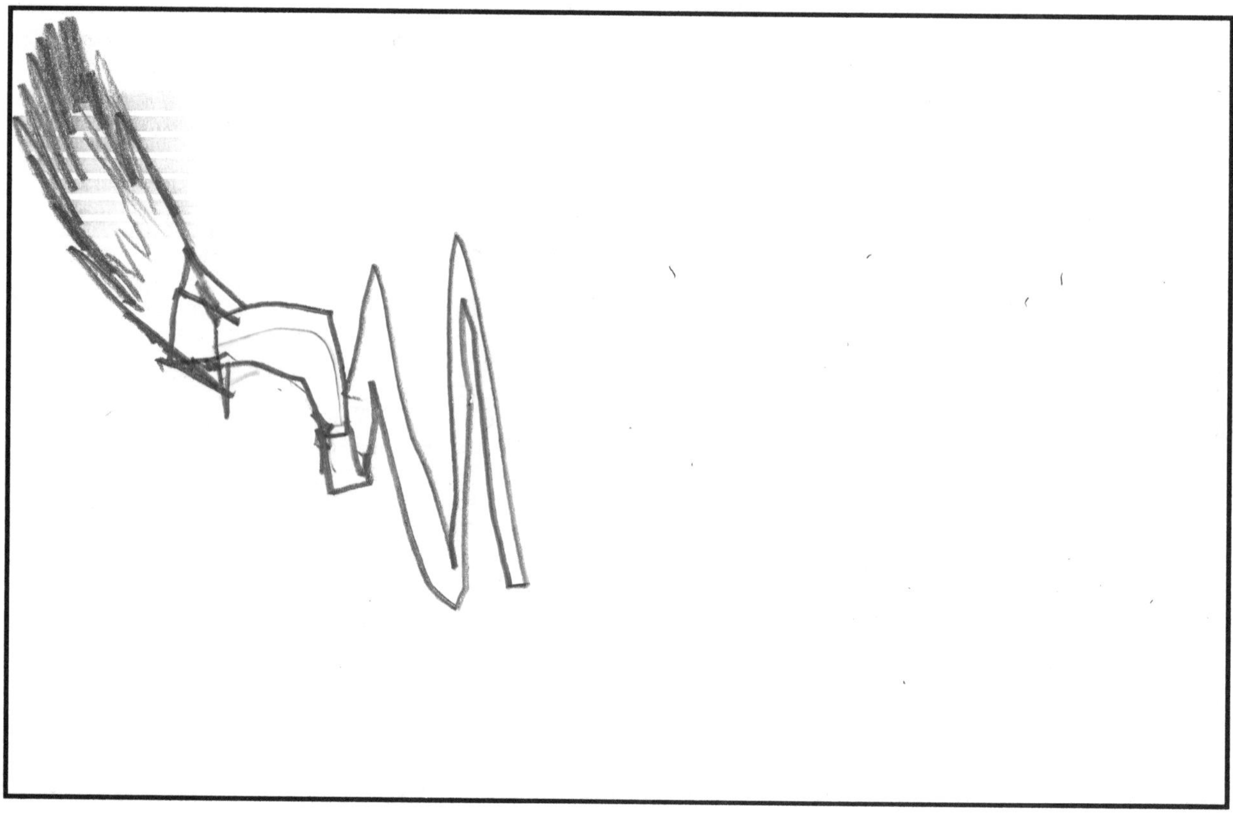

What is in the truck? Is the delivery for the fire station, the store, or the school? Draw a picture of your idea in the box below.

What is caught on the fisherman's line? Draw a picture of your idea in the box below.

Complete the picture by drawing the missing half of the monster.

Complete the picture by drawing the missing half of the troll.

Complete the picture by drawing the missing half of the fairy and then the frog.

On the lines below, write a story about a fairy, a monster, a troll, and a frog. Use additional paper if you need to.

Circle the answer that makes the **most** sense. The first one has been done for you.

Yellow is to banana as red is to	(apple)	pencil
Sour is to lemon as sweet is to	broccoli	candy
Fur is to bear as feather is to	bird	jacket
Hard is to rock as soft is to	ice cube	pillow
Moon is to night as sun is to	day	island
Pool is to swim as bed is to	sleep	read
Chair is to sit as bike is to	push	ride

Circle the answer that makes the **most** sense.

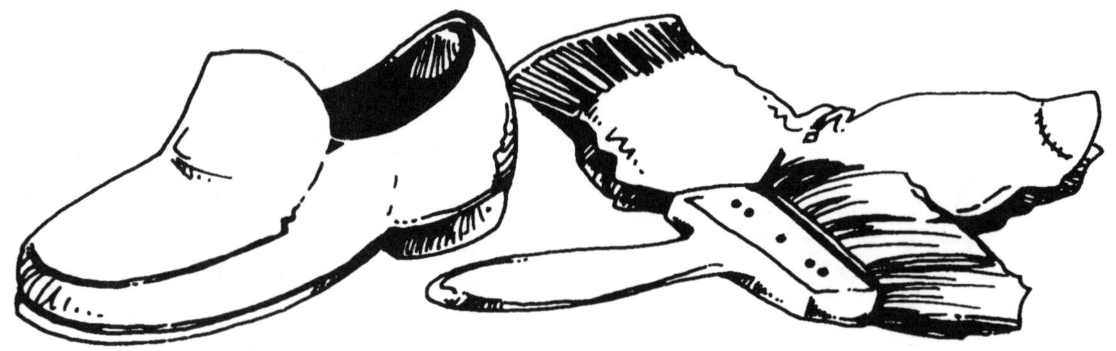

Foot is to shoe as hand is to	sock	glove
Fish is to swim as bird is to	fly	float
Kitten is to cat as puppy is to	bear	dog
Over is to under as high is to	up	low
Friday is to day as January is to	February	month
Pen is to ink as brush is to	paint	write
Eye is to see as ear is to	speak	hear

Circle the answer that makes the **most** sense.

Oak is to tree as poodle is to	pig	dog
String is to guitar as key is to	lock	piano
Bottom is to top as hot is to	water	cold
Pencil is to write as candle is to	burn	draw
Plane is to sky as car is to	road	drive
Kangaroo is to hop as snake is to	bounce	slither
Bark is to dog as quack is to	duck	bird

See how many words you can find in the grid below. Words may be formed by using any letter squares that touch each other horizontally, vertically, or diagonally. Each letter square may be used only once in each word.

T	S	I	P
A	D	O	L
Y	H	T	A
O	E	R	E

On the lines below, list the words you find. The first one has been done for you.

hop

See how many words you can find in the grid below. Words may be formed by using any letter squares that touch each other horizontally, vertically, or diagonally. Each letter square may be used only once in each word.

C	H	L	E
O	B	S	V
B	U	O	T
M	D	F	A

On the lines below, list the words you find.

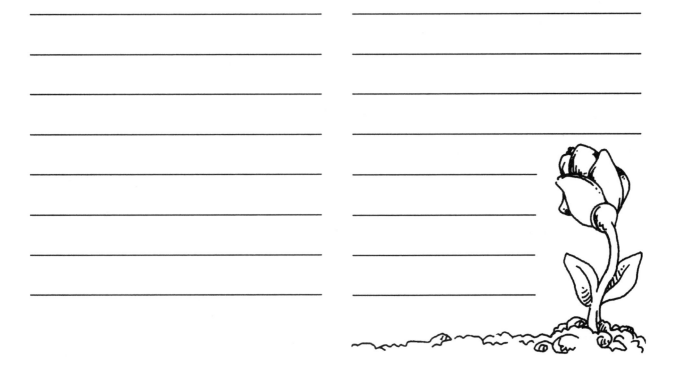

See how many words you can find in the grid below. Words may be formed by using any letter squares that touch each other horizontally, vertically, or diagonally. Each letter square may be used only once in each word.

B	L	L	Y
A	I	A	C
N	F	M	E
K	U	E	S

On the lines below, list the words you find.

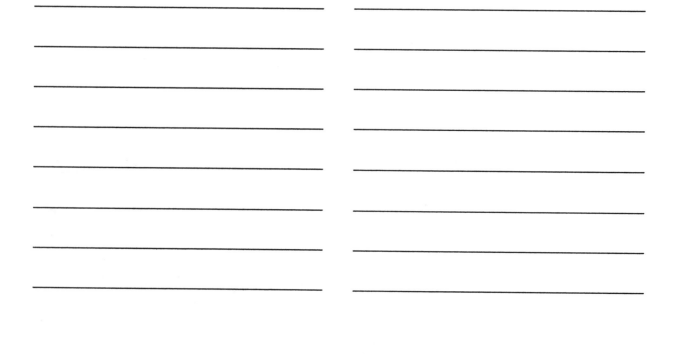

See how many words you can find in the grid below. Words may be formed by using any letter squares that touch each other horizontally, vertically, or diagonally. Each letter square may be used only once in each word.

L	B	I	R
O	G	C	L
I	A	E	K
L	T	X	N

On the lines below, list the words you find.

Use the squiggle line to draw a picture in the frame. Write a story to go with your picture on the lines below it. Use additional paper if you need to.

Use the squiggle line to draw a picture in the window. Write a story to go with your picture on the lines below it. Use additional paper if you need to.

Use the squiggle line to draw a picture in the frame. Write a story to go with your picture on the lines below it. Use additional paper if you need to.

Use the squiggle line to draw a map. Write a story to go with your map on the lines below it. Use additional paper if you need to.

Number the pictures in order so that they tell a story. Draw a picture of your own in the empty box to show what happens next.

___

___

___

4

Number the pictures in order so that they tell a story. Draw a picture of your own in the empty box to show what happens next.

___

___

___

4

Number the pictures in order so that they tell a story. Draw a picture of your own in the empty box to show what happens first.

Number the pictures in order so that they tell a story. Draw a picture of your own in the empty box to show what happens first.

These are bezzuzziks.

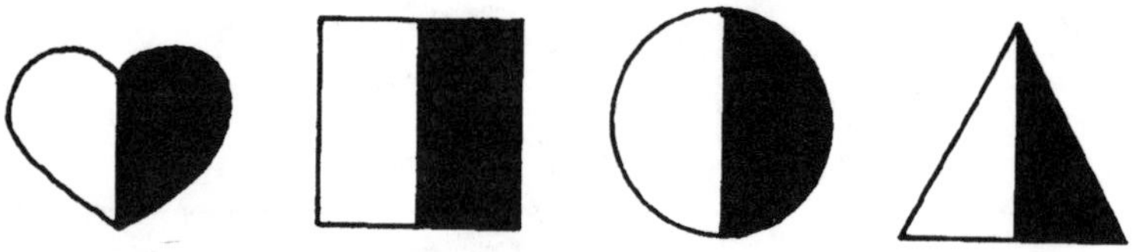

These are **not** bezzuzziks.

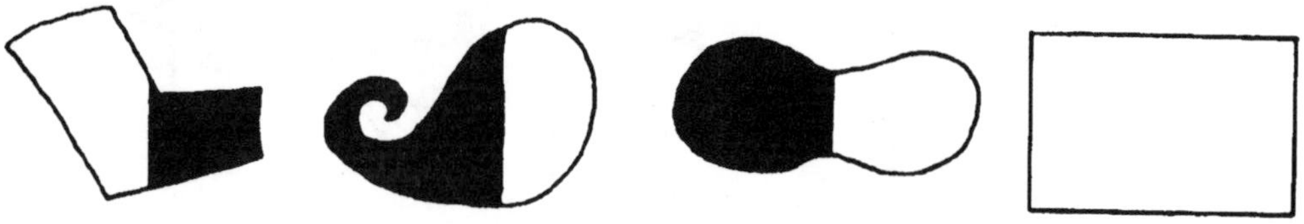

Circle the bezzuzziks in this row.

Draw three bezzuzziks of your own in the box below.

How can you recognize a bezzuzzik? Write your answer on the lines.

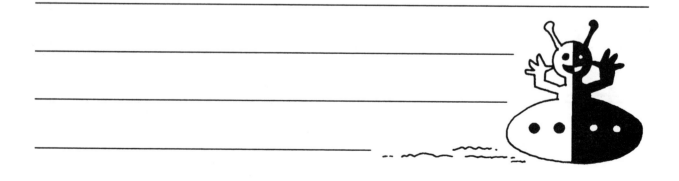

These are dodoloos.

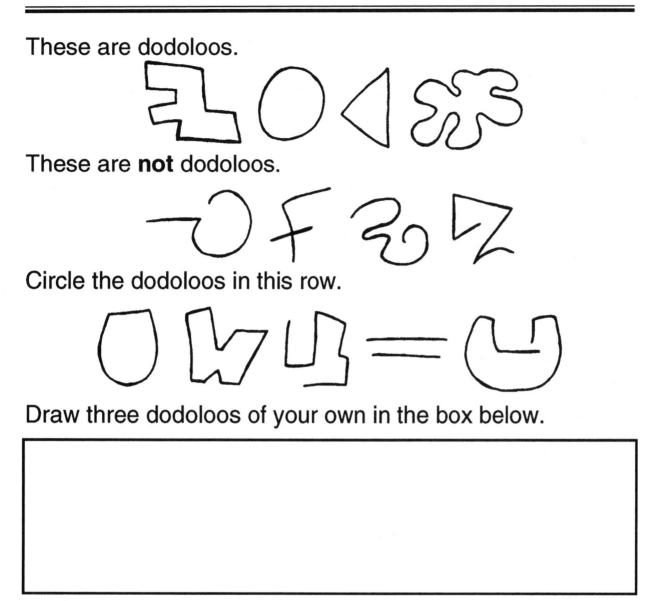

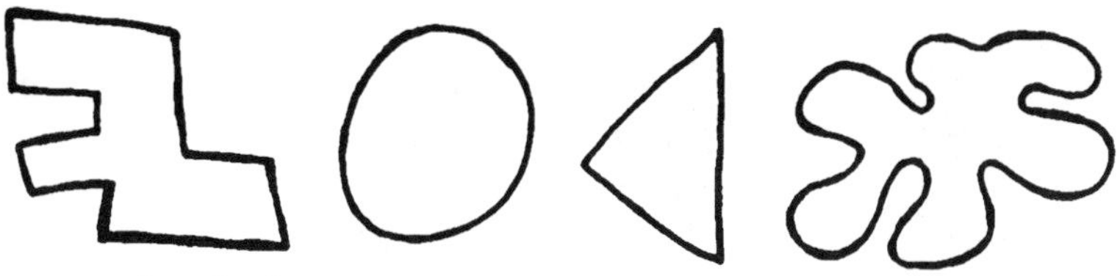

These are **not** dodoloos.

Circle the dodoloos in this row.

Draw three dodoloos of your own in the box below.

How can you recognize a dodoloo? Write your answer on the lines.

These are perkles.

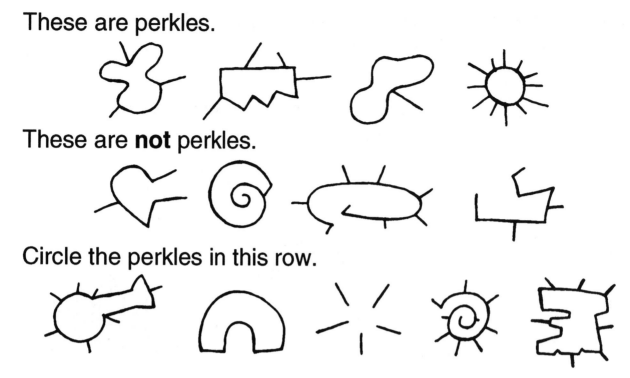

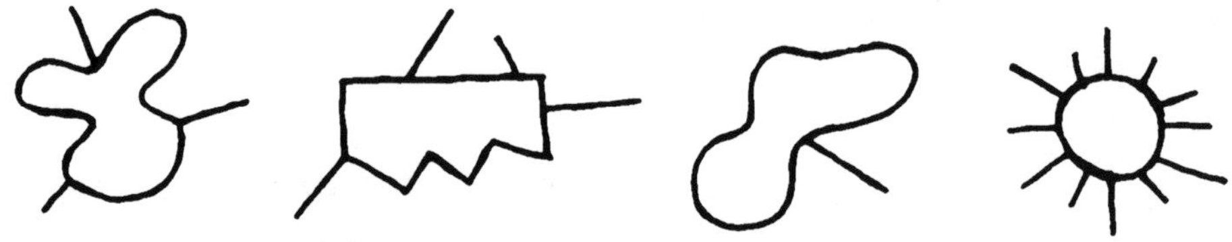

These are **not** perkles.

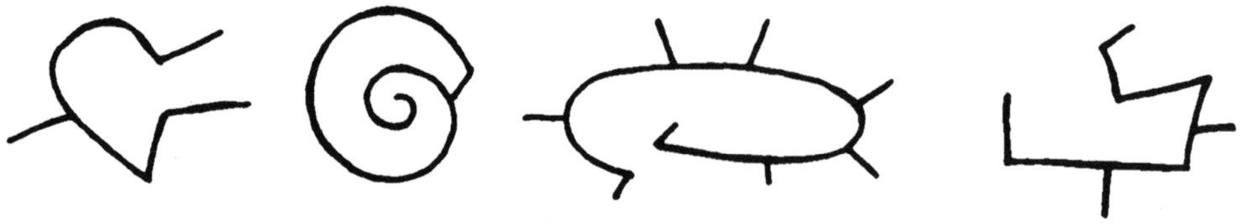

Circle the perkles in this row.

Draw three perkles of your own in the box below.

How can you recognize a perkle? Write your answer on the lines.

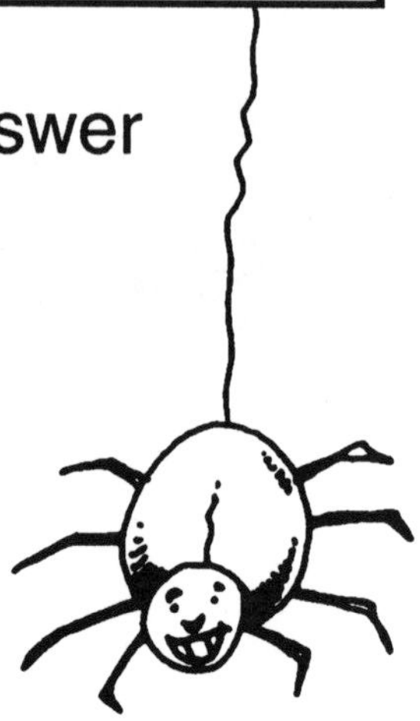

Use the clues to figure out which boy is which. Write each boy's name on the line nearest him.

Freddy only eats things that are shaped like circles.
Eddy only eats things that come in pairs.
Teddy likes sandwiches.

Use the clues to find out who lives in each apartment. Write your answers on the lines below.

Mrs. Pinky lives in Apartment 2.
Mr. Smith does not live next door to Mr. Jones.
Ms. Becker does not live in Apartment 4.
Mr. Jones lives next door to Mrs. Pinky.

Apartment 1: ____________________

Apartment 2: Mrs. Pinky

Apartment 3: ____________________

Apartment 4: ____________________

Maria, Kim, and Allison are sisters. Use the clues to find out which girl is which. Write their names on the lines below them.

Maria is not the shortest sister.
Allison is not the first in line.
Kim is shorter than Allison.

________________ ________________ ________________

What comes next in each pattern? Draw your answers on the lines.

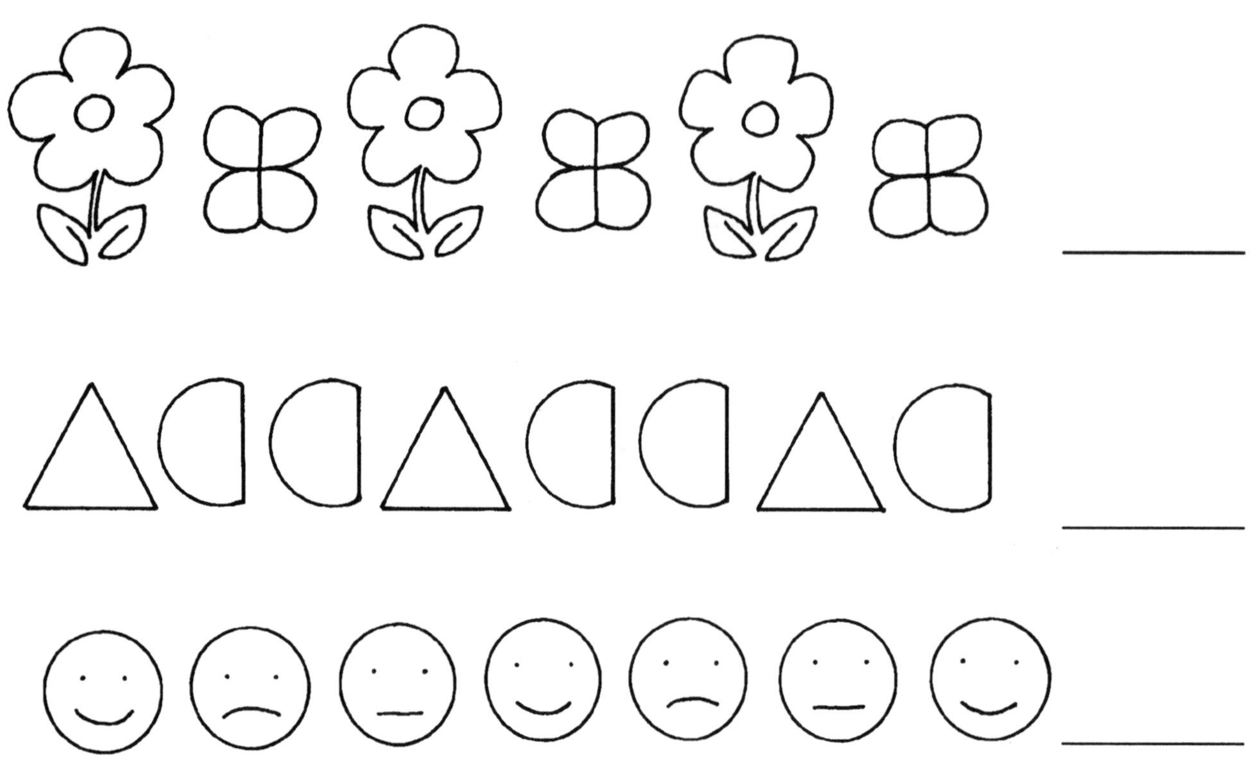

Continue each pattern. Draw your answers on the lines.

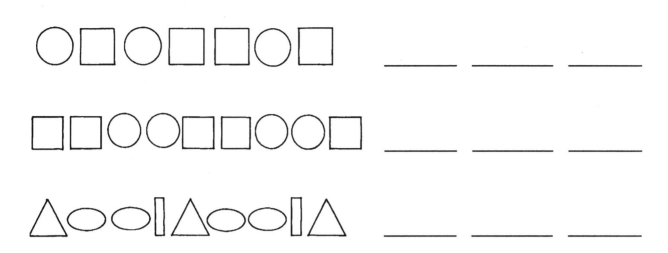

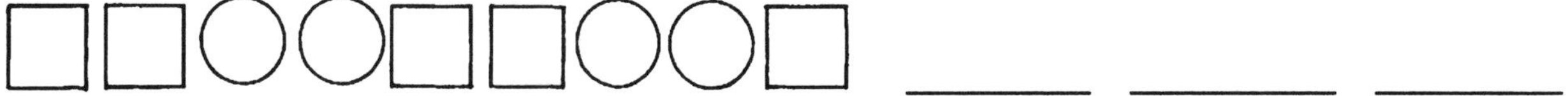

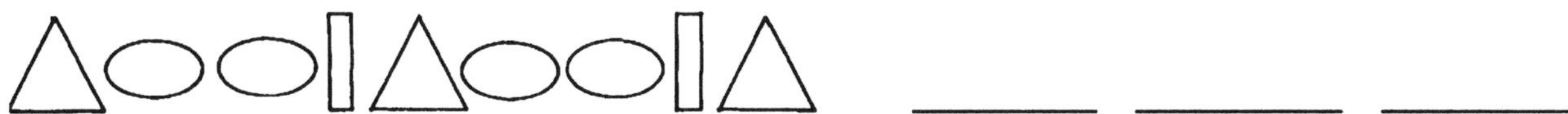

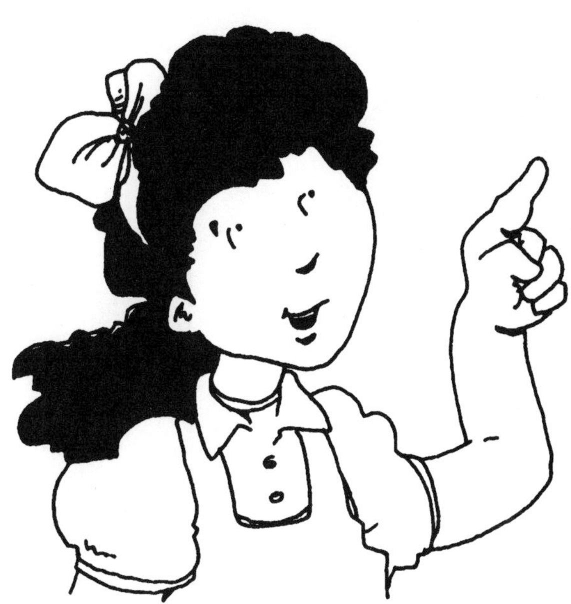

Continue each pattern. Draw your answers on the lines.

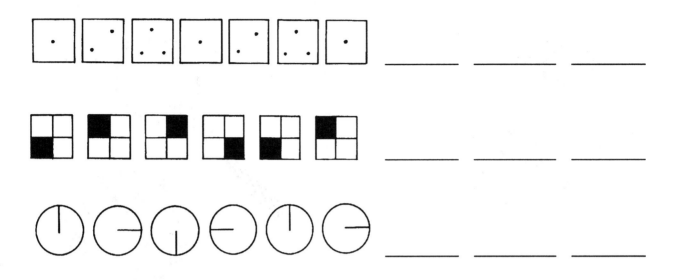

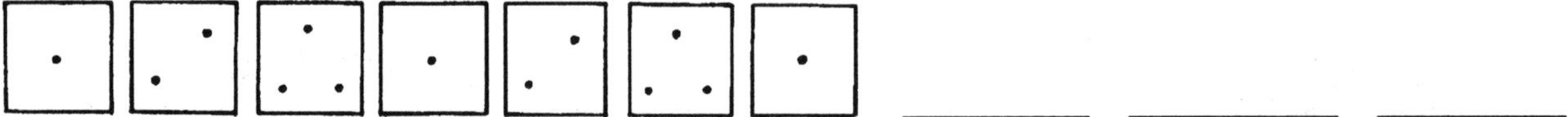

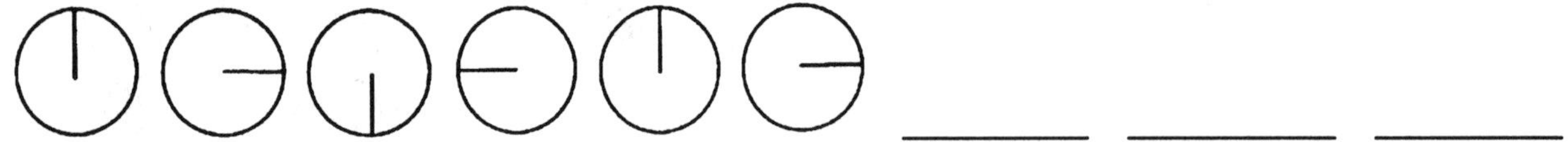

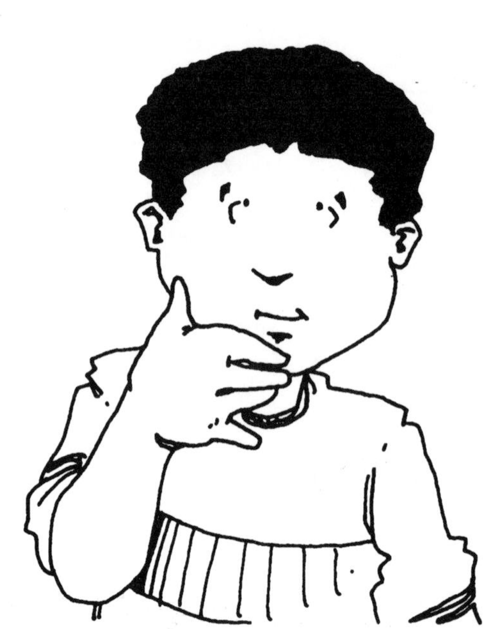

Draw some more items that belong in this group.

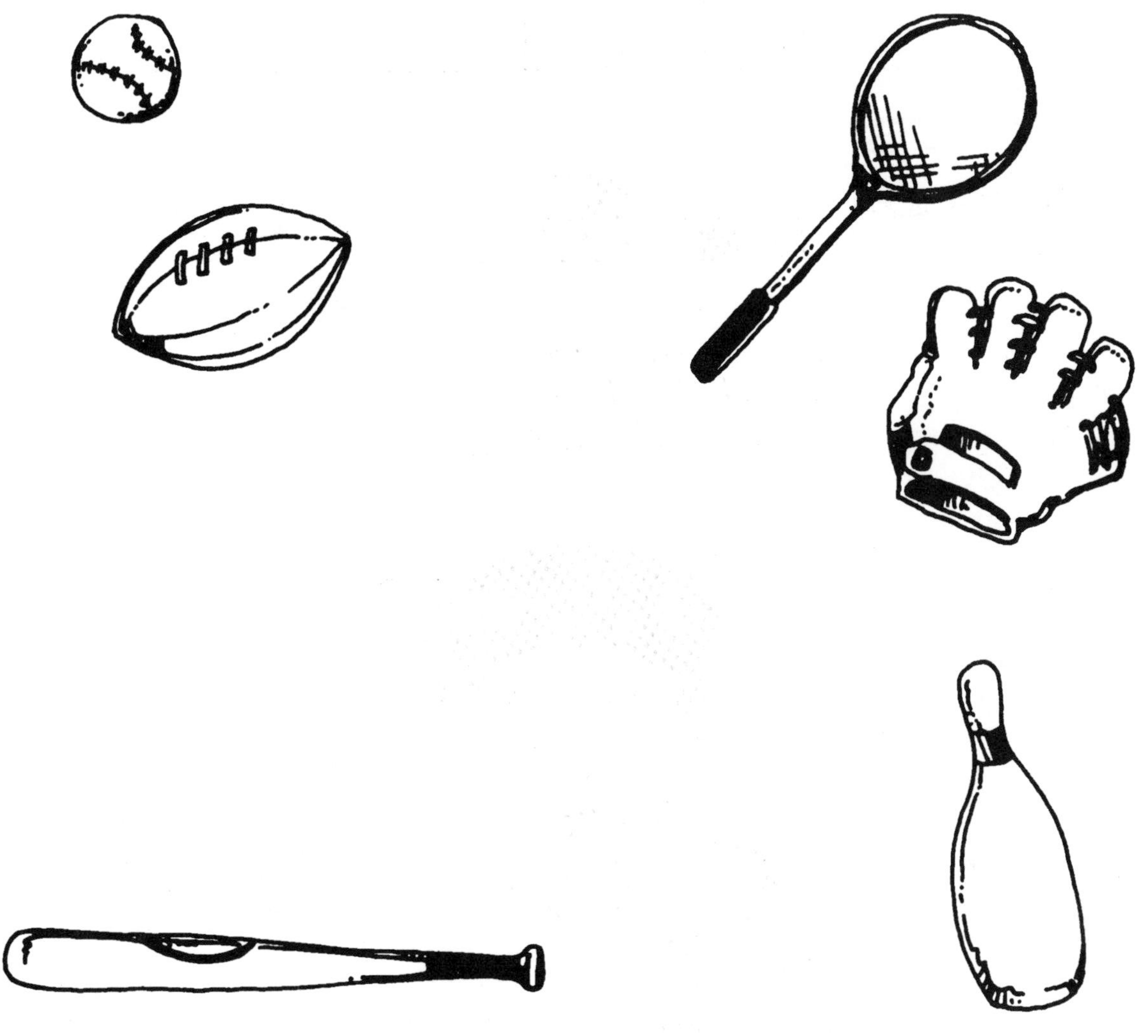

Why do these items belong together? Write your answer on the lines.

____

____

____

Draw some more items that belong in this group.

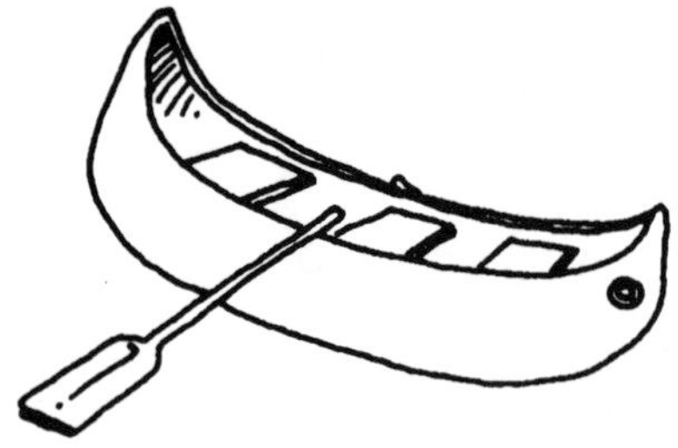

Why do these items belong together? Write your answer on the lines.

____

____

____

These are woozles.

These are **not** woozles.

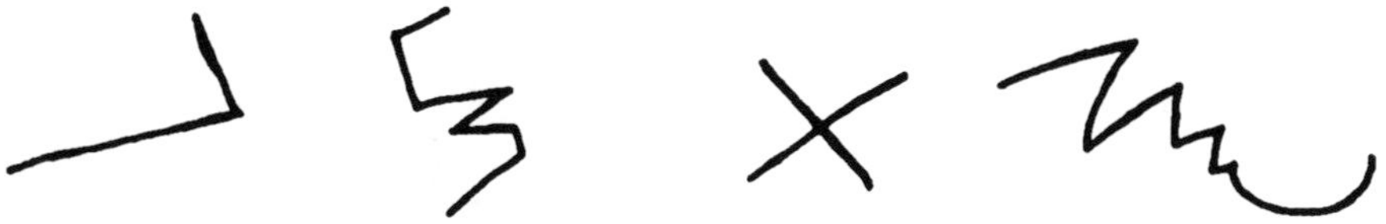

Circle the woozles in this row.

Draw three woozles of your own in the box below.

How can you recognize a woozle? Write your answer on the lines.

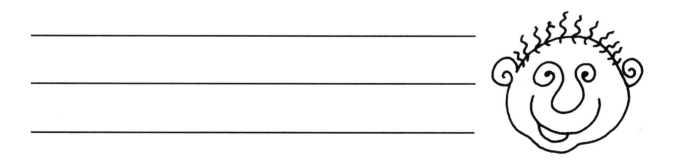

These are smileks.

These are **not** smileks.

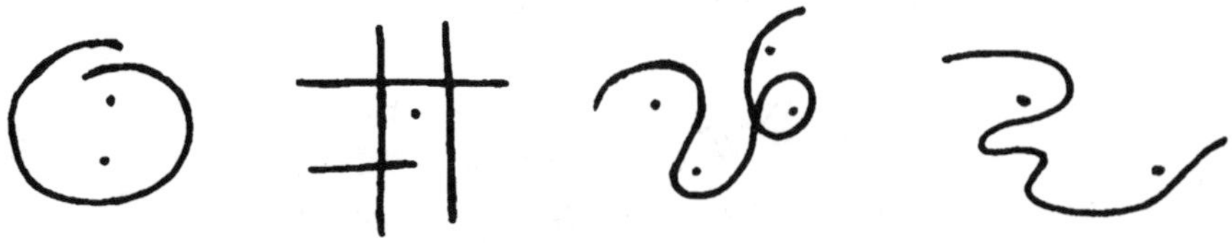

Circle the smileks in this row.

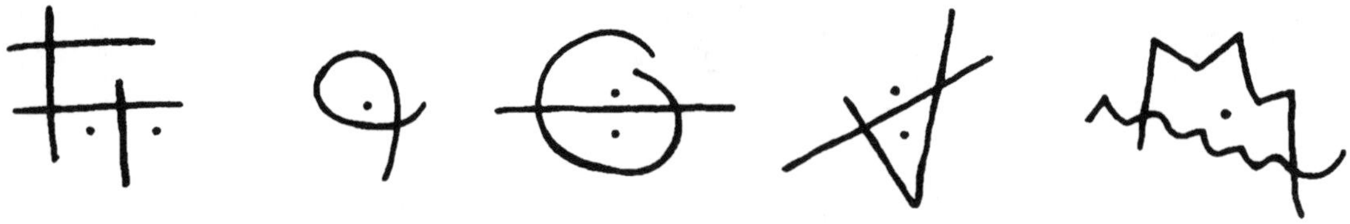

Draw three smileks of your own in the box below.

How can you recognize a smilek? Write your answer on the lines.

What comes next in each pattern? Circle the correct object.

In the space below, draw a pattern of your own. Ask a friend to circle the correct answer.

What comes next in each pattern? Fill in the blanks.

c f i l o r ___ ___

1 2 4 8 16 32 ___ ___ ___

28 26 24 22 20 ___ ___ ___

a z b y c x d ___ ___ ___

85 81 77 73 69 ___ ___ ___

What comes next in each pattern? Fill in the blanks.

3 6 9 12 15 ___ ___ ___

5 10 15 20 25 ___ ___ ___

z y x w v u ___ ___ ___

a 1 b 2 c 3 ___ ___ ___

6 12 18 24 30 ___ ___ ___

What comes next in each pattern? Circle the correct answer.

aa ab ac ad ae ag af

1 1 1 2 1 3 1 4 1 5 1 1 6

2 4 6 8 10 11 12

f h j l n q p

42 38 34 30 26 22 24

In the box below, draw a picture of something you could make using these items:

Write a sentence about your creation.

In the box below, draw a picture of something you could make using these items:

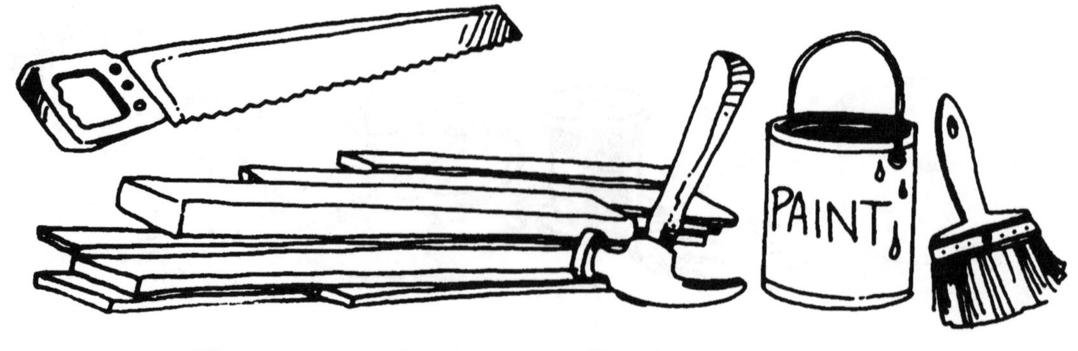

Write a sentence about your creation.

In the box below, draw a picture of something you could make using these items:

Write a sentence about your creation.

Draw some more items that belong in this group.

Why do these items belong together? Write your answer on the lines.

Draw some more items that belong in this group.

Why do these items belong together? Write your answer on the lines.

___

___

___

Draw some more items that belong in this group.

Why do these items belong together? Write your answer on the lines.

Look at the picture. On the lines below, write what the child is thinking.

Look at the picture. On the lines below, write what each character is thinking.

Painter: ______________________________

____

Lady: ______________________________

____

Dog: ______________________________

____

Look at the picture. On the lines below, write what each child is thinking.

Boy: ____

____

____

Girl: ____

____

____

Be a chef. Create a recipe using these ingredients:

orange juice
peanut butter
flour
onion
hot dogs

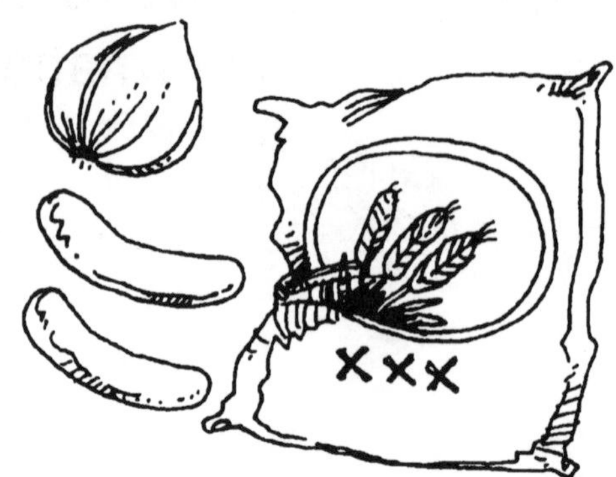

Draw a picture of your creation in the box. On the lines below, describe how you made it.

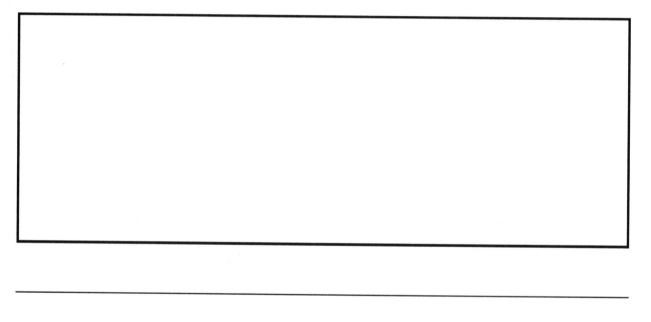

Create a make-believe creature using parts of the animals below. Draw your creature in the box. On the lines below, write some information about your creature. Give it a name.

Be an inventor. Create a contraption using the items below. Draw a picture of your contraption in the box. On the lines below, give it a name and describe what it is used for.

Look at the group of words listed below. Why do they belong together? Try to add more words to the list.

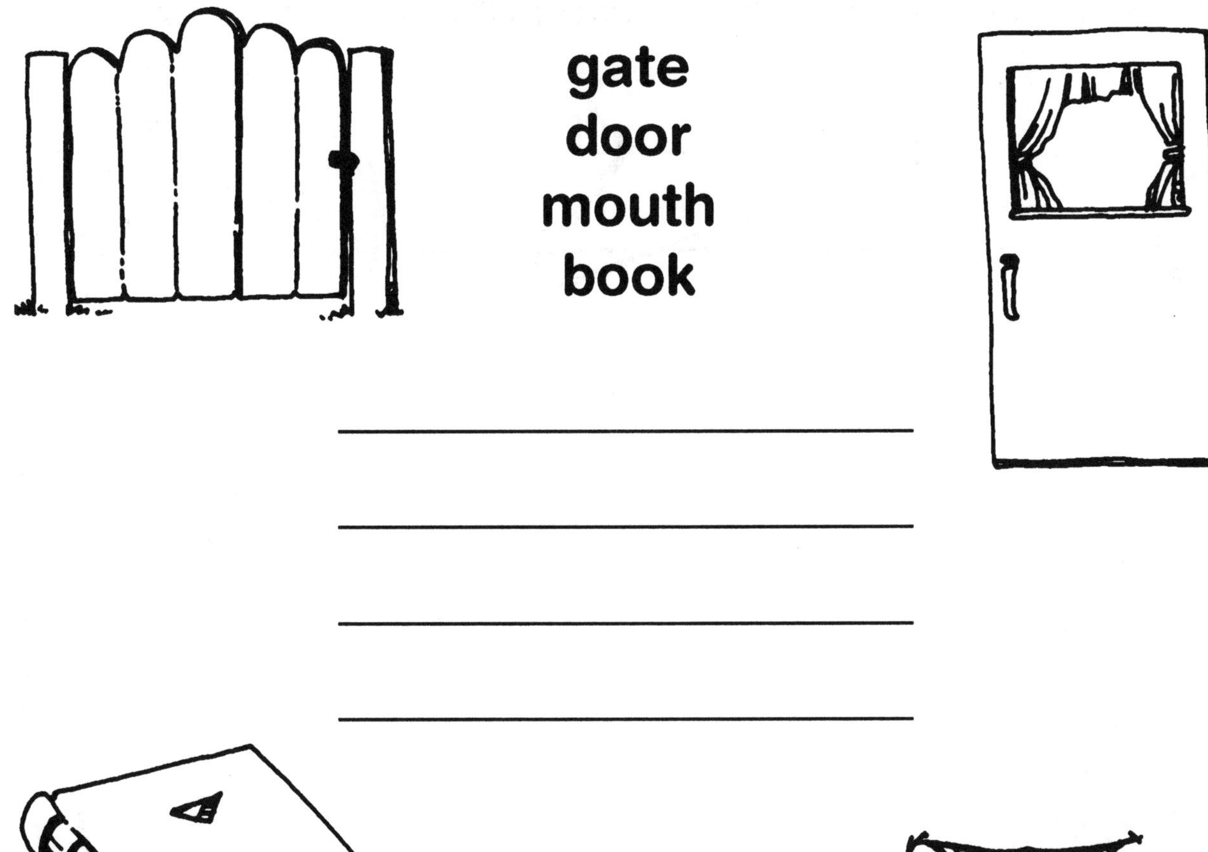

gate
door
mouth
book

____

____

____

____

Write a sentence explaining how all of these words relate to each other.

____

____

____

Look at the group of words listed below. Why do they belong together? Try to add more words to the list.

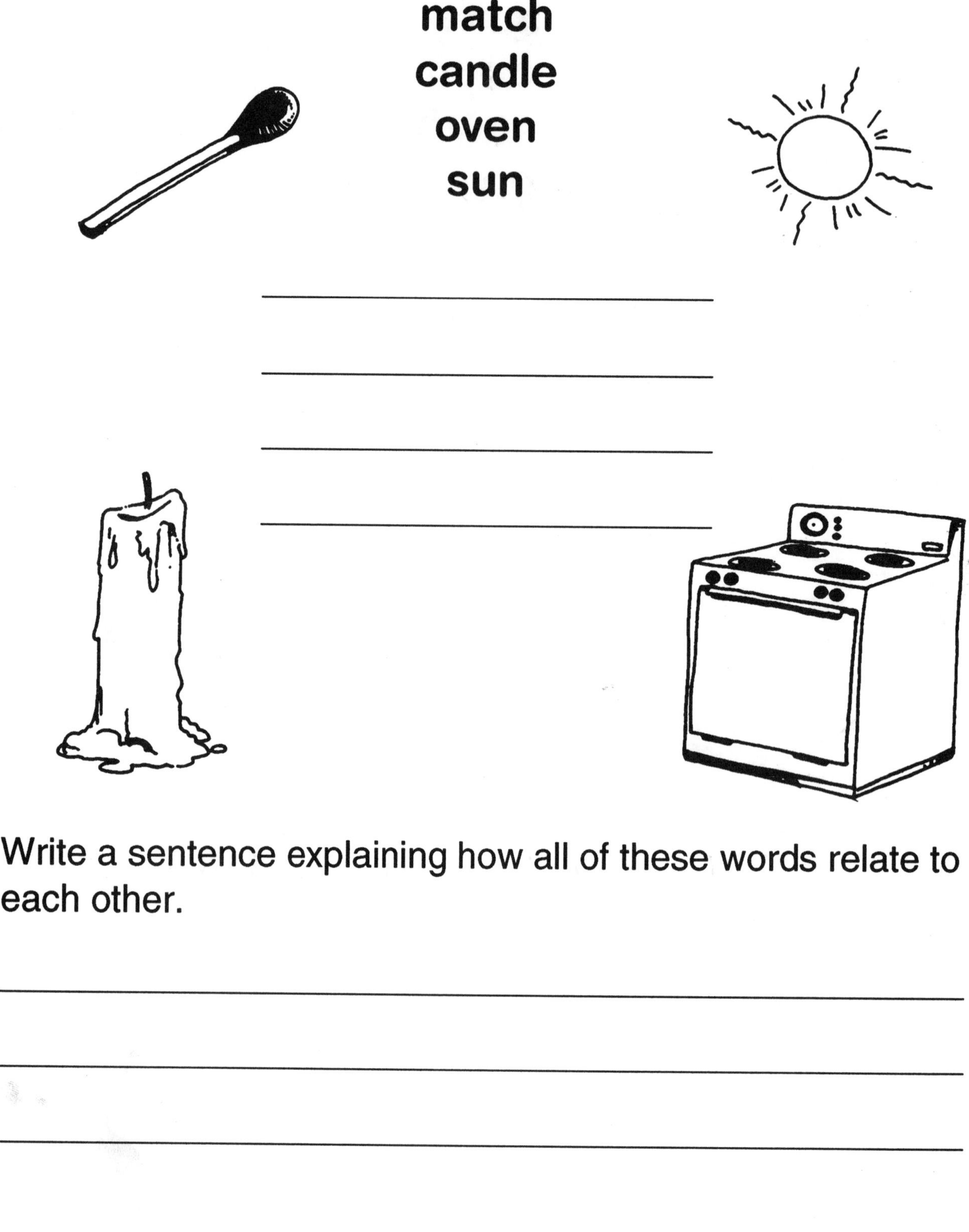

Write a sentence explaining how all of these words relate to each other.

Look at the group of words listed below. Why do they belong together? Try to add more words to the list.

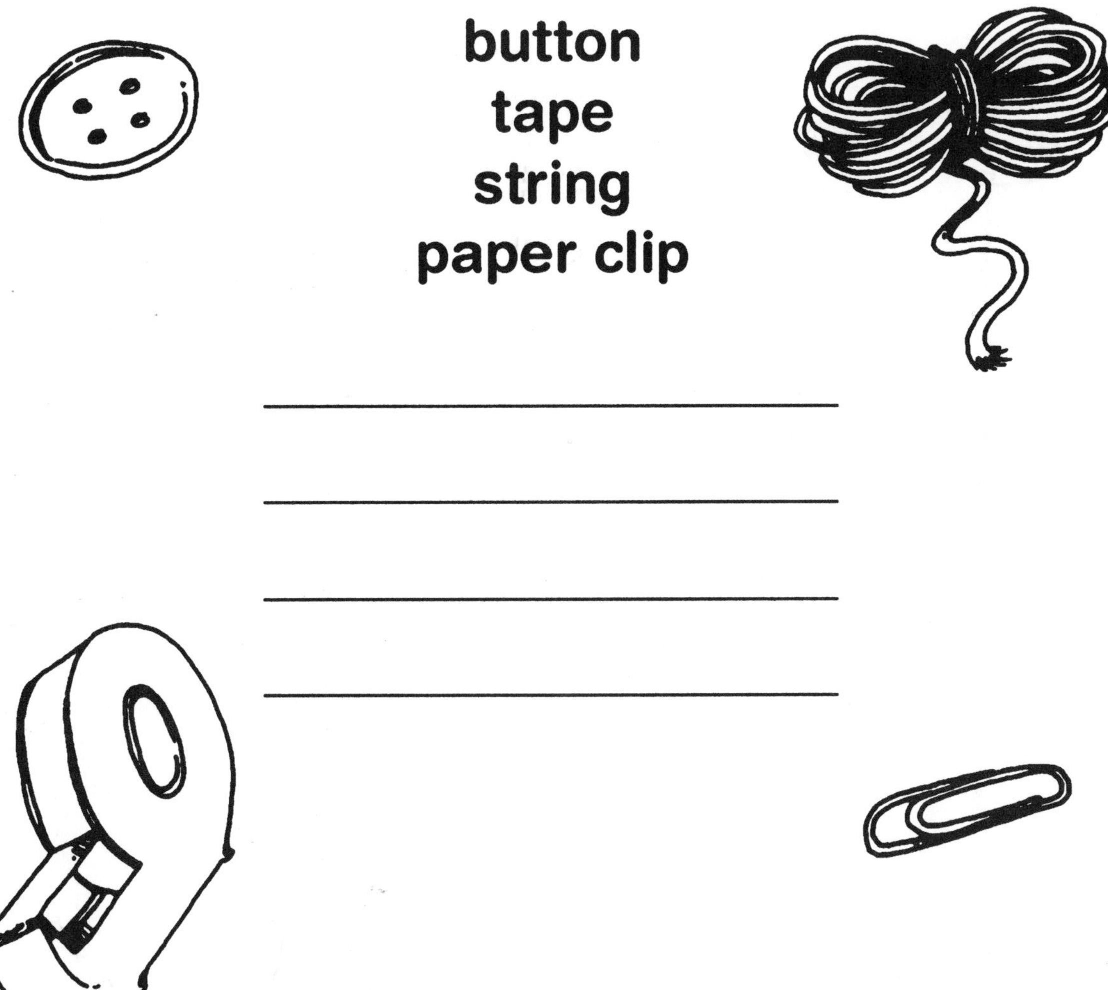

Write a sentence explaining how all of these words relate to each other.

Connect the dots to find a message from the teacher. Write the message on the lines below.

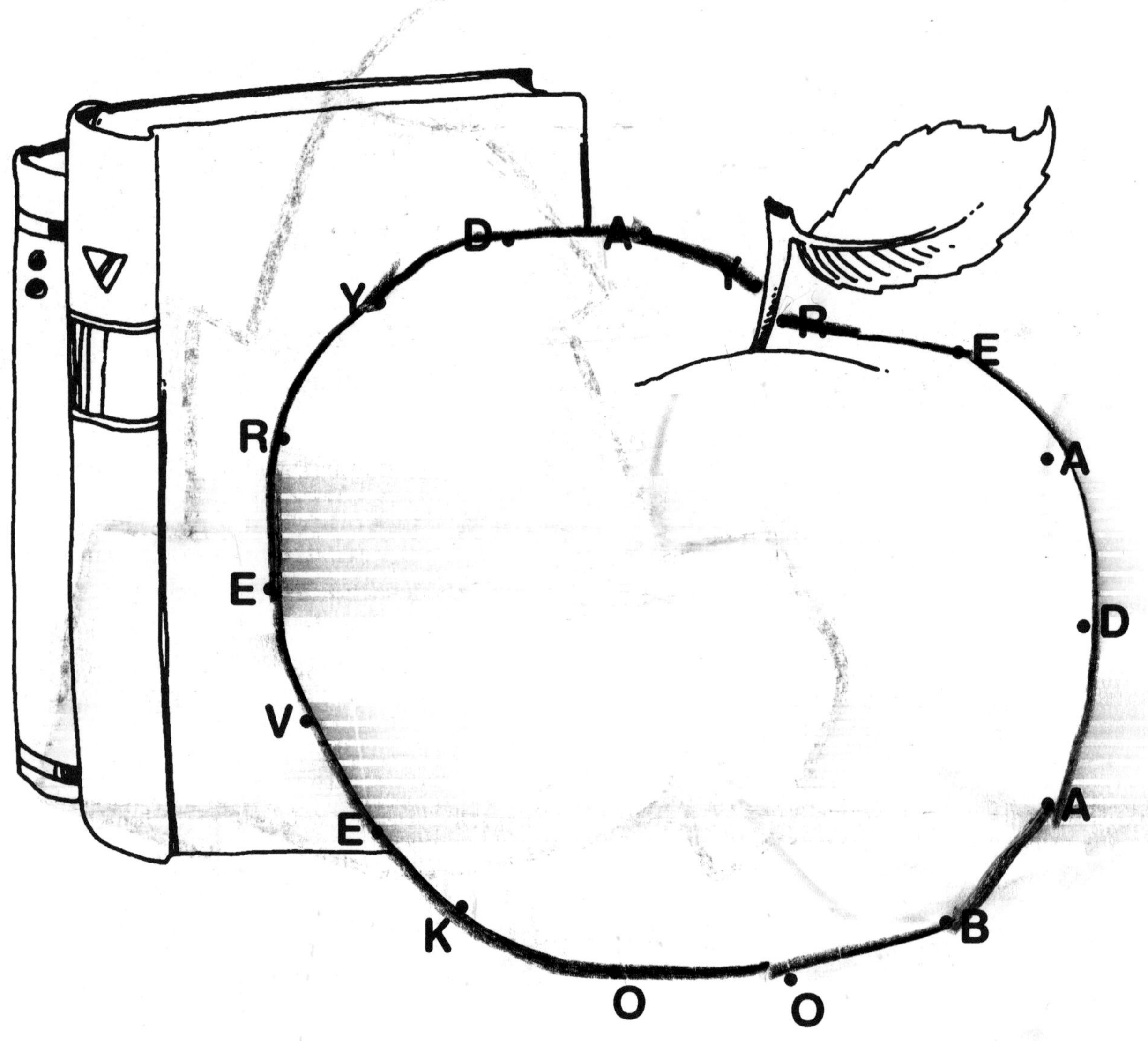

Connect the dots to find a message from the animals. Write the message on the lines below.

Follow the dots in alphabetical order to find a hidden picture.

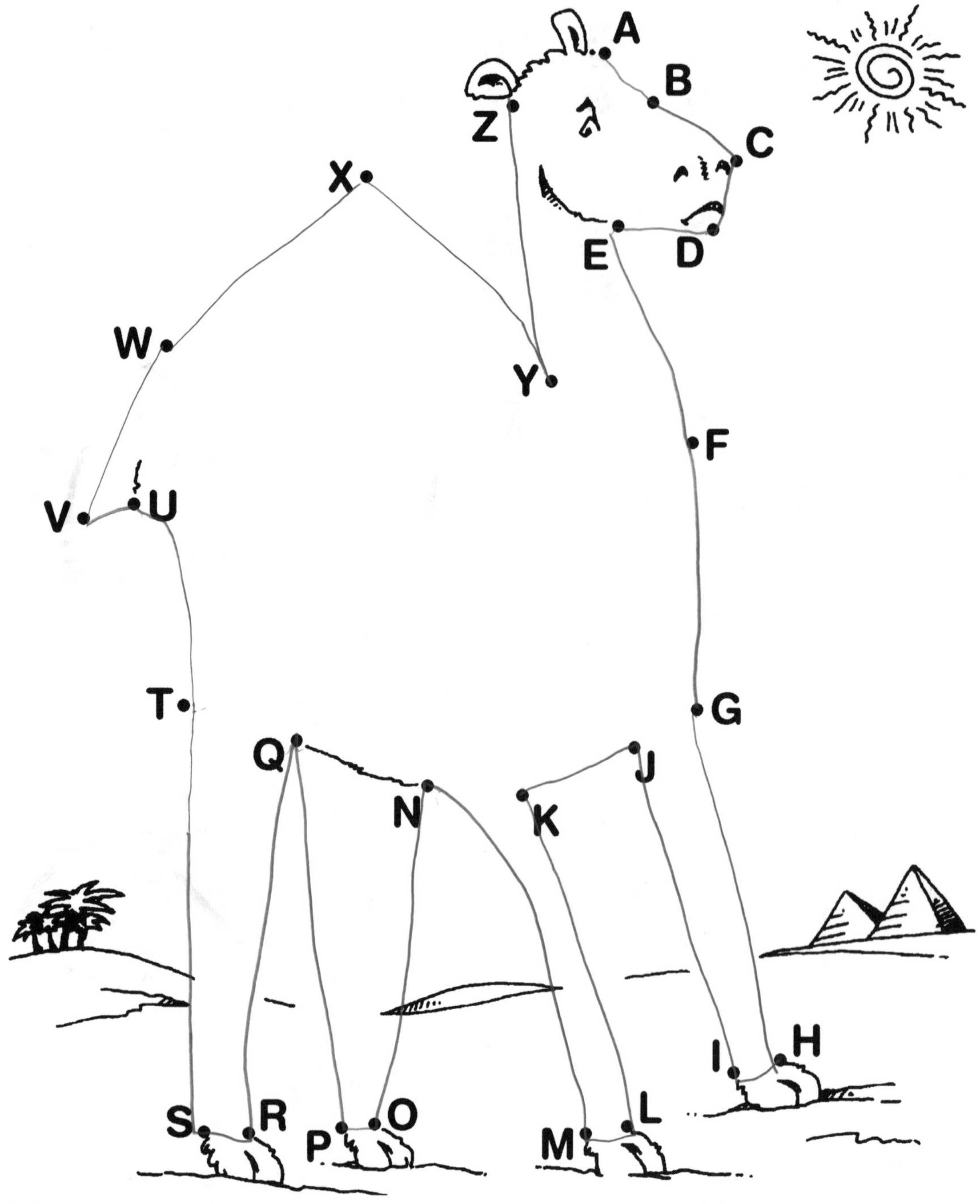

On another piece of paper, make your own dot-to-dot puzzle. Use all the letters of the alphabet. You can ask a friend to solve the puzzle.

Use the code to find the secret message.

1	2	3	4	5	6	7	8	9	10
a	b	c	d	e	f	g	h	i	j

11	12	13	14	15	16	17	18	19	20
k	l	m	n	o	p	q	r	s	t

21	22	23	24	25	26
u	v	w	x	y	z

Write the message on the lines.

___ ___ ___ ___ ___ ___   ___ ___ ___ ___ ___
19 5 3 18 5 20   3 15 4 5 19

___ ___ ___   ___ ___ ___ !
1 18 5   6 21 14

Use the code to find the secret message.

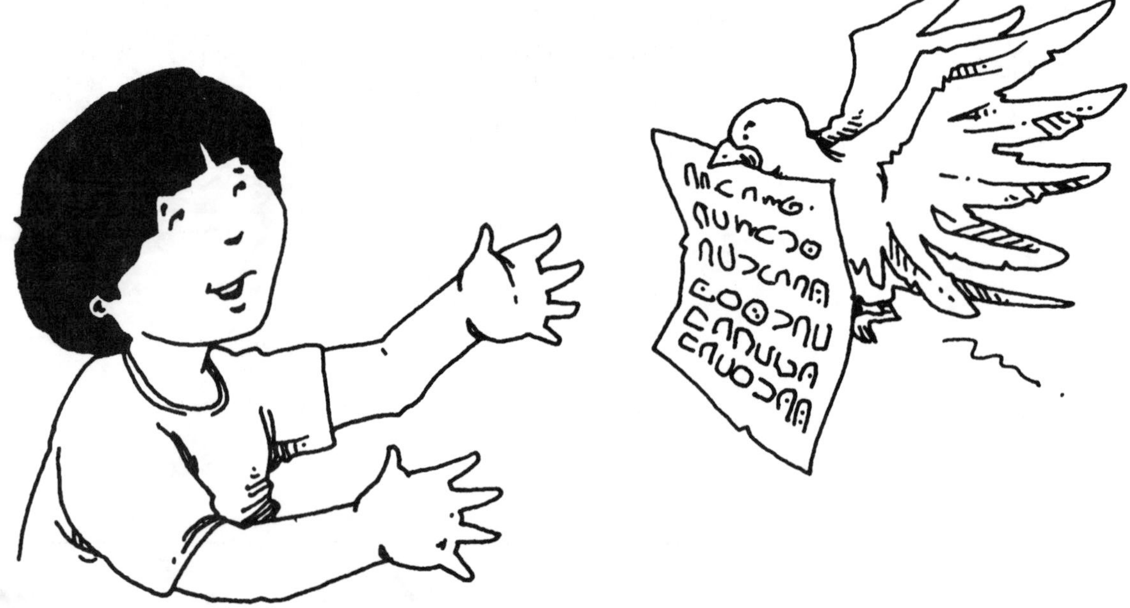

Write the message on the lines.

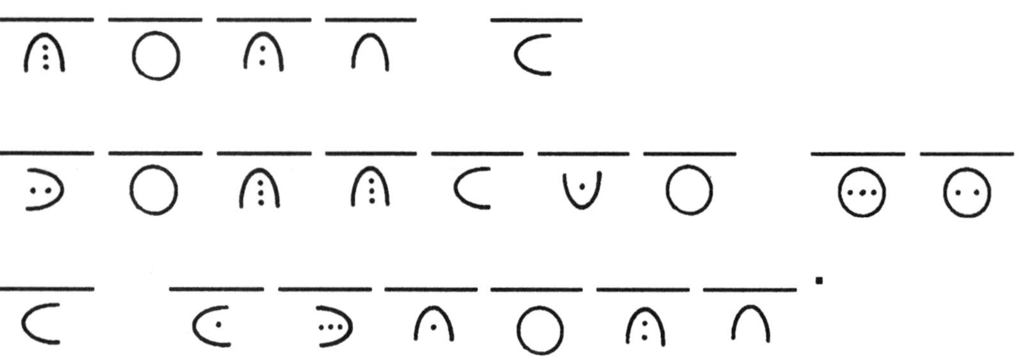

See how many words you can find in the grid below. Words may be formed by using any letter squares that touch each other horizontally, vertically, or diagonally. Each letter square may be used only once in each word.

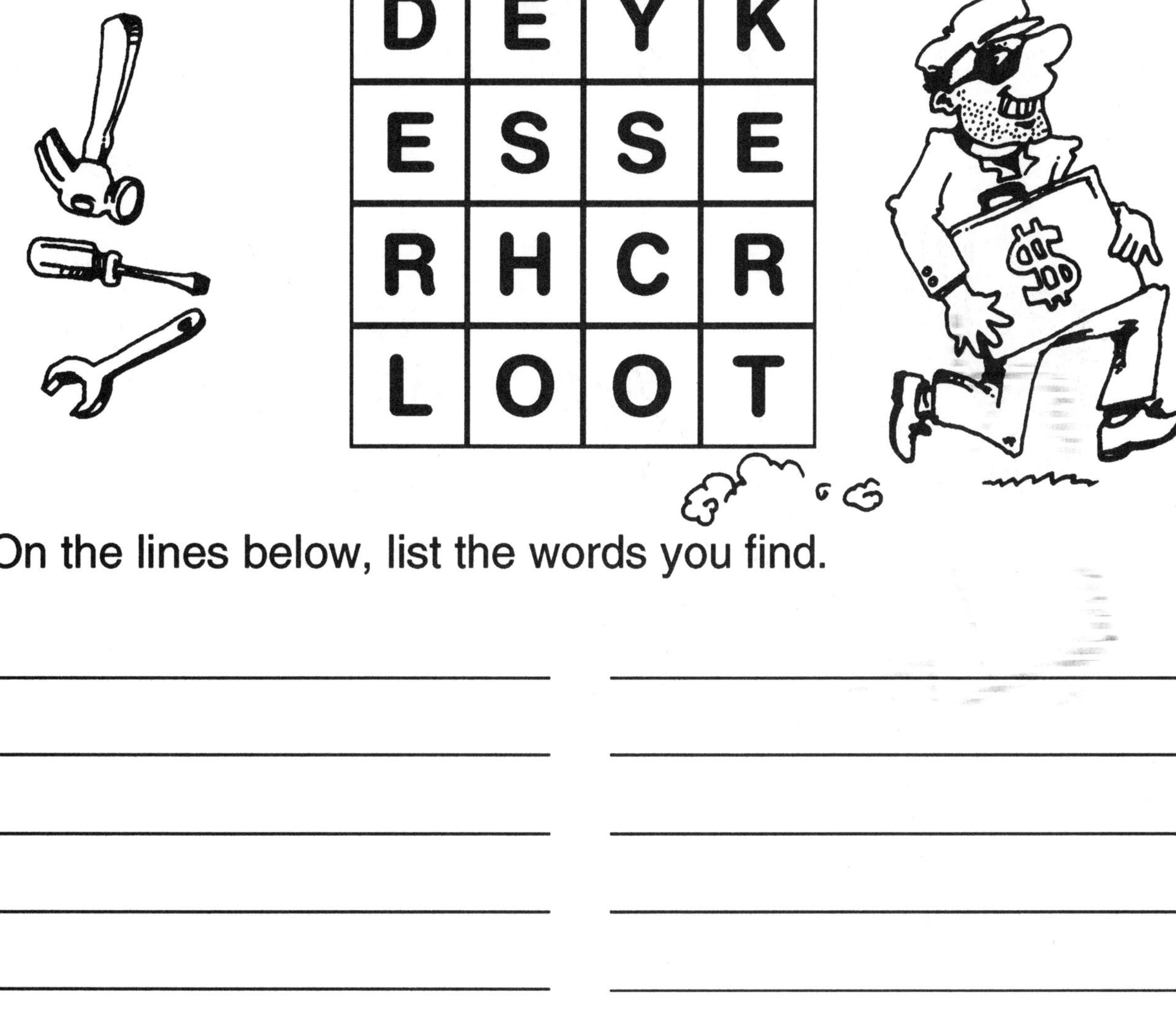

D E Y K
E S S E
R H C R
L O O T

On the lines below, list the words you find.

ANSWERS

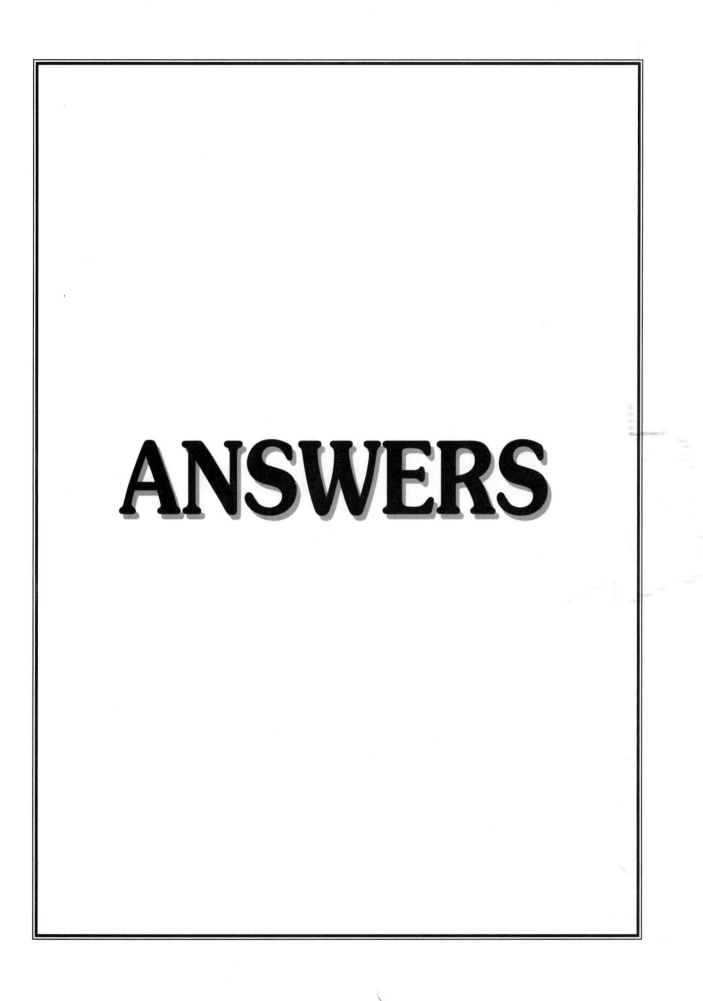

Answers

PHONICS

Page 18
Possible answers include:
mongoose, marmot, mole, mink, mule, muskrat
They are all mammals and begin with **M**.
Possible answers include:
cabbage, celery, cauliflower, cantaloupe
They all grow in a garden and begin with **C**.

Page 19
Possible answers include:
bike, boomerang, book
They are all things to play with and begin with **B**.
Possible answers include:
painter, porter, paratrooper, parent
They are all people and begin with **P**.

Page 20
We can share the fish.
Please bring your brother to the party.
Try to play the trumpet while you ride the tricycle.

Page 21
Which kind of whale is usually white?
I would like a cheese sandwich and some cherries for lunch.
Both of us thought we heard a thump.

Page 22
The blond boy blowing bubbles wore a blue shirt and black shoes.
Sarah played with the plane while she ate a plum.
The flea flung himself across the floor and did a flip.

Page 23
Daniel and his brother had brown bread and broccoli for lunch.
The green plant grows out of the ground.
The dragon drank a soda while he played the drums.

Page 24
Jan and Tom found a box. They opened the lid and peeked in. The two kids could not believe what they saw. At the bottom of the box there was a nest. Sitting in the nest was a gigantic egg. As they watched, the egg began to shake and shiver.
Rest of answer will vary.

Page 25
Laura and Tricia went fishing when the sun was just coming up. They dug some worms out of the dirt in the garden. They packed a lunch to eat at noon. They put on their hats and walked down to the stream.
As soon as Laura put her line in the water, a fish began to tug at it. The pole began to bend.
Rest of answer will vary.

Page 26
Sue and Josh wanted to make (bake) a cake. They got out milk, eggs, flour, sugar, vanilla, and baking powder. They found a great big bowl. They mixed everything together in the bowl and poured the batter into a pan. They put the pan in the oven and waited.
Rest of answer will vary.

Page 27
One Saturday, Gary went for a ride on his horse, Shorty. They went up to the top of the mountain to have a picnic lunch. Gary brought a sandwich and some cookies for himself. He brought a carrot and an apple for Shorty. While they were eating lunch, they heard a loud boom.
Rest of answer will vary.

Page 28
glue
stew
moose
broom
root
Rest of answer will vary.

Page 29
play
eight
train
mail
sleigh
hay
Rest of answer will vary.

Page 30
squirt
dirt
nurse
turkey
surf
fern
Rest of answer will vary.

Page 31
shout
towel
growl
round
house
flower
Rest of answer will vary.

Page 32
Sounds like **S**:
celery
circle
city
cent
Sounds like **K**:
cake
camel
collie
cone

Page 33
Sounds like **J**:
giraffe
giant
gerbil
gingerbread
Sounds like **G**:
guitar
goose
game
gum
Exceptions: give, gill, girl

Pages 34–40
Answers will vary.

Page 41
Silent letters are:

Two little ghosts went for a walk in the darkest hour of the night. They saw a bright light shining from a house so they went up to the door and turned the knob.

Parent: Picture should show two ghosts at the door. There should be a knob drawn on the door. The picture should be colored to represent night. There should be a light in the window of the house.
Rest of answer will vary.

Page 42
Silent letters are:

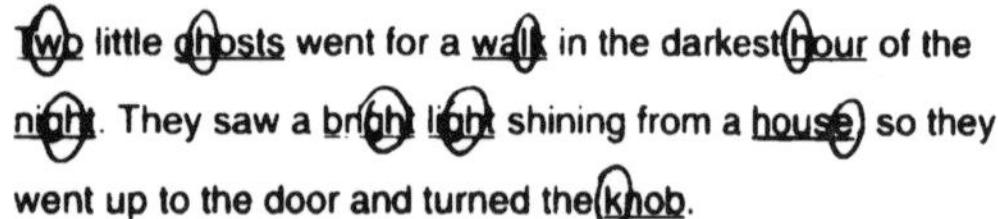
Two little ghosts went for a walk in the darkest hour of the night. They saw a bright light shining from a house so they went up to the door and turned the knob.

Parent: Picture should show that Sally's thumb and knee are hurt. She should be wearing mismatched socks and shoes.
Rest of answer will vary.

Page 43
cherry
fly
Rest of answer will vary.

Page 44
soap
bird
Rest of answer will vary.

Page 45
comb
train
Rest of answer will vary.

Page 46
flower
toast
Rest of answer will vary.

Page 47
goose
moon
Rest of answer will vary.

Page 48
hide
bite
hope
pane
cube
Sentences will vary.

Page 49
same
spine
scrape
plane
hate
Sentences will vary.

Page 50
paste
mints
pants
soccer
tacks
socks
comb
flat
coat
The new words are all articles of clothing.
Rest of answer will vary.

Page 51
home
purse
horse
lamp
cab
lamb
dime
truck
duck
The new words are all farm animals.
Rest of answer will vary.

Pages 52–55
Answers will vary.

Page 56
arm
eye
head
heel
thumb
The hidden words are all body parts.
Rest of answer will vary.

Page 57
apple
lemon
melon
pear
orange
The hidden words are all kinds of fruit.
Rest of answer will vary.

Page 58
horses
over
the
hills
seven
gallop
Seven horses gallop over the hills is the **best** answer.
Some children may put the words in a different order:
Over the hills gallop seven horses.

Page 59
winds
cold
winter
blow
and
wild
Winter winds blow wild and cold.
Or: Winter winds blow cold and wild.

Page 60
some
pumpkins
children
orange
twelve
found
Some children found twelve orange pumpkins.
Or: Twelve children found some orange pumpkins.

Page 61
Saturday
our
cards
family
night
played
Our family played cards Saturday night.
Or: Saturday night our family played cards.

Pages 62–68
Answers will vary.

READING

Page 71
His name is Alan.

Page 72
The thief is Max.

Page 73
A. Alana
B. Leesa
C. Carol
D. Joyce
E. Helen

Page 74
A. Susan
B. Mary
C. Jill
D. Hilary
E. Yolanda
F. Maria

Page 75
A. Carl
B. Willy
C. Sophia
D. Adam
E. Mike
F. Sherry
G. Tony

Page 76
1-b
2-c
3-a
4-b

Page 77
1-b
2-a
3-c
4-a

Page 78
1-C
2-C
3-D
4-A
5-C

Page 79
1-B
2-C
3-D
4-A
5-B

Page 80
1-C
2-B
3-A
4-B
5-C

Page 81
1-B
2-A
3-C
4-B
5-C

Page 82

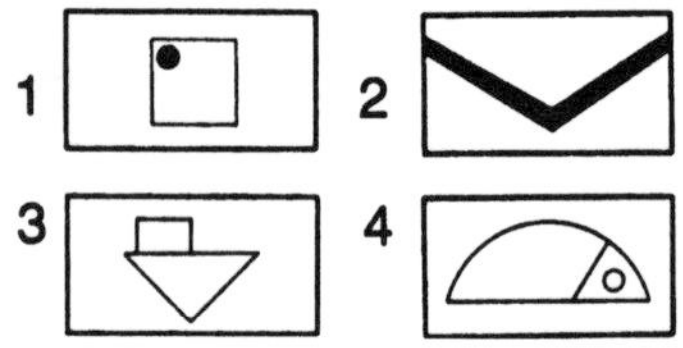

1 2
3 4

Page 83
1. boots
2. walked
3. yellow
4. boat
5. ice-skating
6. melted
7. ✔
8. barked

Page 84
1. capital
2. hear
3. glad
4. talked
5. ✔
6. wasn't
7. great
8. smell

Page 85
1. lost
2. deaf
3. start
4. ✔
5. soaked
6. baseball
7. closes
8. hat

Page 86
A-5
B-3
C-1
D-4
E-2

Page 87
A-5
B-3
C-6
D-2
E-1
F-4

Page 88
Red: A-3, B-1, C-2
Wolf: A-1, B-3, C-2

Page 89
Sam: A-3, B-4, C-1, D-2
Dan: A-3, B-4, C-2, D-1

Page 90
1. green
2. colors
3. fruits
4. buildings
5. sports
6. machines
7. tools
8. babies
9. girls
10. storms

Page 91
1. white
2. fly
3. go around
4. grow
5. countries
6. cities
7. open
8. seasons
9. boys
10. light

Pages 92–93
Answers will vary.

Page 94
1. hands
2. cat
3. foot
4. barn
5. June
6. garage
7. flower
8. eat

Page 95
1. scratch
2. bake
3. Boston
4. cub
5. birds
6. hay
7. high
8. butterfly

Page 96
Answers will vary.

Page 97
1-C
2-E
3-A
4-B
5-D

Page 98
1-C
2-A
3-E
4-B
5-D

Page 99
1. yes
2. no
3. no
4. no

Page 100
1. no
2. yes
3. no
4. no

Page 102
The King loved to cook. He baked a chocolate cake for the Queen. He began to carry the huge cake into the royal dining room. Then the King slipped! The cake fell all over the Queen. The Queen just laughed. "I love upside-down cake," she said.

Mary was a happy witch. But Mrs. Noseup, who lived next door, was not happy. She did not like living next door to a witch. One night Mary heard Mrs. Noseup scream. A robber was tying up Mrs. Noseup. Mary turned the robber into a toad. Now Mrs. Noseup is happy to have a witch next door.

Page 104
There was an old witch named Elaine,
Who thought taking a bath was a pain.
She washed once a year,
And from what I hear,
She won't even go out in the rain!

There was a king from Baltimore,
Who thought being a king was a bore.
He gave up his crown,
And put money down
To open a grocery store!

Page 105
Luisa: cat
Tyrone: goldfish
Jason: dog
Jennifer: parrot

Page 106
Barry: sweep floors
Tom: wash windows
Sherry: paint
Alyson: dust
Wayne: trim trees

Page 107
Wanda: tea
Ellie: plates
Rex: cups
Ralph: cake

Page 108
Dale: bike
Bonnie: scooter
Anna: skateboard
Bert: roller skates

Page 109
Sara: jelly
Milo: vanilla
Ed: fudge
Drew: raisin
Ali: peanut
Rose: cherry

Page 110
Amy got the coloring book.
Mark got the ball.
Tracy got the game.

Page 111
Sukie says "hello."
Flookie says "stop."
Pookie says "wow."

Page 112
Jenny won.
Luke came in last.
(Lulu came in second, and Harry finished third.)

Page 113
A. Bruno
B. Igor
C. Ralph

Page 114
A. Max
B. Jack
C. Ed
D. Fred
E. Joe

Page 115
A. Carlos
B. Cathy
C. Paul
D. Yolanda
E. Betty

Page 116
A. Danny
B. David
C. Sally
D. Luisa

Page 117
A. Erik
B. Jennifer
C. Jon
D. Amy
E. Mike
F. Mary

Page 118
A. red
B. blue
C. purple
D. yellow
E. green

Page 119
A. Pug
B. Rover
C. Fluffy
D. Sam
E. Rex

Page 120
A. Alberto
B. Ann
C. Kate
D. Jill
E. Scott

Page 121
It is a cat.

Page 122
A-3
B-2
D-1
F-4
You don't need C and E.

Page 123
It is a sailboat.

Page 124
A-3
C-5
D-1
F-2
G-4
You don't need B and E.

Page 125
It is Little Red Riding Hood.

Page 126
grape jam
applesauce
peas
cherry pie
banana bread
string beans

Page 127
It was a book.

Page 128
BROTHER
COUSIN
AUNT
FATHER
UNCLE
MOTHER
SISTER

Page 129
KNIFE
AX
SAW
BALL
SUN
WHEEL
JAR
WINDOW
BOTTLE

Page 130
1. ball
2. cloud
3. daisy
4. table
5. top
6. boat
7. banana
8. sun
9. sleep
10. happy

Page 131

1. nail
2. gorilla
3. frog
4. teacher
5. steel
6. box
7. kite
8. sun
9. ice
10. aunt

Pages 132–133

Answers will vary.

Page 134

1. flowers
2. liquids
3. coins

Page 135

1. games
2. baked goods
3. baby animals

Page 136

1. planets
2. materials
3. homes

Page 137

A-2
B-4
C-1
D-3

Page 138

A-3
B-1
C-4
D-2

Page 139

A-2
B-1
D-4
E-3
C does not belong

Page 140

Duck:
1) pond
2) tree
3) barn
Farmer:
1) barn
2) pond
3) tree

Page 141

Peg-Leg:
1) bridge
2) ship
3) cave
Peg-Leg did not go to the treasure chest.

Sam:
1) treasure chest
2) bridge
3) ship
Sam did not go to the cave.

Page 142

The last clown is thin.

Page 143

The first girl has long hair.

Page 144

The last shape is small.

Page 145
The princess is not telling the truth. If the moon was full and the stars were out, it wasn't raining.

Page 146
Nora is not telling the truth. It is unlikely that she could take a violin lesson with a broken arm.

Page 147
Pat is not telling the truth. The oak tree would not have leaves in January.

Page 148
Miss Rollo: 8:30, Mr. Bond: 8:00.
Mr. Bond could be the thief.

Page 149
Mr. Simon: 6:45, Ms. Jones: 6:30, Mr. Smith: 6:00.
Mr. Simon stole the watch.

Page 151
Parent: Check pictures circled against those on page 150.

Page 153
Parent: Check words circled against pictures on page 152.

Page 155
Parent: Check pictures circled against words on page 154.

LANGUAGE ARTS

Page 159
JUMP

Page 160
MARCH

Page 161
SPLASH

Page 162
PIRATE

Page 163
CANDY

Page 164
DRIVE

Page 165
I'm hungry. I will go to the river to catch a fish.

Page 166
Answers will vary.

Page 168
I hiked up the mountains with my friends.
The mountains were cold.
I was happy to hike down the mountains!

Pages 170–174
Answers will vary.

Page 176
Answers will vary.

Page 177

basketball	football
stickball	boathouse
broomstick	candlestick
moonlight	footlight
lipstick	doghouse
houseboat	

(You may find other words, too.)

Page 178
fireman
firebird
snowbird
snowman
raincoat
bedroom
coatroom
starfish
bathroom
goldfish
(You may find other words, too.)

Page 179
downtown
downhill
uphill
uptown
paperboy
paperback
upstairs
backstairs
nighttime
bedtime
backhand
downstairs
(You may find other words, too.)

Pages 180–185
Answers will vary.

Page 186
pail

Page 187
pet

Page 188
book

Page 189
beast

Page 190
1. balloon
2. igloo
3. pear

Page 191
1. ghost
2. elephant
3. robot
4. baboon

Pages 192–194
Answers will vary.

Page 195
meet–meat
one–won
bury–berry
prince–prints

Pages 196–198
Answers will vary.

Page 199
full of beans

Page 200
"I'll keep an eye on the baby!"

Page 201
burned up

Page 202
Answers will vary.

Page 203
FIDLR3–Old King Cole
NO YOLK–Humpty Dumpty
ZZZZZZ–Sleeping Beauty

Page 204
GR8MOM–Old Woman in a Shoe
LV2KS–Georgie Porgie
CAP 10–Captain Hook
LAZBOY–Little Boy Blue

Page 205
Answers will vary.

Page 206
Monday: Fred
Tuesday: Gary
Wednesday: Don
Friday: Susie

Page 207
Tuesday: Jim
Thursday: Angela
Friday: Lisa
Saturday: Rick

Page 208
Whale Show: 10:30 A.M.
Dolphin Show: 2:00 P.M.
Walrus Show: 3:30 P.M.
Seal Show: 11:30 A.M.

Pages 209–210
Answers will vary.

Page 212
Answers will vary.

Page 213
top
want
cake
thing

Page 214
A. bee, egg
B. car, ride
C. lake, kite
D. box, pot

Page 215
b o w l
a i
t a l k
h e

Pages 216–220
Answers will vary.

Pages 222–224
Answers will vary.

Pages 225–226
Parent: Go over answers with child.

Page 228
Answers will vary.

Page 229
cookie sheet

Page 230
"You are odorable!"

Page 231
Meet Max at midnight.

Page 232
icecycles

Page 233
Three monsters are behind you.

Page 234
Answers will vary.

Page 235
an alarm cluck

Page 236
so
saw
best
story
stones

Page 237
no
box
look
socks
window
outside

Pages 238–246
Answers will vary.

MATH

Page 249
6
10
11
9
8

Page 250
6
4
8

Page 251
11
13
21
33
19

Page 252
18
16
14
12
10

Page 253
75
81
99
79
87
93

Page 254
6
12
18
24
30

Pages 255–257
Answers will vary.

Page 258
9

Page 259
16

Page 260
7
2

Page 261
7
6
2
4

Page 262
Answers will vary.

Page 263
A. Jamal
B. Sarah
C. Eli
D. Matt
E. Rachel

Page 264
A. Amanda
B. Kevin
C. Michele
D. Daniel

Page 265
A. Teddy
B. Megan
C. Brittany
D. Tyrone

Page 266
A. Timmy
B. Michael
C. Soraya
D. Tara
E. Nicky

Page 267
A. Erin
B. Damon
C. Josh
D. Courtney
E. Sean

Page 268
Hawks: 9–7–4
Eagles: 12–19–11

Page 269
Top: 4
Middle: 7, 5
Bottom: 3, 6, 8

Page 270
Top: 4
Middle: 6, 8
Bottom: 3, 5, 7

Page 271
357, 375, 537, 573, 753, 735

Page 272
168, 186, 681, 618, 861, 816
lowest score: 168
highest score: 861

Page 273

Dimes	Nickels	Pennies
1	1	0
1	0	5
0	1	10
0	2	5
0	0	15
0	3	0

Page 274

Quarters	Dimes	Nickels
2	0	0
1	2	1
1	1	3
1	0	5
0	0	10
0	1	8
0	2	6
0	3	4
0	4	2
0	5	0

Page 275
9 quarters
7 nickels

Page 276
Ryan: 3
Breanna: 5
Alisha: 7

Page 277
Luis: 5
Henry: 9
Jimmy: 10

Page 278
Erica: 3
Hilary: 5
Morgan: 10

Page 279
Adam: 15
Josh: 7
Teddy: 9

Page 280
Answers will vary.

Page 281
1) watercolors, crayons
2) markers, crayons
3) markers, crayons, paper

Page 282
1) board game, puzzle
2) 2 board games
3) board game, book

Pages 283–284
1) hamburger, fries, milk
2) apple, hot dog
3) 2 hot dogs, 1 milk or
1 hamburger, 2 milks
4) hot dog, hamburger, milk, french fries
5) $2.00
6) 2 hamburgers, fries, milk or
1 hamburger and 3 french fries
7) $10 bill
8) Answers will vary.

Page 285
Answers will vary.

Page 286
6, 2, 2, or 4, 4, 2, or 3, 3, 4

Page 287
7, 4, 4

Page 288
Possible answers:
top: 4
middle: 5, 6
bottom: 3, 7, 2

Page 289
A. 10
B. 10
C. 10
D. 6
E. 8

Page 290
A. 3
B. 10
C. 12
D. 12
E. 8

Page 291
Answers will vary.

Page 292
6 + 2 − 4

Page 293
8 − 4 + 6 or 6 − 4 + 8

Page 294
5 + 7 − 9 + 3 or 7 + 3 − 9 + 5

Page 295
Answers will vary.

Page 297
14 squares

Page 298
30 squares

Page 299
8 triangles

Page 300
11 rectangles

Page 301

1. Clown	10:00 A.M.
2. Magic	10:30 A.M.
3. Dog	11:30 A.M.

Page 302

1. Seal	10:30 A.M.
2. Elephant	11:00 A.M.
3. Lunch	12:00 P.M.
4. Monkey	1:30 P.M.
5. Bird	2:30 P.M.

Page 303

1. Jack and the Beanstalk	10:00 A.M.
2. Hansel and Gretel	11:00 A.M.
3. Beauty and the Beast	11:30 A.M.
4. Lunch	12:30 P.M.
5. Red Riding Hood	2:00 P.M.

Page 304
A = 4
B = 0
C = 2

Page 305
A = 3
B = 5
C = 1
D = 2
E = 4

Page 306
A = 4
B = 10
C = 2
D = 5
E = 6

Page 307

```
   2
1—(5)—4
   3
```

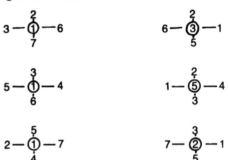

Pages 308–309

```
   2              2
3—(1)—6        6—(3)—1
   7              5

   3              2
5—(1)—4        1—(5)—4
   6              3

   5              3
2—(1)—7        7—(2)—1
   4              5
```

Page 310

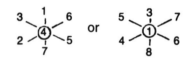

```
3   1   6          5   3   7
  \ | /              \ | /
   (4)      or        (1)
  / | \              / | \
2   7   5          4   8   6
```

Page 311

```
8 — 1 — 6
|       |
4       2
|       |
3 — 5 — 7
```

Page 312
Answers will vary.

Page 313
Answers will vary: strawberry, cherry, tomato, etc.

Page 314
Answers will vary: skateboard, bike, wagon, etc.

Page 315

1, 3, 5, 7, 9, 11, 13, 15, 17, 19

Page 316

42, 44, 46, 48

Page 317

Answers will vary.

Page 318

Hilary
Stephen ○ Valerie
Casey

Page 319

Keith
Max ○ Courtney
Sean

Page 320

Maple City

Page 321

Cherry Town
Hawthorne

Page 322

A. 12 cents
B. 21 cents
C. 30 cents

Page 323

Zoonies	Roonies	Loonies
2	0	0
1	1	1
1	0	3
0	3	0
0	2	2
0	1	4
0	0	6

Page 324

A. 2
B. 4
C. 2

Page 325

Dookles	Nanoops	Pogos
2	1	0
0	5	0
0	0	10
1	2	2
1	1	4
1	0	6
0	4	2
0	3	4
0	2	6
0	1	8
2	0	2

Page 326

Page 327

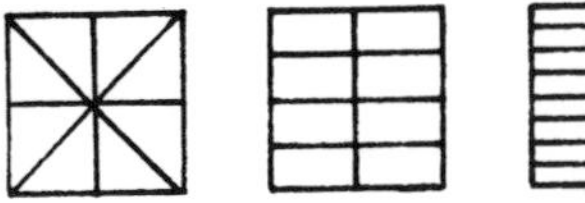

Page 328

A. B. C. D.

Page 329

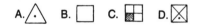

A. B. C. D.

Page 330

A. B. C. D.

Page 331

A. 14
B. 13
C. 1
D. 35
E. 4

Page 332

A. 18
B. 3
C. 7
D. 13
E. 21
F. 17

Page 333

A. 12, 12
B. 32
C. 17
D. 12
E. 12
F. 22

PUZZLES AND GAMES

Page 337

4	3	8
9	5	1
2	7	6

Page 338

Answers will vary.

Page 339

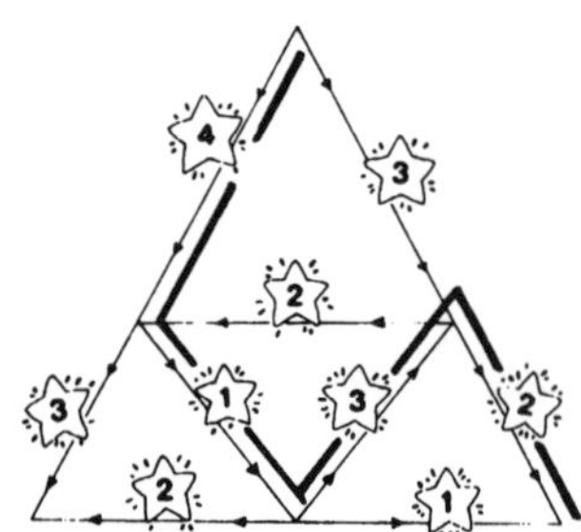

Page 340

yellow kettle – 3 + 4 + 1

7 2 3 1 6
4 3 4 2 5
5 6 1 0 5
7 3 4 1 4

red kettle – 1 + 3 + 4 + 2

1 2 5 4
5 6 2 1
1 3 4 2
8 0 5 4

orange kettle – 4 + 3 + 5

6 1 2 8
3 7 3 5
6 7 0 3
4 3 5 8

Pages 341–342

Answers will vary.

Page 343

10 = H–3–7–C
14 = H–3–5–6–C
19 = H–3–7–2–2–5–C
22 = H–3–5–7–2–5–C

Page 344

Missing numbers: 18, 7
Numbers used more than once: 17, 5, 8
Number greater than 0: 35

Page 345

	over	up
robot	1	1
stuffed bear	5	5
skates	2	6
soccer ball	4	4
fire truck	3	5
pony	1	3
blocks	4	1

Page 346

1. Casey, 332
2. Samantha, 387
3. Jon, 222
4. Benjie, 279
5. Michael, 249
6. Adam, 264
7. Marta, 178
8. Erica, 321

Page 347

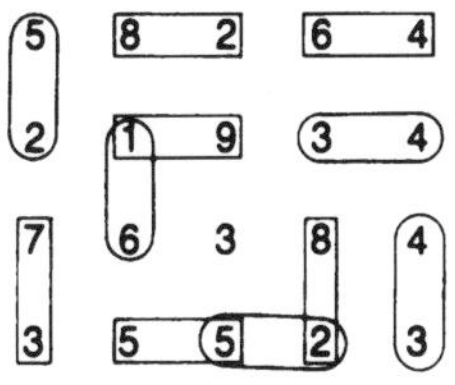

Page 348

Erica's name = 15¢

Rest of answer will vary.

Page 349

1 + 6 = 7	6 + 2 = 8
9 - 5 = 4	5 - 3 = 2
5 + 4 = 9	4 + 4 = 8
7 - 2 = 5	6 + 6 = 12

Page 350

Top road = 6

Middle road = 4

Bottom road = 8

Page 351

Page 356

6 + 5 + 0 = 11

7 + 3 + 2 = 12

8 + 4 + 1 = 13

Page 357

Answers will vary.

Page 358

Greatest–6

Answers will vary.

Least–4

Answers will vary.

Page 359

Page 360

1) 6 1 8

2)

Page 361

1)

2)

3)

Page 362

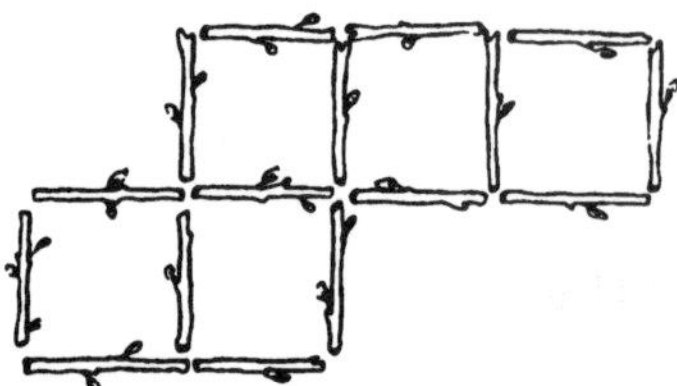

Page 363

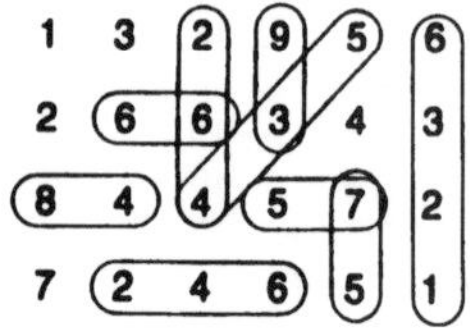

Page 365

48¢

Page 366

Page 369

Page 370

1)

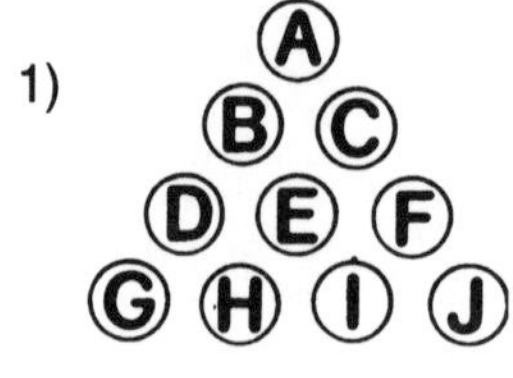

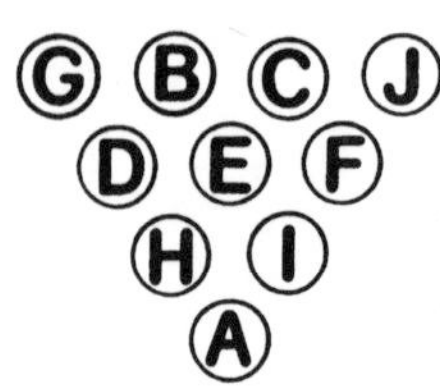

2)

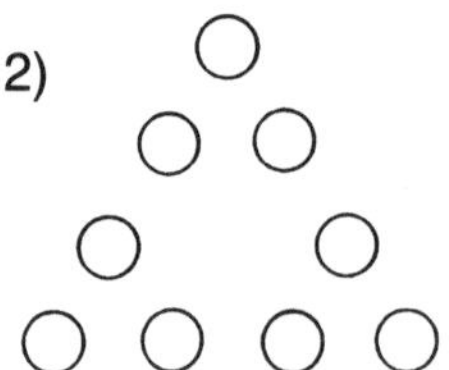

Page 371

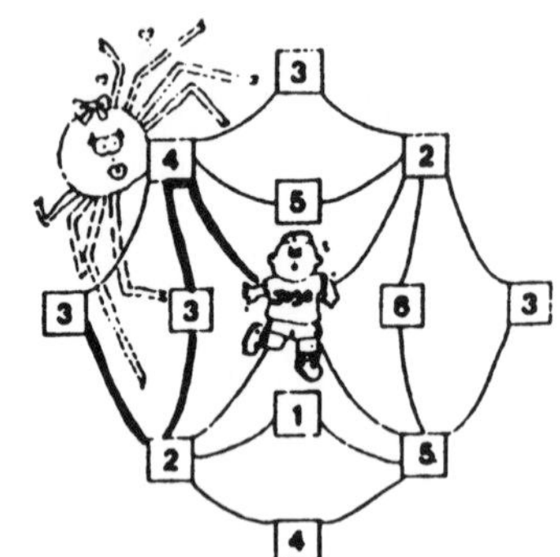

Page 372

14 squares
11 triangles

Page 373

5 + 4 = 9	3 + 2 + 2 + 2 = 9
4 + 2 + 2 = 8	7 + 1 = 8
3 + 3 + 3 = 9	3 + 2 + 3 = 8
10 - 3 = 7	2 + 5 = 7
3 + 3 + 1 = 7	

Page 374

2
5 8 6
3 1 4
7

Page 376

Page 377

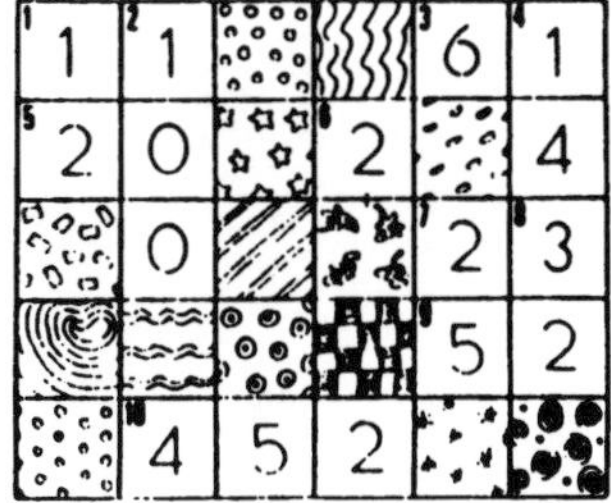

Page 379
MILK AND QUACKERS

Page 380
cat
game
bag

Page 381
swing
green
chain

Page 382
bright
sheet
slim
grapes
Parent: Picture 4 should be colored.

Page 383
chart
drink
frame
prize
Parent: Picture 2 should be colored.

Page 384
stick
ship
trap
wrap
Parent: Picture 2 should be colored.

Page 385
flower
table
snake
store

Page 386
long
drove
beside
bridge
John drove beside the long bridge.

Page 387
I AM GREAT!

Page 388
DRAW A DOG.

Page 389
MAKE A BLUE FLAG.

Page 390
THAT WAS EASY.

Page 391
MAKE A SECRET CODE.

Page 392
SCORE MORE POINTS.

Page 393
LOTS OF LETTERS.

Page 394
AT THE ZOO.

Page 395
I KNOW THE ABCS.

Page 396
Answers will vary.

Page 397
potato

Page 398
glove

Page 399
towel

Page 400
log
dog
dig
pig

Page 401
page
cage
cane
cone

Page 402
flat
flap
clap
slap

Page 403
take
tame
game
same

Page 404
wet
hid
bit
set or sat

Page 405
try
yet
pet
tap

Page 406
1. a, e, i, o, u
2. pig, gag, tag, pot

Page 407
1. bcdfghjklmnpqrstvwxyz
2. bear, read, toad, boat

Page 408
1. dghlmqtxz
2. boat, tied, need, bean

Page 409
goat
tool
pail
grip
Rest of answer will vary.

Page 410
bib
dad
mom
peep
toot
noon

Page 411
BOB
EVE
NAN

Page 412
kayak
madam
level

Page 413

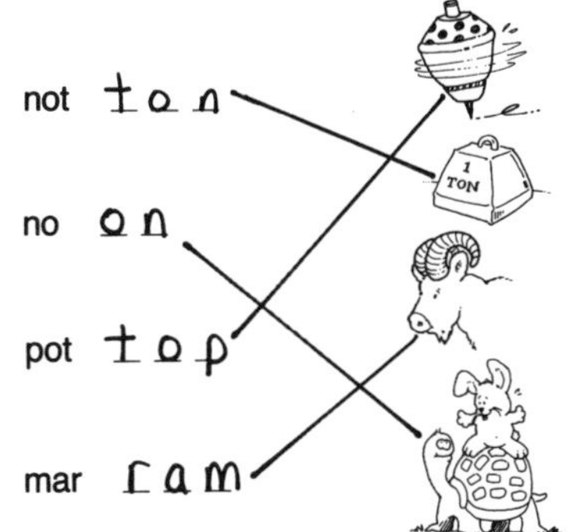

Page 414

Page 415
egg
girl
king
camel
icicle

Page 416
snow
man
pig
apple
boat
spider
sponge

Page 417
fire
rain
hand
basket
night
cloud
staircase

Page 418
coat
lids
name
earn

Page 419

Across	1. BOAT	3. POUR
Down	2. TOP	4. READ

Page 420

Across	1. TABLE	3. EAT
Down	2. BAT	4. APE

Page 421

Across	1. FOUR	2. THREE
Down	1. FIVE	3. EIGHT

Page 422
stop
little
far
work
day
give
pretty kitty

Page 423
hat
bear
tock
jar

Page 424
Answers will vary.
Some of the words are:
SAID
READ
TRIP
FADE
DIP

Page 425
rainbow

Page 426
on the farm

Page 427
pillow
paint
hay
quilt
fuzzy
snow
inch
eight
pajamas
horse
tub
vine
harmonica
gift
candle
bed
xylophone
trumpet
violin
telephone
sheep
snake
top
rabbit
book
drum

Page 428
happy
band
box
letter
yellow
tiger
mother
bubble
puzzle
cookie
pink
jam
duck
little
flower
queen
window
finger
birthday
number
square
seven
stop
friend
funny
other

Page 429

Page 430

Page 431

Page 432

How many foods did you find? 15

Page 433

How many did you find? 17

Page 434

On the lines below, write the name of each item you find.

pencil	note book	globe
crayon	paint brush	apple
book	scissors	lunchbox
desk	flag	map
eraser	computer	bell

Pages 435–442

Answers will vary.

Page 443

Yellow is to banana as red is to	**apple**	pencil
Sour is to lemon as sweet is to	broccoli	**candy**
Fur is to bear as feather is to	**bird**	jacket
Hard is to rock as soft is to	ice cube	**pillow**
Moon is to night as sun is to	**day**	island
Pool is to swim as bed is to	**sleep**	read
Chair is to sit as bike is to	push	**ride**

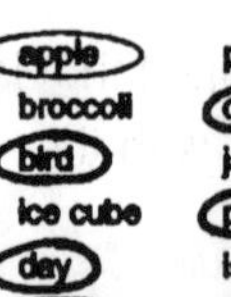

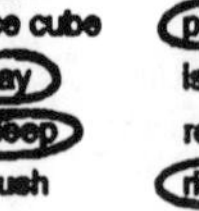

Page 444

Foot is to shoe as hand is to	sock	**glove**
Fish is to swim as bird is to	**fly**	float
Kitten is to cat as puppy is to	bear	**dog**
Over is to under as high is to	up	**low**
Friday is to day as January is to	February	**month**
Pen is to ink as brush is to	**paint**	write
Eye is to see as ear is to	speak	**hear**

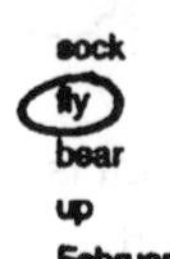
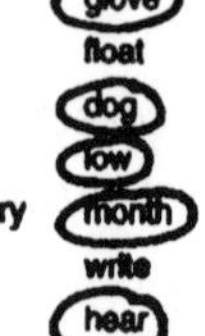

Page 445

Oak is to tree as poodle is to	pig	**dog**
String is to guitar as key is to	lock	**piano**
Bottom is to top as hot is to	water	**cold**
Pencil is to write as candle is to	**burn**	draw
Plane is to sky as car is to	**road**	drive
Kangaroo is to hop as snake is to	bounce	**slither**
Bark is to dog as quack is to	**duck**	bird

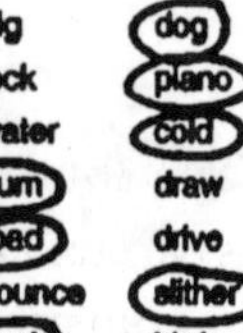

Page 446

Answers will vary. Some of the words are:

SIP
STAY
DAY
HERE
EAT

Page 447

Answers will vary. Some of the words are:

SOFA
FUSE
BUS
MUD
USE

Page 448

Answers will vary. Some of the words are:

MAIL
YAM
FUME
CLAY
LINK

Page 449

Answers will vary. Some of the words are:

BOAT
AXE
NECK
GOAT
RIB

Pages 450–453

Answers will vary.

Page 454

Page 455

Page 456

Page 457

Page 458

A bezzuzzik is an object that is equal on both sides, with the right side colored in.

Page 459

A dodoloo is an object that is closed all the way around.

Page 460

A perkle is an object that is closed all the way around and has lines, or rays, coming out of it.

Page 461

Page 462

Apartment 1: Mr. Jones
Apartment 2: Mrs. Pinky
Apartment 3: Ms. Becker
Apartment 4: Mr. Smith

Page 463

Page 464

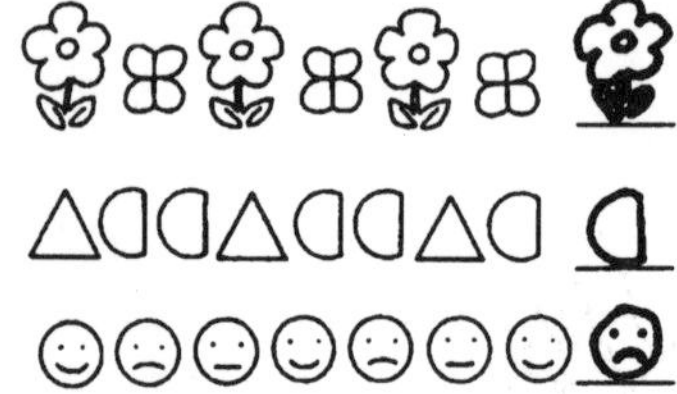

Page 465

Page 466

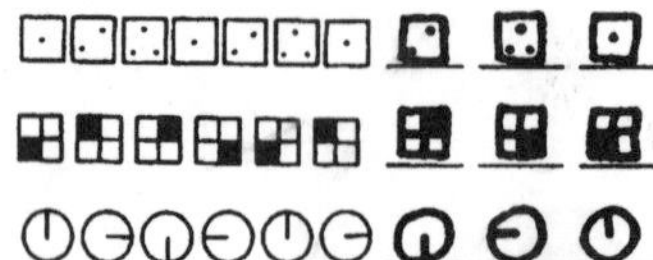

Page 467
All the items are used to play sports.

Page 468
All the items are vehicles that can carry people from place to place.

Page 469

A woozle has curved lines, no straight lines.

Page 470

A smilek has lines that cross over each other, or intersect, and two dots.

Page 471

Page 472

c f i l o r u x

1 2 4 8 16 32 64 128 256

28 26 24 22 20 18 16 14

a z b y c x d w e v

85 81 77 73 69 65 61 57

Page 473

3 6 9 12 15 18 21 24

5 10 15 20 25 30 35 40

z y x w v u t s r

a 1 b 2 c 3 d 4 e

6 12 18 24 30 36 42 48

Page 474

aa	ab	ac	ad	ae	ag	af
1 1	1 2	1 3	1 4	1 5 1	1	6
2	4	6	8	10	11	12
f	h	j	l	n	q	p
42	38	34	30	26	22	24

Pages 475–477
Answers will vary.

Page 478
All of them can be found on a farm.

Page 479
All of them are foods that begin with P.

Page 480
All of them can melt.

Pages 481–486
Answers will vary.

Page 487
All of them are objects that can be opened and closed.

Page 488
All of them are objects that can give off heat.

Page 489
All of them are objects that can fasten things together.

Page 490
Read a book every day.

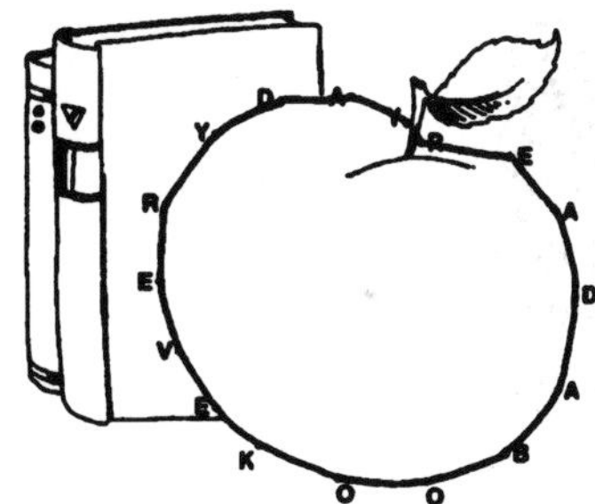

Page 491
Take care of our trees.

Page 492

Page 493
Secret codes are fun!

Page 494
Send a message to a friend.

Page 495
Answers will vary. Some of the words are:
YES
KEYS
TOOL
SEED
DESK